THE MODERN LANGUAGE ASSOCIATION OF AMERICA

MONOGRAPH SERIES

V

THE REAL WAR OF THE THEATERS

Approved for publication in the Monograph Series of the Modern Language Association of America.

Albert Feuillerat
Joseph E. Gillet
Robert A. Law
E. C. Roedder
Robert K. Root
Committee of Award

THE REAL WAR OF THE THEATERS

SHAKESPEARE'S FELLOWS IN RIVALRY WITH THE ADMIRAL'S MEN, *1594–1603*

REPERTORIES, DEVICES, AND TYPES

BY

ROBERT BOIES SHARPE
ASSISTANT PROFESSOR OF ENGLISH IN THE UNIVERSITY OF NORTH CAROLINA

Published by the Modern Language Association of America
BOSTON, D. C. HEATH and COMPANY
LONDON, OXFORD UNIVERSITY PRESS
MDCCCCXXXV

PRINTED IN U.S.A. BY GEORGE BANTA PUBLISHING COMPANY, MENASHA, WISCONSIN

PREFACE

I HAVE ATTEMPTED here a chronological survey of the theatrical events of Queen Elizabeth's last decade, the first study to take up systematically season by season those complex interrelationships among happenings in the nation and on the stage which so intensely concern us in studying the rivalry between Shakespeare's fellows and the other chief London company, the Admiral's men. I have considered each court season by itself in order to bring out the fluctuations of stage vogue and royal favor. The chronological method should make it possible for the reader to see with some clearness the differing literary policies of the companies and their causes in differences of patronage and audience. The most important patrons of dramatic companies, the Admiral, Worcester, and the two Hunsdons, as well as the two Cobhams for their relation to the drama through the Chamberlainship, are here for the first time traced through this crucial decade in their political and personal relationships to each other and to the dominant factions of Essex and the Cecils.

This is far too great a sweep of history to be treated definitively within the scope of this study; but I have tried to draw the outlines so that students hereafter may not have to generalize for the whole decade from some momentary arrangement of the shifting scene, or to apply to the interpretation of a play of 1600 political relationships assumed from those of 1596. I have ventured few generalizations about the censorship; but it appears more subject to partisan influences than has hitherto been assumed. The working out of the study has forced me to hazard some definition, not too dogmatic, I trust, of Shakespeare's politics—not as the private citizen, whose opinions may always remain mysterious, but as the chief play-writing member of a close coöperative producing group which wore the livery of a place-holding noble.

My thanks are due to the Modern Language Association of America, which has made possible this publication, and to the members of its Monograph Committee for a painstaking consideration which was accompanied by many valuable marginal hints on the manuscript. The study was begun in a Yale doctoral dissertation in 1926; its present development was vastly aided by a Sterling Research Fellowship at Yale for 1930–31. I wish to express my gratitude also to the staffs of the Sterling Library at Yale, of the Peabody, Pratt, Goucher, and Johns Hopkins libraries in Baltimore, of the Widener Library at Harvard, and of the Duke University and University of North Carolina libraries for a great many favors; to my wife for untiring clerical assistance; to Professors

Karl Young of Yale, E. P. Kuhl of Iowa, T. W. Baldwin of Illinois, and my colleagues in Chapel Hill, especially Professors G. R. Coffman, G. C. Taylor, and W. F. Thrall, for invaluable backing and heartening interest; to Professors Carleton Brown and P. W. Long for generous editorial advice; and above all to Professor Tucker Brooke of Yale University, at whose suggestion the study was originally undertaken, and whose advice and encouragement have accompanied me all the long way.

The University of North Carolina,
Chapel Hill, June, 1934.

CONTENTS

Chapter VI (1602–1604)

THE STAGE DURING THE TRANSITION FROM ELIZABETH TO JAMES

Chapter VII

CONCLUSION

CHAPTER I (1594–1595)

BEGINNINGS OF THE RIVALRY

The reorganized companies of 1594, their patrons and audiences. Their repertories. The Christmas season of 1594–95 at court.

As the Christmas season of 1594 approached, Edmund Tilney, Queen Elizabeth's Master of the Revels, faced in due course his official task of recommending a select list of dramatic amusements for the court's celebration.[1] He had to deal with a state of affairs on the professional London stage which was to continue essentially unaltered through the remainder of the reign. Two well-matched rival companies, the Lord Admiral's men and the Lord Chamberlain's men, held the situation in a control which, though it was to be challenged now and again during the next eight years, was not to be seriously shaken.

The fact that two companies rather than one ruled the stage during this period, and those two jointly rather than alternately, is oddly typical of the canny and successful dualism of Elizabeth's *political* policy.[2] For the Elizabethan dramatic companies were of course in politics, whether they wished to be or not; they were attached to the persons of the great place-holding nobles. According to the political relations of their patrons, then, there would inevitably exist politically tinged rivalry between the two companies whose repertories were under Master Tilney's consideration. But political bias would not be likely to weight Tilney's choice of one or the other organization for the greater number of performances before the Queen and her court, for although the post of Master of the Revels was officially under the general supervision of the Lord Chamberlain, Tilney himself seems to have owed his position to the influence of his great kinsman the Admiral. He stood in obligation to both. Therefore we can presumably take the choices of the Master of the Revels for this and succeeding years as a sort of criterion of the relative success of the rival companies. We shall find other ways of judging, too; but this, as reflecting after all the best taste of the

[1] Our best glimpse of the way in which this may have been done is given us by Shakespeare in *M.N.D.*, v, i, 36 ff. Philostrate's function here is selective and advisory; but the final selection of amusements for the occasion is in the hands of Duke Theseus.

[2] Cf. *Sydney Papers*, II, 8.—Mr. Lake to Sir Robert Sidney, news from London, 4 Nov., 1596: "The Factions never more malicious . . . if the Stormes breake out from beyond See, . . . great inconvenience must follow,—and yet she whom it most concerneth, doth rather use her Wisdome in Balancing the Weights, than in drawing all to one Assize, which shalbe the wiser way, *docebet dies*."

day (for Tilney's judgment must be in general the court's), cannot but be highly valuable.

Tilney, we may suppose, presented his lists and comments; the Queen chose: the Lord Chamberlain's men performed at court December 26 and 28, the Lord Admiral's on December 28, January 1, and January 6. Why did Tilney favor the Admiral's company with three dates out of five? It would help us greatly if we knew what plays were performed on those dates; unfortunately we may only make some plausible guesses from the 1594 repertories of the companies in question. But first, what did Tilney know of the companies themselves, aside from the lists of plays they had in stock?

Previous court performances could hardly serve Tilney as a guide. The most recent, that of January 6, 1594, had been by the Queen's men, an organization suffering of late from weakened finances and from a habit of provincial barnstorming. These associated evils were due to the long period of plague[3] that had been harassing all players, keeping them from playing in London, where they could make money and could progress dramatically—for provincial tours seem likely to have paralyzed activity in bringing out new plays. The Queen's company, then, although it had possessed a good repertory of well-known plays, was already out of date. In a last effort in April, 1594, this company joined with another, less prominent, of the older organizations, the Earl of Sussex's, in a series of performances at the Rose in Southwark. The venture was not a success, probably on account of the meagre attendance caused by the lingering of the plague in town and the playgoers in the country. A shabbiness of repertory may have been a handicap, too; for Marlowe, who probably wrote for Sussex's men, was dead, and the new organization of the Admiral's must have been drawing to itself the leading playwrights available as well as some of the best actors. On the eighth of May, we learn from Henslowe, the Queen's men "broke and went into the contreye to playe." At the same time, and possibly with them, vanished Sussex's. Neither company returned to London in the autumn. Many plays from the Queen's stock appeared in print within a year or so, a phenomenon suggestive of the financial straits of the company and a resolution to strive no longer to capitalize its sole possession of these older plays in London competition with newer companies using fresher material. These old plays, among them *King Leire*, *James IV*, *The Famous Victories of Henry V*, *Selimus*, and *The Old Wives' Tale*, would still be useful in the provinces, whether allowed to

[3] King James made the considerable gift of £30 to the King's men, formerly the Chamberlain's, to tide them over the plague period of 1603–04. Not so Queen Elizabeth.

escape into print or not;[4] so the Queen's men could raise a little money for drums and banners (and perhaps heavier shoes) by this method of eating their cake and having it too. They seem to have gone into the Midlands and then passed down into the West. Records of 1594 show them at Coventry, Bristol, Bath, and Barnstaple.[5] They could not be considered by Tilney.

The Earl of Pembroke's men also had enjoyed the honor of playing at court—twice in recent years, on December 26, 1592, and on January 6, 1593, giving Marlowe's *Edward II* on one of these occasions. This seems to have been an ephemeral company of those two years only, formed (according to the theory of Sir Edmund Chambers, which seems to fit the facts) by an emergency division of the larger company amalgamated of Lord Strange's and the Admiral's. Under plague conditions London could no longer support so many players. A part of them were sent out on the road under the name of Pembroke's men; perhaps the remaining group had also to "travel with pumps full of gravel." At any rate, this company, taking with it several plays probably worked upon more or less by Marlowe and Shakespeare, had little success in its visits to York, Rye, Ludlow, Shrewsbury, Coventry, Bath, Ipswich.[6] In the late summer of 1593 we hear that they had to pawn their apparel to pay their charges. The players vanished in the provinces or straggled back to London destitute. We hear no more of the group as an organization, though most of their plays, useful at least for revision and revival, probably became ultimately a part of the stock of the Chamberlain's men.[7] They were probably not available for Tilney's selection.

The Lord Strange's men, an old organization several of whose members had once belonged to the Earl of Leicester's men and had gone to the Low Countries with him,[8] had also appeared at court, probably with Shakespeare among them, on December 27 and 31, 1592, and January 1, 1593. Their patron, Ferdinando Stanley, Lord Strange, later Earl of Derby, died April 16, 1594; and the company was playing at Winchester in May under the name of the Countess, his widow.[9] Then came a reorganization which obliterated the old group but produced from it two new, vigorous, and very promising dramatic companies. The leading parts in the performances by Strange's men of the great popular dramas

[4] What right of *production* thus escaped, even in revision? None, I believe, by the mere fact of *printing*.

[5] See Chambers, II, 115, for notes on the records of their provincial performances down to the end of the reign.

[6] Chambers, II, 128.

[7] *Ibid.*, 129.

[8] These were Kemp, the famous clown, and Bryan and Pope, acrobats and musicians. They played before the Danish Court at Helsingör in 1586. Pope and Bryan went on to Dresden, and left there in July of 1587.

[9] She was Alice, daughter of Sir John Spencer of Althorpe, sister of Lady Hunsdon.

of Greene, Kyd, Marlowe, and the new dramatist, Shakespeare, had been taken by Edward Alleyn. But Alleyn did not wear Lord Strange's livery. Something of a financier himself, he had bought up and was retaining the old Lord Admiral's men legally in his own person, apparently preserving the identity of that troop, and at least to some extent the ownership of its playbooks, wholly in himself.[10] He had recently married the stepdaughter of Henslowe, who owned the Rose theater; and so in the late spring of 1594, foreseeing a renascence of the London stage, Alleyn and his father-in-law reorganized the Admiral's men, taking their players presumably from the many former members and hired men of broken companies out of work, and getting together a repertory of plays from broken companies, from those of the old Admiral's stock still owned by Alleyn, and from such of the stock of Strange's men as Alleyn could legally claim. The new organization also, it must be supposed, took immediate measures to insure a supply of new plays from the hands of the best playwrights available.

This action of Alleyn's seems to have left the remnant of what had been Strange's company out in the cold; but it was a tough and stubborn little group of able men, and it had some hold upon the most popular living dramatist. It seems to have lost no time in gaining, possibly through the fashionable acquaintances won for that dramatist[11] by the popularity of his *Venus and Adonis* and *Lucrece*, the patronage of the Lord Chamberlain himself, under which the company appears in June, 1594, in a joint occupancy with the Admiral's men, of the little old theater at Newington Butts, a mile or so south of London Bridge. This joint occupancy was brief and may have broken up in a quarrel, for if Burbadge was with his fellows, friction seems inevitable because of the old Burbadge-Alleyn feud.[12] At any rate, before the middle of the month the Admiral's men returned to the Rose, and the Chamberlain's men seem to have gone on the road, since they were at Marlborough about

[10] Chambers, II, 138.

[11] Though the elder Burbadge had been Hunsdon's man in 1584 (Chambers, II, 394).

[12] See Chambers, II, 392. In May, 1591, there was a dispute in the tiring house at the Theatre with the Admiral's men about some of "the dyvydent money between him and them" which Burbadge had detained. John Alleyn, who Chambers thinks was probably Edward's elder brother, and James Tunstall later deposed that Burbadge was irreverent about the Lord Admiral himself, saying "by a great othe, that he cared not for iij of the best lordes of them all." John Alleyn had also given testimony of a hostile tone in regard to the actions of the Burbadges in repelling Mrs. Brayne and Robert Miles at the Theatre in November, 1590. Chambers thinks that it was the trouble with Burbadge in 1591 which led the Admiral's men to cross over to Henslowe at the Rose. He also (II, 307) makes some remarks on the difficulties this quarrel raises in regard to the "plot" of *The Seven Deadly Sins*. Cf. also W. W. Greg, *Dramatic Documents From the Elizabethan Playhouse*.

September. But this trip may have been by special engagement.[13] On October 8 their patron wrote to the Lord Mayor of London, asking permission for his company to continue an occupation of the Cross Keys inn, Gracious (now Gracechurch) Street, to which it seems already to have laid claim at least for winter playing. For better weather the company had the use of the Theatre, London's first playhouse, just outside London Wall, in Moorfields. Richard Burbadge, one of their leading members and soon to rival Alleyn himself in "straight leads," was son of the owner of the Theatre. I have just spoken of the bitter personal enmity between the Burbadges and the Alleyns and their violent quarrel at the Theatre in 1591. Richard Burbadge is not likely to have played with Strange's while Alleyn was their leading man, and very likely did not rejoin his fellows until the summer or early autumn of 1594, when they first began to appear as the Chamberlain's men at the Theatre. But now the Burbadges, with their great actor, their theater, and their financial resources, could hope to balance the Henslowe-Alleyn combination provided with a popular actor, a theater, and financial backing.

In financing, the Admiral's men had an apparent advantage which was a real handicap—the stronger outside backing, in the person of Philip Henslowe. He was an ignorant man whose spelling bears witness to a complete lack of acquaintance with literature. He apparently first came into association with the drama through his business of pawnbroking and small loans.[14] From dealing in the cloaks and debts of players and dramatists, he had now come to be owner of the Rose theater, father-in law of the greatest actor of the day, and general banker and business manager of the new Admiral's company. His "Diary" or notebook for the theatrical part of his business enterprises over the last dozen years of Elizabeth's reign shows him estimating and taking his share of the receipts, buying properties in the name of his players, lending money to players and dramatists, and even buying plays for the company; at least he was doing so from 1597 on, and there is no reason to suppose he did not do so from the beginning. This last function was the one in which his influence was naturally in the long run most baneful. Down to 1597, at least, he was keeping close account of each performance of each play by his illiterate approximation of its name, together with his share of the gate receipts. Evidently he was taking an interest in drama

[13] Marlborough was on the road to Bath, whither fashionable folk, including at least the younger Hunsdon, as we know from the Gawdy letters, used to resort for their health. On June 5, 1600. Philip Gawdy writes his brother, "Since Bath first smoked ther was never greater nor more worthy companye in that towne. And my Lo. [Hunsdon] kepte the most honorable house that ever was kept ther." (*Letters of Philip Gawdy*, ed. by I. H. Jeayes.)

[14] Greg, *Henslowe;* II, 3, 11, 33, 45. The evidence is not altogether clear, but this seems a reasonable inference.

primarily from the gate receipts point of view, doubtless with much the same influence on the dramatic merit of his productions as that exerted by certain theatrical and motion-picture magnates to-day. Like those producers, he must have developed crude theories of what sorts of things would draw a crowd—with what effect on the courtly fortunes of the company we shall soon see.

The Burbadges, on the other hand, seem to have been financially weak compared with Henslowe; but the financial center of gravity of the Chamberlain's men was within its close corporation of sharing members, all of whom save Cuthbert Burbadge, Richard's brother, were actors, and one of whom, Shakespeare, was the company's chief playwright. Indeed, Shakespeare may already have possessed outside investments which made his financial weight another steadying influence on the company's policies—that thousand pounds, for example, which the Earl of Southampton is said to have given him (about 1593, it would be) "for a purchase which he had a mind to." This would not, as is often asserted, have gone into the purchase of a share in the company. Shares in the new venture cannot have been worth any such sum,[15] and moreover, Shakespeare's standing as poet-playwright[16] was such that the other sharers may very well even have given him his share as an inducement to furnish the new company his services. The money (whether or not it was a thousand pounds) much more probably went into real estate, later Shakespeare's favorite form of investment. At any rate, the Chamberlain's company was firmly centralized and self-directed, and its dramatic policies were guided by men of sound dramatic training, men of taste and foresight.

As for actors, the Admiral's central figure, Ned Alleyn, loomed far above anyone in the rival company. The Queen herself was very fond of his acting in such great Marlovian rôles as Faustus, Tamburlaine, and Barabas.[17] We have not as yet any such careful study of the Ad-

[15] Chambers, I, 352, cites indications that a share in the Admiral's men, 1597–1602, was worth £50; in Queen Anne's, about 1612, £80.

[16] Possibly but newly free from the binding obligation of apprenticeship. Cf. T. W. Baldwin, *The Organization and Personnel of the Shakespearean Company*, 287 (Chambers, *William Shakespeare*, II, 82–86, disagrees with Baldwin's views on the nature of dramatic apprenticeship).

[17] In 1600 Alleyn was having difficulty in building the new Fortune theater for the Admiral's men, whose own patron was overruled by the Council on the protest of Lord Willoughby (a friend of Essex with a town-house in the Barbican) and other local residents. But (I am quoting Chambers, II, 297) "on 8 April the council wrote again to the justices, withdrawing their previous inhibition, and laying special stress on Elizabeth's desire that Alleyn personally should revive his services as a player, 'whearof, of late he hath made discontynuance.' " Doubtless the Queen liked him in Marlovian rôles, for Fuller says, "he made any part (especially a majestic one) to become him"; and of his eight recorded parts:

miral's personnel as Professor T. W. Baldwin has made for the Chamberlain's men; but among the company in 1594 appear to have been Thomas Downton (a capable musician), Richard Jones, Edward Juby, John Singer (a clown), Martin Slater, Thomas Towne, James Donstone or Tunstall, John Pyg or Pigge, and very likely the dramatists Antony Munday and Robert Wilson.[18]

An interesting impression of the Chamberlain's personnel at this time is given by Baldwin's ingenious assignment of parts for *The Taming of the Shrew*, produced, he holds, in the winter of 1594. He has given out the parts according to the "lines" he has built up for the actors, i.e., the types of parts which each habitually took. In this play only one casting, that of Tooley, happens, through a slip of the printer, to be known. Readers of Baldwin's book may differ considerably about these assignments of rôles; but his casting gives in brief compass a great deal of information about the ages, personalities, and relative positions in the company of Shakespeare's fellows:

Gremio—Augustine Phillips.
Lucentio—Richard Burbadge.
Petruchio—Thomas Pope.
Lord—George Bryane.
Tranio—Henry Cundall.
Baptista—John Heminges.
Hortensio—William Sly.
Vincentio—William Shakespeare.
Grumio—William Kemp.
Katherine—Alexander Cooke.
Messenger—Nicholas Tooley.
Bianca—Robert Goffe.
Biondello—William Eccleston.
Widow—Samuel Gilburne.
Page—Ned [?Shakespeare].

Other parts in the play, such as those of Sly, Curtis, Hostess, Tailor, and Huntsmen, were presumably supplied by supernumeraries or doubling. Baldwin does not think that Burbadge should be assigned comic leads. He was at his best in such parts as Richard the Third and Romeo. He was fast becoming the recognized rival of Alleyn; and this reorganization had given him his chance to show his ability in leading rôles.[19] Shakespeare never took important parts; his greatest usefulness was as

---

Faustus, Tamburlaine, Barabas, Orlando Furioso, Sebastian (in *Frederick and Basilea*), Muly Mahamet (in *The Battle of Alcazar*), and the title rôles in *Cutlack* and *Tamar Cam*, three are Marlowe's. We may add with good probability Dunstan (in *A Knack to Know a Knave*) and Hercules (in Heywood's *Four Ages*). Among the plays he sold Henslowe, the "tyrant's vein" appears pretty clearly in *Valteger* (*The Mayor of Quinborough*?), *The Massacre of France*, *Philip of Spain*, and *Mahomet;* can the last have failed to introduce Termagant?

[18] Cf. Chambers, II, 149.

[19] Baldwin's actor-lists naturally do not show Alleyn as appearing with the company at all, for he was never a member of it. But by giving Burbadge Romeo, Talbot, Richard the Third, Hamlet, etc., he probably does not mean to imply that he created all these rôles, for it seems that some of them, at least, must have been created by Alleyn when he was appearing with Strange's men.

stage manager and director.[20] Will Kemp was the most popular clown since Tarleton, and a great box-office asset to the new company. He was also a dramatist, in a way, and supplied comic scenes or "meriments" if desired and probably even if not. (Shakespeare's complaints in *Hamlet* of improvising clowns are far less likely to be aimed at Armin, who had recently joined the company, than at Kemp, who had recently left it.[21]) We know little about the apprentice boys with the Admiral's men. Those with Shakespeare's company can be watched through Baldwin's tables as they develop into skilled actors.

In 1594 when Tilney considered the actors of the two companies, it is likely that in his estimation Alleyn's name easily led all the rest. But the Master of the Revels may have weighed the merits of playwrights too. No sharp rivalry had yet developed; the division into camps was yet uncertain; but there were some names to conjure with among the authors of old plays in stock or new ones of the season. The Admiral's men had old plays by Marlowe, Kyd, Peele, and Greene, most of them still very popular. Their rivals had several of Shakespeare's successes of previous seasons, as well as several in which Peele and Marlowe probably had a hand, and also perhaps some of the work of Kyd, Greene, and Wilson. But even though authorships of many of these plays may have been less dubious in those days than now, still in old plays by recognized masters the Admiral's men had a clear advantage.

And they had a good repertory of new plays of the 1594 season. True, of those listed by Henslowe only one is extant under the same name, and of that one we do not know the author; and we can only guess plausibly at the identification and authorship of the others. But we may be fairly sure that some of the fifteen listed as new were by Heywood, Munday, Peele, Chettle, and Wilson. Of these dramatists, Munday, Peele, and Wilson were already veterans. And young men who may already have been writing for Henslowe, as we know they did later, were Dekker, Drayton, Chapman, and Jonson. Meres' mentioning them in 1598 would indicate that they had already been working up reputations for some time.[22] Although it may be doubted that in 1594 their reputations were sufficient to give these younger playwrights' names

[20] Baldwin, 293, 261–265.

[21] Chambers, II, 300, 326. The change seems to have occurred in 1599. Kempe's introduction in *2 Return from Parnassus*, probably January, 1602, as fellow of Burbadge and Shakespeare does not necessarily mean that he had rejoined the company on his return from abroad; he had a loan from Henslowe on March 10, 1602, and during the next winter he was one of Worcester's men.

[22] Other possibilities from Meres' list are Samuel Rowley, Lodge, Nash, Porter, Hathway. Kyd died some time before the end of the year.

any box-office value, we must remember that some of them, like Shakespeare, were also becoming known for non-dramatic literature.

The Chamberlain's men doubtless had new plays by Shakespeare, since Marlowe's death the leading English playwright. His name must have been an immense attraction. Was he not author of the farcical *Comedy of Errors*, so well advertised by its unexpected playing in the suffocatingly-packed hall at Gray's Inn that same Christmastide? and of the sensational *Richard III* which sent the cry, "My kingdom for a horse!" echoing through the drama of the decade? and perhaps of *Romeo and Juliet*, that incomparable romantic tragedy, still to be ravishing the ears and hearts of London gulls and impressionable Cambridge undergraduates half a dozen years later? His *Venus and Adonis* was flatteringly popular in the world of fashion. Indisputably Shakespeare had a well-established literary and dramatic reputation by the autumn of 1594, so that in him the Chamberlain's men had a name almost, if not quite, as potent as that of Ned Alleyn.

But what other playwrights the company had is, for this and several succeeding years, a mystery. We may feel sure that they had some; they could hardly meet the Admiral's fifteen or more new plays a year with only two or three. But aside from Kemp's bits and improvisations, which should by no means be underrated as drawing attractions, we can only guess that several of the men who were writing for Henslowe were turning off an occasional play for the Chamberlain's company too. The group of eight I have just named could easily have provided half a dozen plays for the rival company, in addition to Henslowe's fifteen.[23] We know that later Henslowe was binding authors[24] under contract to write for his companies only. This being necessary, we can easily surmise what must have been happening, even though this generation of literary serfs was merely a little lacking in unjustifiable loyalty, and not so shifty as Greene, who was said to have sold the same play to two competing companies.[25] We also know that later Dekker and Jonson did write for the Chamberlain's men.[26] And many believe that Chapman was a rival of Shakespeare for the patronage of Southampton at about this time;[27] it is, then, a possibility worth considering that his earliest

[23] I recognize that two plays a year were plenty for Shakespeare, but such an output was nothing to the known and boasted fecundity of Heywood, with his "hand or main finger" in some 220 plays during his working career.

[24] For instance, Porter in 1599, Chettle in 1602. See Chambers, III, 466, 263.

[25] *Orlando Furioso* to the Queen's men, and later, while they were in the country, to the Admiral's. He was taunted with this in *The Defence of Conycatching*, 1592.

[26] Dekker, *Satiromastix*, 1601; Jonson, *Every Man in*, 1598; *Every Man out*, 1599.

[27] Chambers (III, 249) remarks that it would be easier to establish him as a rival of Shakespeare, as Acheson and Robertson attempt to do, if any relation with Southampton

dramatic work (the first recorded work for the Admiral's men was in 1596) was for the company in which Southampton and his friends were interested. However this may be, on playwrights the Chamberlain's men would, I believe, score with Shakespeare over all rivals.

If Tilney had (as the case seems to have been) just five dates for plays in his program for the revels, the question in his mind now would be which company was to have the three and which the two; a more uneven division would not be thinkable. Tilney's regular duties as censor in approving plays for performance[28] kept him in touch with repertories; perhaps he determined to try picking out the plays themselves, and to let this method dictate the final decision. But before we join the Master of the Revels in comparing the two companies' repertories, let us look more closely at their patrons, the politics which they were inclined to favor, and the audiences to which they mainly appealed; for this information should help to make the repertories more nearly as intelligible to us as they were to Tilney, especially in the case of the numerous plays of the year not now extant.

Each city company, of course, under the law had to have a patron, whose livery its members might on occasion wear, to whose household they technically belonged.[29] Thus the Admiral's men would be referred to often as "the Lord Admiral his servants." Because of the strong Puritan opposition to stage plays, especially in the City but also in provincial towns and even at the universities, it was highly advisable for a dramatic company to have as powerful, influential, and withal respectable a patron as possible. The Admiral's men certainly had such a patron in Charles, Lord Howard of Effingham, Lord High Admiral; commander-in-chief against the Armada, first cousin once removed of Queen Elizabeth, full of years[30] and honors. He had himself been Lord Chamberlain from 1574 to 1585, when he was made Lord Admiral; and his wife, daughter of Lord Hunsdon, the present Lord Chamberlain, was one of the Queen's closest friends in an intimacy which increased during the last decade of the reign as the deaths of other old friends among the Queen's ladies left the two more and more alone together in a new generation. This intimate family connection between the Lord Admiral and the Lord Chamberlain seems a little odd in view of the rivalry of their "servants"; and indeed, although there is not necessarily harmony between a man

---

could be established for him earlier than a 1609 dedication shared with several others. He was, however, dedicating in 1598 both to Lady Walsingham, Essex's mother-in-law, and to the Earl himself (see A. H. Bullen in *D.N.B.*). Essex, indeed, appears to have been the chief patron of Chapman's translation of the *Iliad*. Essex and Southampton were so closely associated that this recognition of Chapman can hardly have left Shakespeare unconcerned.

[28] Chambers, I, 318, 86.

[29] Chambers, I, 310 ff.; II, 86, 105; App. D, No. xix.

[30] He was 58 in 1594.

and his father-in-law, the relations of the two men seem to have been amicable enough. Still, certain facts about the beliefs and policies of these men and their associates indicate that in the dualism of Elizabeth's policy their weight was on opposite sides of the scale. The Lord Admiral was perhaps the most distinguished figure of the Cecil party, which was conservatively loyal to Queen Elizabeth, and therefore in general Protestant. He had urged the death of Mary, Queen of Scots, and he was active in anti-Catholic employments. In 1598 he was hunting papists and traitors. In 1602, it is said, the Jesuits feared chiefly the Lord Chief Justice, Sir Robert Cecil, and the Lord High Admiral. He was very friendly to the Cecils, leaders of the peace party, and at increasing personal enmity toward the Earl of Essex, chief jingo and favorite of the decade.[31] But aside from his personal rivalry with Essex for military commands and feudal honors, the Admiral (although a nepotistic aider of his wide family connection and a great grasper of wealth) appears as the able and loyal servant of his Queen and country rather than as a partisan politician. His friends and party associates were among the elder statesmen and nobles, men who had seen Elizabeth's throne shaky and had helped to make it firm, and who now were rather trusted than petted by the Queen. Grown austere and conservative, they were not a group to take enthusiastic interest in dramatic enterprises, whether on land, sea, or boards. It was no new thing to the Lord Admiral to have a company of players in his livery; and if there was any lively interest taken in his reorganized company by the Howard family it may well have been taken by his children: his son William, of marrying age in 1597, his younger son Charles, and his daughters Frances, Elizabeth, and Margaret.[32] But we can only surmise this interest. The

[31] In speaking of the religious and political affiliations of the Howards, we must be careful not to confuse two great branches of the family. The Admiral was grandson of the second Duke of Norfolk by his second wife, Agnes Tilney. The Howards of Effingham had a record of consistent loyalty, and although the lesser branch of the family, were most trusted and honored by the Queen. The other branch, descended from Norfolk's first wife, held, at various times, the titles of Norfolk, Surrey, Arundel, and Northampton. Several of this branch of the Howards were executed for treason, most were Roman Catholics, many were malcontents. Friends of the Earl of Essex are to be found among them. One of them, however, called by the Queen her "good Thomas' in marked contrast to her suspicion of the others, was by her created Baron Howard de Walden in 1597, and encouraged in an attempt to reconcile Essex and Ralegh. He acted as Lord Chamberlain during the serious illness of the second Lord Hunsdon in 1602.

[32] William, 3rd. Lo. Howard of Effingham, m., 1597, Ann, dau. of Lo. St. John of Bletsoe. Charles, his younger brother, m. 1597, Charity, dau. of Robert White and widow of Wm. Leche. They had three sisters: Elizabeth, m. Sir Robert Southwell; Frances, m. Hen. Fitzgerald, 12th Earl of Kildare, who d. 1597—her second marriage, about 1600, was to Hen. Brooke, 11th Lo. Cobham; and Margaret, who m. Sir Richard Leveson, Vice-Adiral. (Gerald Brenan, *The House of Howard*, II, 372.)

Lord Admiral's men, then, enjoyed a patronage which was likely to furnish them very good protection against all manner of interference, but nothing so good in the way of active literary interest or frequent attendance at performances.

The Lord Chamberlain, in charge of Queen Elizabeth's household, was Henry Carey, first Lord Hunsdon (1524?–96). He was the son of Anne Boleyn's sister and thereby first cousin to Elizabeth. Apparently, although loyal, he was at least tolerant in religious matters, and perhaps of Catholic sympathies, for in 1569 he went to Scotland to discuss the possibility of sending Mary Stuart back to her own country while excluding her from the throne (later his loyalty is attested by his presence on the commission which condemned her); in 1572 he was trying to get a pardon for Thomas Percy, Earl of Northumberland; he was favoring the marriage of Anjou in 1579; and he was on a mission to placate James for his mother's execution, in April, 1589. On a later occasion, his son Sir Robert tells us in his *Memoirs*, King James refused to impart some important business he had for Queen Elizabeth's ear to any one but a Carey. Thus he seems to have been looked on by the Queen as a suitable representative of the milder Catholic sympathizers and influencer of the more dangerous ones. Her faith in his loyalty is shown by the fact that at Armada time he was trusted with the command of Tilbury Fort, the key defense of London. His diplomatic methods must have been of bluff openness and sincerity, for he had the reputation of being straightforward and rough, a man of "blasphemous oaths and threatnings."[33] Naunton (in his *Fragmenta Regalia*) says of the elder Hunsdon, "As he lived in a roughling time, so he loved sword and buckler-men, and such as our fathers were wont to call 'men of their hands'—of which sort he had many brave gentlemen that followed him, yet not taken for a popular and dangerous person." Popular report had it that he "took as much delight in hanging Scotch thieves as most men do in hawking or hunting." He was no man of faction; indeed, with his bluntness, he cannot have dealt tactfully with Catholics unless his spirit was sincerely tolerant; and he was not much interested in literary matters. The Chamberlain, like the Admiral, had had players before 1594; and it is not likely that he took much personal interest in the new organization, although when he died it was feared that the players would miss his protective influence.[34] His eldest son George (1547–1603) was

[33] Birch, *Memoirs of Queen Elizabeth*, II, 164.

[34] Nashe, letter to William Cotton, c. Sept., 1596, in McKerrow, *Nashe*, V, 194: . . . "now the players . . . ar piteously persecuted by the L. Maior & the aldermen, & however in there old Lords tyme they thought there state setled, it is now so vncertayne they cannot build vpon it." This seems to apply to all the London actors.

also a military man and shared the family reputation for bluntness. In 1588 he was in charge of the Isle of Wight; the "gentry complained of his arbitrary conduct, and were much offended at his assuming the title of governor." A characteristic action was to order an attorney coming to settle there, "with a pound of candles hanging at his breech lighted, with bells about his legs, hunted owte of the island."[35] Lord Chamberlain from March, 1597, until the death of the Queen, George Carey may have had some interest in his players through his wife, Elizabeth, daughter of Sir John Spencer of Althorpe, probably a relative of Edmund Spenser, and a woman of literary tastes. But for a close interest in the Chamberlain's men felt by a member of the Carey family we should probably look to Sir Henry, a younger son of the first Lord Hunsdon, whose home in Kent was seized in February, 1601, on account of his complicity in the Essex rising, and to Robert, seventh son, born about 1560. Sir Robert Carey was himself a prominent courtier, who "exceeded in making choice of what he wore to be handsome and comely." He was a close friend of his father's grand-nephew, the Earl of Essex, was with him on several of his military adventures, and was knighted by him in 1591 for interceding with the Queen on his behalf. In 1593 he married a West Country lady (the Careys were originally from Devon), Elizabeth Trevannion of Caerhayes, Cornwall, his cousin on his mother's side. He seems to have escaped implication in the Essex rebellion largely because from 1593 on he was employed in the government of the Border and in negotiations with King James. His *Memoirs* mention very few dates, but it is possible to work out from them that he was in London from the autumn of 1591 to the spring of 1593, in the autumn and again in the winter of 1593, until Shrovetide, 1594, from the spring of 1595 to the spring of 1596, in the spring of 1597, and again in the autumn or winter, and yet again at the time of Queen Elizabeth's death in the spring of 1603. We know also that he was M.P. for Callington in 1593; and for Northumberland, 1597–98 and 1601. Thus we have frequent periods at which he could be in touch with the activities of the family players.

As for his position in 1601, he was anxious for leave to come up to London just before the Essex outbreak, but Cecil forbade him,[36] excusing himself by saying the Queen opposed it:[37]

> . . . especially because she hath a principal affiance in you, and she is daily advertised of practices upon the Border; so as I can draw no other resolution than this, that you shall be here at the next term to dispatch any of your business, but not before.

[35] Sir John Oglander, *Memoirs*.

[36] *Sal. MSS.*, XI, 29 (Feb. 6, 1601).

[37] His usual excuse in such cases; cf. Whyte's letters to Sidney, *passim*.

Carey's reply[38] is significant of his attitude toward the Cecil party. He begs again for leave from his post,

> not now for my private affairs, but in these desperate times I desire to be near about her majesty . . . You may have many worthy men that you trust to and that are truly yours, but so long as you are to her Majesty as I know you are, by God, Sir, I will be as honest to you as any he that lives.

He goes on to try to make Cecil believe that he has very private information of plots against his life; but obviously he wishes access to the Queen, fearful of being ruined in his absence at this critical time by stories, true or false, of his relations with Essex and King James. His famous ride, abetted by his brother, then Chamberlain, to notify James of Elizabeth's death, was taken counter to Cecil's apparent policy; and his tastes and friendships form one of the several strong links between the affairs of the Lord Chamberlain's players and those of the romantic and unfortunate Earl of Essex.

The patronage of the Lord Chamberlain promised to his players a prestige but slightly less than their rivals' and a security practically as great. This security was unexpectedly destroyed by the succession of Cobham as Chamberlain in 1596, but restored by the reinstatement of the Carey family the following year—perhaps no longer quite so firmly.[39]

Since I have spoken of the political groupings about Cecil and Essex, and since these had very important bearings upon the dramatic history of the decade, I shall endeavor to state briefly their natures and aims:

The Cecil party was headed by the wise and crafty old Lord Burghley. But he was of comparatively low origin; aristocratically, the party's most distinguished leader was probably the Lord Admiral. The Howards of Effingham were renowned for sternly repressive measures in Scotland and the North, and the party stood for a like policy in Ireland. In governmental affairs, although sometimes harassed by the Queen's caprices in regard to her favorites, the party's situation was that of the "Ins." And as a body it was a party of mature years and old, cool heads: even Sir Robert Cecil was a very old young man. It was the party of conservative Protestantism, and probably to some extent of conforming Catholicism. There must have been puritanism in the party, of an old-fashioned type like Burghley's own; but extremer Puritans dissatisfied with the political bishops would hardly feel at home there. The Cecil party stood for defensive war, and later for peace, with Spain; until after the death

[38] *Sal. MSS.*, XI, 84 (Feb. 26, 1601).

[39] The younger Hunsdon's apparent lack of sympathy for his players when they wished to use Blackfriars in 1596 was probably due to a working relationship with Cecil which helped the company to survive its perilous association with Essex through the performance of *Richard II* in 1601 and come through intact into the long-promised favor of King James.

of Essex it at least appeared to oppose the accession of James, and to favor the English claims, especially that of Suffolk[40] (the Essex party believed the Cecils secretly favored the Infanta); it showed hostility to the Scots; and it stood for the strict upholding of the state religion, with unrelenting harshness to Catholics. Socially the party was conservatively aristocratic, but its high practical respect for money gave it a considerable sympathy for the mercantile classes with their growing bourgeois and plebeian Puritan or (as it became later) "Roundhead" element; and like most parties long in power, it was increasingly, and probably with increasing truth, charged with cynical corruption and even atheism.

Puritanism, as I have said, as far as it represented a conservative upholding of Elizabeth and the Church of England, was in general on the Cecil side. As it sought more toleration and independence (for example, Burghley opposed Presbyterianism), it received some encouragement to look to Essex,[41] as some radical Puritan elements are known to have done in 1600. The party had considered Leicester its chief bulwark against a Catholic marriage; but now that this danger was over, the conservatism of its elder members drew them over to the side of Burghley. Essex's assertion that the Cecils favored the succession of the Infanta proved a fruitless bid for these elder Puritans' support, probably because they did not believe it. The new Puritans of the "precise" sort had little place in either party; as a class they were too inferior socially to count in the aristocratic politics of the day; their most radical wing, however, had a distinct connection with the Essex rebellion.

Such political eccentrics as Cobham, Ralegh, and Northumberland held loosely to the Cecils as the party in power and because they hated Essex. In the uncertainty over the succession in Elizabeth's last years

[40] See the shrewd Sir John Harington, in 1602 (in his *Tract on the Succession*) on the party's treatment of Hertford and especially Arabella.

[41] Essex, often called atheist and papist by his enemies, died in a fervently Protestant frame of mind, under the strongly evangelistic influence of his temporary chaplain Abdie Ashton. That he had ambitions connected with the extremer Puritan party as early as 1595 is indicated by his demonstrations on the death of that faction's champion and candidate for the succession, the Earl of Huntingdon. See Harington, *op. cit.*, p. 41. The Puritans adhered to Huntingdon's title from Clarence; "and the said Earl was so chargeably attended of the pure Gospellers both spiritual and temporal as had well nigh decayed that most honourable house"; "this faction died with my Lord of Leicester," . . . and yet when Essex got news of Huntingdon's death, in 1595, "he tore his hear and all his buttons brake with the swelling of his stomach, as if some great design of his had been frustrated thereby." Huntingdon's widow was a sister of the Earl of Leicester; and *Leicester's Commonwealth* accused its villain of conveying the crown to the Dudleys by advancing Hastings to the throne. Harington hints that Essex had fallen heir to some of his stepfather's ambitious policies.

they tried unsuccessfully to play their own hand; but Cecil raising his truly great powers of secret diplomacy to their loftiest height, outwitted them and what remained of the Essex party, contriving not only to keep on the winning side but also to contribute, one must grant, a great deal to its bloodless and welcomed victory.

Some typical persons of this group are:[42]

William Cecil (74), Lord Burghley, Lord Treasurer.

William, Lord Howard of Effingham (58), Lord Admiral.

Sir Robert Cecil (c. 31), tiny, frail, deformed, coolly Machiavellian younger son of the Treasurer, acting as Principal Secretary of the Queen.

The Cecil and Howard family connections—the latter especially vast. Both Burghley and the Admiral were dynasts, furthering the interests of their relatives by blood and marriage, even quite distant ones, most persistently.

The Brookes, Lords Cobham, elder and younger (67 and 30), connected with the Cecils by marriage, the younger, some years later, to the Admiral also; men of vast possessions and small prowess. Their sway over Kent was almost absolute.

Edward Seymour, Earl of Hertford (57), and his son Edward, Lord Beauchamp (33). The latter, whose mother was Lady Catherine Grey, represented the "Suffolk claim" to the succession.

Gilbert Talbot (42), Earl of Shrewsbury, formerly a friend of Essex, but drawn more and more to Cecil, partly through fear, partly through hopes for his niece, Arabella Stuart, another claimant.

Richard Bancroft (50), Bishop of London from 1597, anti-toleration, active against the Essex rising and the "libels" or satirical leaflets that abounded before and after it.

Sir George Carew (39), President of Munster, Sir Robert Cecil's most intimate friend.

Sir Thomas, Lord Grey of Wilton (18), son of Spenser's "Sir Artegall," and a special enemy of Southampton.

Sir Walter Ralegh (c. 42), rival of Essex as favorite, Captain of the Queen's Guard.

Edward Sutton, Lord Dudley, and other Staffordshire rivals of the Essex connection there. Connections of Cecil in Herefordshire and of the Admiral in Glamorgan opposed the strong Essexian factions in those regions. The parties were distinctly developed, too, in East Anglia, especially near Norwich and Colchester, in Lancashire and Cheshire, in Kent, and in Hampshire and Sussex. The geography of the Essex episode in English history would itself make an interesting study.

William Rider, Lord Mayor of London, and the citizens in general, who failed to rise in aid of Essex, current opinion being that they were held safe to the government by solicitude for their property.

John Lyly (c. 40), literary man and placeless courtier, who, with many others, came forward for loot after the rebellion.

Richard Topcliffe (62), spy, recusant hunter, torturer, profiteer of persecution, an aid of the Cecils and a special hanger-on of Shrewsbury.

Phineas Pett, respectable shipwright, protégé of the Admiral.

[42] I include in parentheses the ages of certain ones in 1594. Edward Alleyn was twenty-eight in 1594, and Philip Henslowe about forty.

The Essex party was led by the warlike, generous, tolerant, impulsive, short-sighted, young Earl of Essex. It had, as we have seen,more than one friend among the younger members of the Carey family, at the head of which was Lord Hunsdon, first cousin to the Queen, great-uncle to Essex, and Lord Chamberlain. The Careys were much used by Elizabeth to further her conciliatory policy in Scotland and the Catholic North. The Essex party favored conciliation in Ireland also. In general, about Essex gathered the ambitious young earls who sought glory at court and in the field, the "younger sons of younger brothers" who sought their fortunes by arms, and all the "Outs" who became more malcontent as it became increasingly apparent that the "ministry" could be changed only by revolution. It was a party of youth and a party of mixed religions. Essex was for toleration. Numerous Catholics were among his friends, and he was encouraging the extreme "independent" Protestants just before the rebellion. His tolerance in religion even went so far as to make him appear sympathetic to Tyrone's demand for the complete religious freedom of Ireland. Essex stood for vigorously aggressive war against Spain, including efforts to set up the independence of Portugal, and effective aid to Holland and France. He was friendly to King Henry and King James and did his utmost to further the Scottish succession.[43] Socially and fashionably the party was brilliant—a sort of forerunner of the Cavalier party, which indeed, even here among the followers of Essex, the rise of Puritanism can be seen forcing into existence.[44]

Some typical persons of this group are:[45]

Robert Devereux (27), Earl of Essex, favorite of the Queen, and her Master of the Horse.

Henry Wriothesley (21), Earl of Southampton, a Roman Catholic, patron[46] of Shakespeare, personal friend of Essex and later connected with him by marriage. A long list might be made of Essex's relatives and family connections who were implicated in his rebellion, and so likewise for the other faction; the clannishness of Elizabethan domestic politics has never been fully brought out.

The Earl of Rutland and his brother (18 and 16).

Sir Charles Danvers (26), a young gentleman of promise, attached personally

[43] Unless one is to accept the assertions of his enemies (strengthened by the wild talk of his rash friends) that he planned merely to use James in order to make himself king. It is difficult to believe this; yet sometimes his policy is greatly obscured by his consuming purpose to ruin, by any means, Cecil and his group.

[44] The term was used for these gallants. Philip Gawdy in his letters of 1593 calls Essex, Mountjoy, and Sir Roger Williams "cavilleros." The modern form of the word occurs in Marston's *Antonio and Mellida*, 1599.

[45] Not all in this list can be proved to have been of Essex's group as early as 1594. Their ages in 1594 are indicated within parentheses—Shakespeare was then thirty, and Richard Burbadge about twenty-five.

[46] Cf. Stopes, 270; also 35, 289, 360.

to Southampton, to whom he owed his life for helping him to escape after killing a man in a family feud.

Anthony Bagot, Staffordshire man, with Essex from college days.

Sir Charles and Sir Joscelyn Percy, younger brothers of the Earl of Northumberland, who was unhappily married to Essex's sister Dorothy.

John Whitgift, Archbishop of Canterbury, a mild sympathizer.

Sir Robert Sidney (31), connected with Essex by the Earl's marriage to Frances Walsingham, Sir Philip's widow, and vainly dependent on him for preferment—but loyal to the Queen at the time of the rising,[47] and later turning to Cecil's side, drawn by his own marriage to a relative of the Admiral.

Vaughans, Lloyds, and Salisburys, Welsh knights.

King Henri IV of France, both personally and politically a friend of Essex.

Antonio Perez, renegade Spanish statesman, enemy of King Philip II for romantic personal reasons and desirous of active war on Spain, an unhappy master of intrigue, fond of giving Essex lessons in statecraft out of Plutarch.

M. de Boississe, French ambassador in London at the time of the rising. Various countries were eager to "recognize" Essex's government if he had been able to set it up: the Earl of Mar, James's envoy, was on his way from Scotland when the rebellion was crushed, lingering to see how it would turn out; the Cecilian authorities were hunting in England for Tyrone's chaplain soon after; and Essex was supposed to have had support in Denmark. Obscure Scots, Irishmen, Frenchmen, may be found in the lists of imprisoned followers of Essex.

Henry Cuffe (31), man of letters aiming at statecraft, secretary to Essex.

Anthony Bacon (36) and his brother Francis (33), both secretaries of Essex, though cousins of Cecil. The former was loyal to him throughout; the latter's turn at a strategic time to zealous loyalty to the Queen has been discussed.

Tracy, Essex's page, killed in the rising. Another of his pages, Thomas Tompkins, became so skilled a pirate as to enjoy, later, the protection of the Admiral.

Dr. Giles Fletcher (c. 45), ambassador, poet, treasurer of St. Paul's, succeeding Bancroft in 1597, when he succeeded Fletcher's brother as Bishop of London.

Henry Hawkins, Doctor of Civil Law.

Mr. Egerton, a very popular Puritan preacher of Blackfriars, in trouble for an Essexian sermon a week after the rising.[48]

Sir John Harington (33), courtier, wit, literary man, a favorite godson of the Queen, who frightened him out of active politics in 1599; but his *Tract on the Succession* (1602) shows Essex sympathies.

Sir Edmund Bainham, martialist, swaggerer, deep drinker, and beater of the watch, leader of the "Damned Crew," later in the Gunpowder Plot.

Robert Catesby (21), Roman Catholic fanatic, of wealthy Warwickshire family and high principles; later in the Gunpowder Plot.

Sir Thomas Smythe, Sheriff of London in 1601, but through fear or other impediments powerless to aid Essex.

Piers Edmonds (c. 30), veteran soldier favorite of Essex and Southampton.

Francis Davison (c. 19), poet, son of the late Secretary, and an intense hater of Cecil, largely because he believed Burghley to have ruined his father to save his own skin after the execution of the Queen of Scots.

One Alexander, apprentice, leader of the Essex faction among the prentices; and one Smith, who held the same position among the watermen.

[47] The *D.N.B.* is wrong in saying he was at his post in Flushing; he parleyed for the forces attacking Essex House.

[48] *Sal. Mss.*, XI, 154.

Except as we can infer it from the personnel of Cecil's party, it is difficult to find evidence of the nature of the Admiral's men's audience at the Rose during those afternoons in the autumn of 1594; but various hints and deductions suggest that they were a somberer, more dowdy, more citizen-like lot than gave tone and color to the assemblage at the Theatre or the Cross Keys. The most costly places would be filled by nobles and courtiers of Cecil's party, older, more responsible, more respectable, soberer; and with those wealthy burghers, whose puritanism, at least with many of the older generation, still allowed playgoing. The cheaper galleries would hold less prosperous citizens, townspeople from the provinces come up to London on business, Malvolios from the more precise of the great households, and so on. The groundlings would be prentices, psalm-singing weavers if they were not too puritanical to attend plays, and menials of the households represented in the galleries. The Admiral's men probably clung to tradition more than did the Chamberlain's, were less eager for innovation. Alleyn very likely felt that his strength lay in the performance of old established rôles before the Queen's own generation; and Henslowe, who shows no indication of having touch with or taste for courtiers,[49] should naturally have felt unqualified to judge their wants (save perhaps for cloaks and loans), and could hardly be expected to see how a comparatively few courtly fashionables could have in the course of the next few critical years more influence on the fortunes of a theater than the multitudes of the bourgeoisie and proletariat. The Admiral's men, then, I believe, aimed their productions at the tastes of the *older*, less sophisticated, more middle-class types, partly out of inertia and the weight of their patronage, and partly as a reasoned policy. Under stress of threatening competition they often wavered in this policy; but, as their repertory lists for successive years show, they never definitely abandoned it. Even after 1600 they were presenting a series of Biblical plays and reviving Kyd and Greene.

The average audience of the Chamberlain's men was, I think, markedly different. Here the pit and cheaper galleries surged with sword-and-buckler servants, hungry "martialists," "younger sons of younger brothers," and other retainers and followers of the warlike Earl of Essex, who, as great an attraction as the play itself, perhaps graced the box balcony at the rear of the stage with an arm over the shoulder of his friend, the gay young Earl of Southampton. With them might be another close friend of Essex, Charles Blount, just become Lord Mountjoy.[50]

[49] Although he had a place, probably nominal, in the Queen's Household from 1592 on, that of Groom of the Chamber (Greg, *Henslowe*, II, 9), a post probably held by members of the Queen's men (Chambers, II, 105), and by Bryan and Singer, while Munday and perhaps Dutton were Messengers of the Chamber (*Ibid.*, I, 45, n. 5).

[50] He was 31 when he succeeded to the title July 16, 1594.

The country squire, up to London for a holiday, could feast his unaccustomed eyes on these meteoric gallants prominent in warlike expeditions and in the intrigues of the Queen's court. All the young men who were or imagined they were or hoped to be of the world of fashion; at least some discreetly masked ladies who wished to interest these young men; and all foreign visitors who desired to see the play with the best society of England—had to contribute to the daily takings of the Lord Chamberlain's men. In a word, here was the center of the new Cavalier party—or, if hardly a party, call it faction, class, group, fashion, or what you will. Such, I believe, was the audience at whose tastes and enthusiasms the Chamberlain's plays, including Shakespeare's plays, were aimed.

This outline of the party groups, however, has to be very rough and tentative, and should be accepted only with many qualifications. During the last decade of Elizabeth's reign the political situation changed radically about every two years. I have tried to visualize the alignments in 1594 as in general their patrons' interests and connections may be surmised to have drawn them. For the contrasting tastes of the two audiences, the best evidence is the trend of the plays themselves, as I shall attempt to bring out in discussing the repertories.

The chief personal dislike at this time existing was that of Essex for the Cecils, with whom as chief favorite of the Queen, he was engaged in an unremitting struggle for preferments for himself and his followers.[51] With the Admiral he was on reasonably good terms until rivalry for the honors and spoils of the Cadiz expedition in 1596 brought them into conflict. The Islands Voyage, next year, roused to a blaze his old bitter rivalry with Ralegh, an ally of Cecil from that time until Essex was dead. In 1596 the first Lord Hunsdon died, and the second lord was kept dangling for his father's honors until he had practically to become a sworn partisan of Cecil before he was made Lord Chamberlain on Cobham's death in 1597.[52] Between Essex and his enemies there were hollow reconciliations now and then—with the Admiral in 1597; with Cecil and Ralegh in 1597 before the Islands Voyage, in 1598, and early in 1599. But these were mere truces, while the struggle for power went on; and it is doubtful whether the drama took them into account, especially because even if we disregard the probabilities of revision, we can date few extant plays accurately enough to parallel these restless changes. After his return from Ireland to disgrace in 1599, Essex's hatred

[51] Bacon, Bodley, and Robert Sidney were among the best-known sufferers by his tactless efforts and their adroit countering by the Cecils.

[52] *Salisbury MSS.*, VI, 286—Geo. Lo. Hunsdon to Sir R. Cecil, 1596, before July 26. Thanks him for his love, "as to one upon whom I will chiefly rely" in suing for his late father's offices, or such of them as he can obtain.

and helpless wrath boiled hotter until the fatal explosion of February, 1601. A realignment followed his death, partly covert, in Cecil's espousing secretly the policy of backing James for the succession, partly open, in the turning of many influential former followers of Essex to the victorious side of Cecil, and accompanied by the complicated and obscure intrigues of the English claimants to the throne. The Admiral was perhaps in the secret of what we may call with Martin Hume Cecil's treachery to his own party;[53] Hunsdon apparently was not, for we see him acting directly contrary to Cecil's overt policy during the critical hours which followed Queen Elizabeth's last breath.

The religious policies of the factions, too, are so complicated and shifting that it is almost surprising to find the dramatic companies as consistent as they are—for instance, the Admiral's men in ridiculing and degrading, the Chamberlain's in making sympathetic and dignified, the figures of their stage priests and friars.

The audiences cannot have been mutually exclusive. A man like Spenser, visiting London in 1596, had sympathies and friends in both camps. Southampton and Rutland in 1599 were "passing their time merely in going to plays every day";[54] they can hardly have confined themselves to one theater, although repeated visits to the same play were apparently common—e.g., take Essex's to *Richard II*, and the numerous references in drama to the practice of getting bits of plays by heart for use in courtly conversation. There are indications that Sir Robert Cecil, his (and Hunsdon's) relative Sir Edward Hoby, and Sir Walter Ralegh saw *Richard II*, during times of truce.[55] Yet the repertories, as I have promised to demonstrate, do show the two companies following tolerably settled policies of catering to distinct tastes in their audiences; and this phenomenon must be due to some such fundamental difference between their habitual, dependable, steady clienteles.

We have spent a good while in going over matters which there would have been no need for Tilney to reiterate. Now we come to the comparison of the repertories themselves, a task over which Tilney himself, with all his advantages over our time-disabled knowledge, may have had to ponder nearly as long as we.

[53] Henry Howard to Bruce, c. July or August, 1602.—Importuning a letter (from King James) for the Admiral, "who thought every day a year till he heard from thence." *Robert Cecil's Secret Correspondence with King James*, ed. by David Dalyrymple, Edinburgh, 1766.

[54] Whyte to Sidney, 6 Oct., 1599.—"My Lord Southampton, and Lord Rutland, came not to the Court; the one doth but very seldome; they pass away the tyme in London merely in going to Plaies every Day."

[55] Hoby to Cecil, Dec. 9, 1595; *Sal. MSS.*, v, 487. Ralegh to the same, July 6, 1597—*S. P. Dom.* 1595–7, 451.

Repertories of 1594

With the exception of three well-known tragedies by Marlowe, no longer new, only one play of the Admiral's repertory for the year is extant, at least under the name given it in Henslowe's diary. This is the comedy *A Knack to Know an Honest Man.* It was published in 1596 in a confused and probably surreptitious text, with no author indicated and no ascription to a company. In the Diary it was marked "ne" (generally interpreted to mean "new") by Henslowe, and was probably written in emulation of[56] the popular older play *A Knack to Know a Knave* published in 1594 as played by "Ed. Allen and his companie," with special mention on the title page of "Kemp's applauded meriments of the men of Gotham." Thus the *Knave* seems to have been a play of Strange's men and not the special property of Alleyn, or he would have taken it to the Admiral's company. Instead, it somehow got into the bookseller's hands; but it may first have been an early asset to the Chamberlain's repertory. *A Knack to Know an Honest Man* might be by Heywood or Munday (Munday more likely; it has a strong Italian flavor), and may even contain work by Wilson, Chettle, and Chapman. It is romantic and tragi-comic in type, with a slight resemblance to *Antonio and Mellida* in its Venetian setting and in the dispossession of women from forfeited property, and a strong resemblance to *Measure for Measure* in its fundamental situation—the key to the whole plot lurking about in disguise to tell the sheep from the goats.

This play appears to give us our first example of competition between the playwrights of the rival companies; the difficulty is that we are not sure *A Knack to Know a Knave* was ever played by Shakespeare's group after it came under the patronage of the Chamberlain. There are some slight resemblances to *Richard III* and *The Comedy of Errors*, but they are too slight to base an argument on. The resemblances to *The Merchant of Venice* are very interesting: Sempronio gibes at his uncle Servio for blindness, as Gobbo at his father; and the following passage must, it seems, have influenced Shakespeare's play:

> *Ser*[*vio*]. Most mighty Duke, most worthy Senators,
> Walking abroad as is my vsuall wont:
> I found Lelio clothed in a base disguise:
> Him when I saw, I seazd . . .
> And in humble wise request the largis which the state alowes
> Which is a thousand Crowns to him that brings
> The head of Lelio to the Senators.
>
> . . . .

[56] The chief points of likeness are the title, a direct allusion in the text to the title of the rival play, a moralistic purpose to separate good from evil characters, and the presence of characters going under the names of abstract qualities, as in the morality plays.

Lelio. Give sentence Prince, delay not by my death
To rid me from a world of miseries.
Du[*ke*]. Law must have course, though pittie plead for thee:
. . . .
Enter Annetta and Lucyda.
An. Stay cruell man, traynd up in cruelty, . . .
Great Iudges of the state, heare me but speake:
Pyttie for Lelio, grant my husband life.
Du. It may not be, Iustice will have no pause.
Lu. Yet mercy Prince, should moderate the Lawes.
Le. Who spares the guyltie, anymates the bad.
Lu. Who spareth none, doth hate to Iustice adde.
Ser. Pittie with Iustice neuer wel agrees.
Lu. Yes when it moderates seuere decrees.
Du. What cause of plea hath this audacious mayde?
Lu. Such cause as vertuous men may wonder at:
I clayme the pension of a thousand crownes,
For I my Lords present my fathers head.
Se[*nator*]. Seruio presented Lelio vnto vs,
And he deserues the pension of the state:
Lu. Lelio first discouered vnto vs,
And we deserue the pension of the state. . . .
And Seruioes seruice was but treachery:
Your lawes command, that on the first surpryse,
Who met with Lelio should disclose him strayght,
But Seruio three dayes space did keepe him close.
An. And therefore Seruio merits not the gold.
Du. This was the certayne hope of my desire.
. . . .
Se[*nator*]. I, so the Foxe was taken in the net,
And nygardnes was caught by sutteltie.
Du. Then do the Senate presently decree,
That Lucida shall haue the promist coine,
And Seruio for breaking of the law,
Shall be imprisoned for a twelue-month space.
This pretty accident doth make me laugh.[57]

As for influence in the other direction; though one cannot, after reading this play, point to definite imitation of Shakespeare, one can hardly escape the impression that its author wrote in rather keen consciousness of his early work.

The most popular of Henslowe's new plays this year was *The Wise Man of West Chester*, played thirty-two times between December 3, 1594,[58] and July 18, 1597, with a high average of gate receipts. This play is quite reasonably identified with Munday's *John a Kent and John a Cumber*, extant in a signed holograph copy dated (in another hand)

[57] *A Knack to Know an Honest Man*, Sgn. G 3.

[58] Observe that it was practically new for the Christmas season, just long enough on the boards for polished acting and a demonstrated success.

December, 1596. With its Welsh border setting, its rival magicians, its pairs of troubled lovers, its rustic-sylvan atmosphere, and its folkways, it is a highly interesting as well as amusing production. Munday could have brought together many of its imitative elements without going to the works of a rival company, finding them rather in *Doctor Faustus*, *Friar Bacon and Friar Bungay*, *The Old Wives' Tale*, and *George a Greene*. Some of these same elements descended within the Henslowe organization to Munday's own Robin Hood plays and to *Look About You;* and one of the characters, Ranulph or Randal, Earl of Chester, gives the title to a lost play by Middleton mentioned by Henslowe in 1602. But *John a Kent* also shows important relations with the Chamberlain's plays. Collier points out the resemblance in one of its scenes to that in *A Knack to Know a Knave* between Miller, Cobbler, and Smith. Much more important as evidence of early rivalry expressing itself in imitation of the other company's successes, even if we do not consider the doubtful ownership of the *Knave*, is the patent exploitation of the vein of *Love's Labour's Lost* in the rustic clowning of Shrimp, Turnip, Hugh Sexton, Tom Taberer, and their choice of Turnip to make their speech to the lords in a sort of masque:

Omnes. Turnop, Turnop, weele haue none but Turnop.

Turnop. Then let vs set forward, for now it is upon the Lordes coming. Thomas, firk it with your fiddle. Spurling, you play the Moore, vaunce vp your Tun, and Robert, holde your porrenger right, least you spill the conceit, for here they come.

Enter Pembrook, Moorton, Oswen, Amery, *to them this crew marching, one drest lik a Moore, wth a Tun painted with yellow oker, another with a Porrenger full of water an a pen in it,* Turnop *speaketh the Oration.*

Turnop. Lyke to the Cedar in the loftie Sea,
or milke white maste vppon the humble mount:
So hearing that your honors came this way,
Of our rare wittes we came to giue account.
ffor when as princes passe through pettie townes
they must be welcomed, least they tearme vs clownes.
Our presents precious, first the golden Tunne,
borne by that monstrous Murrian black a Moore,
Mortonus Earlus in thy prayse is doone.
This shining brook hemd in with this fierce shoare
That hath [The manuscript is incomplete here.]
Is peerelesse Penbrook, if I roue not wyde . . .
This princely pen vp prauncing by the sydes,
And so we wishe ye bothe two blessed brydes.

Oswen. My Lordes, my fathers tennants after their homely guise,
Welcome ye with their countrey merriment,
How bad so ere, yet must ye needes accept it.

Pemb. Else Oswen were we very much to blame,
thankes, gentle freendes, heere drinke this for my sake.

Notice also the resemblance of Shrimp, John a Kent's boy, to Puck and Ariel in his power to become invisible and mislead persons by magical music. Interesting influences of the play in a direction of which we can feel more assurance are on Shakespeare's depiction of Glendower in *1 Henry IV*,[59] and, perhaps through the Robin Hood plays, on the sylvan atmosphere of *As You Like It*. And of course we meet again the clownish players and their condescending audience at a wedding in Athens.

Another item in the Henslowe list for 1594 which we may reasonably identify with an extant play is *Godfrey of Bulloigne*, which seems likely to have been Heywood's wondrous romance, almost a better burlesque of itself than Beaumont could do upon it in his *Knight of the Burning Pestle*—*The Four Prentices of London*.[60] Sussex's men too, had presented that spring a play called *Huon of Bordeaux*. These plays of chivalrous romance were common. But a highly popular element which was especially characteristic of the Admiral's men's productions was the democratic appeal in Heywood's play, the catering to London 'prentices.[61] Nothing makes the comparatively aristocratic trend of the Chamberlain's men stand out more strongly than to consider the tone of this play in contrast with the attitude toward the "base mechanicals" which Shakespeare habitually shows. All that we know of the repertory of his company supports the belief that they left this field of proletarian appeal to the tribe of Henslowe, and made their bid for favor in another quarter.[62] This is not to deny that Heywood showed in this play that stimulating vein of his which so often influenced dramatic history. Perhaps with an eye upon the success of *Two Gentlemen of Verona*, he developed the girl-page motif to a new piquancy of situation and complication which may in some applauded revival have encouraged Shakespeare to work the vein again in *As You Like It* and *Twelfth Night*. But of this particular chain of influences more later. Heywood's young man who prefers horsemanship and war to the lady who woos him reminds us of Adonis, Hotspur, and Bertram:

[59] See Collier's introduction to his edition of *John a Kent* for the Shakespeare Society (1851) upon John a Kent's traditional connection with Kentchurch, Herefordshire, and with Owen Glendower, who is mentioned in the play (p. 35) as an even more learned magician. There are Welsh songs. That Sidanen, a Welsh princess, omits articles may indicate dialect. Kent calls Griffin "my hotspur" on p. 13.

[60] S.R. 1594 (June 19); quartos 1615, 1632.

[61] For an account of the Nine Worthies of London, legendary figures whose careers closely resemble those of the Four Prentices, see the *Harleian Miscellany*, VIII, 437 (an account dated 1592).

[62] Beaumont's burlesque, by the way, dating c. 1607 or later, and therefore outside our period (and after the time when any company was likely to look for much help from the proletarians?) was written for a company of boys. But Beaumont did most of his dramatic work for the Shakespeare company, in his day the King's men.

Lady. Fie niggard, can you spend such precious breath,
Speake to your selfe so many words apart;
And keepe their sound from my attentiue ear,
Which saue your words no musicke loues to heare?
Guy. What would you haue me say?
Lady. Would I might teach thee!
. . . faire Knight do you loue?
Guy. To ride a horse as well as any man:
To make him mount, curuet, to leape, and spring:
To chide the bit, to gallop, trot the ring.
Lady. I did not aske you if you loue to ride.
Something I meane; which though my tongue deny,
Looke on me, you may reade it in mine eye.
Guy. To march, to plant a battle, lead an Hoast,
To bee a souldier, and to goe to Warre, . . .
By heauen, I loue it as mine owne deere life.
Lady. I know all this; your words are but delaies:
Could you not loue a lady that loues you?
Tis hard when women are enforced to woo. *Priuate.*
Guy. Where is my man to bring me certaine newes,
The Kings Commission sends me to the warre:
The villaine loyters in my businesse.
Lady. All this is from the matter, gentle Knight:
The Kings Commission may be signd at leasure.
What say you to my question? . . .
Guy. Tis pretty for some foole that could endure it:
How neere am I vnto this loue, sweete Lady?
I loue to mount a Steed, whose heavy trot
Crackes all my sinewes, makes my Armour crash:
I loue to march vp to the necke in snowe:
To make my pillow of a cake of ice, . . .
I loue no Chamber-Musicke, but a Drumme
To giue me hunts-vp. Could your Grace endure
To lye all night within a sheete of maile,
By a drawne sword that parts not from my side,
Embrace a body full of wounds and skarres,
And heare no language but of blood and warres?
Such is my life, such may my honour proue:
Make warre a Lady, I that Lady loue.[63]

The young bachelor earls of Southampton and Pembroke showed Guy's disposition, the former about 1593–98, the latter in 1597–1601.

Another play marked by Henslowe in 1594 as "ne" is *The Set at Maw*, four performances in December and January, very doubtfully identified, as material underlying a much later revision, with Dekker's *Match Me in London*, published in 1631. The extant play gives no considerable evidence of being earlier than 1600, and it may easily be much later. *The Set at Maw* may have been quite satirical in its nature; the Chapel

[63] Heywood, *The Four Prentices of London*, Act II.

children had played a satirical "Comedie or Morrall devised on A game of the Cardes" as early as 1582.[64] Another lost play which may have been not only a satire but an offensively biting one is *The Merchant of Emden*, played for the first and only time on July 30, with receipts which were very good even for a new play.[65] The foreign merchants in London were causing much irritation at about this time, and the expulsion of the Dutch traders had been warmly urged by Ralegh in Parliament the preceding year. The subject was dangerous, for it was liable to excite riots; and the same administrative policies which interfered with the licensing of *Sir Thomas More* may have commanded the withdrawal of *The Merchant of Emden* from the boards, particularly as the theaters attracted a large attendance of the hot-headed disorderly 'prentices.

The Venetian Comedy may be the same as Dekker's lost *Jew of Venice*, and if so is likely to have had an important relation to *The Merchant of Venice*, put on by the rival company within a year or two. It is true that through a German *Jew of Venice* play in which a personage disguises as a French doctor, *The Venetian Comedy* has been identified with *The French Doctor* of Henslowe's 1594 list. But *The French Doctor* is not marked "ne," while *The Venetian Comedy* is. Greg and Fleay, the latter much less responsibly, try to do a good deal of this telescoping of the Admiral's repertory. Henslowe's slipshod methods of entry and his weirdly diverse spellings of what ought to be the same play-titles encourage these speculations, but we should accept them sparingly. At all events, *The French Doctor* rather suggests satirical portraiture of a racial sort, perhaps under influence of Armado in *Love's Labour's Lost*.[66]

There remain of the new plays which seem to belong to the comedy classification *Galiaso*[67] and *Philipo and Hippolito* (Italianate romances?)[68]

[64] *C.H.E.L.*, VI, 322.

[65] Greg, *Henslowe*, II, 166: "The same story, no doubt, as Collier suggested, appears in a Pepysian broadside ballad entitled, 'A most sweet Song of an English Merchant born in Chichester,' printed in T. Evans' collection (1810, I, p. 28)." Its story of the saving of the English merchant from death on the gallows for murder by an Emden maid who "begs" him in matrimony very possibly served as the romantic portion of the play.

In the spring of 1595 (*Sal. MSS.*, V, 163, April 1) the burghers of Emden revolted against their Earl, "doubting the Earl practiseth to alter the religion and place the Lutheranism." Numerous intelligences to Cecil and Essex during the year attest the English sympathy with the rebels, who seem to have gained their point. It is possible that there already existed in July, 1594, a strained situation of which the Council did not wish any cognizance to be taken on the London stage.

Another delicate situation connected with the Emden traders is indicated by a spy's information to Cecil, July 11, 1593 (*ibid.*, IV, 336), that English Jesuits habitually passed to Rome via Emden. Cf. also F. S. Boas (ed.), *Dr. Faustus*, II, i, 23 and note.

[66] Cf. Dr. Caius in *Merry Wives*.

[67] Possibly an Italian form of the Galahad story? Or see Deloney's *Joyful new Ballad declaring the happie obtaining of the great Galleazo*, etc., an Armada ballad, S.R. Aug. 10,

and *The Love of an English Lady*, which smells of Heywood as the other two titles do of Munday. Old plays in the same repertory[69] are *The Ranger's Comedy*, which may have come from the Queen's men, and *The Grecian Comedy*, which some think is Peele's unfortunately lost drama, *The Turkish Mahomet and Hiren the Fair Greek*, so ringingly quoted by Pistol—whose quotations, however, together with other references make the play seem at least as likely to have been a ranting tragedy like *The Battle of Alcazar*. It may be *Mahomet*, also 1594.

Taken as a group then, as we observe, the Admiral's comedies of the year show a strongly romantic trend—what is more, a trend toward the romantic types of the eighties or earlier.

Our reconstruction of the Chamberlain's repertory of comedies for 1594 is more a list of extant plays, largely because no Henslowe has preserved for us a list of the lost ones. But it commences with a name he has saved in his account of the joint occupancy in June of the theater at Newington Butts by the Admiral's and the Chamberlain's men. *Hester and Ahasuerus*[70] belongs to a considerable list of Biblical plays, of which it is the only one ascribed to Shakespeare's company, and all of which (unless we count Peele's *David and Bethsabe*)[71] are lost. Henslowe's diary shows that Sussex's men had presented *Abraham and Lot* three times in January of this same year.[72] It may be noteworthy that all three subjects so far mentioned have sex interest which would be attractive to a dramatist with an eye to what makes a popular play, and that *Abraham and Lot* offers a good opportunity for satirizing London (or better, Rome) as Sodom.[73] Apparently the Chamberlain's company did not feel that plays on Bible subjects would appeal to their clientele; after these first days at Newington Butts we never hear of their presenting such material. But the Admiral's men, with their cater-

1588, especially praising "our Lord High Admirall," *Roxburghe Ballads*, VI, 384. A "Galeatzo" in *Antonio and Mellida* is a very flighty, changeable character. The name also occurs among the Sforzas of Milan, famous for their tragic fall.

[68] Greg, *Henslowe*, II, 165.

[69] I have speculatively classified *Cutlack* among the Histories and shall there give my reasons for suspecting that it was a play on St. Guthlac.

[70] Possibly this play had some connection with the old *Godly Queen Hester*, plausibly assigned by Mrs. Stopes (*William Hunnis and the Revels of the Chapel Royal*) to Hunnis (d. 1597), who was connected in various ways with the Devereux family and with Sir Thomas Heneage, vice-chamberlain (d. 1595, 17 Oct.), Southampton's stepfather since 2 May, 1594. See Chambers, III, 349. Heneage entertained the Queen at the Savoy on December 7, 1594.

[71] Properties for its revival were perhaps purchased by Henslowe in 1602.

[72] Cf. also Chambers, II, 95

[73] London is satirized as Nineveh in *A Looking Glass for London and England* (Q. 1594), a play which might as well be entitled *Jonah* from its leading character. See below.

ing to the more old-fashioned Puritans, those not "precise" enough to stay away from the play no matter what its subject, had a play on Nebuchadnezzar in 1596, one on Judas in 1600, and no less than five Biblical plays in 1602: *Pontius Pilate, Jepthah, Tobyas, Samson,* and *Joshua.* One wonders whether they had very special reasons for such great piety at this late date. We may note that at this time Cecil's party was pretending to favor certain English candidates for the succession, partly on patriotic religious grounds, King James having done a great deal of coquetting with Rome. Moreover, they had been frightened by Essex's accusation of plotting for the Infanta.

Another old play in the 1594 repertory of the Chamberlain's men—at least the play-book was in their possession, and the play may have been revived by them—was *Love's Labour's Lost,* probably written at least as early as 1590. Possible influences of its pastoral and satirical elements on the Admiral's plays have already been mentioned. They had also *Two Gentlemen of Verona,* written two or three years earlier—another influential, much imitated play.

We learn from the *Stationers' Register* that in 1600 the Chamberlain's men still possessed a "Moral" called *Cloth Breeches and Velvet Hose.* This is not the sort of thing which the company had been doing since their organization in 1594. I suspect that it was Strange's men's and was produced in 1592, because its title is also the sub-title of Greene's tract, probably of that year, *A Quip for an Upstart Courtier, or a quaint Dispute Between Velvet-Breeches and Cloth Breeches,* which is in a form easily adaptable into a satirical drama. Pamphlets, like everything else in print (except, I think, plays actually in the repertories of active London companies), were considered fair game for the dramatist hunting material. What could be a more apt allusion, in the famous complaint about the "upstart crow beautified with our feathers," than one to an appropriation by the youthful play-cobbling Shakespeare of Greene's Velvet Hose? Other remarks of the dying dramatist on the players indicate clearly enough that he felt they should more suitably be walking in cloth breeches. If this did contain any work of Shakespeare's, one would rather see it than his lost *Cardenio,* for we have no idea what he would have done with such a general social satire[74] as Greene's pamphlet, which is an estimate of the relative values to the State of the several

[74] A drama of this type may have been Sussex's *God Speed the Plough* of Henslowe's 1594 list. S. R. March 1, '01, but not extant. The tillage laws, calling for certain acreages in foodstuffs, caused acrimonious discussion from time to time. In November, 1601, Ralegh said in Parliament, "I think the best course is to set corn at liberty, and leave every man free; which is the desire of a true Englishman." Cecil replied, "Whosoever doth not maintain the plough, destroys the kingdom." The issues included national defense as well as economics. (See D'Ewes, 299.)

classes of society, trades, and professions. A hint for the costuming may be found in the old pictures of "Nobody" and "Somebody" in the play they give their names to—Nobody "all slops" and Somebody all bombasted doublet. It is not clear that *Cloth Breeches and Velvet Hose* was ever acted by the Chamberlain's men but if not it is hard to see why they retained the play as a valuable property until 1600.[75] Perhaps they had altered the "Moral" into a burlesque of democratic propaganda.

In 1594 and again in 1598 and 1602 our period saw quartos of Lodge and Greene's *A Looking Glass for London and England*. This is a fascinatingly sensational conglomeration of the story of Jonah, the fulminations of the prophet "Oseas" against Nineveh (London thereby satirized), romantic tragedy of horrors, glittering pageantry, and realistic clowning. The play belonged to Strange's men in 1591–92, and may have strongly influenced Shakespeare; although as it was probably in print early in 1594 (S. R. March 5), it may never have been played by his company after they became the Chamberlain's men.[76] The escape of a play into print did not, however, necessarily destroy its value in a repertory. We know that during our period the Admiral's men were playing profitably *The Battle of Alcazar* (Quarto 1594, revival 1597 or 1600–02), *Friar Bacon and Friar Bungay* (Quarto 1594, revival for court, Christmas, 1602), *Tamburlaine* (Quarto 1590, playing 1594–5), and *The Spanish Tragedy* (Quarto 1594 or earlier, revival 1597 and probably 1601 and 1602) although they were all in print. There is a mystery here; what kept the Chamberlain's men from presenting these same plays, if the Admiral's monopoly was lost on publication? Yet we never hear of their doing so in any case—at least if we follow Chambers in believing that *The Spanish Tragedy* was an Admiral's play; that *Don Horatio* or *The Comedy of Jeronimo*, revived for Henslowe by Strange's men in February, 1592, is lost; that the extant *1 Jeronimo* was motivated by the revival of *The Spanish Tragedy* by the Admiral's men in 1601–02; that it was the property of the Chamberlain's men and was pirated by the Revels boys, thus causing Shakespeare's company to retaliate by taking their *Malcontent*, as the Induction of that play indicates. I think myself that the Chamberlain's *Jeronimo* was written and played as a burlesque on the old-fashioned *Spanish Tragedy*, and that the boys when they took

[75] Whyte writes Sidney, 9 Feb., 1600, that Essex walks in the garden at York House, where he is confined, all in cloth—"cloth Gown, cloth Jerken, cloth Hose, cloth Stokins, cloth Mittins." Was this to express melancholy and retreat from the things of the world? Whyte goes on, in the same sentence, to speak of his imminent trial.

[76] The Quarto of 1600 ascribes another play of doubtful date and authorship, *An Alarum for London*, to the Chamberlain's men. This, based on the sack of Antwerp by the Spaniards (1576), may have been written by Lodge as early as 1590–94, and revived at the Spanish scares of 1597 and 1599.

it added the burlesque touch of giving the part Jeronimo to one of the smallest among them.[77] Chambers remarks on this problem:[78]

It is often held that what they feared was the appropriation of their plays for acting by other companies. About this I am rather skeptical. It is, of course, impossible to hold, with Miss Albright, that there was a common law stage-right, which would have prevented appropriation . . . But it is reasonable to suppose that there was some comity among London companies in the matter.

He thinks that the plays were stolen for the two pounds or so which a publisher would give for one. In the case of Slater's sale of an Admiral's playbook, however,[79] the damages awarded were ten guineas.

Perhaps the "additions" so often mentioned in the case of revivals had some effect of renewing the "copyright." But if so, additions being easily provided, why did the companies make such efforts to keep their plays from the publishers? Perhaps, again, the real danger was such a rehandling as Shakespeare gave to the printed plays *The Taming of a Shrew* and *The Famous Victories of Henry V*,[80] completely superseding the older play as a valuable property. If so, the fears of Henslowe were better justified than those of Burbadge.

Before leaving *A Looking Glass* we might remark that the tragic part of the action revolves about the proposed incestuous marriage of a king with his sister, an unusual plot somewhat like the father-daughter motives in *Pericles* and in Green's *Pandosto,* source of *The Winter's Tale.* The use of stage-lightning may have inspired the same device in Heywood's *Golden Age. As You Like It* (IV, i) seems foreshadowed in Remilia's and Alvida's practicing coyness on one another. The latter is evidently a comedienne of deliciously swaggering mimicry:

Aluid. Madam, vnless you coy it trick and trim,
And plaie the ciuill wanton ere you yeeld, . . .
You marre the market, beautie nought availes.
You must be proud, for pleasures hardly got,
Are sweete, if once attainde.
Remilia. Faire Aluida,
Thy counsell makes Remilia passing wise.
Suppose that thou weart Rasnes mightinesse,
And I Remilia Prince of excellence.
Aluida. I would be maister then of loue and thee.
Remil. Of loue and me? Proud and disdainfull king,
Dar'st thou presume to touch a Deitie,
Before she grace thee with a yielding smile?

[77] See Boas, ed. Kyd, note on *I Jeronimo*, I, iii, 103, and Introduction, xliii.

[78] *Shakespeare*, I, 147.

[79] See Wallace's article in *Englische Studien*, XLIII, 382.

[80] Neither of which can be shown to have belonged to the Admiral's men. The former belonged to Pembroke's men, the latter to the Queen's.

> *Aluida.* Tut my Remilia, be not thou so coy,
> Say nay, and take it.
> *Remilia.* Carelesse and vnkinde,
> Talkes Rasni to Remilia in such sort . . .
> I tell the Flora oft hath wooed my lips,
> To lend a rose to beautifie her spring,
> The sea-Nymphs fetch their lillies from my cheekes.
> Then thou unkind, and hereon would I weepe.
> *Aluid.* And here would Aluida resigne her charge,
> For were I but in thought Th' assirian King,
> I needs must quite thy teares, with kisses sweete . . .[81]

Strange's men had a new play in 1593, *The Jealous Comedy*, which did not reappear in the Admiral's repertory and may have come to the Chamberlain's. It has often been identified with *The Comedy of Errors*, but not on fully convincing grounds; although that play does have striking scenes of jealousy, as has also *The Merry Wives of Windsor*, with which Baldwin identifies this lost (?) play. Of the two identifications I prefer the former, as it does not necessitate our making our first version of *The Merry Wives* (the "bad" quarto of 1602) a revision. In neither case is jealousy the most striking feature of the extant play, and the naming of plays from minor elements and characters does not seem to have come into vogue until much later. *Cosmo* (Cosimo de Medici?), also Strange's, may possibly be the same as *The Jealous Comedy*, an identification which would throw it into the classification of romantic Italian intrigue plays of unknown authorship.

Coming to comedies which may have been new, we find *The Taming of a Shrew* in Henslowe's Newington Butts list. A play of this title, different in many respects from Shakespeare's *The Shrew*, was published in 1594 as played by Pembroke's men. It seems likely that the Chamberlain's men at Newington were already performing Shakespeare's play; Henslowe was no man to make fine distinctions between "a" and "the." *The Taming of the Shrew* was doubtless a great hit. It must have been one of the leading candidates for court performance that Christmas, and its career must have been long and prosperous. Long after our period it still had so much vitality that Fletcher provided for it a sequel with subtitle *The Tamer Tamed.* The lasting effectiveness of this great piece of farcical comedy is perhaps less due to Shakespeare's handling than is the case with any other old play he worked over; but surely it was a great stroke, if by a rewriting with its "additions" of underplot and so on he made the favorite version of the play definitely the property of his company.

[81] Thomas Lodge and Robert Greene. *A Looking Glass for London and England*, Sgn. C. I follow here the Students' Facsimile, which reproduces the 1598 quarto.

The Comedy of Errors, although probably at least three years old,[82] was still a very popular farce, to judge by its use in the practical joke, perhaps Southampton's, "on Innocents' Day (December 28) at night,"[83] when the hall of Gray's Inn was so jammed at the time of the scheduled performance of some masque that both the masquers and the guests from the Temple were crowded out, the latter mightily offended thereby, so that the Prince of Purpoole, Lord of the Christmas revels of the Inn, deprecated the bringing in of common players to embroil still further such a "night of errors" and had a special Masque of Friendship[84] devised for January 3 to placate the Templars. With its strong thread of romance woven into the classic farce, *The Comedy of Errors* must have been a valuable property of Shakespeare's fellows for years. It does not seem likely to have been selected for court performance in 1594, because it probably already had been played before the Queen when new. Although in joking mood, Southampton would not have wished to expose his favorite players to obloquy for presenting a stale play; but we should remember that for being truly up with the latest fashion, the Court was one thing and the Inns of Court quite another. The Earl of Southampton belonged to both; but remember that Justice Shallow had been of Clement's Inn. The very latest dramatic fare does not seem to have been demanded by the "Grayans." Perhaps it was Southampton himself who inserted in the rules of their mock Order of the Helmet, conferred at these revels, an injunction to "frequent the Theatre."

A not unusual dating for *A Midsummer Night's Dream* is 1594, although one may appreciate Chambers' desire to have it regarded as written for the wedding on January 26, 1595, of the scions of two player-patronizing houses, those of Derby (Strange) and Oxford.[85] Of course the play could have been given on that occasion without having been especially written for it. It has been observed that "summery" plays were

[82] T. W. Baldwin, *William Shakespeare Adapts a Hanging*, dates it 1588.

[83] The *Gesta Grayorum* was written (at least in part) by Francis Davison. For general information see Chambers, IV, 55 ff. For a discussion of the dating problem involved, cf. Greg's ed. of the *Gesta* for the Malone Society and Chambers in *M.L.R.*, II, 10; Stopes, 73.

[84] Some speeches delivered Jan. 3, 1595, as part of the *Gesta Grayorum* were almost certainly by Francis Bacon, at this time one of the Earl of Essex's secretaries (Spedding, *Bacon*, VIII, 342).

[85] For Shakespeare's slighting of Derby and Oxford in *Henry V* see R. B. Sharpe, "We Band of Brothers," *S.P.*, XXVI, 166. Southampton, because of a heavy breach-of-promise payment to the bride, cannot have looked happily on the couple's prosperity. Essex disliked the Cecils, relatives of the bride, and had been recently (1594) quarreling with the brother of the groom (Lodge's *Illustrations*, Vol. III). Oxford, the bride's father, a generally unpopular man, hated all who caused Norfolk's fall, including, of course, Leicester, Essex's late stepfather. Hunsdon, the bluff Borderer, must have disliked the Italianated Oxford, who, in turn, disliked Southampton's stepfather, Vice-Chamberlain Heneage.

usually first produced in the summer, wintry ones in the winter. Now if the play had been given at court a few weeks before, it would not be likely to be thought suitable for this extremely fashionable wedding, because of the practically identical audiences; therefore, if we wish to think of it as presented at the wedding, we must consider Tilney barred from choosing it for the Christmas season. The most effective barrier, of course, would be that it was not completed, although it may have been "bespoken" for the wedding. The problem is a hard one. The arguments based on the weather are well known, and need not be discussed here.[86] My own preference for the occasion of the Berkeley-Carey wedding on February 19, 1596, is based on considerations which can best be discussed when we reach the dramatic season of that winter (pp. 162–68). The resemblance of its clowns' theatrical efforts to passages in *John a Kent*, and the identification of that play with Henslowe's *Wise Man of West Chester* may indicate Shakespeare in this case as the imitator. We should not omit to remark, however, that this supposed 1596 performance may have been a revival with hymeneal revisions, and that therefore we are not barred from believing in some form of the play as an item in the Chamberlain's 1594 repertory. It is hard not to believe that the version we possess was used at some occasion for a noble wedding; it is practically impossible to believe that it can have been used for more than one.

A glance over the Chamberlain's repertory of comedies as it has just been discussed shows its great strength in farce. On a quantitative estimate of the available data we cannot concede it anything like equality with the Admiral's list in romance.[87] In satire there is little to choose.

Well-marked differences in the nature of the chronicle plays to be found in the rival companies' repertories appear from the start. For instance, one of the Admiral's list is *Guise*, reasonably identifiable with Marlowe's *The Massacre at Paris*, which had belonged to Strange's men. This sensational tragedy from recent French history was, of course, good strong Protestant propaganda, hardly the sort of thing the Chamberlain's men went in for. In fact, the horror of French Catholicism which this revival was calculated to instil may have worked against the policies of Essex—an enthusiastic supporter of Henry of Navarre, who had just decided that Paris was "worth a Mass." *Warlamchester* also is not marked "ne." It may have been of the type which mingles folk-lore and chronicle with a strong comic element. So probably did the new and popular play *Bellendon*, which we may safely assume from an entry in

[86] Cf. Chambers, *Shakespeare*, I, 360.

[87] I do not think we should assume that a "Burbadge's Diary" corresponding to Henslowe's would show lost plays to make up this difference.

the Stationers' Register dealt with a personage of the time of Rufus, Belin Dun, "the first thief ever hanged in England." Camden tells us:

we mounted up by a whitish chalkey hill into the *Chiltern*, and streightwaies were at *Dunstable*. . . . But heare the very words out of that private History, although they savour of the Barbarisme of that age. *Note that the plat of ground where the two high waies* Watling *and* Ikening *meet, was first by* Henry *the elder*[88] *King of England cleered, to keepe under and bridle the wickednesse of a certaine most notorious Theefe named* Dun, *and his Companions, and of that* Dun *the said place was named* Dunstable. *The King our Lord built there the Burgh of* Dunstable, *and made for himselfe a royall Manour, or house neere under that place. The King had in the same Towne both Faire and Mercat.*[89]

That "Chiltern" was once noted for thieves is also testified by Camden:[90] "it was altogether unpassable in times past by reason of trees, until that *Leofstane Abbot of Saint Albans* did cut them downe, because they yeelded a place of refuge for theeves." Dunstable, as a place well known to travelers, and of comic connotations somewhat like those of Gotham,[91] was especially celebrated by Henslowe's dramatists in *Sir John Oldcastle*. That the legendary etymology of Dunstable was alluded to in the play is well established by the entry in Henslowe's 1598 inventory of "Belendon Stable."[92] The historical material dealing with Rufus in Dekker's oddly and hastily put-together *Satiromastix*, done for the Chamberlain's men years later, may be somehow influenced by *Bellendon;* indeed, it may have been prepared as a tragedy about 1594–96.[93]

Two more old plays remain, *Cutlack* and *The Siege of London*. That Cutlack was one of Alleyn's famous heroic rôles we know from Guilpin's *Skialetheia:*[94]

OF CLODIUS

Clodus me thinks lookes passing big of late,
With *Dunstons* browes, and *Allens Cutlacks* gate:
What humours haue possest him so, I wonder,
His eyes are lightning, and his words are thunder:
What meanes the Bragart by his alteration?
He knows he's known too wel, for this fond fashion:
To cause him to be feared: what meanes he than?

[88] Henry I, brother and successor of Rufus.

[89] Camden, *Britannia*, trans. ed. of 1637.

[90] *Ibid.*, 393.

[91] Cf. E. H. Sugden, *A Topographical Dictionary of the Works of Shakespeare and his Fellow Dramatists*. He does not mention *Bellendon*, Belin Dun, or the Camden etymology. There is a pun, aimed at certain lawyers, in Manningham's Diary, Duns-table = Duncetable.

[92] Greg, *Henslowe*, III, 117.

[93] A *Rufus I* appears in the *Stationers' Register*, Nov. 24, 1595. What Dekker was doing before his appearance as a writer for the Admiral's in 1598 is unknown, although he may have been working for them as early as 1594. He was born about 1572.

[94] 1598; Epigram 43.

> Belike, because he cannot play the man.
> Yet would be awde, he keepes this filthy reuell,
> Stalking and roaring like to *Iob's* great deuill.

Note the graphic descriptions here of Alleyn's habitually robustious acting, and the interesting allusion to Job's devil—quite possibly still another of his rôles, for Warburton's cook is said to have destroyed a play of Greene's on Job. The "Dunston" referred to should, I believe, be considered another Alleyn rôle, and be identified with that of St. Dunstan, who calls up and controls devils in masterful fashion in *A Knack to Know a Knave*—at any rate, whether Alleyn played him in that or another play (perhaps in some version of the Grim the Collier legend), Dunstan, of course, was famous for his devils. Now one naturally suspects that the epigrammatist is bringing together two similar characters to point his jab at "Clodius"; hence my desire to see in the mysterious "Cutlack" the renowned St. Guthlac of Croyland or Crowland Abbey in the Lincolnshire fens. Guthlac's life presented fine opportunities for an Alleyn interpretation. As a young man a wild warrior, looting and killing, he was forced by conscience always to restore a third of his plunder, and finally to turn hermit on a remote island in the fen, the favorite retreat also of legions of demons, who tormented him until he was rescued by his patron saint, Bartholomew.[95] On one occasion he was nearly murdered by a rival who was shaving him, but saved himself by his powers of mind-reading, of which on other occasions he made humorous use, such as telling two simple visitors about a couple of bottles they had cannily hidden on their way to Crowland, so as to be sure to have them for solace on the journey home.

Camden[96] uses Felix's *Life of Guthlac* with a relish for its comic possibilities; indeed, may not some of the graphic touches in this paraphrase by his translator give us a glimpse of the Admiral's play itself?

> If I should exemplifie unto you out of that Monke Felix, the Devils of Crowland, with their blabber lips, fire-spitting mouths, rough and scaly visages, beetle heads, terrible teeth, sharpe chins, hoarse throats, blacke skinnes, crump-shoulders, side and gor-bellies, burning loines, crooked and hawm'd legges, long tailed buttockes, and ugly mishapes, which heeretofore walked and wandered up and downe in these places, and very much troubled holy Guthlake and the Monkes, you would laugh full merily: and I might be thought a simple sily-one full worthily.

Alleyn's company had among their properties devil-costumes for such plays as *Faustus*, *Friar Bacon*, *A Knack to Know a Knave*, *Like Will to Like*. But this establishes no more than an interesting possibility.

[95] Is it significant that of the twelve performances of *Cutlack*, 16 May–26 Sept., 1594, six were on the next day to *The Massacre at Paris*, i.e., that of St. Bartholomew's Day?

[96] *Britannia, re* Crowland, quoting Felix's life of "Guthlake."

As for *The Siege of London*, a play on such a subject might give good scope for the prentice-flattering propensities of Heywood. It is amusing to think of it as perhaps opposing the cynical views of the masses given us in Shakespeare's account of the Jack Cade disorders in *2 Henry VI*. Or it may be identified[97] with Heywood's *1 Edward IV*,[98] which refers to Cade's rising but stresses "the besieging of London by Bastard Faulconbridge." *Edward IV* shows a rather careful picking-out of incidents not used in *Henry VI* or *Richard III*, either through a kindly deference toward Shakespeare, of which I think Heywood capable, or through fear of being taunted with plagiarism. (His treatment of the Troilus and Cressida story in *The Iron Age* exhibits, I think, the same phenomenon.)[99] Heywood here stresses the patriotism of the London citizens and their interesting organization by craft companies to defend the city. The streets are chained, lights hung out in the streets, the walls and Tower strongly manned. Falconbridge, outside, comes off second-best in an altercation with prentices on the walls:

> *2P.* You are those desperat idle swaggering mates,
> That haunt the subburbs in the time of peace,
> And raise up ale-house braules in the street,
> And when the rumor of the war beginnes,
> You hide your heads, and are not to be found . . .
> *Fa.* Who can endure to be so braude by boyes?
> *1P.* Nay scorne us not that we are Prentises,
> The Chronicles of England can report,
> What memorable actions we have done,
> To which this dayes achievement shall be knit,
> To make the volume larger than it is . . .
> *Here is a very fierce assault on all sides, wherein the Prentises do great seruice.*

Other writers who usually work for Henslowe may be represented by rhymed traces of Munday's balladizing hand (the prose seems full of ballad scraps), and by a "three-man song" from Drayton's *Agincourt*. A comic character named Jockie uses Scots dialect, a kind of speech which the Chamberlain's men seem comparatively careful not to make fun of.[100] There seem to be references to *King John*, *Henry VI*, and *Rich-*

[97] See Greg, *Henslowe*, II, 173. [98] Q. 1599, ascribing it to Derby's men.

[99] It is noteworthy how, on his part, Shakespeare avoids doing more than refer to the story of Shore's Wife. Was this prudence or courtesy? (And see note on *The True Tragedy of Richard III*, below.)

[100] The Scots are satirized also in *Black Bateman* (if I am right in identifying it with Sampson's *Vow-Breaker*), *James IV*, and *George a Greene*. The chief examples of the sort in the Chamberlain's plays occur in *Henry V*, coming in oddly enough at a time when Essex and Mountjoy were secretly treating with King James for the establishment of his claim to the succession by armed intervention; cases where propaganda is used to disguise real motives are, however, not unknown. The Carey family's close and friendly associations with the Scots have already been noticed.

ard II; the dramatic irony of Jane Shore's protestations of loyalty to her husband reminds one of *Hamlet.* The fun of the disguised king with the tanner of Tamworth is like parts of *Henry V* and *Sir John Oldcastle;* indeed, there are numerous touches in this play, especially in Part Two, which make a revision about 1598–99 seem likely.[101] Altogether, though ill organized, it is an interesting play.

Whether or not *Edward IV* was theirs, the Chamberlain's men may have had *Richard II*[102] and *King John* as early as 1594. And doubtless they possessed the three Henry VI plays, in one form or another. Of course *1 Henry VI* had not yet been adapted to join on smoothly to the end of *Henry V*, or *Richard II* to connect with *1 Henry IV*. *Richard III*,[103] a sensational success, can hardly have been more than a year old at most. The influence on Shakespeare's *Richard II* of Marlowe's *Edward II*,[104] which does not appear to have been played after 1592 or 1593 (unless by the Chamberlain's men) has often been discussed. As a reason for its disappearance from the stage, we should consider the resemblance of its deposition of an unworthy ruler to the case of *Richard II*, where the faction of Cecil made as much as they could of what they declared sedition in the use of very similar historical material in print and on the stage. We can trace the beginnings of the issue back to about 1597, perhaps even to 1595, if Cecil's visit to the play at Hoby's was one of inspection. Surely they could not afford to allow the other faction such a splendid opportunity to point out that they were tarred with the same brush as would have been provided if the Admiral's servants were rivalling *Richard II* with a piece of practically identical political implications.

[101] The complimentary references to the Captain of the Isle of Wight thus may be an attempt to flatter the new Lord Chamberlain, after the Falstaff—Cobham unpleasantness. (The scene is Part One, Sgn. G, the discussion between Vice Admiral Sir Harry Moorton and the unnamed Captain of the Isle of Wight and Falconbridge, whom they are escorting to the block.)

[102] With it should be considered the manuscript *1 Richard II* which may have been a property of the company, written after Shakespeare's play to take advantage of its popularity. In *The Death of Huntingdon* we have an example of a second part written largely by a different hand from that which composed the first, and in *Cardinal Wolsey* (see Greg, *Henslowe,* II, 218) an instance of a first part written later than a second. *The Merry Wives,* which deals with events occurring before those of *Henry IV*, seems to have been written after it. The revision of the close of *Richard II* to make it fit on to *1 Henry IV*, apparently for successive performance in a revival of the former play encouraged by the success of the latter, may serve as an example of somewhat the same sort of linking.

[103] Chambers (II, 95) suggests a connection with Sussex's *Buckingham,* listed by Henslowe in December, 1593; but he seems to prefer identifying *Buckingham* with a hypothetical early version of *Henry VIII*, which would then be in the Chamberlain's possession in 1594. I prefer the *Richard III-Buckingham* identification, or none at all.

[104] S.R. July 6, 1593, Quarto 1594, ascribed to Pembroke's men.

An anonymous *True Tragedy of Richard III*[105] belonging to the Queen's men was published in 1594 (S. R. June 19). This may have been considered, since the Queen's men had become a provincial company, as releasing the subject to the first dramatist to take it up again; if so, *Richard III* was new in 1594. The atrocious Richard, of course, had a great influence on subsequent villains.

The Reign of King Edward the Third, published in 1596 as "sundrie times plaied about the Citie of London," seems the more likely to have been a Chamberlain's play because of the passages which, if not Shakespeare's, are in sincerest flattery of his style, and the line "Lilies that fester smell far worse than weeds," found also in Sonnet XCIV. In editing the play,[106] Farmer says "from internal evidence it is clearly shown that the play was written early in 1589." If so (I am not convinced, but the style does not absolutely belie it), it was no longer fresh enough to be a valuable property in 1594, and was naturally let go to the publishers a year or so after.[107] It seems to me that the play was really in two parts; for it is very long and has a distinct break at the change of scene to France marked by large type in the quarto.[108] That Shakespeare was familiar with the play is indicated by many reminiscences of it in his handling of martial events in *Henry IV* and *Henry V*.[109] The second quarto appeared in 1599, the year of *Henry V*.

With this survey, a distinction between the history plays of the Admiral's and those of the Chamberlain's men begins to appear: The Ad-

[105] This play is usually declared to have left little trace of its use on Shakespeare. I do not agree, but think there are marked traces. See Richard's opening soliloquy revealing illegitimate ambition, Richard's dream of ghosts "gaping for revenge," the reference to gloomy weather for the battle, his cry "a horse, a horse, a fresh horse." There seems to be a bit of satire on some writer's fondness for Jane Shore, perhaps added on publication:

Jane Shore. I Lodowicke, I am she that begged thy lands of King Edward the fourth, therefore I pray thee bestow something on me.

Lod. A gods what is this world, and how uncertaine are riches? . . . I will shun her company and get me to my chamber, and there set downe in heroicall verse, the shameful end of a Kings Concubin, which is no doubt as wonderfull as the desolation of a kingdome. *Exit.* (*The True Tragedy of Richard the Third*, ll. 1068 ff.)

[106] As a Tudor Facsimile Text.

[107] S.R., Dec. 1, 1595.

[108] There is large type at the beginning of the next scene, too, but this may have resulted from a natural error of the printer.

[109] Some passages in *Edward III* which may have influenced the martial side of Shakespeare's King Henry plays: (1) *Henry IV:* John Copland refuses to deliver King David, his prisoner. News brought by Percy. "The mightier that their number is The greater glory reaps the victory." Refusal of the French offer of mercy before the battle of Poitiers. Ominous darkness before the battle. (2) *Henry V:* Bearing of the Salic Law on the English monarch's claim to France. Disloyalty of the Scots. Account of the numbers slain on each side. The burghers of Calais (compare Harfleur). Taunting gifts of a horse and a prayer-book (compare the tennis balls). The shame of the French (compare *Henry V*, IV, v).

miral's had one French topical play, of strongly Protestant spirit; the rest of the plays on their list seem to have been of the romantic and legendary type in their dealing with English history. Their rivals, on the other hand, had a remarkable repertory of patriotic, warlike English historical plays, calculated by their martial and dynastic characteristics to delight their courtly audiences, in which the war party headed by Essex was strongly represented.

In the tragic section of the Admiral's repertory an unusual number of plays can be identified. The doubtful one among the old plays is *Mahomet;* this may be Peele's *The Turkish Mahomet and Hiren the Fair Greek*, or Greene's *Alphonsus, King of Arragon.* The former is lost; but it probably influenced *Selimus*, and it certainly is burlesqued by Pistol. *Alphonsus*, written of course before 1593, was published in 1599 as played by the Admiral's men, and may have seen revivals in 1594 and 1601. It has a brazen head, perhaps "owld Mahemetes head" mentioned in Henslowe's inventory of 1598. It is called a "Comical History" on the title page probably because, although it is wholly ranting and sensational and has no comic relief, it is written in imitation of the first part of *Tamburlaine.* Like that play, it probably had a tragic sequel, promised by Greene's words, "when I come to finish up his life."

The Admiral's men were also playing three mighty works of Marlowe, still profitable attractions down at least to 1597: *The Jew of Malta*, which influenced *Titus Andronicus* and *The Merchant of Venice;* both parts of *Tamburlaine*, which influenced *Selimus* and numerous other plays; and *Doctor Faustus*, also long influential on the Elizabethan stage (revived with additions by Birde and Rowley for the Admiral's men in 1602). Another valuable property was Kyd's *Spanish Tragedy*, usually spoken of by Henslowe as *Jeronimo*, revived in 1593 and 1597, and with additions by Jonson in 1602. It does not appear to have been performed, however, in 1594. It came out in quarto that year, and an undated quarto is thought by Boas to be still earlier.

The new tragedies of the season are all lost. *Tasso's Melancholy* looks as if it might have been a Chettle-Munday imitation of the early *Hamlet.* If later than *Romeo and Juliet, Palamon and Arcyte* can hardly have escaped its influence in atmosphere and treatment. The use of material from *The Knight's Tale* may have a relation to that in *A Midsummer Night's Dream* (the wedding of Theseus and Hippolyta). Heywood probably had "a hand or a main finger," to use his own expression, in this play.[110] Shakespeare's company apparently did not bring out their ver-

[110] Heywood's fondness for Chaucerian material may be deduced from his *Lucrece, Iron Age* (Troilus story), *Brazen Age* (Jason and Medea), and *Appius and Virginia;* not that he necessarily had to use Chaucer in any of these cases; a careful source-study would be useful on this point, which A. M. Clark does not take up in his *Thomas Heywood.*

sion of the story until about 1613, in *The Two Noble Kinsmen*. The two[111] remaining are Roman plays,—*1 Caesar and Pompey* and *Dioclesian*. Of course the former may have influenced *Julius Caesar*, though at considerable distance. Chambers rejects the identification of this play with Chapman's *Caesar and Pompey*, published long after, but it does not seem impossible to me that for the published play Chapman rewrote in his later style some early work of his for Henslowe.[112] *Dioclesian* has been identified with *The Virgin Martyr* (Quarto 1622), by Massinger and Dekker, the latter of whom may have been writing for Henslowe in 1594. The extant play is full of horrors, indicating that *Dioclesian* may have been written to compete with *Titus Andronicus*. A burlesque of the style of Stanyhurst and Gabriel Harvey may indicate an early date for some of the material of *The Virgin Martyr*.[113]

Shakespeare's company had a list of tragedies which rather closely matched the Admiral's in type and theme. The Senecan horrors-type was represented by the popular *Titus Andronicus*, which is marked as new by Henslowe at a performance by Sussex's men on January 24. It appears in the joint Chamberlain's-Admiral's repertory in June at Newington and was doubtless then a Chamberlain's play. I have no doubt that this is the so-called Shakespeare play as we have it. It was published in 1594 with a puzzling ascription to Derby's, Sussex's, and Pembroke's men (the second quarto, 1600, ascribes it to the Chamberlain's).

[111] We might add Lodge's *The Wounds of Civil War*, a Roman play published 1594, as belonging to the Admiral's men. But it was probably written in 1588, and its stage usefulness was past. Its politics may have been considered useful enough to encourage its publication, since the succession debate was a constant and dangerous irritant. For instance, as early as 1593 gossip had it (*Sal. MSS.*, IV, 336) that Sir Robert Cecil planned to marry Arabella Stuart and advance her to the throne—odd, for his wife, Lord Cobham's daughter, did not die until 1596 (Jan. 24). The rumor persisted until the end of the reign; see Hume, *Treason and Plot*, 502.

[112] In *Caesar and Pompey*, I, 1, the description of Caesar's army by Cato would not apply so very ill, in the minds of a hostile audience, to the followers of Essex, whom they feared, especially in 1599, he might lead home from foreign parts to assert his rights and claims:

> Impostors, flatterers, favorites, and bawds,
> Buffoons, intelligencers, select wits;
> Close murtherers, mountebanks, and decay'd thieves,
> To gain their baneful lives' reliefs from him.
> From Britain, Belgia, France, and Germany,
> The scum of either country (choosed by him,
> To be his blackguard and red agents here)
> Swarming about him.

A little later comes a mention of "the damn'd crew"—Baynham, leader of a group so called, was an Essexian. May the play, originally or in a revision, belong to 1599–1601?

[113] "Ile come upon her with rounce, robble-hobble, and thwick-thwack thwirlery bouncing." Compare Stanyhurst's *Vergil*, "With peale meale ramping, with thwick thwack sturdelye thundring."

Scholars have thus been led to deny that the play really was new in January and to try to identify it with *Titus and Vespasian*, of which ten performances were given by Strange's (Derby's) men between April 11, 1592 and January 25, 1593. There is a clear statement of this matter by A. M. Witherspoon in his edition of *Titus Andronicus* for the *Yale Shakespeare*.[114] It seems to me possible that *Titus and Vespasian* was a chronicle play based on a portion of legendary British history of especial interest to the Earl of Southampton. Let me cite from Holinshed, Book One: In Chapter II, under the valiant leadership of Plautius,

> Titus the sonne of Vespasian also won no small praise for deliuering his father out of danger . . . being beset with a companie of Britains, which the said Titus bare doune, and put to flight with great slaughter.

There follows, so closely that a reader might take it for granted that Titus and Vespasian were concerned, the following passage:

> Claudius at his comming aland at Porchester, besieged that towne, to the rescue whereof came Guiderius, and giuing battell to the Romans, put them to the woorse, till at length one Hamo, being on the Romans side, changed his shield and armour, apparelling himself like a Britaine, and so entring into the thickest prease of the British host, came at length where the King was, and there slue him. But Aruiragus perceiuing this mischiefe, to the end the Britains should not be discouraged therewith, caused himselfe to be adorned with the kings cote-armor, and other abiliments, and so as king continued the fight with such manhood, that the Romans were put to flight. Claudius retired back to his ships, and Hamo to the next woods, whom Aruiragus pursued, and at length droue him vnto the sea side, and there slue him yer he could take the hauen which was there at hand; so that the same tooke name of him, and was called a long time after Hamons hauen, and at length by corruption of speach it was called Hampton, and so continueth vnto this day, commonlie called by the name of Southhampton.

Chapter III relates with apologies the "feined tale" of Arviragus' marriage to Claudius' daughter. In Chapter IV "Aruiragus denieth subjection to the Romans, Vespasian is sent by Claudius to represse him and his power, the Romane host is kept back from landing" at Sandwich: they land at Totnes, and besiege Exeter. A battle with Arviragus is indecisive. Then Queen Genissa makes them friends. Holinshed here takes pains to quote Suetonius and Sabellicus on Vespasian's capturing the Isle of Wight. Chapter XVI tells how Vespasian deputes Iulius Agricola to govern Britain, and Chapter XVIII how Vespasian, deprived of his command by the envy of Domitian, becomes emperor after the death of Titus, whom Holinshed calls his brother.

Thus we see that the adventures of Titus and Vespasian cover a great deal of ground, at least three plays about them being possible: a chronicle

[114] 112–114.

history of their exploits in Britain; a political history of intrigues at Rome;[115] and a tragical history of the fall of Jerusalem—to the Middle Ages Vespasian was a Christian, whose war against the Jews was a sort of crusade.

That *Titus and Vespasian* and *Titus Andronicus* were two distinct plays is, I think, made clear by certain references in *A Knack to Know a Knave*, given during the same season as *Titus and Vespasian* by "Ed. Alleyn and his Companie," i.e., Strange's men. In the opening speech of the play a mention of "wise Vespasian" with flattering mention of his laws, such as the punishing of seduction by death,[116] looks like a "puff" by the company of another of its own plays, and hints that if this lost play of Vespasian and his son had any influence on Shakespeare's work it was upon *Measure for Measure*. In an entirely different part of the play we have the simile, "As Titus was unto the Roman senators When he had made a conquest on the Goths." Since the *Knave* was not published until 1594, this reference may have been inserted as another puff, this time of *Titus Andronicus*, when both plays were in the Chamberlain's repertory. Another of these advertising references in the same play is to "Locrin, eldest son of Brute," who kept an "Almaine maid" seven years underground in the life of Guendolin, "which made the Cornish men to rise in arms." Strange's men had a *Harry of Cornwall* in 1592–93; and this reference seems to fix the otherwise unknown ownership of *Locrine* (Quarto 1595, no company named) and to hint that this rather Senecan tragedy,[117] too, may have descended to the Chamberlain's men. *Selimus*, which imitates *Locrine*[118] more closely than seems likely for two plays belonging to the same company, was

[115] It will be remembered that Vespasian, like Bolingbroke, reached the throne by deposing his predecessor, Vitellius, and that Titus like Prince Hal, on coming to power, "falsified the pessimistic prophecies of his detractors"; *Encyclo. Brit.*, XIV Ed., "Titus."

[116] *King Edgar*. Dunston, how highlie are we bound to praise
The Eternall God that still prouides for vs,
And giues vs leaue to rule in this our land
Like wise Vaspasian, Romes rich Emperour:
Suppressing sinue [?sinne], that daylie raignes in vs:
First, murther we rewarde with present death,
And those that doe commit fellonious crimes,
Our lawes of England doe awarde them death:
And hee that doeth dispoyle a Virgins chastitie,
Must lykewise suffer death by lawes decree,
And that decree is irrevocable.

This reference may perhaps be taken to indicate that some portion of the lost *Titus and Vespasian* centered upon events at Rome.

[117] Of course it might be classified rather as a chronicle play, if preferred.

[118] Chambers, IV, 27: "I agree with Cunliffe (*C.H.*, V, 84) that the evidence is clearly in favor of *Selimus* being the later of the two plays."

published in 1594 as a Queen's play, and may well have remained in the provincial repertory of that company.

The Senecan attractions of the Admiral's tragic repertory, then, represented by work of Marlowe and probably also of Kyd, Greene, and Peele in the same vein, we may consider rivalled by the Chamberlain's men with *Titus Andronicus* and *Locrine*. We can tell, too, from the Henslowe record of the Newington performances, that Shakespeare's company had a *Hamlet*. Whether we believe this to have been Kyd's Ur-*Hamlet* or already a rewriting by Shakespeare, this was certainly a successful play and a great asset to the company. Another tragedy in the Senecan vein which should be mentioned here is Chapman's (?) *Alphonsus, Emperor of Germany*. The quarto (1654) tells us that this play belonged to the King's men, as the Chamberlain's men became on the accession of James. Chapman is not unlikely to have written some early things for Shakespeare's company; but the main reason for placing the play early is that some see in it the hand of Peele, who was dead by 1598. The verse seems to me rather old-fashioned and unlike that of *Bussy d'Ambois*. T. M. Parrott, *The Comedies of George Chapman*, 676, points out the merits of Chapman's early comic style in *The Blind Beggar of Alexandria*, so markedly different from his later, tragic manner. The verse of *Alphonsus Emperor of Germany* has, it seems to me, somewhat the same clear, easy, rapid movement. The play has many resemblances in wording and situation to dramas of the nineties; its parallels to *Faustus*, *The Jew of Malta*, *Tamburlaine*, *The Massacre at Paris*, *The Spanish Tragedy*, and *Hamlet* indicate its imitation of Marlowe and Kyd. It may well be by the same playwright, whoever that may have been, as *Lust's Dominion*, one of the Marlowe apocrypha. There is a striking scene based on Nash's *Jack Wilton* (1594).[119] I think this perhaps a 1595 play, and Chapman not its sole author.

Romeo and Juliet, even if not a 1594 play, was very likely filling the playhouse for frequent performances. The usual datings range from 1593 to 1595.[120] The play was, of course, immensely influential, with a vogue which spread gradually out from London; the impression it was still making on university students at the end of the century is interestingly indicated in *1 Return from Parnassus*, presented by students of St. John's College, Cambridge, at Christmas, 1599, which has a sample-wooing performance, full of bits from *Venus and Adonis* and *Romeo and Juliet*, with a reference to "sweet Mr. Shakespeare." On the basis of

[119] Alexander binds Alphonsus and gives him his choice between abjuring God and dying. After securing an abjuration resembling that of Faustus, Alexander kills him, having insured his damnation by this device. The idea occurs in *Hamlet* in modified form.

[120] Chambers, *Shakespeare*, I, 345, places it 1595 (*Eliz. Stage*, III, 483, "1594–95?").

these amorous works the author of the academic play considered Shakespeare over-sensuous and over-popular.[121]

With the Senecan type so well represented in the tragic repertories of both the rival companies, with the villainous Jew of Malta balanced by the atrocious Moor Aaron, with Tasso's melancholy perhaps resembling that of Hamlet, and the woes of Palamon, Arcyte, and Emily plaintively echoing those of Romeo and Juliet, we perceive a balance in tragedy with which the Admiral's possession of a couple of Roman plays and the Chamberlain's of a tragedy of British legendary history can interfere but little. One side had Marlowe, the other Shakespeare. Perhaps the Chamberlain's men had a slight advantage in that their tragedies, though fewer, were on the average newer.

It is now fairly easy to summarize the problem of the Master of the Revels. Equally obligated to both court factions and distributing his favors nearly equally, he may well have found that in comedy his choice lay between the Admiral's two most successful plays of the season, *A Knack to Know an Honest Man* and *The Wise Man of West Chester*, and Shakespeare's clever new version of a sure-fire farce, *The Taming of the Shrew*, and his *Comedy of Errors*. As the *Errors* confused the lawyers on December 28, *The Shrew* seems to be Tilney's probable choice from the Chamberlain's list. To go on to histories, *Belin Dun* looks the most promising in the Admiral's repertory, and *Richard III* in the Chamberlain's. Of Henslowe's new tragedies *Tasso's Melancholy* was far more successful than *Palamon and Arcyte*, to judge by the number of performances. It would be hard to choose among Marlowe's well-tried plays; perhaps *Faustus*, with its fine spectacular qualities and strong religious emotions, would be most suitable for Christmas performance at court. Among the rival offerings, *Titus Andronicus* seems really too bloody for the Christmas revels even of a Queen fond of amusing herself with bull- and bear-baitings; *Hamlet*, unless recently renovated by Shakespeare, would be out of date, for Kyd's version was probably before 1592. *Locrine*, because of recent plague conditions, may still have been new to the court. But *Romeo and Juliet*, also if fairly recent new to the court, far excels the other entrants.

If we may assume that Tilney knew in advance what dates he had available, let us supply them as Chambers[122] gives them from the records of payments for court performances, none of which this season unfor-

[121] These academic playwrights may have known political considerations, for Essex, who was of Trinity College, succeeded Burghley as Chancellor of Cambridge, and served 1598–1601, being in turn succeeded by Sir Robert Cecil. This alternating of parties in the office resembles the case of the Chamberlainship.

[122] IV, 108, 109.

tunately gives the name of the play, though they do give us the company. We may then suggest this as a possible dramatic program, the ultimate decisions to be made by the Queen, doubtless with some advice from her courtiers as well as from the Master of the Revels:

December 26, 1594, the Chamberlain's men—*The Taming of the Shrew* or *Richard III.*

December 28 (afternoon), the Chamberlain's men—*Romeo and Juliet.*

December 28 (evening), the Admiral's men—*John a Kent* or *Belin Dun.*

January 1, 1595, the Admiral's men—*Doctor Faustus.*

January 6, the Admiral's men—*A Knack to Know an Honest Man* or *Tasso's Melancholy.*

Considering the flattering outside engagement (curious and informal but good advertising) of the Chamberlain's men at the Gray's Inn revels on the evening of December 28, the rival companies ended their first year with almost equal success, an even start in the race for the supremacy of the London stage. It proves to be a contest worth watching.

CHAPTER II (1595–1597)

THE CHAMBERLAIN'S MEN RISE TO SUPREMACY

Repertories of 1595. *Disguise plays, 1594–1603.* Satire on the 1595 stage. *Friars in the plays of the rival companies, 1594–1603.* History plays and their political bearings. The court season of 1595–96. Repertories of 1596. Satire against the Admiral's men in "A Midsummer Night's Dream." "Henry IV" and the Hunsdon-Cobham rivalry. The turning of the river Trent. "The Tinker of Totnes" and the Suffolk claim to the succession. *The Jew on the stage, 1594–1603.* Satire against Essex in "The Blind Beggar of Alexandria." The Christmas season of 1596–97.

IT is not difficult to see how Tilney's survey of the competing repertories could have led him to give the Admiral's men a parity with the Chamberlain's men at the Christmas season of 1594. Neither is it hard to see how this competitive series of court performances in the last few days of 1594 and the first few of 1595 must have given Shakespeare's company an advantage at court which a man like Henslowe—or even an Alleyn, misled by the warmth of a personal triumph—would not at once realize. The best Elizabethan taste, thus given an opportunity for close comparison of the best of the two repertories, seems to have awarded the palm to the Chamberlain's men in a quiet but decisive way. This preference must soon have become evident in the attendance at public performances; it was fairly clear at the next Christmas season, and overwhelming at the following one, that of 1596.

But for a time, at least, there seemed to be no reason for the Henslowe-Alleyn company to be apprehensive; and the year 1595 saw their production of a normal number of new plays, sixteen, normally enough distributed among their usual dramatic types: romance, satire, legendary British history, Roman history, mythology, realistic comedy, romantic tragedy. Moreover, at least seventeen plays of the previous year's repertory are shown by Henslowe's records to be still running in 1595.[1]

I am not sure that the company had a new play based on the popular romances; *Barnardo and Fiammetta* looks as if it might be of that nature. Anyhow, *Godfrey of Bulloigne* was still running. The way the

[1] *Tamburlaine* to 12 Nov., *The Venetian Comedy* to 8 May, *Mahomet* to 5 Feb., *Tasso's Melancholy* to 14 May, *Godfrey of Bulloigne* to 16 Sept., *The Ranger's Comedy* to 19 (18) Jan.; *The Grecian Comedy*, *1 Caesar and Pompey*, *Warlamchester*, *The Set at Maw*, and *2 Tamburlaine* ran through 1594 and into 1595; *Belin Dun*, *Faustus*, *The French Doctor*, *A Knack to Know an Honest Man*, *The Wise Man of West Chester*, and *The Siege of London* ran through 1594 and 1595.

Admiral's men handled this "matter of romance" is shown by the very titles to be consistently different throughout our period from the policy of the Shakespearean company. The latter organization had an audience which considered the romance bourgeois and old-fashioned; and with the single exception of *Troilus and Cressida*, which was satirically treated, they never advertised in their titles the fact that romance material might be found in their plays. Of course romance material is often there, but disguised and adapted—a rose by some other name often does smell sweeter to the followers of literary fashions.

But Henslowe's titles show that his company's audiences had a taste for the romances: *Orlando Furioso*, *Godfrey of Bulloigne*, *Palamon and Arcyte*, 1594; (*Valentine and Orson*, registered 1595, belonged to the Queen's men, another unfashionable company); *Chinon of England*,[2] *Fortunatus*, 1596; *Uther Pendragon*, *Alexander and Lodovick*[3] 1597; *Arthur*, 1598; *Four Kings*,[4] *Tristram of Lyons*, *Patient Grisell*, *Troilus and Cressida*, 1599; *Seven Wise Masters*,[5] *Fair Constance of Rome*,[6] 1600; *The Four Sons of Aymon*, 1603. The last-named play may have been an old one, and there appears to have been a change of heart about 1601. Why at this time the Admiral's men were giving up the romances and at the same time stressing another old-fashioned speciality of theirs, the Biblical play, it is difficult to imagine, especially since none of the latter type is extant to tell us whether some way of fitting them to the taste of the time had been discovered. The secret is perhaps the current vogue of satire, always employable with scriptural material but not so easily to be combined with romance. And of course a glance at those of this list of romances which are extant shows none to be entirely simple and unmixed with sophistication;[7] the catchpenny titles tell the story.

An interesting case of a play based on what might be classified as romantic material, and possessing both a literary and a popular title, is

[2] Greg, *Henslowe*, II, 178, refers to the romance by C. Middleton, S.R. 20 Jan., 1596, pub. 1597, *The Famous Historie of Chinon of England, with his strange adventures for the loue of Celestina daughter to Lewis King of Fraunce. With the worthy Atchiuement of Sir Lancelot du Lake, and Sir Tristram du Lions for faire Laura, daughter to Cador Earle of Cornewall, being all Knights of King Arthurs round Table.*

[3] The story of Amis and Amiloun (*ibid.*, 182). A story of identical twin brothers. There is a ballad on the subject, and a reference in *The Duchess of Malfi*.

[4] Greg rejects Fleay's identification with *Sir Clyomon and Sir Clamydes*, but perhaps it is safe to classify as romantic a play that stresses such a number of kings.

[5] Greg (*Henslowe*, II, 211) says, "Nothing is known of this play"; but doubtless it is a form of the medieval romance of the Seven Sages.

[6] The romance used by Chaucer in his *Man of Law's Tale*.

[7] Heywood's *Four Prentices* is more naïve than any of them; but it was very likely played as *Godfrey of Bulloigne*. The most primitive thing of the type in our period is *Sir Clyomon and Sir Clamydes*, published in 1599 with an ascription to the Queen's men.

Munday's *Downfall of Robert, Earl of Huntingdon*, 1598, generally referred to by Henslowe as *Robin Hood* and doubtless so advertised. In such cases the more pretentious title may also have been useful for court performances.

Of course in the long run this, like other "popular" policies of the Admiral's men, was a bad one. Henslowe's tastes were probably vulgar and Alleyn's old-fashioned; it would take serious adversity to force the company to make any effective efforts to come abreast of the vogue.

But there are indications that they had writing for them a dramatist of genius who was to give them the leadership in certain types of plays—George Chapman, author of *The Blind Beggar of Alexandria* and *A Humorous Day's Mirth.*

Disguise Plays, 1594–1603[8]

On October 2 Henslowe records a new play called *Disguises.*[9] The company had played it five times more by the tenth of November. This play is lost, but it evidently belonged to the same general type as *The Blind Beggar of Alexandria* (1596) and *Look About You* (Quarto 1600), stressing quick changes, confusions, and grotesqueries of make-up. It may appear rewritten as Chapman's play the following year, but the interval before rewriting was customarily much longer; *Look About You,* which shows resemblances to plays of about 1595 and also to several about the end of the century, is a more probable identification. The latter play does not appear in Henslowe's Diary but may be the same as *Bear a Brain* (a phrase used in *Look About You*), for which Henslowe paid Dekker on the first of August, 1599.

Plays in which disguising constitutes a prominent feature became sufficiently numerous to be recognizable as a separate class. Robert Greene's *Orlando Furioso*, written before 1592, a drama of the Admiral's men and a favorite character of Alleyn, appeared in quarto form in 1594 and 1599. (Note that *Disguises* appeared in 1595, *Look About You* in 1600.) *Orlando* abounds in rather pointless disguisings stressed apparently for their own sake. It may be more than a coincidence that Shakespeare's version of the Shrew farce, prepared about 1594, adds considerably to the disguises in the play.[10] *John a Kent and John a Cumber*, which we have assigned to the Admiral's repertory of 1594, among many disguisings introduces the striking situation where both magicians appear, each in the other's form;

[8] Cf. V. O. Freeburg, *Disguise Plots in Elizabethan Drama, passim.*

[9] Fleay (*London Stage,* 388) identifies this play (as an earlier version) with Chapman's *May Day,* which most critics agree to belong in style to about 1601 as we have it in the 1611 quarto, and to show no clear traces of revision.

[10] *The Wit of a Woman,* a play of uncertain provenance which was published in 1604, makes extensive use of the same type of disguises—lovers as tutors of various sorts.

this is cleverly varied in *Look About You*, possibly only a year later, in the excellent scene where the two great disguisers, Skink and Gloster, disguised as the same deceased hermit-friar, are brought face to face.

Chapman's highly successful disguise play, *The Blind Beggar of Alexandria*, had a run of twenty-two performances between February 12, 1596 and April 1, 1597. This is so extravagant a tale of multiple disguises that I suspect Chapman of burlesque, a mood in which, it seems to me, his essentially serious, mystical spirit more than once approached comedy. Cleanthes, banished claimant to the crown, beguiles his leisure, distributes his caresses, and turns many a dishonest penny by disguising as the beggar Irus, the usurer Leon, and the elegant but eccentric Count Hermes. The projection of this material against a romance background appears to burlesque Greene; some martial elements take off Marlowe; some bits of folk-lore, Peele. I rather think that Leon, the big-nosed usurer, now and then casts a sly leer in the direction of Shylock, who was probably on the boards in 1596. Of a possible element of contemporary satire I shall defer speaking until considering the Admiral's 1596 season as a whole.

Machiavellus, an Italianate comedy in Latin verse given by the students of St. John's, Cambridge, December 9, 1597, belongs to this type. It contains a comic Jew, Jacuppus, with a desirable daughter, and has many disguises, including an uncommon one as a ghost—compare Falstaff as Herne the Hunter in *The Merry Wives of Windsor*, about 1599, a play with much disguised roguery and intrigue. Other plays of 1598–1600 in which Shakespeare employed disguise more or less extensively are *Much Ado*, *As You Like It*, and *Twelfth Night;* but none of these is truly of the disguise-roguery type, the picaresque element not being sufficiently strong.

The publication of the Admiral's play, *Look About You*, in 1600 put into print what I consider the cleverest and jolliest play of the type. It is anonymous and has been ascribed to Anthony Wadeson; my opinion is that it is Dekker's *Bear a Brain*, which, I think, was a rewriting of Munday's *Disguises*.[11]

Chettle and Day wrote another disguising play for the Admiral's men in 1600, *The Blind Begger of Bednal Green*. Note the similarity in title to Chapman's play. The Chettle-Day production was so popular that it was followed in 1601 by Parts Two and Three. Momford, the Blind Beggar, supposed banished, is staying in disguise to "try" his brother; thus we have an adaptation of the grotesque-disguise type, with its oppor-

[11] The closing lines, read in the light of the play's marked anti-abdication propaganda, seem designed to foster those bitter suspicions of Essex which the party hostile to him were diffusing from 1597 until his downfall:

> Beseeching grace from Heaven's eternal throne,
> That England never know more prince than one.

tunities for slapstick action, to the moralistic motivation of *A Knack to Know an Honest Man* and *Measure for Measure.* At this sort of juggling and recombining of dramatic elements Henslowe's group of journeyman-playwrights was exceedingly adroit.

The boy companies next take up the type. Marston's *What You Will,* probably given in 1601 by Paul's boys, has a character, supposed dead, lurking about in disguise to spy on his wife. The general tone of burlesque[12] is characteristic of the boys' productions during the period when the adult companies were feeling their competition and when Shakespeare was resenting it in his well-known remarks in *Hamlet;* and this burlesque tone is still stronger and still more definitely aimed at Shakespeare himself in Chapman's *May Day,* which, following Fleay's commonly rejected dating, I am inclined to place among the boy's productions of about 1601. Here we have pointed burlesque of *Romeo and Juliet,* Falstaff, *The Rape of Lucrece,* and *Twelfth Night.* Chapman even goes so far as to satirize himself by his evident reference to his own *Blind Begger*—"the stale refuge of miserable poets, by change of a hat or a cloake, to alter the whole state of a Comedie."[13]

Wily Beguiled, an evidently old play which seems to have been revived by Paul's boys about 1602, contains a sound beating of a character disguised as Robin Goodfellow, as does another old play revived about this time, *Grim, the Collier of Croydon,* begun for Henslowe in 1600, transferred to some other company, and published in 1602. This taking advantage of a character's disguise to misuse him was prominent in Shakespeare's *Merry Wives,* about 1599; later examples are innumerable.

The anonymous *Fair Maid of the Exchange* with its "pleasant humours of the Cripple of Fanchurch" belongs to the type we are discussing. Its imitations of Shakespeare and Jonson place it about 1602. Its authorship and ownership are unknown; it is sometimes assigned to Heywood's work for the Admiral's men or Worcester's men, both Henslowe companies at this time; but it may as well be someone burlesquing other dramatists (and especially Chapman) for one of the companies of boys. It is an interesting combination of bourgeois romance (like that in *The Shoemakers' Holiday*) with "humours" and a benevolently intriguing cripple who resembles the Blind Begger of Bednal Green. There is much disguising, including that device beloved of Elizabethan dramatists, a masked marriage;[14] and a counterfeit cripple is confronted on the stage with the true one, in apparent imitation of *Look About You.*

[12] Specific instances can best be considered in the seasons when they occur, because of the topical character of many of the allusions.

[13] *May Day,* II, i, 480.

[14] Other "romantic conventions" of Elizabethan drama, such as feuds and street frays, single combat in war, private assassinations, early marriages for the alliance of houses, the

The marriage part of the disguisings here somewhat resembles *The Wise Woman of Hogsdon.* But that play—as well as *Measure for Measure* with its disguised Duke; *The Fair Maid of Bristow* with its multiplicity of disguises, given by the King's men at court at Christmas, 1603; *The Wit of a Woman;* and Marston's *Dutch Courtesan* with the rogueries in disguise of Cocledemoy—is perhaps outside our period.

In general harmony with the policies of the rival companies, the Admiral's men are seen to have based their most striking disguise plays on folk-lore and legendary British history (*John a Kent* and *Look About You*), and the Chamberlain's men (in such plays as *Twelfth Night*) to have appealed skilfully to a more cultivated taste through sophisticated adaptations of the disguise motive. The Admiral's men seem to have possessed two actors who were remarkably adroit at lightning changes of costume, at least one of whom was excellent at grotesque make-up. Shakespeare's company had no one it cared to feature in these specialties, at least until *The Fair Maid of Bristow.* By the date of this play one of the clever boys who had been trained to imitate the Admiral's star disguiser may have been available to the King's men.

These years 1595 and 1596 were tempting and dangerous years for satire, years full of trouble and tension. England was under the fearful shadow of another Armada. The Spaniards raided the Cornish coast, and were known to be continually intriguing in Ireland and elsewhere. They were preparing the fleet which was to be delayed by Essex's raid on Cadiz in 1596 and finally shattered by storms in 1597.

In England the issue of the succession was unusually tense. Doleman's book on this fascinating and dangerous subject came out in this year, with a dedication to Essex which many thought malicious. The coming year, 1596, was looked on as especially dangerous to the Queen as being her "grand climacteric."[15] King James, probably desirous to counteract the Cecils' favoring of Lord Beauchamp as the "Suffolk Claimant," and somewhat frightened by succession gossip arising from the Shelford Weir case (I shall discuss both matters in this chapter) was negotiating with Spain and the Pope to help him to the English throne on condition that he become a Catholic.[16]

---

practice of witchcraft and consultation of astrologers and soothsayers, disguises (including girl-pages and claimants to thrones), the use of token rings, substitution in bed of bride for mistress, etc., can be shown to have had exemplars in real life among the Elizabethans, most of them frequently; but I know of no masked marriage, although the use of masks—for the complexion, as in riding, or for the reputation, as in the theater—was common among ladies, and there were many secret, irregular, and repudiated weddings.

[15] G. B. Harrison, in *Times Literary Supplement,* Nov., 1930.

[16] For the state of their negotiation in 1596, see *Winwood's Memorials,* I, 1–15.

With France and the Low Countries Elizabeth was carrying on rather acid negotiations over loans, and efforts to gain the aid of Denmark against Spain were proving unsatisfying. At home continual alarms were arising over suspected Papist plots against the Queen's life; Essex had been prominent in the accusations against her own physician, Lopez, which had brought about the latter's execution the year before. Jesuit-hunting was active; Robert Southwell's execution occurred in 1595. Even within the English Church there was a serious friction over predestination, which Whitgift favored in a theological dispute that centered at Cambridge and which seemed sufficiently serious to draw in old Lord Burghley, in spite of his failing health, against the Calvinistic doctrine. It was a year of dearth, and of bread riots in Wiltshire and in London. These were years when satire's violent delights might have violent ends.

Several lost plays of the Admiral's men in 1595 perhaps made a more than incidental use of satire. They had a "*French Comedy*"; and they were habitually unkind to the French, as I hope to show later, partly because of King Henry's apostasy and partly because of Essex's cordial relations with him. Their own patron's relations were by no means so cordial, for the Admiral, partly through his prerogative of a tenth share in all the reprisals for which he issued the official permits, was a considerable upholder of privateers, who seemed to their victims plain pirates. The sufferers from their enterprises being frequently French, King Henry was concerned; for instance, in 1599 he was complaining bitterly to the English ambassador of the injustice of the English Admiralty.[17] And we may perhaps judge the Admiral's general feeling toward the French by his remark that with such an army as Essex had in Ireland the French King might have been driven out of France.[18]

Seven Days of the Week, a very successful play, was probably of the moralistic, didactic type, like *The Seven Deadly Sins* before our period, of which the "plot" is extant.[19] *Crack Me This Nut* was successful, too; the title a little resembles some used in satirical pamphleteering,[20] but the play's subject is a complete mystery. *A Toy to Please Chaste Ladies* had a long run; it and *A Wonder of a Woman* probably had a strong element of social satire.[21] The latter may possibly underlie Rowley's *A New*

[17] *Winwood's Memorials*, I, 26 (May 15, 1599; Ambassador Sir Henry Neville to Cecil).

[18] Whyte, Nov. 4, 1599, The French ambassador complained to the Queen.

[19] Greg, *Henslowe*, II, 176, "A piece of this name forms part of the Christmas Prince . . . Oxford entertainments of 1607 . . . but . . . probably had nothing but the title in common with the Admiral's play."

[20] It was a proverbial phrase, and occurs as the subtitle of one of the anti-Martinist tracts (promoted by Bancroft and subsidized by Burghley), *Pap with a Hatchet*.

[21] Cf. Nash's obscene *Choice of Valentines*. It is not for nothing that Marston names his page "Dildo" in *Antonio and Mellida;* see especially Sgn. C 3.

Wonder, of a Woman Never Vex'd; the satirical implication of Rowley's title is obvious. *The Welshman* arouses our suspicions by its single performance, on November 29; but it was not a new play, and the receipts were small enough to explain its not being repeated. But *The Mack*,[22] played only on February 21, when it was marked "ne" by Henslowe, gave him a very good revenue of three pounds. *Seleo and Olympo*, the next new play, gave Henslowe the same return for its first night, and ran ten performances; *The French Comedy*, ran six, although its first-night entry is only fifty shillings. It appears that *The Mack* gave offense and was suppressed; else why was its run cut short?

In the strictly consored state of Elizabethan public opinion, historical writings almost always had political implications read into them, whether the author intended them or not. So we are only joining Shakespeare's contemporaries when we suspect partisanship in his remaking of *The Troublesome Reign of King John* into his own *King John* in 1595. The older play, resembling somewhat in Protestant zeal the still older *Kynge Johan* of John Bale, was published in 1591. It calls for applause for its Christian champion in contrast to "Scythian Tamburlaine," and violently satirizes monks, nuns, and friars in justification of the spoiling of the abbeys, which it depicts. Much is made of a monk's revenge on King John by poisoning him, after first being absolved by an equally-revengeful abbot. Shakespeare in his version throws the stress on the purely political aspects of John's defiance of the papal legate, and suppresses as much as he can of the monastic material, even to the extent of leaving the poisoning of the King an abrupt and seemingly unmotivated event. He seems, also, to be comparatively gentle with the French. A comparison of the *dramatis personae* shows a few matters of interest:

Shakespeare omits three friars and Alice, the nun found in the monk's cell, in doing away with the coarse satire on the monastic system. He comes very near cutting out the Earl of Essex, leaving him only three lines; but it should be observed that he retains William Longsword, Earl of Salisbury, one of the most illustrious ancestors of Robert Devereux.

More significant omissions are the Earls of Chester, Clare, and Beauchamp. Ranulph, Earl of Chester, about whom clustered many legends, was almost a property of the Admiral's men, prominent in several of their plays; he was related by marriage to the Earl of Huntingdon, celebrated

[22] Fleay identifies *The Mack* as *The Wonder of a Kingdom*, a disconnected piece of composite work published in 1636 as by Dekker, which appears from the closing lines to have been a "card play." A renowned example of this sort of thing's being used for offensive political allegory was Middleton's *A Game at Chess*, objected to by the Spanish ambassador in 1624. as a "verv scandalous comedy acted publickly by the king's players" which displayed "in a rude and dishonourable fashion" both King James and King Philip, as well as Gondomar, the latter king's recently retired ambassador.

by the Admiral's men in their Robin Hood plays; and his lands had descended to Hastings, Howard, Stanley, and Paulet—mostly Cecilian families. The titles of Clare and Clarence were considered the same. The Huntingdom claim to the succession derived from the Duke of Clarence, another connection between these omitted characters and the Admiral's men; and the fact that the Earl of Clare in King John's time was also Earl of Hertford gives us still another, for the Elizabethan Earl of Hertford's wife was the Admiral's sister. Moreover, the Cecil faction was supposed to favor the "Suffolk claim" to the succession, vested in Hertford's son, Lord Beauchamp, who thus gives us a reason for the omission of the Earl of Beauchamp from *King John*.[23] I shall have a little more to say about this claim and its connection with the drama when we come to the 1596 season; it was proclaimed in November, 1595, that the title "Lord Beauchamp" should be no longer used.

Shakespeare adds the slightly sentimental part of the Dauphin, and the brief one of James Gurney, servant of Lord Faulconbridge. The latter addition has seemed to me curious. Why should a dramatist under the stern necessity of compression add this slight but circumstantial bit? Just for realism? It is possible. But we ought, in considering the effect Shakespeare looked for in using the name, to have in mind that the Gurneys or Gournays were a great Norman family, with descendants of the name in several parts of Elizabethan England, and blood in the veins and possessions in the hands of several great houses.[24] It would be interesting to discover which of Shakespeare's contemporaries quartered the Gournay arms.

Although it is hard to say whether Gurney's appearance in *King John* was meant to be complimentary or not,[25] at least it was a historical bit of sufficient interest to be of value to the play; and I am inclined to think that Shakespeare, in making him the servant of the Faulconbridges, intended a slight slur. The lands of Hugh de Gournay, who was with Richard Coeur de Lion in Palestine, descended to Lord Bardolph, and some of them thence to the Stanhopes of Shelford, Nottinghamshire, Cecilians, whose connections with *1 Henry IV* will appear later. But probably the best known of all the family was a Gurney of the Somerset branch (related through Newton to the Cobhams, who objected to Shakespeare's making fun of their ancestor Oldcastle), Thomas de

[23] *The Bold Beauchamps*, a lost play by Heywood (See Chambers, III, 347), may belong to a later period.

[24] Daniel Gurney, *The Record of the House of Gournay*. It is curious that in these two large volumes I have nowhere been able to find James used as a Christian name by this very numerous family.

[25] Anthony Gurney, Anne Boleyn's second cousin, married a Tyrrell, supposed descended from the Tyrrell honored by Shakespeare's company in *Satiromastix*.

Gournay, who joined Maltravers in the murder of Edward II at Berkeley Castle. It is possible that in Marlowe's *Edward II*, in which Gurney is a character, the Admiral's men owned a valuable property which for political reason they dared not use; the policy of the Cecilians—at least as it appeared later—being to connect *Richard II*, the Chamberlain's story of the deposition and murder of a king, with Essex's supposedly treasonable ambitions. Thus they may have refused to let their own players perform a dramatic story so very similar in its political implications. At least we have no evidence that the Admiral's men ever performed *Edward II* during our period. Can Shakespeare's Gurney embody a sly allusion to this situation?

As if in direct reply to *King John*, the Admiral's men produced *Longshanks* on August 29, and played it fourteen times in the ensuing twelvemonth. It is lost; but it is almost as certain that it was built on Peele's *Edward I* as that Shakespeare's play was based on the older one. Peele's play, published in 1593, satirized the strolling friars. The rival companies were demonstrably different in their treatment of friars, as might be expected from their religious and political leanings; and this seems a good point at which to discuss the difference.

Friars in the Plays of the Rival Companies, 1594–1603

That Peele was a patriot of a violently narrow-minded type is impressively shown in *Edward I*. Marlowe, on the other hand, cannot be accused of narrow-mindedness, but his *Jew of Malta* is by no means gentle in its treatment of friars. The Admiral's men revived this play in 1596 and again in 1601. Henslowe enters a *Friar* (?) *Francis* in his account with Sussex's men in 1594.[26] Greene gives a kindly impression of Friar Bacon and Friar Bungay, but as magicians they were doubtful characters. The play belonged to the Admiral's men, and was revived by them in 1598. Lost plays which their playwrights seem to have based on folk tales and fabliaux of a discreditable sort are *Friar Spendleton*, in Henslowe's accounts with Pembroke's men, 1597; *Friar Fox and Gyllen of Brentford*,[27] 1599; and *Friar Rush and the Proud Woman of Antwerp*,[28] written by Day and Haughton in 1601 and "mended" by Chettle the

[26] But this was very likely not a friar play. Heywood's *Apology for Actors* informs us that "the old History of Feyer [Fair?] Francis," performed by Sussex's men at King's Lynn, Norfolk, was the story of a woman who murdered her husband in order to enjoy her lover, and was haunted by his ghost.

[27] See *Jyl of Breyntfords testament*, by R. Copland. Gillian was a disreputable character of the type of Elynour Rummyng, and her "testament" like Chaucer's *Somnour's Tale*.

[28] See Greg, *Henslowe*, II, 218. An English chapbook on Friar Rush was entered in the Stationers' Register 1569, and there is an extant edition of 1620. "The Rush story also supplied the plots of Dekker's *If it be not Good, the Devil is in it*," and *The Devil is an Ass*,

following year. They had also the jolly but disreputable Friar Tuck of the Robin Hood plays, and the unlovely Clun,[29] the summoner, in *Sir John Oldcastle*, to say nothing of that play's hedge priest, John of Wrotham, and his model in *Edward I*.

There are wicked friars in *Lust's Dominion*, very likely an Admiral's play of about 1600; and Chapman's curious friar-pander in *Bussy d'Ambois* was at least a creation of a graduate of the Henslowe group of playwrights.[30]

It is hardly possible to say anything new about Shakespeare's kindly friars. They are uniformly benignant, and even their tendency toward matchmaking intrigue, so cynically perverted by Chapman, is made admirable by the dramatist of the Chamberlain's men. The hint that the lovers are to meet "at Friar Patrick's cell" in *Two Gentlemen of Verona* is magnificently developed in *Romeo and Juliet*, where Shakespeare retains from Brooke the lovers' marriage in Friar Lawrence's cell.

In *Blurt, Master Constable* lovers meet by stealth to be married by a friar, and *The Wit of a Woman* has Sir Laurence, a priest; it is possible that both of these plays belonged to the Chamberlain's men. A much less kindly echo of *Romeo and Juliet* is Dekker's *The Wonder of a Kingdom*, published in 1636, and possibly based on Henslowe's *Wonder of a Woman*, 1595. Much of Dekker's play reads like a cynical burlesque of Shakespeare's great drama of young love; and in it Angelo (whose name is almost as ironic as the Angelo's in *Measure for Measure*), disguising as a friar for purposes of intrigue, promises to "prove a lustie Laurence."[31] As if in answer to such attacks, the indispensable friar of *Much Ado* is made older and more trusted than Friar Laurence. The later friars of *Measure for Measure* and *The Fair Maid of Bristow* are connected with disguise plots. Friar Benedic and Friar Hildersham in *The Merry Devil of Edmonton*, which belonged to the King's men in 1603, should be noted, with the fact that the play contains an element of satire on monks and nuns which seems out of keeping with the company's policy. But the religious situation in England had changed with the revealing of a

[29] The Lordship of Clun in Shropshire went with the Earldom of Arundel, from Fitz Alan to Howard in the sixteenth century. For its connection with Philip, Henry, and Thomas Howard, see Cockayne's *Peerage*. The Earls of Arundel, as Catholics, were natural targets for some of the propaganda in *Oldcastle*. Lord Henry Howard, Catholic and (unreliable) Essexian, may have held Clun in 1600, or Thomas, Lord Howard de Walden, another Catholic but in general non-partisan.

[30] *Bussy* was performed by Paul's boys, probably about 1604. Greg (*Henslowe*, II, 198) points out a possible connection with *The Civil Wars of France*, 1598.

[31] A legendary Lancashire character, famous for his great number of bastards. A ballad on him was entered S. R., June 14, 1594; and Wm. Blackwall was fined April 10, 1598, for selling it. For numerous allusions see H. E. Rollins, *Analytical Index to the Ballad-Entries*, 137.

definitely Protestant policy by King James. In general it is clear that to see a friar in an undignified, an immoral, or a demonologically dubious position, one would see the Admiral's men. If one's bias was to prefer them in "sympathetic" rôles, he would see the Chamberlain's men.

Of all Shakespeare's plays the one which is most closely and interestingly connected with Elizabethan politics is *Richard II*. It was probably first produced in 1595. It was entered in the Stationers' Register August 29, 1597, and quartos appeared in that and the following year. The deposition scene, however, was not printed until 1608. The great success of this play is attested by Queen Elizabeth herself, who remarked to W. Lambarde on August 4, 1601, that it had been played "40tie times in open streets and houses." This must have been about 1596–97, and is a run longer than any recorded by Henslowe.[32] The Queen's reference at the same time to the ingratitude of the "most adorned creature" Essex, and her identification of herself with Richard II arose, I think, from an impression carefully instilled in her naturally rather suspicious mind as late as 1597, a slander which may have had much to do with the turning of the tide of favor against the Earl in that year. I believe it was a slander at the time, and a most ingenious perversion of Shakespeare's intention, which may not have been political at all.

The great Lord Burghley was failing; and various high posts in his possession or control were coveted by the Essex party, some by Essex himself, urged by his somewhat Machiavellian secretary, Francis Bacon. Lord Burghley's younger son, Robert, undersized and deformed and of no official standing, was fatally underestimated by his political opponents. Although he was not formally named Secretary until 1596, he had, with his father's astute advice, been doing much of the work since Walsingham's death in 1591; and in the constant clashes between the Essex interests and the Cecil policies the latter were seldom compelled to give way. Sir Edward Hoby, son-in-law of Lord Hunsdon and nephew of Burghley, an anti-papist controversialist and probably strongly attached to the Puritan party, wrote to his friend Sir Robert Cecil inviting him to his house in Canon Row on December 9, 1595, promising, "as late as shall please you, a gate for your supper shall be open, and K. Richard present himself to your view." I surmise that this was a visit of inspection; that Cecil's acute mind continued to work on the matter is shown by Ralegh's writing to him on July 6, 1597:

Pray pardon me if I write but little, in such haste and confusion, and further our demands for a supply, or the multitude of men will prevent our reaching the place of our hope. I acquainted the Lord General [Essex] with your letters and

[32] The longest run is that of *The Wise Man of West Chester*, 32 performances.

kind acceptance of your entertainment; he was wonderful merry at the[33] conceit of Richard II. I hope it will never alter, and shall be glad of it, as the true way to our good, quiet, and advancement, and most of all for her sake whose affairs will thereupon find better progression. I will always be yours, and will perform what you may require with my life and fortune.[34]

Was not this "conceit" something involving a playful identification of Elizabeth with Richard, Essex with Bolingbroke?[35] I think I hear something forced in Essex's laughter. Ralegh too, as rival courtier and later rival commander, was an enemy of Essex, though at this time a political reconciliation had made him into a treacherous friend. The hint seems to have fermented in the minds of Essex and his followers, as Cecil intended that it should; the result was the historic revival of *Richard II* by the arrangement of Sir Gilly Meyrick, Charles Percy and other Essex partisans, on the eve of the Rebellion in February, 1601.[36] By this time, in the minds of Essex's henchmen, at least, Richard was certainly identified with the Queen and Bolingbroke's career interpreted as of happy augury for Essex.[37]

The exact nature of the political competition through history plays between the two rival companies would be made much clearer if we could find a copy of the *Henry V* listed as new by Henslowe on November 28, 1595, and performed thirteen times to July 20, 1596. The availability of the old *Famous Victories* as a source is debatable; it was entered in

[33] Chambers, *Shakespeare,* I, 353, reads "y^e^"; Stopes, 106, "your," (apparently "y^r^").

[34] *S. P. Dom.*, 1595–97, 451.

[35] *Sal. MSS.*, XI, 49. Capt. Christopher Levens (wounded by rebels) to Cecil, Feb. 13, 1601.—"Something has come to my hand which would have forced fouler understanding if God had not destroyed the wicked councils and devilish devices of the seditious, imitating Bolingbroke's unripened strategems, from further proceeding. Please it you to send some sure man to find out here on the Bankside one Smith, a waterman, Essex's servant, that 'scaped out of the house on the Sunday night, a desperate fellow." It should be remembered also, that Essex had another link with Bolingbroke in his title of Viscount Hereford, his "style" from 1572 to 1576.

[36] *S. P. Dom.*, 1598–1601, 578.

[37] Essex's trouble in 1599 over Sir John Hayward's *Life of Henry IV* has been recently investigated for its connection with *Richard II.* Most of the important documents are reprinted by Ray Heffner, "Shakespeare, Hayward, and Essex," *PMLA*, XLV, 754–780; and Margaret Dowling, "Sir John Hayward's Troubles over his *Life of Henry IV*," *The Library*, XI, 212–224. The incident is of importance because it shows how the public mind gave political interpretations to historical writings. Camden (*Annales*, for 1599) says that Essex's "Pages and followers, would boast of great matters up and downe, viz. That he descended from the family of the Kings of Scotland by the eldest daughter of Alan of Galloway. . . . That, he also was of the English blood royall, which came by Cecill Bourchiere, his Great grandmother, whose stocke was first, Thomas of Woodstocke youngest son vnto Edward the Third: and Richard Earle of Cambridge. And that by vertue thereof his right was better to the Crowne of England than any of the competitors; for their rights had beene confuted (all but the Spanish Infantaes) by Doleman's bookes."

1594; and the earliest known quarto, 1598, assigns its ownership to the Queen's men. The dramatist for Henslowe's company may have taken advantage of a lost earlier quarto, of course; or the Admiral's men may have laid claim to its actual ownership as a play on some grounds resembling those which made *Orlando Furioso* a property of both companies. We have seen Heywood to be adept at making plays out of unpreempted portions of well-known subjects; perhaps he did this with the Henry the Fifth saga. But Agincourt is in *The Famous Victories*—and what would a Henry the Fifth play be without Agincourt? Then, too, there is to be considered the action of Shakespeare the next year, in using part of *The Famous Victories* for *1 Henry IV*. This action, it seems to me, might be explained as a counter to a high-handed appropriation by the Admiral's men of a useful subject which was the rightful property of the Queen's men, absent in the provinces.[38]

I shall take up later, in connection with Shakespeare's *Henry V*, those indications of political partisanship in the selection of Agincourt heroes for *The Famous Victories* which lead me to suspect the hand of some dramatist of the Admiral's group in the latter play as we have it; indeed, *The Famous Victories* may thus be identical with the *Henry V* of the Admiral's men.

The next move in this game of politico-dramatic chess belonged to the Chamberlain's men. But before we pass on to 1596 and *1 Henry IV* let us pause at the Christmas season to estimate very briefly the repertories of the competing companies and to sketch their second season at court.

The Admiral's men had several new plays to which we have not yet given specific attention. It is a great pity that their popular *Long Meg of Westminster* is lost; it appears to have been a realistic comedy of contemporary London life; perhaps it was the first venture of Dekker in that field.[39] *Selio and Olympo* and *1* and *2 Hercules* evidently dealt with the Greek mythology; it is highly probable that they represent the first appearance of some or all of the material[40] later published by Heywood as

[38] Greg says (*Henslowe*, II, 178) that probably the Queen's sold the MS. to the printer Creede, 1594, but the Admiral's appropriated and revised the play, and stayed publication until '98, when Creede printed it from the original MS. But what right or precedent had the Admiral's men for such an action?

[39] See the well-known chapbook, 1620, and the ballad-entry, S. R. 27 August, 1590. Both it and the Admiral's play, *Oldcastle* (1599), feature old Lancashire carriers—*Long Meg* "Father Willis," *Oldcastle* "Gaffer Club" and "old Dick Dun." Alleyn claimed connection with the Towneleys of Lancs. For the playwrights engaged on *Oldcastle*, little is known about Wilson, but Munday claimed to belong to a Staffordshire family, and Drayton and probably Hathaway were of Warwickshire; so any one of the three was no doubt familiar with the Northwest Road and the Lancashire carriers who used it. See my remarks on *Oldcastle*, later.

[40] A. M. Clark, *Thomas Heywood*, 63, denies all possibility of this, but gives no reason.

The Golden Age and *The Silver Age* in his *Four Ages*. Few plays throw more interesting light on Elizabethan staging when it was aimed at spectacular effects; it is very fortunate that old Thomas Heywood thought them worthy of preservation. But *The New World's Tragedy*, which had eleven performances, alas, has vanished. What a loss to Americana![41]

As for the Chamberlain's men, their chief dramatist's new plays in 1595 are given by Baldwin[42] as *King John*, summer, and *Richard II*, winter. *Edward III* and *A Midsummer Night's Dream* may belong to either this or the preceding year; *The Merchant of Venice*, to this or the following one. It must not be forgotten that both companies' chief successes of 1594 were still running, and probably several more still older plays possessing lasting qualities given them by such playwrights as Shakespeare and Marlowe and such actors as Burbadge and Alleyn.

The positions of the companies were reversed at this Christmas season, the Chamberlain's men having five court performances to the Admiral's four; the former company's dates being December 26, 27, and 28, January 6, and February 22; the latter's January 1 and 4 and February 22 and 24.[43] Tilney may quite reasonably have chosen the Chamberlain's five plays out of the following seven: *King John; Richard II* (in which the Queen may not yet have construed any malice toward herself; she would be apt to recognize her own character as more like Bolingbroke's than Richard's); *Edward III; A Midsummer Night's Dream; Romeo and Juliet; Richard III; 1 Henry IV*.[44] The Admiral's men may have given their four plays from the following six: *Henry V; A Toy to Please Chaste Ladies; Longshanks; Selio and Olympo; Seven Days of the Week; Long Meg of Westminster*. But some or all of these may have seemed too satirical, too old, or too common for the court: *Henry V*, if the same as *The Famous Victories*, crude in treatment as well as old-fashioned, possibly hampered by factional politics in the court intrigues of the season; *A Toy to Please Chaste Ladies*, if on the subject I suspect, satire of too advanced, too Marstonian a type to please the court this season; *Longshanks*, probably a slightly refreshed form of the antiquated *Edward I; Selio and*

[41] It is possible, however, that the expression was used as by Cecil to Carew, 1601, August 12—his friends lost, the Spaniards threatening, the Secretary wishes that he and his friend "might once confer in this new world."

[42] Baldwin, 229 (tables).

[43] Why do the dates group together thus? A possible explanation might be that the moving of scenery, costumes, and properties must have been an item on which the Revels Office could economize by furnishing carts only for a group of performances at a time. The giving of series-plays, such as those in two parts, or the Falstaff group, on successive evenings (or afternoons and evenings) is another possibility, and one which is borne out more or less by the evidence of Henslowe's diary for the practice in the public theater.

[44] It may have been ready by the end of the season.

Olympo, mythology popularized, which the learned Elizabeth's court could not dare not to scorn; *Seven Days of the Week*, probably morality on an old-fashioned plan like that of old John Heywood's *Play of the Weather; Long Meg of Westminster*, crude realism ahead of its time, and aimed at the lower-class citizens' taste. Several more new plays had been launched by the company before February 24, among them *Pythagoras* and *The Blind Beggar of Alexandria*. But the former, to judge from hostile references to the Pythagorean philosophy by Shakespeare, was notorious for heretical speculations upon the immortality of the soul; and the latter, doubtless a much better play than in its present mangled form, may have been interpreted as containing ill-timed references to the dangerous ambition, unstable character, and multiple love-affairs of the Queen's favorite.

Our general impression of the Henslowe repertory from the point of view of its suitability for a season at court is that 1595 had been a year of too specialized an appeal to a rather low-grade audience, and that of the company's numerous popular plays few or none would be likely to appeal to the fashionable. That few or none of those given did appeal seems clearly enough indicated by the fact that the season of 1596 saw the Admiral's men at court not at all.

The Admiral's men produced on the third of January, 1596, a new play called *Chinon of England*. It is lost, but the title of the prose romance already quoted, and the play's creditable run of fourteen performances make it look like a fairly successful attempt to combine with the type of popular romance in which the company specialized some of that patriotic appeal which had taken so well the previous year.

Another play on the boards early in 1596 was, I believe, *A Midsummer Night's Dream*, written at least as late as the summer of 1595, and the whole play adapted, especially at the end, to serve at the wedding[45] on February 19, 1596, of Elizabeth Carey, only child of the Chamberlain's eldest son Sir George, to the eldest son and heir of Henry, Lord Berkeley.

The usual intricate marriage negotiations had preceded the match, and their shiftings and disappointments may have been felt to be prettily romanticized in the adventures of the two young couples in Shakespeare's play. Rowland Whyte gives us some of the gossip:

December 5.—Sir *George Carey* takes it very unkindly, that my Lord of *Pembroke* broke of the Match intended between my Lord *Herbart* [probably Pembroke's eldest son] and his Daughter, and told the Queen it was because he would not assure him 1000 £ a yeare, which comes to his Daughter, as next a Kinne to Queen *Ann Bullen*. [Note the probability that the Queen would attend her young

[45] Probably at Hunsdon's house in Blackfriars.

cousin's wedding.] He hath now concluded a Marriage between his Daughter and my Lord Barkleys Sonne and Heire . . . Truly I hard, that if my Lord of Pembroke should die, who is very pursife and maladife, the tribe of *Hunsdon* doe laye waite for the Wardship of the brave young Lord.

In connection with this wedding, too, we have further evidence that the Hunsdons were in sympathy with Essex about 1596. Pembroke and Essex were having an angry controversy which drew in both Berkeley and the Queen. Whyte tells us on December 8, 1595 that her Majesty

takes the Matter in Hand . . . is angry with 1000 [Essex] for taking so violent a course, and tells 2000 [Pembroke] he shall goe without the thing in Question, who sware vnto her Majestie, that he would never deliver up the Covenants and Assurances he had, and that to be denied the Cours of Law, was an Injury donne to the meanest Subject. But away is he gonne . . . and here hath he now no Frend to leane vnto; 500 [Carey?] truly touched with a Scorn, as he thinkes donne unto him, by refusall of the intended Marriage, and indeed bent to favor all that are his adversaries.

One of these adversaries was, of course, Essex.

It seems to be generally believed that the naïvely inflated style of the Pyramus and Thisbe interlude in *A Midsummer Night's Dream* is a general literary burlesque of an outmoded dramatic form and manner of performance. If this is the case, we may imagine some out-of-fashion Elizabethan company such as the Queen's men, long relegated to the road, in place of the Victorian players we now parody. Another possibility, of course, is burlesque of the amateur histrionic efforts which greeted the Queen frequently on her progresses through the kingdom or her visits to the universities. But I should like to bring forward some evidence that Shakespeare's satire here was not remote, general, and literary, but immediate, specific, and personal, motivated by a really vital rivalry and applying directly to a current series of productions by the rival company, the Admiral's men, to the author of these plays, Thomas Heywood, and to the principal actor in them, Ned Alleyn[46]—and not without general satirical implications against the typical audience and whole popular policy of the Henslowe-owned and Alleyn-dominated company.

In a recent article[47] Miss Margaret Farrand makes out an interesting case for Dr. Thomas Moffett's poem, *The Silkwormes and their Flies* as the object of some of Shakespeare's burlesque in *A Midsummer Night's Dream.* It is noteworthy in view of the Careys' anger at Pembroke that Moffett was a dependent of the Herberts, with whom he lived at Wilton and Ludlow; and that he dedicated the poem on silkworms to the Countess of Pembroke.

[46] Cf. G. B. Harrison, *An Elizabethan Journal*, 392; and *Shakespeare and the Theatre*, 76.

[47] Margaret L. Farrand, "An additional Source for *A Midsummer Night's Dream*," *Studies in Philology*, XXVII, 233 ff.

But are we accumulating too many objects for Shakespeare's burlesque? I think not. The combination, in the Pyramus and Thisbe interlude, of a general archaic literary flavor, a specific esoteric literary burlesque on one or more contemporary poems such as *The Silkworm*, and a broad popular burlesque of the leading actor of a rival company, seems to me quite possible. No one denies Shakespeare's aptitude for appealing to everyone in a varied audience; to do this, even in a partisan gathering, he would have to use varied devices. Some would miss the literary parodies, some the gossipy personal allusions; yet those who did not miss the one sort or the other would enjoy them all the more in the knowledge that their appreciation belonged to the few.

It seems to me probable that the satire on Alleyn[48] as Bottom took advantage of a waning interest in his acting on the part of his royal patroness, and that his temporary retirement from the stage in the summer of 1597 was due to his disappointment at the lack of court favor for his company in the preceding winter season. He returned to the stage in 1600, apparently, as Chambers remarks,[49] partly in deference to the expressed desire of the Queen to see him again in some of his favorite rôles. That he revived numerous old plays during the next year or two seems certain;[50] that "Ercles vein" was among them may be suspected from these words of Hamlet, in which I have italicized reminiscences of *A Midsummer Night's Dream* and the first three of Heywood's *Four Ages:*

> O, it offends me to the soul to hear a *robustious* periwig-pated fellow *tear* a passion to tatters, to very rags, to *split* the ears of the groundlings, who for the most part are capable of nothing but *inexplicable dumb-shows* and *noise:* I would have such a fellow shipped for over-doing *Termagant;* it out-herods *Herod:* pray you, avoid it.[51]

The word "inexplicable" furnishes a brief and pungent complaint of such clumsy efforts to explain dumb-shows as those of Homer in Heywood's plays. Herod, of course, was the great prototype for the "tyrant's vein." Notice also Hamlet's references to the bad work of "nature's journeymen" a few lines below. Alleyn's most renowned rôles were those of Faustus, Tamburlaine, Barabas, and Orlando Furioso; but it is in that of "Hercles" that he would be most vulnerable to satire on his mannerisms and general style of acting. As for the essential justice of pillorying

[48] The Alleyn-Burbadge friction was personal as well as professional. See Chambers, II, 307, 392; C. W. Wallace, *The Children of the Chapel at Blackfriars*, 101, 127.

[49] Chambers, II, 173.

[50] Chambers, II, 177. "The succession of new plays is not quite so rapid during 1600–3 as in the previous periods. . . . It may well have been the case that Alleyn, who 'created' parts in the 80's and early 90's, had a tendency toward revivals."

[51] *Hamlet*, III, II, 15–17.

him as Bottom, his biographer in the *D.N.B.* admits that "of literary ability and taste he gives no sign." We do not know that he was ever actually a weaver; indeed, he seems to have been apprenticed as an actor; but his father was Porter to the Queen, and his mother, for whom he dubiously claimed good descent, remarried John Browne, a haberdasher. Would not an Elizabethan haberdasher have in stock "a bottom of brown thread"?[52] It may be remembered that the common taunt of "bricklayer" at Ben Jonson was a sneer at his stepfather's trade.

So much for the general nature of the burlesque on the Heywood plays and their leading actor. Perhaps the best way to take up the specific points of the burlesque will be to cite them in order as they occur in Shakespeare's play:[53]

> *Bottom.* My chief humor is for a tyrant [Alleyn, as we have seen, specialized in tyrants]: I could play Ercles rarely [doubtless he did], or a part to tear a cat in . . .

In *The Silver Age*[54] Hercules, entering with the head and skin of the Nemaean lion, brags:

> Thus Hercules begins his jovial tasks.
> The horrid beast I have torn out of his skin.

As far as I am aware, no annotator of this "part to tear a cat in" passage has mentioned the curious fact that in the Latin comedy *Silvanus*, given at St. John's, Oxford, January 13, 1597, an actor, supposedly mad, actually twists the necks of two cats upon the stage,[55] thinking them to be two other characters, the idea for the scene probably coming from the classical inroads of the mad Ajax upon the defenseless herds.

In *Histriomastix*, perhaps written about 1595 for an academic or legal audience and revived in 1599 by Paul's boys, we have a satirical reference which seems to connect Alleyn with this burlesque by implying that the same actor who played Tamburlaine was also a dismemberer of the harmless, necessary cat:

> *Soldier* [who has just pressed the touring professional players into the army]. Slid, how do you march?
>
> Sirha, is this you would rend and teare the cat
> Vpon a Stage, and now march like a drown'd rat?
> Look vp and play the Tamburlaine: you rogue you.[56]

Is it likely that an audience would fail to think of Alleyn when the rôle of Tamburlaine was mentioned?

[52] *The Taming of the Shrew,* IV, iii, 138. *N.E.D.* gives as one sixteenth-century meaning of *haberdasher,* "a dealer in small articles appertaining to dress, as thread. . . ." Of course Bottom in his trade used *bottoms* of thread to weave from. [53] *M.N.D.*, I, ii, 29 ff.

[54] III, i. [55] See F. S. Boas, *University Drama in the Tudor Age,* 298 ff.

[56] Act V (Sgn. G). "Tear-Cats" are alluded to later in *Isle of Gulls* and *Roaring Girl.*

For what follows, "The raging rocks," etc., Rolfe seems to have given the right model,[57] until we come to the last two, more than jovially audacious lines:

And make and mar
The foolish Fates.

Heywood, inconceivable as it may seem, actually has Hercules do this.[58] In *The Silver Age*, v, i, after many lines of thunderous rant, we have the following stage direction:

Hercules sinks himself: flashes of fire; the Devils appear at every corner of the stage with several fireworks. The Judges of hell and the three Sisters run over the stage, Hercules after them: fireworks all over the house.

Heywood always becomes comical when he tries to be terrific, but this play does make all split. Notice that, to drive the point of the burlesque home, after his bit of ranting parody Bottom repeats with vast complacency, "This is Ercles' vein, a tyrant's vein."

Bottom's desire to play many parts may glance at the necessary doubling in any company presenting the *Ages*, plays in which the number of parts runs from fifty to over a hundred per cent greater than in *A Midsummer Night's Dream*.[59]

To pass on to Act Five, the passage in which Theseus rejects various offerings of entertainment and finally chooses "Pyramus and Thisbe" appears to glance at the selection of current dramatic offerings for court performance, and his rejections appear to be satirical in the playwright's intent. "The Battle with the Centaurs" is in *The Silver Age*. This savage conflict certainly is not a theme suited "to be sung by an Athenian eunuch to the harp." Perhaps Shakespeare thought Heywood's treatment of it equally unworthy. "Pyramus and Thisbe" is called "merry and tragical, tedious and brief"—surely not a bad description of the strange mixture of moods in Heywood's series, especially in the *Golden* and *Silver Ages*, tedious aggregations of brief scenes, with comedy that usually sinks to farce and tragedy that doesn't quite come off, so mingled as to leave no unified general effect.

[57] W. J. Rolfe, ed., *M.N.D.*, 133. He gives extracts from a 1581 translation of Seneca's *Hercules* which should be compared with Heywood's *Silver Age*.

[58] He seems to have been misled by the language of ecstasy—cf. *1 Tamburlaine*, I, ii, 174, and *Old Fortunatus*, V, ii, 357—failing to realize how different a thing it is to represent such hyperboles on the stage.

[59] Puck's promised transformations, III, i, 110 ff., can be paralleled closely in those required of some of the lesser actors in Heywood's company: a horse—a centaur; a hound—Cerberus; a hog—a boar; a headless bear—a dehorned bull; fire—Jove destroying Semele. Heywood's Epistle to *The Jew of Malta*, 1633, celebrates Alleyn as "Proteus for shapes." And see Hercules's battle with the protean Achelous, *Brazen Age*, I, i.

In the interlude itself, Quince's explanatory Prologue burlesque those of Homer in the *Ages*. Heywood has no actor play a wall, but makes Earth rise through the stage with self-descriptive lines:

> I have spread
> My arms from sea to sea, look'd o'er my mountains,
> Examin'd all my pastures, groves, and plains,
> Marshes and wolds, my woods and champain fields,
> My dens and caves; and yet, from foot to head
> I have no place on which the Moon doth tread.

The river Arethusa follows. And in the same scene (*Silver Age*, III, i) Proserpine appears "attired like the Moon." With the lines:

> Whereat with blade, with bloody blameful blade,
> He bravely broach'd his boiling bloody breast,

compare *The Golden Age*, II, i:

> *Jupiter*. Down with the tyrant and that hateful crew,
> And in their murderous breasts your blades imbrue.[60]

Pyramus' and Thisbe's garbled references to Leander, Helen, Cephalus, and Procris may well serve as general burlesque on Heywood's manglings and distortions of Ovid. With the much-annotated line,

> Now is the mure all down between the two neighbors,

compare *The Golden Age*, III, i (the Titans against Olympus):

> *Enceladus*. What but to spurn down their offensive mures.

A little later we have Demetrius, Theseus, and Hippolyta cheering on the actors; Theseus exclaims, "Well moused, lion." (Notice that the lion is a cat here.) This bit seems to burlesque the killing of the Nemaean lion[61] again, a horrific combat which Heywood manages in a naïvely unconscious burlesque of the classic manner by having it happen off-stage, described concurrently to Juno, on the stage, by Iris "above in a cloud," like a military observer in a captive balloon, Juno, of course, is strongly partisan to the lion, while Iris favors Hercules. The scene is richly comical. Hercules brags:

> You might have heard the lion roar to heaven,
> Even to the high tribunal in the spheres;

but the off-stage roaring must have been in ludicrous contrast.

I have omitted to mention many of the points of burlesque and parody

[60] Thisbe also parodies this line; Shakespeare seems to have abhorred the old-fashioned wooden type of alliteration.

[61] *Silver Age*, III, i.

that may be observed by an attentive eye which makes a careful study of Heywood's *Four Ages* with Shakespeare's play in mind—to say nothing of the abundant opportunities for Shakespeare's fellows, by means of costume, intonation, and action (even as Aristophanes presented Socrates) to ridicule their rivals. Heywood seems to have taken Shakespeare's laughing criticism in a way that was both sweet-tempered and wise, making it lead, not to bitterness, but to a friendly emulation which did both dramatists good.

And in general, in regard to the satire in *A Midsummer Night's Dream*, we should consider this: that Shakespeare in his jibes at Heywood's *Four Ages* and Ned Alleyn's acting therein is in both cases poking fun at a good man doing something inept. Heywood was good at some things, but could not wear the grand manner; Alleyn, a fine "robustious" actor of the elder school, was splendid in Marlowe's magnificent bombast, but ludicrous in Heywood's bathos. Of course the comedy of *A Midsummer Night's Dream* has always been loved for its own sake, and always will be; but for those who see the Elizabethan literary sunrise as the ideal school of creative minds, a school in which each man who amounted to anything was teacher and student at the same time or by turns, sometimes consciously and sometimes unconsciously, it is significant that when Shakespeare took the conscious rôle of teacher through literary satire he filled it in what we should now consider the best, because the most potent, way—by administering correction to those who were well able to profit by it, and who had transgressed only momentarily; not, like Pope, by wasting much of his ridicule on hordes of petty scribblers, the "hopeless students" of the great university of letters.

Such burlesque in *A Midsummer Night's Dream* surely gave it importance in the stage rivalry. But as I have already said, I believe that the Chamberlain's men replied to the challenge thrown down by the rival company in their production of *Henry V* by producing *1 Henry IV*, probably by the middle of 1596. This great play with its new and effective combination of heroic and realistically comic elements and its hugely successful creation of the fat knight, Sir John Oldcastle, must have been a staggering blow to the Admiral's men, whether or not it was a rebuke to the Henslowe playwright who had made unauthorized use of *The Famous Victories*.

William Brooke, tenth Lord Cobham, Lord Chamberlain from July, 1596, until his death early in 1597, was descended through the female line from Sir John Oldcastle, the Lollard martyr, ancient Lord of Cobham. (And, by the way, the wife of Humphrey, Duke of Gloster, was a Cobham.) In spite of his family's Catholic sympathies in Elizabethan times, which produced his imprisonment in 1572 on suspicion of being concerned in a plot to wed Mary Stuart to the Duke of Norfolk[62] and which brought about his eldest son's imprisonment and the execution of his younger son George in the Catholic plot of 1603, he was trusted as Warden of the Cinque Ports and Constable of the Tower. His daughter Elizabeth had married Sir Robert Cecil, who was the friend and ally of her brother, Henry Brooke, the eleventh Lord Cobham. One of the objects of the Essex Rebellion was this Lord Cobham's removal from court; and when arrested Essex charged him with scheming to assassinate him, and to sell England to the Infanta. Henry Brooke became about 1601 the second husband of Lady Kildare, a daughter of the Lord Admiral. His enemies describe him as henpecked and a good deal of a fool. He appears to small advantage in the intrigues over the succession in Elizabeth's last years, when with Ralegh and Northumberland he formed the "Triplicity of Hell" to oppose James as claimant, while Lady Kildare was an aggressive Jacobean. The three went over finally to the side of James, but were never trusted by him after his accession. Cobham and Ralegh were both enmeshed in the plot which cost George Brooke's life, and Cobham died in obscure poverty in 1619.

The tendency of recent criticism has been to set aside the possibility that a slur on the Cobhams was intended by Shakespeare when he gave the name of the historical character Oldcastle to the "Jockey" of *The Famous Victories*, and to look for the "original" of Falstaff in such more-or-less well known figures of the dramatist's environment as John Florio or Nicholas Dawtrey, or to reduce such speculations to absurdity with a plea for Robert Greene, and fall back upon the familiar theory that Falstaff is without individual prototype but is taken from the Elizabethan braggart soldier in general.

It seems to me that the time is ripe for a return to the only hypothesis which has any support in external evidence—for we know that Shakespeare changed the name of his character from Oldcastle to Falstaff; and the Jacobean testimony that the change was made under pressure from Oldcastle's descendants (the Cobhams)[63] is supported by the obvious aim of the rival play, *Sir John Oldcastle*, produced by the rival company

[62] Lodge, *Illustrations*, II, 506 n., remarks that his consequence was derived entirely from his birth and great fortune. From the Tower "he obtained his liberty by a full discovery of all he knew of that ill-fated affair. We find by letters in this connection [see especially one from his son in 1603, pleading for mercy from King James on the ground of his father's attachment to the Queen's mother], and by several scattered passages in other papers of his time, that he was always suspected, and probably with justice, of an attachment to Mary's interest." His father, however, had been imprisoned for giving up Cowling Castle too easily to the forces of Wyatt, with whom were his sons, including this Sir William.

[63] R. James, in the dedication of his MS. *Legend of Sir John Oldcastle* (c. 1625)—"offence being worthily taken by Personages descended from his title."

in 1599, to rehabilitate the Lollard martyr's memory. This evidence has been presented by every editor of the play: what has been lacking is evidence of a motive for Shakespeare's malice against the house of Cobham. And yet such a motive is not difficult to find if we look for it in the interests of the dramatist and his company in 1596.

Henry Carey, Lord Hunsdon, Lord Chamberlain and the players' patron, died in July. As his death was seen approaching, members of the rival factions at court began to "beg his offices," an invariable practice; and among the candidates for the Chamberlainship were his eldest son Sir George,[64] and Sir William Brooke, Lord Cobham,[65] Lord Warden of the Cinque Ports. Loyalty to their patron and fear of what might happen to them in case the Chamberlainship fell to a member of the faction backing their rivals, the Admiral's men, would quite naturally cause the Hunsdon family players to feel enough dislike of Cobham to lampoon him if they dared.

The rivalry for the Chamberlainship between the families of Brooke and Carey continued through our period. Hunsdon dying, July 23, 1596, Cobham won the post, but died March 6, 1597,[66] and was succeeded (March 17) by the younger Hunsdon, himself in failing health. During his illness, April–June, 1600, a leading candidate for his white staff was the younger Cobham[67]—there appears to have been provocation for his having his players give "Sir John Oldcastle" before the Flemish ambassador that spring. Still another probable cause of dislike between Sir George and Sir Henry was a rivalry at court, paralleling that of Essex and Ralegh. Moreover, Hunsdon had a place at Stone, in Kent, a county ruled by the Cobhams with a high hand.

Somewhat more insight into the application of Shakespeare's lampoon

[64] *Sal.* VI, 304 (July, '96)—the new Lo. Hunsdon to Cecil, with list and valuations of his late father's offices, which he sues for, not omitting the Chamberlainship.

[65] Cobham had already acted as Chamberlain, doubtless in Hunsdon's absence: *Sal. MSS.*, V, 19 (H. Maynard to Sir R. Cecil, 1594, Nov. 8).—"I am scared with a message that hath been sent to me from Clapham by a man of mine that I have left there, that one of the guard hath been at my house this day to see it, signifying her Majesty's meaning to drive there on Thursday next . . . I doubt not, by Lord Cobham's favour, being now the director of these removes as Lord Chamberlain, and your good means . . . but to be rid of this fear."

[66] Apparently in a spirit of "tit for tat," the younger Hunsdon was a candidate for the Cobham post of Warden of the Cinque Ports in February (Whyte to Sidney, 21 Feb.).

[67] Whyte to Sidney, 15 March, 1600 (a week after the banquet for the Flemish ambassador)—"My Lord Chamberlain is very sicke at *Draiton*, being seised with an apoplexy; if he shuld die, I hear 400 [Cobham] wold stand for his office." But Henry, Lo. Cobham, especially after Essex's death, was becoming disliked by Cecil, who transmitted his feeling to King James; hence Hunsdon's successor in 1603 was not Cobham, but Lord Howard de Walden, who had acted as Chamberlain during Hunsdon's illness in 1602.

to Cobham's personality may be had from another contest at about this time, that of Essex on behalf of his brother-in-law, Sir Robert Sidney, for the Cobham office of the Cinque Ports. The only clue I have been able to find to the physical proportions of the elder Cobham is in a letter from Whyte to Sidney, 21 February, 1597:

My Lord *Cobham* is ill in Deed, and much fallen away, and now as I heare, his Sonne Mr. Harry comes daily to the Queen, and the Father is willing to make Resignation of such places he holds by the Queen, to his Sonnes, especially of the *Cinque Ports.*

Hunsdon and Buckhurst, he goes on to say, are also candidates; but Essex may be willing to beg the Cinque Ports for Sidney:

yf my Lord of Essex wold deale, *tanquam pro seipso,* he were the fittest man of all others; because feare to offend, might make others fearefull to deale for you.

On February 27 Whyte reports a conference with Essex about the Cinque Ports, Essex saying:

Neither due I here that any Body stands for yt, but 30 [A. Collins, the editor, glosses "Lord Brooke"; but the reference is to Henry Brooke, soon to succeed as Lord Cobham], who, of all Men, is the unfittest; and such hath his base villanies bene towards me, which, to the World, is to well known, that he shalbe sure never to have yt, if I can keape hym from yt. I make no Doubt but that great Meanes wilbe used for hym; and at this Instant he hath a stronge Party for hym.

The course of this struggle would make a long story. As late as 22 March, 1598, Essex promises Sidney, through Whyte, that "As a Favoryt, he (Essex) will take all Opportunities to hynder your competitor, ever laying before her Eyes his Unworthines, and his ill dealing towards him." But the Queen "would give yt my Lord *Cobham* in Respect of his Frends, and the particular good Opinion she conceaved of hym, whom she used in some Kind of Services"; and the Cinque Ports eventually went to Cobham.[68] Some extracts from letters of Sidney to Essex[69] give us a little more light on the origin of Essex's dislike, and a glimpse from his hostile viewpoint of the character of the elder Cobham:

Do not forget to lay before the consideration of the Queen the nearness of Calais and Dunkerck, and the easiness to do a skorne or a spoil if he that hath the charge of those places be not a man of war. I doubt not your Lordship remembers how slenderly you were assisted by the late Warden in the service of

[68] John Chamberlain to Dudley Carleton, August 30, 1598 (*S. P. Dom.* 1598–1601, 85)—"Lord Cobham is installed Lord Warden of the Cinque Ports; 4000 horse were assembled at the solemnity, and he kept the feast magnificently, spending 26 oxen. It is said that he . . . [is] to be sworn of the Council." Probably Cobham's appointment was prepared during Essex's absence on the Islands Voyage in 1597, but he returned in time to prevent its signing or sealing, and managed to hold it up until the middle of 1598.

[69] *Sal. MSS.*, VII, 115 (March 15, 1597).

Calais [which fell about April 15, 1596].[70] The like occasions or worse may come, and your Lordship like much worse to be seconded by the son than you were by the father,[71] who, you may boldly say, is beloved by never a man in Kent. Truly, I pity my poor countrymen [of Kent] who are ready to leave their houses[72] upon the sight of every small fleet for want of somebody among them to tell them what they have to do.[73]

But her Majesty will have a baron in that place: I would to God that the Spaniards would run away at the title of a baron, or that it would keep our men from running away, otherwise I fear me our country of Kent and Sussex will be honourably left to be spoiled and burnt.[74]

It is clear from these quotations that Essex's dislike of the Cobhams antedated 1597, and that his faction considered William, the elder Cobham, if not cowardly, at least lazy and inefficient as a military leader.[75]

And thus if Shakespeare and his fellows gave intentional offense to the Cobhams in 1596 by presenting the martyred ancestor of their house[76] as a buffoon, it was with the delighted approval of both their patron and the Essex faction. That we have in their productions no other case of personal lampooning so clear as this, is no doubt at least partly due to the fact that the interests and sympathies of the Essex party and the house of Hunsdon so frequently failed to coincide.[77]

[70] *Sal. MSS.*, v, 492 (1595, Dec. 10).—A letter from Cobham to Essex, putting him off about reinforcing Ostend against a threatened siege. For Essex letters telling of his efforts to relieve Calais in time, see *S. P. Dom.*, 1595–97, 196–208. He does not make any complaint of slackness on Cobham's part; but he is being much more tactful and conciliatory than usual, and pressing with all his power for the Queen's permission to sail (cf. p. 204).

[71] Cf. Whyte, 16 March, 1597;—"When the great Invasion [1588] was threatened from Duncarke, the little Assistance that then was given by the Lord Warden."

[72] As evidence that something of this sort was going on under the elder Cobham, see the Queen's orders to him, June 7, 1596 (*S. P. Dom.*, 1595–97, 227): "You are to let the inhabitants upon the sea coasts know that if any of them, in this doubtful time, leave their habitation, they shall not only be severely punished, but their houses and lands shall be seized, and the whole profits thereof applied for the defence of the said houses."

[73] *Sal. MSS.*, VII, 115 (March 15, 1597). [74] *Ibid.*, 133 (March 28).

[75] Sir Thomas Randolph, Master of the Posts, wrote his friend Walsingham, Nov. 28, 1588 (*Cal. Scottish Papers*, IX, 638), accusing Cobham of nepotism in appointing as captain in the Kentish forces of that year a younger brother, Sir John, who acted in a very Falstaffian manner in selling discharges from the "press," and stealing the soldiers' pay. Moreover, he accuses Cobham of abetting his son "Sir Harry" and a servant in extorting illegal tribute from a recusant in return for his freedom. Randolph's tone of extreme caution in making these revelations proves the tyrannous sway of the Cobhams over Kent.

[76] There was a lively sixteenth-century controversy between Protestants and Catholics, as to whether Oldcastle was martyr or traitor, participated in by Foxe and others (cf. James Tait, "John Foxe," *D.N.B.*

[77] For the dependence of the Careys upon Cecil at this very time, see the letters to the Secretary from Sir George's brothers, Sir Edmund, Sir John, and Sir Robert, from Henry Lord Hunsdon's widow, and from her daughter, Lady Margaret Hoby, *Sal. MSS.*, VII, 261, 277, 286, 297, 301, 313, 322, 339, 342.

Yet in asserting that the character of Oldcastle was a lampoon on Cobham, I do not wish to be misunderstood to mean that he was only that. Much of the objection raised by conservatives against any and all contemporary identifications in Shakespeare's plays is based on a sound feeling that Shakespeare was not a writer of political and personal squibs. May we not believe that the character we know as Falstaff was sketched in as a braggart soldier type, elaborated with all the resources of genius aided by an appreciative observation of many of the contemporaries who have already been suggested by seekers for his prototype—and doubtless of others who remain still to be suggested—and at last given, under some pressure from outside, enough identification with the historical Oldcastle and the contemporary Cobham to make the allusion cause especial delight in the one camp and resentment in the other? By pressure from outside, I mean influences working upon those loyalties to persons which any man must have, however non-partisan his philosophy, however great his devotion to his art: in Shakespeare's case his loyalties to his personal patron, company's patron, fellow-sharers, and audience.

Another sort of contemporary allusion in the play, one made, it appears, only to give delight and encourage good feeling between the exacerbated parties referred to, has long lain unsuspected in the famous scene of the division of England among the conspirators; all north of Trent to Percy, south to Mortimer, west of Severn to Glendower.

> *Hot.* Methinks my moiety, north from Burton here,
> In quantity equals not one of yours:
> See how this river comes me cranking in,
> And cuts me from the best of all my land
> A huge half-moon, a monstrous cantle out.
> I'll have the current in this place damm'd up,
> And here the smug and silver Trent shall run
> In a new channel, fair and evenly:
> It shall not wind with such a deep indent,
> To rob me of so rich a bottom here.
> *Glen.* Not wind! it shall, it must; you see it doth.
> *Mort.* Yea, but—
> Mark how he bears his course, and runs me up
> With like advantage on the other side;
> Gelding the opposed continent as much,
> As on the other side it takes from you.
> *Wor.* Yea, but a little charge will trench him here,
> And on this north side win this cape of land;
> And then he runs straight and even.
> *Hot.* I'll have it so; a little charge will do it.
>
> . . . .
>
> *Glen.* Come, you shall have Trent turn'd.
> *Hot.* I do not care: I'll give thrice so much land

To any well-deserving friend;
But in the way of bargain, mark you me,
I'll cavil on the ninth part of a hair.[78]

As early as 1590 there was an old quarrel between Gilbert Talbot, Earl of Shrewsbury, and Sir Thomas Stanhope of Shelford, on the south side of the Trent a little below Nottingham;[79] and by February, 1592, partisan feeling had risen so high that the Stanhope coach was defaced and someone set up "certain vile pictures of the Talbot."[80] In August the Privy Council received an elaborate petition[81] that Stanhope's new weir, between the upper curve of his great oxbow (called on modern maps "the Holmes") at Shelford and the other shore at Stoke Bardolph, lands to which Shrewsbury had some sort of claim,[82] be pulled down as obstructing the navigation of the Trent. Through the potent influence of Burghley and the Admiral this petition was shelved, some of the most influential signers being forced to withdraw with the excuse that they had been misinformed.[83] Importuned by Shrewsbury, the Council refused to consider the matter further, and referred it to a Commission of Sewers,[84] but in November the Earl was still striving to have one appointed.[85]

On Easter morning, 1593, a large crowd "riotously" attacked the weir, and made it useless as well as harmless by diverting the river to a new trench, cut through the low meadows at the Stoke Bardolph end of the dam. Stanhope's complaints of the outrage brought the Council into action at once, but they had difficulty in bringing the officers, friendly to Shrewsbury, to find and send up the chief offenders, and had to reprove them.[86] In April a sanguinary riot in Fleet Street between Stanhopes and Cavendishes (the latter, of course, Shrewsbury's relatives) brought the disturbance, really a survival of feudal petty warfare, close to the Londoners.[87] On May 25 the weir case was heard in the Star Chamber, and heavy fines awarded to Williamson, Shrewsbury's estate agent, who had led the rioters, and others.

The oxbow of which I have spoken may be clearly seen on the map of the region in Bartholomew's Atlas,[88] where the Trent swerves northward

[78] *1 Henry IV*, III, i, 97–139.

[79] Lodge, *Illustrations*, III, Calendar of Unpublished Talbot Papers, H. 151.

[80] *Privy Council*, 21 February, 1592.

[81] *Ibid.*, 22 August.

[82] Cf. *Rutland MSS.*, I, 306.

[83] *Ibid.*, and see *Hist. MSS. Com.*, *Portland MSS.*, IX, 74, a letter (misdated "1599") from Sir John Holles to Lord Sheffield, advising him to withdraw his signature lest he offend his friend the Admiral.

[84] Lodge, *op. cit.*, H. 389.

[85] *Ibid.*, 499.

[86] *Privy Council*, 1592–93, 201, 239, 267, 279, 352.

[87] *Ibid.*, 181, 206.

[88] Or see the map in J. B. Frith's *Highways and Byways in Nottinghamshire*, p. 109, based on the Ordnance Survey.

just before it reaches Shelford, cutting "a huge half-moon" out of the lowlands to the north, almost reaching Burton Joyce before it winds southward again in its general course toward the northeast. A usual way from London to Nottingham avoided the deep clay of the more direct route through Gotham by turning off from the North Road at Newark and passing through Burton Joyce (Burton "Goose" in Speed's account of this road);[89] hence Shakespeare, writing these lines, may have remembered the fertile oxbow seen across the Trent to southward, and imagined that the trench diverting the river had been cut on the Shelford side, as Hotspur would have wished it. That he wrote "North from Burton" may be mystification or a slip; but the whole region is north from the large town of Burton-on-Trent, suitable for locating the allusion in the minds of an audience. Worcester's "and on this north side win this cape of land" is ambiguous. Bernard Smith[90] connects the whole incident with still another tiny Burton, some miles down the river toward Newark, which did once have a large meander, since cut off, to the north of it. However, there is no political significance connected with this place, or with Willington, above Nottingham, mentioned by the editors of the (English) *Arden Shakespeare*[91] in annotating this passage, without giving any evidence that the local "tradition" did not grow out of the play.[92]

For over a year the "riot" was seemingly forgotten. Meanwhile Williamson drifted abroad on some mysterious business, returned, and was arrested for associating with Jesuit agents. Shrewsbury was seized with panic, repudiated him, and sent men to ransack his papers, apparently to remove anything that might incriminate his Lordship. As a result, by midsummer of 1595, probably not long before Shakespeare began writing *1 Henry IV*, we find Shrewsbury under arrest for this "contempt" and generally thought to be in grave danger of being tried for treason.[93]

[89] Speed, John, *Theatre of the Empire of Great Britain*, 1676 edition. Speed's map of Notts. distorts the directions so that the loop lies east of Burton (Joyce), not south. His chart (about the middle of the volume, unpaged) "The North-Road from London to Barwick; and its Branches to several of the principal Towns, with their computed distances," gives the itinerary (turning to the left at Newark) as "Stoake 3" (not Stoke Bardolph, but the place where Henry VII defeated the Earl of Lincoln and Martin Swarte), "Gunthorp, Burton goose 5, Charlton, Notingham 2." For the clay of the more direct road to London, see Charles Deering, *Antiquities of Nottingham* (1751), 168.

[90] "Some Recent Changes in the Course of the Trent," *Geographical Journal*, XXV, 568 ff.

[91] R. P. Cowl and A. E. Morgan.

[92] Cf. also *Notts. Notes & Queries*, 1895, 176. Can this affair be the source also of Shakespeare's comic Bardolph? Camden, a partisan of Cecil, speaks highly of the lords Bardolph, former owners of Shelford, as well as of the Stanhopes, present owners (*Britannia*, 1637 translation, 549).

[93] Cf. *Sal. MSS.*, v, 526.—"Memorial of the Earl of Shrewsbury's Causes"; and *Ibid.*, 273.—Sir Thomas Cecil to his brother Robert, July 9, 1595: "I am very glad to hear by

Williamson, abandoned by his master, now offered to testify to help the Stanhopes if they and their friend Cecil would get him free and into Essex's service.[94] Elaborately examined by Coke, he brought to light much interesting gossip regarding the sore subject of the succession to the crown,[95] the claims of Arabella, James, Stanley, and Hastings all being mentioned with pungent comments reported from Shrewsbury's "imperious" lady. For example:

> My lady also one day told me of the manner and forcible death of my late lord of Derby, saying that some were of opinion that my lord that now is, his brother, had procured him to be poisoned; 'but,' saith she, 'I believe it not, but those foolish speeches that he spake to Mr. Fr. Hastings, saying that they two should one day fight for the crown, the shew of his great will and haughty stomach, his making of himself so popular and bearing himself so against my lord of Essex, I thought would be his overthrow: . . .

To bring this high-tempered family into still greater notoriety, early in July, 1595, Lord Keeper Puckering, Lord Treasurer Burghley, Essex, the Admiral, Sir Robert Cecil, Sir John "Wollye," Sir John Fortescue, Lord Chief Justice Popham, and John Whitgift, Archbishop of Canterbury, were hearing in the Star Chamber the scandalous case of the Earl of Shrewsbury's brother, Edward Talbot, against a quack physician named Wood, who had accused Talbot of instigating him to poison the Earl with a pair of gloves. With this same brother the Earl had wished to fight a duel the year before, and had been with difficulty dissuaded by Essex and the Admiral.[96] The general aim of the Star Chamber judges seems to have been to clear the nobility by concentrating all the scorn and punishment upon Wood; so he was condemned "per totam curiam (th'erle of Essexe & th'archebishope onely excepted, for which they were checkte by her Matie afterwards)" to punishments[97] sufficiently public to bring still further notoriety to the "causes" of this hot-headed noble of the North.[98]

Wood had implicated Lady Shrewsbury deeply in his examination, but Whyte professes to disbelieve him as a perjured fellow; still, on December 13 he reports, "I heare yt feared, my Lady *Shrosbery* wilbe called in publique Question for Wood's Perjuries; yet hath she here many great Frends of both Kinds." I think he means "both Catholic and Protestant"; the Countess was a Catholic, and her influence on Arabella's faith was suspected.

---

your letters that the Earl is not to be touched *in capite*, whereas here it was in common report doubted, by reason of Williamson's committing to the Tower."

[94] *Ibid.*, 227. [95] *Ibid.*, 251 ff. And see *S. P. Dom.*, 1595–97, 64, 65.

[96] Lodge, *Illustrations*, II, 463 ff.

[97] Carting, pillory, ear-clipping, branding on the forehead.

[98] John Hawarde, *Les Reports del Cases in Camera Stellata*, 13 (July 2), 16 (July 4). For the distinguished group of counsel present, see p. 14.

Through 1596 Williamson languished in the Tower, sending frequent imploring letters to Cecil. Something of a shadow appears to have continued to hang over Lord and Lady Shrewsbury, although the Earl was in sufficient favor that autumn to be sent to carry the Garter to King Henri. On October, still in France, he was aiding the Danvers brothers, Southampton's friends.[99] When we add to this fact Southampton's connection by marriage to the Willoughbys of Wollaton,[100] near Nottingham, whose relations with the Stanhopes of Shelford were intimate, although not always altogether friendly,[101] we can still better understand the impartial, conciliatory character of the reference to the weir affair in Shakespeare's play this spring or summer. Moreover, Sir Thomas Stanhope died this year.[102]

On November 6, 1598, Williamson was free, but estranged from his wife, who wrote Cecil to ask his aid.[103] That summer had appeared the the Admiral's *Black Bateman of the North*, a play which, in its Caroline reincarnation as William Sampson's *Vow-Breaker*, gives us another dramatic allusion to the Trent weirs. At the end of *The Vow-Breaker* we have Queen Elizabeth, on progress, visiting Nottingham, and there greeted by the Mayor, Aldermen, and citizens:

> *Queen*. On, to your former motion made for *Trent*. . . .
> *Mayor*. *Edward* the first from [whom] we beare our armes,
> Three Crownes displaied in an Azure feilde,
> First 'gan to make our River navigable,
> Small barks it bore, but not of that full weight,
> That were transportable for our affaires;
> In the two *Edwards*, the second, and third,
> Vnto the second *Richard* it continu'd
> Till *Bulling-brooke* began! then *Harry* the fift,
> And *Pearcy* fell at odds; in which division,
> Dividing of the land, *Glendower* began
> To stop the water-courses of flowing Trent;
> By what meanes our navigable course was stop'd.
> And where before we usually transported
> With things un-numerous from *Hull* to us
> And in returne releiv'd the neighbour coaste
> With fuell, and commodities of great use,
> As Wool, Lead, Corne, fruits, and Iron,
> We now have neyther, but with double cost;

[99] Lodge, *Illustrations*, II, 496.

[100] In 1585 his sister married Thomas Arundel, whose mother was daughter of Sir Henry Willoughby of Wollaton. In 1590 Sir Thomas Stanhope disclaimed to Burghley that he was trying to marry his daughter to Southampton.

[101] *Hist. MSS. Com.*, *Middleton MSS.*, 544, 546, 551, 552, & *passim*.

[102] At "his house called Stoke," August 3. Cf. Thoroton's *Nottinghamshire* (ed. Throsby, 1797), I, 292. He was buried at Shelford, Sept. 27.

[103] *Sal. MSS.*, VIII, 430.

This is the cause why we entreate your Grace
To signe our pattent, and, by *St. Lucy*, *Besse*,
Wee'le pray for thee, and that's thy full reward.
Qu. You shall enjoy your wishes.[104]

If this scene occurred in *Black Bateman of the North*, the source of the tragic portion of *The Vow-Breaker*, it at first seems odd that the Admiral's men, who produced the former play in 1598, should be issuing propaganda on the navigation or antiweir side of the controversy. But their patron had recently been created Earl of Nottingham, and ordinary politics would naturally dictate his appearing to favor Nottingham's commerce. Note the fact that the obstruction of the river is below Nottingham; and especially that Glendower here is the one who stops the watercourses, just as in Shakespeare he sides with his son-in-law, Mortimer, in the interest of the lands to the south of the Trent, as were Stanhope's at Shelford.

Shrewsbury himself, although still inclined to be turbulent where others were concerned, seems to have been thoroughly cowed by Cecil somewhere in the course of the investigations of Williamson and Wood. On August 8, 1598, he wrote the Secretary,

For the falcon, she soars too high for my compass, and therefore God speed you well with her, but for the goshawk that flies near the earth more humbly like my nature and fortune, I have her in my custody, with meaning that you shall never see her.[105]

In the almost formal division of factions at Essex's return from Ireland in 1599, he sided with the Cecilians.[106] M. de Boississe, the French resident ambassador, in his pro-Essex account of the treason trial names among the judges, "le Conte Shrevesbery, grand Ennemi du Conte d'Essex."[107] In 1602 he was working hand-in-glove with Cecil, in Sir Robert's feint at supporting the claims of Beauchamp and Arabella, to cover his secret attachment to James.[108]

[104] *The Vow-Breaker*, Q. 1636, by William Sampson, a gentleman retainer of Sir Henry Willoughby of Richley, Derbyshire. This play appears to be a reworking in the reign of Charles I of *Black Bateman of the North*, produced by the Admiral's men in 1598, not long after their patron had become Earl of Nottingham. Sampson himself was probably not born until 1600; see Hans Wallrath's edition of *The Vow-Breaker* for Bang's *Materialen*, Louvain, 1914. Schelling (*Elizabethan Drama*, I, 348; II, 546) suggests the identification with *Black Bateman* (two parts, Chettle, Dekker, Day, and Wilson, for Henslowe, May–July, 1598). Also centering on this region were the Admiral's Robin Hood plays (1598), *Martin Swarte* (1597), and probably *The Spencers* (1599) and *Mortimer* (1602).

[105] *Sal. MSS.*, VIII, 297. I think the falcon stands for Elizabeth, the goshawk Arabella.

[106] Whyte, 30 September, 1599.

[107] *Winwood's Memorials*, 296 (February, 1601).

[108] See E. T. Bradley, *Lady Arabella Stuart*, I, 157, and Sir John Harington's *Tract on the Succession*.

Shakespeare's allusion to the diversion of the Trent, then, was of the non-malicious type which, merely in passing and without the slightest distortion of dramatic characterization, touches the spark of delighted recognition to a great mass of an audience's current interests in striking personalities and scandalous doings.

To return from these details to the general fortunes of the Chamberlain's men. On July 23, 1596, the first Lord Hunsdon died at Somerset House, of which he was keeper. Fuller says his death was caused by disappointment at not being made Earl of Wiltshire, the title of his grandfather, Sir Thomas Boleyn, and that, the title and robes being offered to him by the Queen in person, he refused, saying that he did not care to accept on his deathbed an honor he had not been considered worthy of in his lifetime. His son George succeeded him as second Lord Hunsdon; but Lord Cobham was given his post as Chamberlain.

Perhaps it was as a result of the political tension caused by the Lord Chamberlain's illness that the Admiral's men stressed satire that month. They produced *The French Doctor*, *Longshanks*, *Henry V* (twice), and two new plays—each of which drew a good house but was given only once—*Paradox*[109] and *The Tinker of Totnes*. The former was given on July 1, and brought Henslowe forty-five shillings; the latter, on July 23 (Greg's correction of Henslowe's date), three pounds. This was the last performance by the Admiral's men at the Rose until October 27. Was *The Tinker of Totnes* so offensive as to provoke an "inhibition"? If it contained any slur on the Careys[110] it was very unfortunate to be playing on the day of the death of Elizabeth's old friend and kinsman.

There was, moreover, plentiful opportunity for political allusion in a play about Totnes, Devon, in that town's connection with the Seymours, whose seat was at Berry Pomeroy, nearby. Edward Seymour, Earl of Hertford, eldest son of the Protector, who had been in the Tower for his marriage to Lady Catherine Grey, was now living at Berry Castle[111] with his second wife, Frances Howard (died May 14, 1598), a sister

[109] Among the Elizabethans who published "Paradoxes" were Antony Munday (1593), George Silver, Thomas Scott, Thomas Lodge, Thomas Digges, John Hall, and John Donne. There is interesting information on this class of writings in R. E. Bennett's "John Manningham and Donne's Paradoxes," *M.L.N.*, XLVI, 309–313. That they often tended to be political we may judge from Andelocia's definition in Dekker's *Old Fortunatus*, "A dish of Paradoxes is a feast of straunge opinion, tis an ordinarie that our greatest gallants haunt nowadaies, because they would be held for Statesmen." (Ed. for John Pearson, London, 1873, p. 114.) And see Bennett's "Four Paradoxes by Sir William Cornwallis the Younger," *Harvard Studies and Notes in Philology and Literature*, XIII, 219 ff.

[110] Who probably originated in Somerset, and flourished long at Cockington, Devon, where the family was still represented at this date.

[111] *Sal. MSS.*, V, 444—Hertford to Cecil, from Berry Castle, Oct. 18, 1596.

of the Admiral, whom he had married before 1582. His eldest son, Edward, Lord Beauchamp, had been born to Catherine Grey in the Tower in 1561, and was inheritor of the "Suffolk claim" to the succession.

But it was the contention of Queen Elizabeth that Hertford's marriage to Catherine Grey was illegal owing to lack of witnesses, and that Edward Seymour was therefore illegitimate. In November, 1595, Hertford rashly brought suit to establish the validity of the marriage, taking the first steps very quietly by the aid of the Stanhopes, at least one of whom was prominent in the legal profession. When the matter was brought to the Queen's ear—perhaps by Essexian friends of the Scottish succession—there was a storm which hurled Hertford into the Tower,[112] whence he emerged January 3, 1596, considerably chastened.

Perhaps the Admiral's men had been preparing to bring out in *The Tinker of Totnes* some mild, complimentary propaganda in the Seymours' favor, imbedded in a play about some merry Tinker and the landing of Brutus on the stone still to be seen in the town; but about a month before the play was ready, any reference to the family was made too risky by the occurrence at Colchester of a farcical event which might very easily have been tragic, and which illuminates the political conditions under which dramatists were writing. Sir John Smith, a man of some distinction and a connection of the Seymours by marriage, was at Colchester with Sir Thomas Lucas, training the county militia against the threatened Spanish invasion; and on June 13 he called upon the soldiers to leave their colonel, promising to save them from being pressed "out of the land," and calling the Lord Treasurer "a traitor of traitors." "You shall go," he said, "with a better man than myself or Sir Thomas Lucas; here is a nobleman of the blood royal,[113] brother to the Earl of Beauchamp, that shall be your captain, under whom I am assistant."[114]

The soldiers did not respond. Lucas immediately informed, and Smith found himself in the Tower, where he was examined in a very gingerly manner, considering his open treason and the insults to Burghley. In due time he was let off with banishment to his home at Little Baddow, the authorities seeing fit to accept his excuse that he had eaten too freely

[112] Whyte writes November 7, "The Lord of *Harforde* was yesterdaye carried to the *Tower*, and two of the *Stanopes*, and dyvars other commetted about that Matter;" and on November 12 reports it has been commanded that Hertford's son be no longer called Lord Beauchamp, but Seymour. There is a rumor that Lady Hertford "is become starck Madde. . . . The doctor *Stanhop* and *Stanhope* the Lawier of *Graies Inn*, that were comytted about that Matter, as being acquainted with Thappeale, with divers others, are put at Liberty, and, for a day or two Mr. *Michael Stanhope* came not to the Court. Yt is muttred here that 200 [Sir R. Cecil] had some inckling in these Cawses, which doe trouble 900 [Burghley]."

[113] Thomas Seymour, Hertford's second son, who was present.

[114] *S. P. Dom.*, 1595–97, 235 ff.

of the famous Colchester oysters, washing them down with wine. An attempt was made to draw a red herring across the trail by asking Smith if he had been influenced by Doleman's book on the succession, which had been making Essex trouble by its dedication (see Whyte, November 7, 1595); but he denied that he had ever seen the book.[115]

The Cecil faction was too deeply involved to permit an open treason trial of Smith, or indeed to allow any allusion on the stage, no matter how friendly, to the Seymour claim, after this contretemps. For the political situation, allow me to cite summarily the pungent observations of some unknown student of succession politics:

The "old fox" [Burghley] counselled his cub "never, if possible, to be at the King of Scots' mercy." The Cecils attempted to draw King James "from depending on any other saint in Court but themselves, but they served him to little purpose . . . now where should they find a tree to shade themselves under in England?" The Infanta "threatened too sharp a reformation for their honour or safety . . . Touching Arabella, . . . Shrewsbury, her great kinsman, till of late was wholly Essex's, and had a deadly feud with the Stanhopes, which lasts yet." As for Derby, "The right of that branch must be maintained with those quirks of law which cannot carry the people, and is besides in a female [Lady Strange, niece of the present Earl], fit enough to make a Queen Jane of, but has not yet been thought of for such purpose I dare say on this side." The Cecils are beholden to the claim of Suffolk, and have made it much beholden to them. There is also the "inclination of our country to keep out strangers, and particularly an old beggarly enemy, the Scot, in whose mother's blood the whole State seems to have washed their hands." The death of James would be a great advantage to the Cecils' plans, the heir being a child, "and garboils ensuing in that mutinous country. You say he has been fair for it more than once [the allusion is probably to suspected Cecil support of the plots of Gowrie and Bothwell]; you know where the suspicion has alighted. All the world takes notice of the occasion taken to lay blocks in his way." Burghley protected the house of Suffolk against Leicester at the time of the Seymour-Grey marriage. "Beale's negotiation in Germany, about the validity thereof, is winked at." Great leniency was shown to Stanhope and Hertford for the appeal; the latter was allowed to name his own fine. Beauchamp is confined only among his own kindred. Sir John Stanhope is kin, and also in credit with the Queen and in ward with Cecil. The "Admiral's love to the house, tho' his sister, Hertford's wife, be dead, "is another great asset, and it is likely that Ralegh concurs, seeing Essex leans to the Scot, and Ralegh is seated in Hertford's region [Devon, Wiltshire, Hampshire]. "Essex being suppressed, which is not unlikely, the party, though his alliance be not with the nobility, will be greater than you think for, of noblemen and gentlemen of good worth, drawn in by the Secretary, the Admiral, and others, if their credit continue, as he [Beauchamp] may have the start of all other competitors when the Queen dies, which will be a great advantage—before men can or dare declare themselves—to have the principal force, and the treasure of the realm put into his hands, with the name of a King."[116]

[115] *S. P. Dom.*, 1595–97, 251.

[116] *S. P. Dom., Addenda, 1580–1625;* 406–408. The views expressed by Sir John Haring-

The second Lord Hunsdon, George Carey, became patron of Shakespeare and his fellows on his father's death. If the chief interest of the Carey family in the players was taken by Robert, the seventh son, and another younger brother, Henry, as I have surmised, it is quite possible that this change of patrons, even considered as merely a family matter, was an unfortunate one for the company; since the change of the headship of the household from an indulgent father to a domineering elder brother was a somewhat unpleasant one for Sir Robert,[117] as he testifies in his *Memoirs*.[118] Thus the fact that the post of Lord Chamberlain, with its power over dramatic affairs, was no longer in the family may not have been the only respect in which the loss of their old lord was disastrous to the players.

It was probably soon after he became Lord Chamberlain that Cobham forced the jovial Sir John to change his name from Oldcastle to Falstaff;[119] but this change cannot have troubled Lord Hunsdon's men extremely —indeed, the advertising probably brought ridicule upon the hapless Cobhams and drew increased audiences to the play. In practice the new name seems to have been only for public and official use. As late as March 6, 1600, the Chamberlain's men gave *Sir John Oldcastle* for their lord at a dinner to the Flemish ambassador.[120]

---

ton in his *Tract on the Succession*, 1602, are much the same. Cecil's turn to James in 1601 was a deep secret, even to most of his own party; indeed, Cecil probably kept the Suffolk claim afoot anyway, mindful of the old fox's sage injunction not to trust the Scot.

[117] That the new Lord Hunsdon was by no means in love with his brother's friends of the Essex party is indicated by Sir Gilly Meyrick's sneering remarks on the hostile influences of Ralegh and "Carey" at court in 1599, and after the Irish failure by a pro-Essex lampoon pillorying the "Chamberlain."

[118] Absolute Warden of the East March after his father's death, Sir Robert could get no allowance from Secretary Cecil for his expenses, nor could be secure leave from his post; so he came up to London, without leave. Warned by Cecil to return, he went to his brother George, now Chamberlain, and "found him far worse than the other." But he was helped to the Queen's presence by Mr. Killigrew of the Privy Chamber, pleaded his way back into her good graces, and astonished Cecil and his brother by getting aid from the exchequer.

About 1593 he had had serious trouble with George over a piece of land in Suffolk.

[119] Cf. Chambers, II, 196, especially n. 2.

[120] Chamberlain to Carleton, March 5, 1600.—Ralegh is showing the sights to Verreyken, the Archduke's Ambassador from Catholic Flanders [peace negotiations were under way, fostered by the Cecilians, who were inclined to England's traditional policy of alliance with Burgundy against France]. To-morrow he is to be feasted at the Lord Chamberlain's, "where methinckes it shold be som what straunge to see carowses to the King of Spaines health." Whyte to Sidney, March 8.—"All this weeke the Lords have been in London, and past away the tyme in Feasting and Plaies, for Vereiken dined upon *Wednesday* with my Lord Treasurer [Buckhurst, a Cecilian], who made him a Roiall Dinner: upon *Thursday*, my Lord Chamberlain feasted hym, and made hym very great, and a delicate Dinner, and there in the After Noone his Plaiers acted, before Vereiken, *Sir John Old Castell*, to

But more serious troubles arose about playhouses. The former Lord Chamberlain had consistently protected the players' rights to act in the City; now growing Puritan opposition to stage plays took advantage of the new Chamberlain's weakness or his partiality to expel the dramatic companies, in 1596, from within its walls. Thus Shakespeare's company apparently lost the use of the Cross Keys as their winter house, and had only the old Theatre, which was neither comfortable nor accessible in bad weather. Perhaps foreseeing this eventuality, the Burbadges had secured the lease of some large apartments in Blackfriars, and toward the close of the year had completed the remodeling of them as a covered playhouse for winter use, within the walls but not under the City jurisdiction. But their enterprise was blocked as the result of a petition of the residents of Blackfriars, with the name of their own patron, Lord Hunsdon, on the list! Very likely politics forced Hunsdon to sign the petition against his will; he was playing for larger stakes than the interests of his band of players—his late father's offices, doubtless including the post of Lord Chamberlain itself, and his dependence on the Cecils[121] seems to have forced him to humor his Puritan and Cecilian neighbor, Lady Russell, whose name leads the signatures. Cobham is mentioned

---

his great Contentment." [Was the choice of a play intended to injure Cobham, on religious grounds, as a diplomat? He went with Ralegh to the Low Countries in July, probably with some secret mission to the Archduke.] The same to the same, 15 March.—"My Lord Chamberlain is very sicke at Draiton, being seised with an apoplexy; if he shuld die, I hear 400 [Cobham] wold stand for his office." [There must have been some jealousy in the situation.] "400 seeks something for his better Maintenance, upon his Marriage [to Lady Kildare, the Admiral's daughter]; he hath not been at 160 [court] these many Daies." This staying from court may be taken as a sign of disgruntlement in the case of such a man as the younger Cobham, who was something of a favorite with the Queen. He was still away the 22nd, complaining that his foot was out of joint. On April 3 Whyte reports that the Chamberlain is not well and there begins to be suing for his place.

[121] His dependence on the Cecils at this time appears in the following extracts from his correspondence: *Salisbury MSS.*, VI, 286.—George, Lord Hunsdon, to Sir Robert Cecil, 1596, before July 26.—Thanks him for his love. "And though beggars may be no chusers, yet to make my mind plain to you, as to one upon whom I will chiefly rely and by whose means I hope your father will be pleased to yield me the more favour, of all my lord's [i.e. his late father's] offices I do least affect Barwicke, as a place far from her Majesty, subject to many jealousies, and where I would be as loth to live as to make a benefit of it by my absence. Of his other offices, the captainship of the pensioners and the justice en oyer, I do chiefly affect, not so much for the benefit, which is less by one half than Barwicke, as for the honour, and desire I have to be near about her person." (*Ibid.*, 280, 286—interesting letters of George's brother Sir Edmund to Cecil, showing a former dependence on Essex, but beseeching Cecil's favor in this his "wretched estate" since his father's death.) *S. P. Dom.*, 1595–97, 509 ff.—Lord Hunsdon writes a long letter to Burghley, October 6, 1597, setting forth his claim to the Earldom of Ormonde. Calls himself, on Queen's mother's side, "her next kinsman and heir."

in the petition as a Blackfriars resident, but did not sign, since he was a member of the Council, to which it was addressed.[122] The result of the petition was a sad blow to Shakespeare and his fellows.

It seems reasonable that Shakespeare's next work should have been the writing of the second part of *Henry IV* in order to capitalize at once the popularity of the first part,[123] although it is possible to find instances in Henslowe's accounts of popular plays not followed by their sequels until a year or so later.[124] Baldwin places *2 Henry IV* in the winter of 1596, but I shall discuss it with the season of 1597.

Efforts by the Admiral's dramatists to meet the competition of Shakespeare's new type of history play seem to have produced nothing better this season than *Valteger*, new on December the fourth, and *Stukeley*, on the eleventh; at least the plays are poor enough if we are right in identifying them with *The Mayor of Quinborough* and *Captain Stukeley*, respectively. The former, a "comedy" with plentiful Senecan horrors, was published in 1661 as by Thomas Middleton. On the dubious ground that "Raynulph Higden, Monk of Chester" serves as chorus it has been identified with T. Middleton's *Randall, Earl of Chester*, written for Henslowe in 1602. This date, at least for one of its incarnations, seems to be supported by its resemblance to *Histriomastix* in its treatment of players on the road; and like that play it has underlying it older material, perhaps to be identified with Henslowe's *Valteger* and *Hengist* of 1596 and 1597, Vortiger and Hengist being characters in the play. Some of the most amusing things in the play as we have it may be late; but that the Mayor of Quinborough in the play had an Elizabethan real-life prototype we may gather from a letter of Sir George Carew to Cecil, June 7, 1595 (as a joke arranged by Cecil he has placed under arrest in his own Castle of Queenborough their friend Sir Edward Hoby):

> The mayor of Queenborough, whom you willed me to call for my assistance, when I beheld his foolish gravity and threadbare robe, I presumed upon my own discretion, and have so far accomplished your commandment as my Lord Admiral may be assured his wager is won. . . ."[125]

Hoby wrote Cecil, May 31, 1596:

> If I perish in this action [the Cadiz voyage, on which he was the oldest knight], I beg you to sue that George Carew may have the keeping of Q. Castle. Though it be nought worth, yet as it delighted me, so do I think for my remembrance it would be agreeable to him. But what! I mean to come home again and play the wag once again. But no more writing of books."[126]

[122] Chambers prints the petition, IV, 319.

[123] See R. A. Law, "Structural Unity in the Two Parts of *Henry IV*," *S.P.*, XXIV, 223 ff.

[124] *Seven Days of the Week*—Part 1, 3 June, 1595; Part 2, 22 Jan., 1596. *The Blind Beggar of Bednal Green*—Part 1, May 1600; Part 2, May 1601; Part 3, July, 1601.

[125] *Sal. MSS.*, V, 235.

[126] *Ibid.*, VI, 202.

Hoby was a friend of Ralegh, whom he called "the Guiana Knight." The play's anti-Puritanism is interesting, for Hoby was an anti-Papist controversialist. He seems a middle-of-the-road man.

Captain Thomas Stukeley was entered in 1600 and published five years later. The text is incoherent, indicating combination or revision. The relation to Peele's *Battle of Alcazar* is curiously close, a considerable fragment of that play being used. A "Tom Stucley" was on the stage at the time of Peele's Farewell in 1589,[127] and perhaps his exploits suffered one or more revisions and combinations with Peele's other play to produce the stuff we have here, some of which bears interestingly on English expeditions to Ireland. Stukeley's fiery devotion to "honour" reminds one of Hotspur, Essex, and Bussy.

Of course it is merely a truism to say that Shakespeare's *1 Henry IV* and *Henry V* represent the culmination of the English chronicle play, but the height by which all the chronicle plays of Shakespeare tower above anything of the type extant from the repertories of the rival company cannot be overestimated. I do not wish to seem obtuse to the charms of plays on Friar Bacon or Robin Hood, but it seems to me that such plays are classified as historical only by courtesy; their dramatic aims are fundamentally different from those of Shakespeare's histories. Perhaps the nearest thing to the Shakespearean type[128] is Heywood's *Edward IV*, but that patchwork of things left over from Shakespeare's work is only doubtfully given to the Admiral's men. In general, as I have said before, the Admiral's men aimed at the groundlings and the citizens through folk-lore and legendary romance; Shakespeare's company, at a cavalier audience through the stirring dramatization of actual history which was still very much alive to their hearers through the intensely genealogical social and political issues of Elizabethan England.

We must leave the chronicle play for the time, to consider an enterprise of the Admiral's men which soon showed results in Hunsdon's repertory—the revival of Marlowe's *Jew of Malta* for a number of performances from January to June. The effectiveness of Marlowe's usurer-Jew seems to have impressed Shakespeare powerfully; at least Baldwin dates *The Merchant of Venice* in the summer of 1597, and it may have been first produced even earlier. (A later revival of Marlowe's play may have influenced *Othello*.) This important dramatic figure of the usurer-Jew merits a pause for the sake of following his type through our period.

[127] Bid theatres and proud tragedians,
Bid Mahomet's Poo and mighty Tamburlaine,
King Charlemagne, Tom Stukeley and the rest
Adieu. (Peele, *A Farewell* to the Portugal expedition, 1589.)

[128] I disregard Marlowe's *Edward II* because I do not consider *Richard II* a typical Shakespearean history play.

The Jew on the Stage, 1594-1603

The wicked Jew as we see him in Marlowe's play or in Shakespeare's can be traced back as far as the mystery plays as a stock type in English drama. Marlowe gives him a bloodthirstiness which comes from such medieval legends as that of Hugh of Lincoln, and adds an indefinable grandeur of character which is achieved by no other example of the type excepting only Shylock. The usurer was of course not necessarily a Jew, but he made a more satisfactory stage villain when he was one. A big nose was part of the conventional make-up,[129] and sometimes appears as a characteristic of usurers who are not otherwise indicated to be Jews; for example, Pisano, "a Portingale," in *Englishmen for My Money*. Numerous pamphlets show the concern of the rising commercial nations about usury in the nineties.[130]

We have noticed the speculations concerning the lost *Venetian Comedy* and its possible relation to *The Merchant of Venice*. *A Knack to Know an Honest Man* contains Servio, a miserly old man with an amiable daughter. Shakespeare's play, coming out two or three years later, appears to owe something to this play of the Admiral's men as well as to their revival of *The Jew of Malta*. Of the two speeches of Shylock most frequently echoed in later plays, "My ducats and my daughter!" and "Hath not a Jew eyes?" the former is itself an echo of Barabas. Jonson's *The Case is Altered*, probably written for Pembroke's men in 1597, appears to imitate both these speeches, and may have been prepared in direct competition with *The Merchant of Venice*. Characteristically, its strength lies in satirically treated "humours," though there is lively farce also. The Marlovian grandeur of Shylock and the romantic magic of Belmont are not attempted. I have mentioned in another connection the university play *Machiavellus*, in which Jacuppus is Jewish chiefly in name.[131] Haughton's *Englishmen for My Money*, mentioned above, belongs to the same company and year. We come to a usurer in the Chamberlain's repertory once more with Sordido of Jonson's *Every Man Out of his Humour*, 1599. The boy companies took the character over, as they did everything else they could lay their little hands on;

[129] When the hero of Chapman's *Blind Beggar of Alexandria* (1596) disguises as Leon the usurer, he dons "a great nose."

[130] For example, Mosse's *Arraignment and Conviction of Usurio*, 1595, and T. Bell's *Speculation of Usurie*, 1596. See also Lodge's *Alarum Against Usurers*, Chettle's *Kind Hart's Dream*, and Breton's 24th and 32nd "Characters." For the legal status of usury, see Greg, *Henslowe*, II, 33.

[131] Perhaps we should notice the odd character, Warman, avaricious and faithless steward, in *The Downfall of Robert Earl of Huntingdon*, written by Munday for the Admiral's men in 1598. He is not really a Jew, but may be intended to demonstrate the fact that the stock "Jewish" characteristics may be found outside that race.

so that *Jack Drum's Entertainment* has Mammon, a big-beaked usurer, in 1601, and *Wily Beguiled*, perhaps about 1602, has a palpable imitation of Shylock in Gripe's "My daughter, my money," and even of the "on such a night" passage in Shakespeare's play. *The Fair Maid of the Exchange* (about 1602, author and company unknown) has an old usurer by the name of Berry. The type, of course, had lost none of its vitality by the end of our period, although it had perhaps become unfashionable to represent the usurer as Jewish; very powerful later conceptions of usurers are found in *Volpone* and *A New Way to Pay Old Debts;* their usurers' grandeur lies not in a Marlovian lofty simplicity of aim, but in their terrific energy.

There are few if any points in which the rival companies met so clearly in competition in which Shakespeare's superiority is less evident than in the usurer type; that is, if we admit Marlowe among the playwrights of the Admiral's men, for practically he was, of course, a most important factor in the dramatic competition for at least a decade after his death. The usurer type had been well established in Roman comedy. Marlowe added grandeur as a possible attribute of a miser. Shakespeare's unique contribution was humanity.

There must have been a dull period for Shakespeare's company during the summer, very likely necessitating a tour, for most of the gallants were abroad on the expedition against Spain which culminated in the gloriously successful attack on Cadiz and the burning of the Spanish fleet there. It was Cadiz which brought the Earl of Essex to the apex of his career in his triumphant reception with almost royal honors, when he quite outshone the Lord Admiral, naval commander of the expedition, and when even Burghley had to kneel to him; but these same honors drew on jealous disputes over the distribution of the spoils and credit for the victory, and intensified the jealousies[132] which led to his downfall. Lord Thomas Howard's wife complained that the Vice-Admiral's share of the loot was unjustly small,[133] and neither the Admiral himself nor his friends could see why Essex and his land forces should monopolize the glory and the booty. Perhaps it was the psychological reaction from his triumph which made Essex "melancholy" and retiring in the late autumn, perhaps it was Sir Robert Cecil's formal appointment to the Secretaryship in his absence, perhaps it was the ague which recurrently afflicted him; at any rate, he left too clear a field for the intrigues which before long began to bear fruit against him.

[132] At the time of the fall of Calais, about April 15, the Admiral was already jealous of Essex; cf. *S. P. Dom.*, 1595–97, 204.

[133] W. B. Devereux, *Lives and Letters of the Devereux Earls of Essex*, I, 381.

At the court at Christmastide the triumph of Essex was accompanied by an even more complete triumph for the Shakespeare company. At court that winter season they gave six performances (the dates were December 26 and 27, January 1 and 6, February 6 and 8), the Admiral's men not one. The total shutting-out of the Admiral's men is hard to understand. It must have been a great shock to them, when they had been counting on a double hold over Master Tilney, now that his chief, the Lord Chamberlain, was one of their faction. But Cobham had not long to live; the Lord Admiral, to whom the Master of the Revels owed his appointment, was in temporary eclipse; and if Shakespeare's depiction of the selection of plays for court performance in *A Midsummer Night's Dream* is to be relied on, royalty had a great deal to do with the process—and the Queen just at present seemed completely under the influence of her favorite, Essex. We surmise that political hints in the Admiral's *Tinker of Totnes* had offended the Queen herself sorely; the Essex party resented the whole political and social policy of the company. Moreover, the company's plays at court the preceding season had been unfashionable, and its 1596 repertory was disgustingly so to the elegant tastes of such courtiers as Southampton: *Chinon of England* based on an outmoded romance; *2 Seven Days of the Week*, bourgeois moralizing, and old-fashioned, too; *1 Fortunatus*, vulgar folk-lore; *Tamar Cam*, an imitation of *Tamburlaine*, itself passé; *Phocas*, probably of somewhat the same type; *Valteger* and *Stukeley*, old-fashioned chronicle plays, the former mythical, the latter an old play refurbished; *That Will Be Shall Be*,[134] an old play, its very title a truism; and *Julian the Apostate*[135] and *Nebuchodonozar*,[136] pap for Puritans! If *Troy* was satirical,

[134] *Che sara, sara;* what will be, will be; the family motto of the Russells, Earls of Bedford. The contemporary Earl had friends on both sides. He was drawn into the Essex rebellion by Lady Rich, but deserted at the first opportunity. The attitude toward Bedford of the Admiral's men in 1600 was hostile, if we may judge from the treatment of a character of that name by John Day in *The Blind Beggar of Bednal Green*. Hence the play built on his motto may have been satirical; the reference in *Faustus* (1604, sc. i), another Admiral's play, seems to disapprove of the motto's philosophy: "What doctrine call you this, *che sera, sera*, what will be, shall be?"

[135] Greg, *Henslowe*, II, 180—*Julian the Apostate*. "Hazlitt states that a play of this title was acted in the seventeenth century at Quarry, near Shrewsbury, but does not give his authority." I think Hazlitt used William Cartwright's entry, in his *Chronological History of Shrewsbury*, for 1556: "The Play of Julian the Apostate played in the Quarrell." See *Shrop. Arch. Soc. Trans.*, 4th Series, IV, 49. The Quarry is now Shrewsbury's public park, with a pretty rock garden where doubtless the Apostate's workmen were scared by balls of fire when they tried to rebuild Solomon's Temple.

[136] The name of Nebuchadnezzar served as a not uncommon political reference. Perez applied it as a nickname to King Philip of Spain, in writing to Essex, November 17, 1595 (Birch, Thos., *Memoirs of Queen Elizabeth*, I, 317); and Essex applied it to himself in a

its bias would be unpleasant to the ruling party; if not, it was outworn and naïve, suitable for the instruction of the groundlings in a set of stale allusions. One play, however, *Pythagoras*, seems to have had a considerable influence on the thought of the times, through a discussion of the Pythagorean doctrine of metempsychosis. Shakespeare's attitude toward the doctrine[137] shows that it was probably considered too dangerously unorthodox for court showing at the Christmas season; indeed, the possession of the play by the Admiral's men could have been used by the Essex faction as ammunition against the notoriously "atheistic" Ralegh, close friend at this time of Cecil and the younger Cobham.

Another play which may have contained offensive satirical matter is *The Blind Beggar of Alexandria* (twenty-two performances, February 12, 1596, to April 1, 1597), the Admiral's only noteworthy play of the season. Its riot of disguisings is not likely, however, to have appealed to a sophisticated taste; and its spirit of burlesque does not seem to have been appreciated. Note that the girls, Elimine, Samathis, Martia, are "Isis' nymphs," and to marry must "leave the pleasant maiden chase." This, of course, is a common way of pointing to an allusion to Queen Elizabeth and her maids of honor; here it may indicate some adventures of the maids with a nobleman who makes miscellaneous love under various guises. It is interesting to observe that Chapman takes care to describe the girls' looks: Elimine has a thin face, Samathis one shaped like the ace of hearts, Martia a round one and a thin skin. This device should have aided identification.

Now, late in 1596, the redoubtable Lady Bacon was scolding Essex for relapsing into some of his scandalous affairs with numerous ladies

---

message by Lord Henry Howard to the Queen, at the time of his release from custody in 1600, saying "that now he had resolved to repent earnestly, and to say with Nebuchadonozor, that my habitation is amongst the wilde Beasts of the field, that I may eate Hay like an oxe, & be watered with the dew of heaven, till such time as it shall please the Queene to restore my sence to me againe." Camden, *Annals of Elizabeth*, trans. 1629, 294.

[137] Thou almost mak'st me waver in my faith
To hold opinion with Pythagoras
That souls of animals infuse themselves
Into the trunks of men. (*The Merchant of Venice*, c. 1597, IV, i, 130.)

Feste. What is the opinion of Pythagoras concerning wild fowl?
Malvolio. That the soul of our grandam might haply inhabit a bird.
Feste. What thinkest thou of his opinion?
Mal. I think nobly of the soul, and in no way approve his opinion.
(*Twelfth Night*, IV, ii, 56.)

And see *As You Like It*, III, ii, 188; and Lyly's *Endimion*, IV, iii, 60. In his *Damon and Pythias*, Edwards, perhaps prudently, omits to mention the fact that his pair of heroic friends were Pythagorean philosophers.

of the court.[138] Among these may be identified with some certainty Elizabeth Southwell, a daughter of the Admiral (by this sprightly lady, the wife of old Sir Robert Southwell, Essex is said to have had a son named Walter, to whom he left Essex House);[139] Mary Howard;[140] "Mrs. Russell";[141] Elizabeth Brydges, daughter of Lord Chandos;[142] and the young Countess of Derby, Elizabeth Vere.[143]

Admittedly, this sort of satire was dangerous business.[144] Even with the Cecil faction in working control of the censorship, it seems hardly possible that *The Blind Beggar of Alexandria* could escape suppression if this allusion to Essex was seen in it. For if Cleanthes is Essex, who is the wicked Queen Aegiale (αἰγιᾶλός, the sea-shore?) who is so infatuated with him that she has put his wife out of the way? And what about Cleanthes' hatred of her, and banishment, and lurking about to overthrow the government and attain the throne? This might be passed off, perhaps, as an allegory of Leicester and the Queen of Scots; *The Faerie Queene* is sufficient evidence that the Elizabethans did not require their allegories to be clear or consistent.

But *The Blind Beggar of Alexandria* is a mysteriously bad play to be so popular unless it contained personalities, and the mangling omissions from the version which survives also hint at topical satire. On the whole, I am inclined to think that this was a case where Chapman's tendency toward satirical personalities proved costly to him, by spoiling his chance of making a success at court.

As for the Admiral's company's chief asset with the Queen, the acting of Alleyn, perhaps she had wearied temporarily of seeing him strut and rant in the same old Marlovian rôles. In 1597 he ceased acting, and his return to the stage three years later is thought to have been due largely to an expressed desire of the old Queen to see him again in his favorite parts. But a revival of favor implies a lapse of favor; and in 1596 Alleyn as an actor was very likely outmoded, too.

[138] Lady Bacon to Essex, Dec. 1, 1596, quoted by W. B. Devereux, I, 406. Essex replied, "Since my departure from England towards Spain, I have been free from taxation of incontinency with any woman that lives."

[139] Devereux, *op. cit.*, I, 475 and note.

[140] Violet Wilson, *Queen Elizabeth's Maids of Honour*, 212 ff., Devereux, *op. cit.*, Harington, *Nugae Antiquae*, I, 233.

[141] Wilson, *op. cit.*, 222. Devereux, *op. cit.*

[142] *Ibid.*

[143] *Sal. MSS.*, VII, 392. Thos. Audeley to Ed. Smythe, Sept. 20, 1597.—"My Lord of Essex in no great grace, neither with Queen or Commons: with the Queen for that he lay with my Lady of Darbe before he went [on the Islands Voyage], as his enemies witness." For the Earl of Derby's jealousy, see pp. 339, 334.

[144] But good politics: see Birch, II, 140. Essex writes Perez that, failing to discredit him over the Cadiz booty, his enemies have revived old accusations and "watch 't his looks" to impute "a vicious gallantry." He asserts that he has returned to England "*coloratus, barbatus*," and with a mind free of its former passions and devoted merely to business.

What six plays could Lord Hunsdon's men have given at court that season? They had the two parts of *Henry IV* and *The Merchant of Venice*, probably, by February, 1597. *Richard III* was doubtless still popular, and there were *King John* and *Richard II* from the previous season. *The Shrew* and *Romeo and Juliet* were perennial possibilities. The company had been playing a *Hamlet*, but not a version we have, to judge by the well-known reference in Lodge's *Wits Miserie*, registered May 5, 1596, to the ghost which "cried so miserally at ye Theator like an oister wife, Hamlet, reuenge!"[145] There is only the slightest reason for supposing that they may have had an early version of *The Dumb Knight*, by Machin and Markham, at about this time.[146] The play as we have it appears distinctly to belong after 1600. *Sir Thomas More*, the politics of which may have kept it from the stage, seems to me to belong in authorship, general tone, and social sympathies to Pembroke's or the Admiral's men; I should be very much surprised ever to see it proved that Shakespeare had anything to do with it, unless his share belongs to the days before the organization of the Chamberlain's men.

To the discussion of the court season should be added the fact that Essex entertained the French king's envoy, Bouillon, on November 13. A dramatic performance would be the natural program, perhaps *Love's Labour's Lost*. At least it is amusing to think that this may have been the play chosen, for besides the fun in its comical distortions of French affairs, its title applies well as an allusion to the efforts of King Henri and Bouillon through Perez to divert the Cadiz expedition, before it sailed, from Spain to the direct aid of the French against the Spanish invaders on their soil. Bouillon appears to have been a good friend of Essex, too good for his own comfort after the downfall of the Earl.

This court season of 1596–97 was the greatest triumph of Shakespeare's company before 1603. A disturbed and dangerous period, but dramatically a richly productive one, was to intervene.

[145] Sgn. H3. Lodge is describing malicious Envy, who "walks for the most part in black vnder colour of grauity, & looks as pale as the Visard of ye ghost which," etc. In 1602 he dedicated his translation of *Josephus* to the Admiral.

[146] Chambers, III, 418.

CHAPTER III (1597–1599)

THE STAGE RIVALRY INTENSIFIED

Essex's glory begins to wane. *Rivalry in history plays, continued through 1597–98.* Repertories of 1597. Pembroke's men. *The rival companies' attitudes toward the French, 1594–1603.* The Christmas season of 1597–98. 1598 repertories. *The domestic crime play, 1594–1603.* The Christmas season of 1598–99 at court.

IN the early spring of 1597 the elder Cobham died, leaving the office of Lord Chamberlain vacant. On the seventeenth of April Lord Hunsdon became Lord Chamberlain.

Through the year the struggle over the glory of Cadiz went bitterly on. The controversy was waged even in print; but we may be sure that there was preparing beneath the surface a still more dangerous attack on Essex, of which we get a hint in Cecil's "conceit of Richard II" in July, already mentioned. A reconciliation which produced "general good feeling" among the Queen, Essex, Cecil, and Ralegh was as hollow as if it had been arranged by Richard III himself. The "Islands Voyage" of this season, unsuccessful, cost Essex much in reputation; he had commanded the expedition rather against his will, for although he had Ralegh along to quarrel with openly, he knew all too well that his enemies at home were poisoning the mind of Elizabeth. Moreover, the Queen had characteristic personal reasons for her growing unkindness. She was always irritable when her favorites were thus absent, apparently blaming them for the anxiety they caused her. She disliked the usual flocking of the gallants to Essex's standard, being especially annoyed on this occasion as on several others that the Earl of Southampton insisted on going. And it was during this year that Essex's attentions to Elizabeth Brydges, a maid of honor, got that young lady a beating by the Queen's own hands; while his affair with the Countess of Derby was notorious.

Late in October, Essex still absent on the Islands Voyage, the Lord Admiral was created Earl of Nottingham and Lord Steward.[1] These honors gave him formal precedence over the Earl of Essex; still worse, the wording of the patent gave the new Earl of Nottingham chief credit for the victory at Cadiz. Essex returned a few days later to find himself in disfavor and the rival party greatly strengthened in his absence. The Queen took such treasure as he had captured, and expressed the opinion that he might have done better.

[1] Whyte, Oct. 23 and Nov. 5. His players were now the Earl of Nottingham's men; but let us continue, for convenience, to know them as the Admiral's.

On St. Thomas's Day Whyte reports that Essex's sense of injury has burst out into demands that the Admiral's patent be altered and proposals of combat "either against thearle of *Nottingham* himself, or any of his Sonnes, or of his Name that will defend it . . . Here is such a doe about it, as it troubles this Place and all other Proceedings." Ralegh is "emploied by the Queen to end this Quarrell." The Queen blames the wrong done to Essex upon the Cecils, "though they doe with infinit Protestations, Execrations, and Vowes, deny it."

Soon after, Elizabeth restored Essex to precedence over the hated Howard by appointing him to the office of Earl Marshal. Since his last predecessor in this office had been George Talbot, the Earl of Shrewsbury's father, the appointment cannot have improved his relations with the Talbot family. The Admiral was so angry that he gave up (temporarily) the staff which was his sign of office as Lord Steward. The Admiral's cousin, Lord Henry Howard, who was looking into the powers of the Earl Marshal for Essex, wrote him with a characteristic salting of malice that the last Earl of Shrewsbury had been able to make no other use of his marshal's staff than to measure his fat oxen between the horns.[2] Essex proposed to the Queen that he make use of the office to pick and choose among the candidates for peerages, so numerous that Elizabeth was refusing to make any new barons at all. "Madame, sayd the Earle, let their titles be first examined by me; I will not doubt but to fynd Cause to keape them backe, and let the Fault be myne."[3] But apparently his partisan aims were too obvious to please her. He did hold one or two inconclusive marshal's courts on questions of disputed titles. The episode in his career has a certain significance to the drama, I think, because of its intensification among his partisans of those genealogical interests to which Shakespeare's historical plays appealed.

Cheered by this triumph, Essex returned to court about the end of the year; and the Earl of Nottingham, offended in his turn, "resigned his staff of Lord Steward, retired to his house at Chelsea, and was very sick, according to the approved practice of discontented courtiers in that age."[4] Early in January, however, all had been smoothed over by the Cecils for a purpose which will soon appear, and Whyte gossiped:

Yt is exceedingly wondred at by the World, to see the to to great Familiarity, that is grown between 1000 [Essex], 200 [Cecil], 24 [Ralegh], and 27 [?]; none but they enjoy him, they carry hym away as they list. 500 that now is [the Chamberlain, I think] is in great Favor with the Queen, and leanes to no Party, and her Majestie likes the better of it, and uses hym very well.[5]

On January 28 he tells us that Southampton is "now at Court, who

[2] Birch, II, 336.
[3] Whyte, Feb. 1, 1598.
[4] W. B. Devereux, I, 472.
[5] Whyte, Jan. 3, 1598.

for a while, by her Majesties Command,[6] did absent himself;" and two days later that Compton, Henry Brooke, now Lord Cobham, Ralegh, and Southampton "doe severally feast Mr. Secretary before he depart, and have Plaies and Banquets." Cecil, off for France on a diplomatic errand, could not afford to leave behind him a hostile Essex; hence the reconciliation. "He had no Fancy to goe, till 1000 did assure him, that in his Absence, nothing should be donne here, that might be disagreeable unto hym."[7]

Rivalry in History Plays, Continued through 1597–98

We may take advantage of this apparent lull in the personal hostilities of these great warriors by land and sea to continue our study of the rivalry of the playing companies in the field of the chronicle through the next two seasons, beginning with a Chamberlain's play written, probably, during the winter of 1596–97.

The Second Part of *Henry IV* is now being studied for the scenes at the Gloucestershire residence of Justice Shallow.[8] In Sir Charles Percy's letter from Dumbleton in that county, comparing himself to Shallow and Silence, we have a reference to the play shortly before the Essex rebellion by a prominent participant in it—indeed, the chief procurer of the playing of *Richard II* on the day before the outbreak. On October 10, 1595, Essex spoke on the side of mercy in the case of two Gloucestershire justices, Davers and Hayes, fined £1000 each at the assizes for admitting highwaymen to bail, but brought up to the Star Chamber for sentence;[9] and on February 4, 1596, he was vehement in the same court against the offence of certain persons in Norfolk who, "when men were being mustered there, did take money to discharge certain men when they were pressed for service, and to appoint others in their places."[10]

A hint that there was some mysterious connection between Ancient Pistol and Sir Thomas Heneage is in a letter from W. Nichols (?) to "Mr. Peter Hallins," December 2, 1594:[11]

I am not employed to be factor for any since my master died, in which respect I cannot do for some friends as I would. Further, if I had been acquainted with

[6] Probably because of his affair with Essex's cousin, Elizabeth Vernon, which could no longer be concealed. [7] *Ibid.*, Feb. 11.

[8] See E. A. B. Barnard, *New Links with Shakespeare,* (Camb. Univ. Press), 1930, especially his chapter on Sir Charles Percy, pp. 62–73; M. A. Taylor, "Shakespeare and Gloucestershire," *The Review of English Studies,* VII, 200 ff.; and Leslie Hotson, *Shakespeare versus Shallow.*

[9] Hawarde, *Camera Stellata,* 22. [10] *Ibid.*, 32.

[11] *Sal. MSS.*, V, 26; words in italics originally in cipher, interpretations supplied in another hand.

Pistol's man (*Mr. Vice-chamberlain,*[12] *Poley*[13]) or that matter by him or *Paget*, I would never have written to you about it . . . The said *Paget* laboured hard of late to have permission for Pistol's man to come hither, assuring he would find means to discover much of Wilk's secrets if he come to these quarters; but he could not obtain the suit.

The letter concerns the business of spying on Catholic plotters abroad. A postcript adds, "Your old friend *Filsher* is here long since" . . . Could this be Nym? "To nym" is, of course, Elizabethan slang for "to filch."

Another letter from the same to the same—at least it uses the same code—is headed, "W. Nichols to Sir Peter Hallins" and dated "?1594–95" January 28. Nichols still desires copies of Perez's book against the King of Spain, and wishes to "spread them abroad . . . by hundreds . . . to the disgrace of whom it toucheth." He ends, "Please to signify unto my good Lord of Essex how ready I am to serve him."[14]

Heneage was Vice-Chamberlain, Treasurer of the Household, and Master of the Rolls. His friendship for Philip Sidney and John Foxe seems to indicate Puritan tendencies. His first wife, Anne Poyntz, died November 15, 1593; and on May 2, 1594, he married Southampton's widowed mother. On December 7 he entertained the Queen at the Savoy. He died October 17, 1595. Through the Poyntz family (which quartered the arms of Bardolph) Heneage was a connection of the Cobhams. He was not a military man, and the fun of the jest must have lain in the incongruity of hearing some tricks of speech characteristic of the dignified Vice-Chamberlain from the moth-eaten old soldier, Pistol.[15]

Pistol shows an interesting fondness for mottoes, too. His own (for he quotes it twice) seems to be a garbled Italian form of Westmorland's *Esperance me comforte,—Si fortune me tormente, sperato me contento;* and in one place he comes out with a whole group of others:

> 'Tis *semper idem*, for *absque hoc nihil est:*
> 'Tis all in every part.[16]

The first of these was the motto most used by Queen Elizabeth;[17] and the third resembles Southampton's "*Tout par ung, ung par tout.*" The second reminds one of that of Lord Petre, married at Essex House on Nov-

[12] Sir Thomas Heneage.

[13] Robert Poley, spy, present at Marlowe's death. Cf. Tucker Brooke, *The Life of Marlowe*, 73–77; Ethel Seaton, "Robert Poley's Ciphers," *R.E.S.*, VII, 137 ff.; and E. de Kalb, "Robert Poley as a Messenger of the Court," *R.E.S.*, IX, 13.

[14] Cf. p. 97. I judge from the contents of these letters that the writer was pro-Essex. Certainly Perez was Essex's ally, and the book mentioned must have been war propaganda. The nicknames used as a code seem definitely satirical.

[15] Perhaps Heneage was really fond of the plays of Peele, Marlowe, Kyd, and other elder dramatists—which were mostly in the Admiral's repertory—and liked to quote them.

[16] *2 Henry IV*, II, iv, 194.

[17] Camden, *Remains*.

ember 8, 1596 (the occasion of Spenser's *Prothalamion*) to a daughter of the Earl of Worcester—"*Absque deo nihil.*" I do not find Heneage using a motto like any given by Pistol, although Woodward and Burnett (*Heraldry*, 586) say that he had as a private badge a heart-shaped knot with the motto, "Fast tho' untied," which would serve equally well for an enamoured widower or a roving husband. He did bear a greyhound on his arms: Falstaff says of Pistol, "He's no swaggerer, hostess; a tame cheater, i'faith; you may stroke him as gently as a puppy greyhound."[18]

Still I do not feel at all certain that Pistol must be identified with Heneage. A great objection is one's natural dislike of seeing Shakespeare make fun of a man who had died we suppose, a year before he wrote the play. It may be that (as the "Pistol's man" reference in December, 1594, would hint) the burlesque character of Pistol had been created a couple of years before for the private solace of an unwilling stepson. Southampton did object strongly a few years later to his mother's remarriage to Sir William Harvey.[19]

I have mentioned the Heneage-Poyntz and Poyntz-Bardolph connections. The best pedigree of the Poyntzes of Gloucestershire, in the Visitation of 1623,[20] shows that Heneage's first wife had a brother Edmund and a nephew Edward, either of whom may have furnished the name of Prince Hal's companion, Ned Poins. Another brother, William, for seventeen years a follower of Leicester, displays in certain letters to Sir Robert Cecil several of the traits we find in the group that surrounds Hal and Falstaff: faithful and hopeful service, a dislike of "strict citizens," impecuniosity and dread of catchpoles, a capacity for "odd shifts" to fill "a wardrobe with pied clouts," and a disposition to use good resolutions to impress favorably those in power.[21]

It may be remarked that in his long service of Leicester Will Poyntz must have come into contact with the Warwickshire Bardolphs and Peytos or Peitos, and also with the Falstaffian Richard Brooke of Warwick who was expelled from the corporation in 1582, his fellow-burgesses accusing him of calling them "gorballied choorles, gowtye wretches, craftye knaves." This Brooke seems to have been a miller and large farmer, occupying Temple Farm and probably the Castle mill.[22]

[18] *2 Henry IV*, v, v, 31, 32.

[19] Note the appearance of "Harvey" as a minor thief in the 1598 quarto of *1 Henry IV*. This was the year of Southampton's greatest protests. See Chambers, *Shakespeare*, I, 382.

[20] Harleian Society, c. 135.

[21] Cf. *Sal. MSS.*, VII, 419; VIII, 345; X, 421; XII, 402.

[22] Shakespeare was eighteen at this time, and may through association of ideas have recalled this picturesque character when engaged in lampooning another Brooke as Sir John Oldcastle. For these Warwick persons and affairs see *The Black Book of Warwick*, ed. by Thomas Kemp, 373 & *passim*.

But this whole play, *2 Henry IV*, cries out for a careful and detailed study. There is a political reference in the words of King Henry the Fifth, just after his father's death:

> Brothers, you mix your sadness with some fear:
> This is the English, not the Turkish court;
> Not Amurath an Amurath succeeds,
> But Harry Harry.

Mehemet, sometimes called Amurath, the Third, succeeded his father in 1595, and had his nineteen brothers strangled, as was the Turkish custom. He was crowned on January 7, 1596. During the autumn of 1595 Ambassador Sir Edward Barton was writing letters to Vice-Chamberlain Heneage urging the sending of a present to the new Sultan (the famous organ did not reach him until 1599). This urgency was accompanied by propaganda to make the new Grand Turk appear a mild and amiable ruler; involved was the Elizabethan beginning of the English policy of supporting the "Sick Man of Europe" and condoning Turkish savageries. The French and Venetians, with whom the Essex party sympathized, do not appear to have considered this policy to accord with their best interests; and from their representatives we get much darker views of conditions at the Sublime Porte.[23]

Observe, too, in this play, as also in *1 Henry IV* and *Henry V*, the notable favoring of Westmoreland. Here "Shakespeare follows Holinshed closely in describing the 'subtill policie' whereby the rebels are disposed of; but he transfers the odium attaching to this action from the earl of Westmoreland to Lord John of Lancaster."[24] Shakespeare's contemporary Earl of Westmoreland was a Neville, a Roman Catholic fugitive abroad, with whom Southampton must have had some sympathy.[25]

The jesting of the Chief Justice with Falstaff is quite in character with what we know of the contemporary Chief Justice, Sir John Popham, a (partly) reformed highwayman, inclined to be friendly to Essex.

It is probable that for this play Shakespeare changed his character's name to Falstaff. Some rather good reasons for the choice of the name are given by Fitzpatrick,[26] who points out Sir John Fastolf's office of Chief Wine-Butler in Ireland, his close connection with the Duke of Norfolk, his feud with Talbot (the ancestor of the Earl of Shrewsbury), his house in Southwark, and a connection with the Scropes which is of especial interest, because of the elder Hunsdon's daughter's marriage

[23] H. G. Rosedale, *Queen Elizabeth and the Levant Company, passim.*

[24] S. B. Hemingway, ed. *2 Hen. IV* for *The Yale Shakespeare*, 138.

[25] Southampton and, more distantly, Shakespeare himself, were related to the Nevilles.

[26] W. J. Fitzpatrick, "The Original of Sir John Falstaff," *Gentlemen's Mag.*, Jan.—June 1887, 428 ff.

to a Scrope: Fastolf married a widow, heiress of the Tiblot family, "whose rich estates in Gloucestershire and Wiltshire he seized and kept in his own possession to the prejudice of his stepson," Stephen le Scrope. The stepson complained that Fastolf had sold his wardship to Chief Justice Gascoigne, to his disfigurement through a long illness. Gascoigne wished to marry Scrope to one of his own daughters, but Fastolf bought him back. "He bought and sold me as a beast," writes Scrope of Fastolf, "against all right and law, to mine hurt more than 1000 marks."

The same Elizabethans who saw Essex in the character of Bolingbroke in *Richard II* could readily have envisaged him in Prince Hal, playing about dissolutely, then distinguishing himself in battle, reforming on coming to power in the state, and promising new martial leadership abroad for great public ends.

How much of such identification Shakespeare intended is quite another question: probably very little, even secretly, and of course none at all openly. His company, for the sake of gate receipts, very likely were pleased by it as long as the loose talk of the Cadiz veterans flocking to the play did not too greatly endanger them. After all, much of the world's successful drama has always skated on thin ice, political or moral; and there is plenty of evidence that the Elizabethan stage was no exception to the general rule that the more piquant the performance is, the more profitable it is likely to be.

Our chief interest, the literary rivalry with the Admiral's men, appears most obviously here in the quotations of Pistol; among the rival company's productions thus satirized seem to be Heywood's *Four Ages*, Peele's *Hiren* and *Alcazar*, Marlowe's *Faustus* and *Tamburlaine*, plays on Caesar, Hannibal, Troy, Cophetua (?), Robin Hood, a "Spanish fig," etc. But these burlesques have been well canvassed by editors.[27]

The Admiral's men continued in 1597 their usual policy of exploiting the legendary and the mythical. The long careers of *Bellendon* and *The Wise Man of West Chester* came to an end at last this season, as did also the shorter runs of *Valteger* and *Stukeley*.

Among their new plays this year was *Uther Pendragon*, which may be the extant *Birth of Merlin or The Child Hath Found His Father* (1662), by William Rowley, a rather scurrilous comedy dealing with Merlin's outwitting his father, a devil. Uther Pendragon is a character, and so also are Vortiger and various Saxons. Thus the piece is related to the Admiral's Arthurian plays on the one hand, and to *The Mayor of Quinborough* on the other. The spectacular staging, with its lightning, comet, fighting dragons, and so on, points to the same approximate date as

[27] See the notes on the play in the editions of W. J. Rolfe and R. P. Cowl (the English *Arden Shakespeare*).

Heywood's *Golden Age* and *Silver Age*, which I suppose to have been first presented about 1595. Merlin's clownish uncle displays corpulence, Falstaff's most easily imitated trait. The prophetic dumb-show of kings, princes, and crowns may have suggested the same device in *Macbeth*. The Elizabethans were greatly interested in the so-called prophecies of Merlin, especially in connection with Queen Elizabeth's death and the doubtful succession to ensue.[28] Lodowick Lloyd wrote Cecil, October 31, 1600, that the old Romans were not so addicted to their Sibyls, the Egyptians to the priests of Memphis, nor the Frenchmen to their superstitious Druids, as many in Wales to the prophecies of Merlin. Were he sheriff this year in Cardigan he would bring such volumes of prophecies that after reading them Cecil should make better fire of them in London than Duke Ogis made in Athens of all the writing tables of usurers.[29]

A curious letter of March 20, 1601, connects the ambitions of Essex's followers to make him king with certain "dreams" which are really allegorical prophecies of the Merlin type.[30] And see Thomas Heywood's *Life of Merlin*, 1641, in which he furnishes a "small Manuell" of British history from Brute to Charles I by the odd method of giving a few lines of "Merlin's" prophecy in verse, and then showing how they came true in history.[31] Shakespeare, of course, has Hotspur pay his scanty respects to Welsh soothsaying in *1 Henry IV*. What Essex thought of such matters we do not know. He was born in Herefordshire and spent much of his childhood in Pembrokeshire; and his great following in Wales may have been strengthened by dark prophecies. He himself possessed second sight, if we are to believe his secretary, Henry Cuffe, who wrote Edward Reynolds in 1599, after the disaster in Ireland to Radcliffe and Clifford, "This disaster I know not how his Lordship presaged . . . but it is true that things fatal may well be foreseen and feared but cannot be avoided."[32] His favorite horse was said to have died at pasture at the moment of his master's execution.

Henry I and *The Famous Wars of Henry I and the Prince of Wales*, next year, must at least belong to the same group of plays as *William Rufus* and the old chronicle material underlying *Satiromastix*. If based on Deloney's prose tale, *Thomas of Reading*,[33] the Admiral's *Six Yeomen of the West* and *Six Clothiers of the West* were also set in the reign of the First Henry. This ruler's "famous wars" were in Normandy against his

[28] Cf. C. B. Millican, *Spenser and The Table Round*, and note the skeptical attitude of Cecil's friend Camden.

[29] *Sal. MSS.*, x, 369. Cf. also Harington's *Tract*, 120, 121.

[30] *Ibid.*, xi, 132. John Garnons of Garnons, Herefords. to Cecil.

[31] Cf. C. B. Millican, "The First English Translation of the *Prophecies of Merlin*," *S.P.*, xxviii, 720 ff. Mr. Millican does not mention Heywood's work.

[32] *Sal. MSS.*, ix, 289.

[33] Cf. Greg, *Henslowe*, ii, 217, 219; and *M.L.R.*, xiii, 102.

brother, Duke Robert; so *Henry I* probably contained scenes on the familiar theme of English victories over the French. The Welshman that Henslowe tells us was in the play need not necessarily have remained in Wales, any more than did Fluellen.

"*Henges*" or *Hengist* is, as we have seen, probably to be identified with *The Mayor of Quinborough* and "*Valteger*." Henslowe may have had one play or a group on the invaders of Kent; see Greg, *Henslowe*, II, 181.

Martin Swarte, as the title informs us, concerned a foreign soldier of fortune in Simnel's revolt against Henry VII, defeated and slain at the battle of Stoke, near Newark-on-Trent, after his Irish troops ran away.

Hardicanute, listed in the joint accounts with Pembroke's men in the autumn, may be the same as "*Knewtus*," which occurs once. If not, *Knewtus* (i.e., *Canutus*) may underlie the extant *Edmond Ironside, or War Hath Made All Friends*.[34] Eleanore Boswell, in editing the manuscript *Ironside* for the Malone Society, quotes the following lines, marked for omission in the MS., as possibly referring to Essex:

> England yf ever warre thy face doth spoyle
> Thancke not thy outward foe but inward frind
> For thou shalt never p[er]ishe til that daye
> When thie right hand shall make thie hart awaye.

The tone of this whole play, centered as it is upon the villainies of the traitor Edricus, Duke of Mercia, in assisting Canutus, Danish claimant to the English throne and opponent of Ironside, suggests reference to James; but of course, as the odium is merely against a foreign claimant, the fact that James's queen was Danish could be disregarded and the propaganda, if any was admitted, declared to be against the Infanta. In the play Southampton is made to favor Canute, as is also the Archbishop of Canterbury. There are various reminders of historical and literary matters of about 1598: The villain engages Stich, the clown, as his chamberlain because a stupid man makes the best tool—compare *Antonio's Revenge* (1599), II, i, 583 ff., and Richard the Third's, "I will converse with iron-witted fools."[35] Edmond is vehement against pinching soldiers of their pay so that commanders may go gorgeous while their companies starve. "These nothinge-fearinge hotspures" are mentioned. An eclipse is taken by Canute to presage the fall of Ironside: the only total eclipse visible in England during our period occurred on March 6, 1598, and had been considered ominous to Elizabeth.[36] Stich, who, like

[34] Can the subtitle refer to the surface reconciliation of the conflicting factions at the beginning of 1598?

[35] *Richard III*, IV, ii, 28–30 (S.R. Oct. 20, 1597, quartos 1597, 1598, 1602, 1605).

[36] *S. P. Dom.*, 1598–1601, 585. A book on the subject seems to have been "called in" at the time of the Essex rebellion.

Falstaff, is a tall man "at the end of a fraye and begininge of a feast," says that Edricus (Essex?) has "dipt his pen in many a man's inckhorne besides his own." As in *1 Henry IV*, there is a proposal to substitute single combat for a battle. And in the end, a reconciliation scene, Edricus, like the villain in *Antonio and Mellida*, seems to promise renewed treacheries for a sequel.

Hardicanute may have been a different story. Camden[37] says that Lambeth (very near the Bankside of the theaters) was

famous in former times for the death of *Canutus the Hardie* [glossed in margin "Hardy-Cnute"], King of England, who there amid his cups yielded up his vitall breath. For hee, being given wholly to banqueting and feasting, caused royall dinners foure times every day . . . to be served up for all his court.

The old Coventry Hock-Tuesday play managed by Captain Cox for the Queen's amusement at Kenilworth in 1575 (see Laneham's famous letter),[38] was to represent the massacre of the Danes in the time of Ethelred and to show "how valiantly the English women for looue of their cuntree behaued themselues." But some think that the Hock-Tuesday (second week after Easter) celebration commemorated rather the deliverance of the English from the tyranny of the Danes by the death of Hardicanute, on Tuesday, June 8, 1042. He died suddenly, not without suspicion of poison, at the wedding feast of a Danish lord and the daughter of a Saxon nobleman.

Alice Pierce appears to have dealt with a mistress of Edward III. She was really a Perers of Perers, Norfolk,[39] who was attainted by act of Parliament, 1 Richard II, but later was given back some of her lands. Perers Manor came to the Greshams, and Sir John Gresham made it a school under the patronage of the London fishmongers. Since *Edward III* is usually accepted as a Chamberlain's play, we have here another of the many cases where the companies emulated each other in their treatment of different events in the same king's reign.

As for the Chamberlain's men, unless *2 Henry IV* was written in 1597, the year has left us no new history play of theirs. Neither does 1598 give us a new history from Shakespeare's company, although the farcical *Merry Wives of Windsor* which belongs, I believe, to this year, is very closely connected to the Henry IV histories.

The Admiral's men in 1598, in addition to reviving *Friar Bacon*, a play set in the days of Henry III, produced their two interesting Robin Hood plays, Munday's *Downfall* and *Death of Robert Earl of Huntingdon*, the latter play in collaboration with Chettle. These were first

[37] *Britannia*, trans. 1637, 303.

[38] John Nichols, *Progresses of Queen Elizabeth*, I, 446.

[39] Blomefield, *Norfolk*, IX, 396.

played about March, during the truce between the factions, and altered by Chettle late in November, perhaps for the court season.

Although, in spite of the truce with Cecil, Essex had probably not been fully reconciled to the Admiral, we need not be surprised to find in the Robin Hood dramas little anti-Essex material in comparison with the large amount of matter complimentary to the new Earl of Nottingham. By late autumn the Cecil group were doing their best to bring Essex to accept the Irish mission.[40] Naturally the chief compliment to the Admiral is in the localization of the plays, which has been done very carefully. Munday was in a position to give the first part its Nottinghamshire local color, through his association with the recusant-hunter Topcliffe, who did much of his work in this region. Note such graphic bits as "Notingham's red cliffes" and Farnsfield's "miry mead." The villain Warman has a cousin of the same name who dwells at Bingham, which is only three miles from Shelford; and George, Gaoler of Nottingham, gets his dog-meat at Redford, just outside the town. Much of the action of the second part is at Windsor, where the Admiral held the offices of Constable and Chief Seneschal of the Castle and Keeper of the Forest.

The dynastic material in these plays is particularly complicated because it is based on the disputed right to the earldom of Huntingdon in King John's time.[41] Munday's preference for Fitzooth's claim may possibly be taken as slightly anti-Scottish. But let us avoid becoming entangled in these intricacies, and merely note the Admiral's family interest in a few of the chief characters in the Robin Hood plays:

1. Robin's Maid Marion is here Matilda Fitzwalter. The family held the barony of Dunmow, in Essex, where Matilda dies, poisoned by John. Dunmow Priory came to their descendants, the Ratcliffes, and the barony of Fitzwalter in 1593 to Robert Ratcliffe, Earl of Sussex, connected with the Admiral by the latter's aunt's marriage to the second Earl. Another connection of the Fitzwalters was with Baliol, awarded the Scots crown by Edward I, a scene the Admiral's men were doubtless showing in 1595–96 in *Longshanks*, for the event is made prominent in Peele's *Edward I*.

2. Mowbray belonged to the family from which the Admiral derived his new earldom of Nottingham.

3. Salisbury is here Alberic or Aubrey de Vere, Earl of Oxford. The contemporary Earl's daughter (Cecil's niece) had married the Earl of Derby, whose grandmother was the Admiral's aunt.

[40] It is interesting that a descendant of Hubert de Burgh, and the Lacys (characters in the plays), Thomas, Lord Burgh, had died in Ireland as Lord Deputy on October 14, 1597.

[41] Cf. *Notes and Queries*, 7th Series, III, *passim*, "Who Was Robin Hood?"

4. William de Braose or Bruce, whose wife and son are starved to death by John in Windsor Castle, was connected with the Fitzwalters by marriage and had possessions in Totnes, now held by the Earl of Hertford, married to the Admiral's sister; at Barnstaple, now belonging to the Earl of Bath, a connection through Martha Howard, another sister; and in Wales, especially Glamorgan, whence came the Admiral's mother, a Gamage of Coity.

5. Leicester here is Robert de Beaumont, High Steward at King John's coronation, who married a daughter (or sister) of William de Braose. The Admiral had a considerable interest in the earldom of Leicester, chiefly through his sister Douglas, now Lady Sheffield, who had borne the Earl of Leicester his only son, Sir Robert Dudley. Sir Robert's claim to the earldom, opposed by Essex, Sidney, and others on the ground that Leicester had never admitted marrying Douglas Howard, came up in the Star Chamber in 1604, at which time he was supported by the Admiral's eldest son, William, Lord Howard of Effingham,[42] who had been married in 1597 to a St. John, and thus was related to the Countess of Warwick (her mother was a St. John), widow of Ambrose Dudley and an inveterate enemy of that Lord Berkeley who was allied to the Hunsdons by marriage in 1596. Much is made in the play of the well-known device, the bear and the ragged staff. This badge was formed by combining two separate devices of the Beauchamps, Earls of Warwick,[43] for whose relation to drama see my remarks on *The Tinker of Totnes*.

6. George Hastings had become Earl of Huntingdon on the death of his brother in 1595. Essex's grief on this occasion appears to have been connected with the late Henry's strong Protestantism and claim to the crown, from his great-grandmother, Margaret, Countess of Salisbury, last of the Plantagenets and sole heir of George, Duke of Clarence, brother of Edward IV.[44] But it may also have been partly due to a dislike of the new earl. The late Earl had been a connection of both Essex and the Admiral through his marriage to Catherine Dudley, sister of the late Robert Dudley, Earl of Leicester. His brother George was thus only slightly connected with the Admiral; but then, as I have pointed out, there was not necessarily much intention to honor contemporary Earls of Huntingdon in the Robin Hood plays, since the Fitzooth claimant was not an ancestor of the house of Hastings.

These plays exemplify a rather common method of advertising by referring in the text to other attractions in the Admiral's repertory—

[42] Hawarde, *Camera Stellata*, 170.

[43] Woodward and Burnett, *Heraldry*, 584.

[44] And add the loss to the Essex faction in the fact that he was President of the Council of the North. Cf. Rachel R. Reid, "The Political Influence of the 'North Parts' under the Later Tudors," *Tudor Studies*, London, 1924.

George a Greene, *Earl Godwin*, *The Funeral of Richard Cordelion*, and probably *Faustus*. And their rivalry of Shakespeare's *King John* follows the form which we are beginning to see as customary, treating the same period and characters while avoiding as far as possible the identical historical events. The characterization of Hubert de Burgh is especially ambitious and forms a very interesting comparison with Shakespeare's.

The Admiral's dramatists used pseudo-history to crowd out true folklore, much to the disappointment of the modern reader; but I have shown how the Elizabethan playwright could appeal to the special interests of his audience by exploiting history as the romantic record of families.

The Admiral's other chronicle plays of 1598 have vanished. We know that *The Famous Wars of Henry I*, by Chettle, Dekker, and Drayton (Henslowe is now recording payments to playwrights instead of receipts from performances), contained the part of a Welshman, and there is an entry of properties for a play called *The Welchmans Price* in the 1598 inventory. *Earl Goodwin and His Three Sons*, in two parts, by Chettle, Dekker, Drayton, and Wilson, deals with the Earl of the West Saxons under Canute, who supported Hardicanute, and was later outlawed for a while by Edward the Confessor; it thus seems to be part of the same cycle as *Edmond Ironside* and *Hardicanute*.

As for *Pierce of Exton*, Greg says,[45] "The position of this entry and the identity of authorship almost force us to believe that it was the first payment for *2 Earl Goodwin*. If so there must be some strange confusion of titles, for Sir Piers Exton was the supposed murderer of Richard II."

The Admiral's men had, too, *King Arthur*, by Hathaway, which fits naturally into a cycle after the prophecies of his reign in *The Birth of Merlin;* and *Richard Cordelion's Funeral*, by Chettle, Munday, Drayton, and Wilson, very likely one of the Robin Hood sequence.[46] Nothing is known of *Pierce of Winchester*, by Dekker, Drayton, and Wilson. It may not have been a chronicle.

The company's dramatists went back to the very beginnings of mythical British history for *The Conquest of Brute with the First Finding of the Bath* and *Brute Greenshield*, apparently by Day and Chettle. Greg[47] sees no reason for Fleay's treatment of these titles as belonging to distinct plays; but it seems somewhat improbable that any one play, even in two parts, could have covered quite so much ground as to include: Brutus, great-grandson of Æneas, who landed at Totnes, subdued the giants, founded Troynovant; Brutus Greenshield, his great-great-great grandson, who fought the French in Hainault, and was buried at York;

[45] *Henslowe*, II, 192.

[46] A spectacular funeral is promised by the Epilogue of *The Downfall*.

[47] *Henslowe*, II, 195.

and the magician-king Bladud, Greenshield's great-grandson, who made the hot baths at Bath by necromancy, and broke his neck at Troynovant (London) in an attempt to fly. It is possible that another "finder" of "the Bath" was meant, but the character of Bladud was a tempting one for the actor of Faustus, Friar Bacon, John a Kent, and Merlin. In this same group of dramas with early settings were Rankins' *Mulmutius Dunwallow* (he was a renowned law-giver and road-maker, the rebuilder of London, and the father of Brennus), and probably *Connan Prince of Cornwall*, by Dekker and Drayton. This Connan may have been Aurelius Conanus, who slew Constantine, the successor of Arthur. According to Stowe[48] he was a cherisher of sycophants and talebearers—types by no means uncommon as objects of Elizabethan satire, from *Damon and Pythias* down.

Important history plays published in 1598 were *Edward II* (first printed in 1594), *1 Henry IV*, and *The Famous Victories of Henry V*.

The remaining Falstaff play, Shakespeare's *Merry Wives of Windsor*, is not, of course, a chronicle; yet it is so closely linked through its characters to *Henry IV* and *Henry V*, plays which do belong to the type, that I am tempted to remark a little here on certain points in which it seems to satirize the Cecil faction. It belongs, I think, most probably to 1598, and appears to contain an oddly spiteful little dig at Cobham in the name Brooke taken by the jealous Ford when he disguises himself to spy upon his highly independent and masterful wife. Although Henry Brooke was not married at this time, his name was being spoken with those of several court ladies, there being an especial rivalry for the wealthy bachelor lord between Mrs. Ratcliffe and the recently widowed Lady Kildare, daughter of the Admiral. The latter finally won him, after a long chase, in 1601, and proceeded to domineer over him, to frustrate his political schemes, and finally to abandon him to his poverty and disgrace under King James. If the part was made up and played as a lampoon on Cobham—which would indeed look queer in scenes filled by Falstaff, whose figure we suppose the audiences to have been accustomed to identify with that of Cobham's late father—the Brookes seem to have been able to do nothing about it, for the alias stands as "Brooke" in the quarto of 1602. The Folio editors changed it to "Broome," perhaps because they saw no reason to perpetuate an ancient grudge.

I should like to point out the coincidence that in Heywood's (?) *2 Edward IV*, published in 1599 with an ascription to the Earl of Derby's men, Master Shore, in disguise to observe his unfaithful wife, King Edward's mistress, takes the alias "Flood" and puns upon it:

[48] *Annales of England*, 61.

> To die unknown thus is my greatest good—
> That Matthew Shore's not hanged, but Matthew Flood;
> For floods of woe have wash'd away the shore
> That never wife nor kin shall look on more.[49]

Compare Falstaff's pun, "Such Brooks are welcome to me, that overflow such liquor."[50]

Conscious as they must have been of the give-and-take between the Chamberlain's men and the Admiral's, especially at this time of the Oldcastle-Falstaff plays, can the audience have helped thinking, during the scenes in and about Windsor, of the Admiral's own posts there? Such an association of ideas, must have been, however, somewhat inconvenient when the time came to introduce the legend of Herne the Hunter (orignally Horne[51]), for such an adornment of the brows as Herne suffered was, of course, the inevitable Elizabethan allusion to cuckoldry—and the Admiral's wife happened to be the Chamberlain's sister. Shakespeare took especial pains to disclaim contemporaneity:

> There is an old tale goes . . .
> The superstitious idle-headed eld
> Receiv'd, and did deliver to our age
> This tale of Herne the hunter for a truth.[52]

A mysterious reference by Carleton, October 13, 1600,[53] connects succession politics, the drama, and some frequenter of Windsor Forest, where, he says, "Sir Sprintado" is hunting "with a bendbow in his hand like Little John;" while Sir Edward Norris has spoiled a reconciliation with the Queen by a friendly visit to Essex and a return to "his climacterical talk."[54] Whoever Sir Sprintado was, the name looks much like the invention of a dramatist.

The title, *The Merry Wives of Windsor*, has the appearance of a retort to the Admiral's title, *Two Angry Women of Abingdon*, by Henry Porter, probably in 1598. Note, as another point of probably intentional contrast, that the women are victorious in the intrigue of Shakespeare's play, as they are losers in that of Porter's.

Having now carried the chronicle play through to its culminating year, 1599, let us return to the situation of the rival companies in the

[49] II, iv.

[50] *Merry Wives*, II, ii, 158. —Observe, too, that Ford recommends himself to Falstaff as one Brooke who has spent much money. Cobham's lavish expenditures on being inducted as Warden of the Cinque Ports in 1598 and as Knight of the Garter a year later were the talk of the court.

[51] Qq. 1, 2; "Disguis'd like Horne with huge horns on his head."

[52] IV. iv. 27–30.

[53] *S. P. Dom.*, 1598–1601, 478.

[54] Cf. G. B. Harrison, on Queen Elizabeth's "climacterical year" (1595–97), *T.L.S.*, November, 1930 *et sequitur, passim.*

spring of 1597. On February 2 James Burbadge, builder of the Theatre, was buried at Shoreditch. His theatrical interests were thenceforth in the hands of his sons, Richard and Cuthbert. In the same month the prospect of greater independence and better returns in a new theatrical venture appears to have drawn players from both the Admiral's and the Chamberlain's companies to form a new organization under the patronage of the Earl of Pembroke.

Henry Herbert, second Earl of Pembroke of his family, was the sot of a sister of Queen Catherine Parr. He had been a partisan of Leiceste and in 1586 succeeded his father-in-law, Sir Henry Sidney, as Presiden of Wales, spending thenceforth much time at Ludlow Castle. In 1597 he was about sixty-three years of age, "pursife and maladife," and involved in a quarrel over money with the Earl of Essex, of which Whyte reports the official settlement at the end of April, "Upon *Monday* did my L. of *Essex's* officers pay 4000£ to my L. of *Pembroke* in *Baynards* Castell." The dispute is obscure as we read of it in the correspondence of the preceding year or two, but it somehow involved Lord Berkeley; and this conclusion was, I believe, a victory for Essex, the returning of the binding installment of a payment Essex considered inadequate.[55]

Pembroke's eldest son and heir, William, Lord Herbert, may have had the new company as a sort of plaything for his first experience of independent living in London, for which he won his father's consent this spring.[56] He was seventeen, and apparently not entirely *persona grata* to Lord Hunsdon, who had been offended at Pembroke's breaking off a proposed match between him and the daughter who married, later, the heir of Lord Berkeley.[57] In September his father was negotiating with Burghley to marry him to the latter's grand-daughter, Bridget Vere, aged thirteen, and saying, "My son shall come up himself at the beginning of Parliament, both to attend Her Majesty's pleasure for his intended travel, and to perform what shall be agreed upon for his proposed marriage."[58] (Ill-health made it impossible for Pembroke himself to come up.) But Lord Herbert did not marry at this time. In 1599 he was borrowing Bay Leigh of his uncle Robert Sidney to play at war in the invasion scare of that summer,[59] and in the autumn was a "continuall courtier," but too cold a one to please Whyte, who hoped for aid to

[55] Cf. especially Whyte, Nov. 29 and Dec. 8, 1595.

[56] *Ibid.*, April 19.—"My lord Harbert hath, with much adoe, brought his father to consent that he may live in London, yet not before the next springe." But this delay does not preclude an extended visit in 1597; apparently he wanted to set up independent bachelor quarters.

[57] *Ibid.*, December 5, 1595.

[58] *S. P. Dom.*, 1595–97, 497; cited by Frances Berkeley Young, *Mary Sidney, Countess of Pembroke*, 64.

[59] Young, *op. cit.*, 84 and *passim.*

Sidney's fortunes if he should become a favorite. The old Earl died on January 18, 1601. The new Earl was in trouble with Mary Fitton, but refused to marry her, although the Queen sent him to the Fleet. Later he got the Queen's permission to travel beyond seas. On November 4, 1604, he married Mary Talbot, daughter of the Earl of Shrewsbury.

We are not certain of any extant play from the repertory of Pembroke's players' brief London season. Perhaps we may infer from the notoriously satirical nature of *The Isle of Dogs* that the family made use of their players to pay off some old grudges, and hence that personal hits at Essex, among others, might be found in many of their plays. But let us consider first the record which Henslowe has left us of their season. The new company entered an agreement with Langley, builder of the Swan theater, to play twelve months there. Of the five men making this contract, two, Richard Jones and Thomas Downton, had been with the Admiral's men; and their transference coincides with a three weeks' break in Henslowe's record of performances at the Rose after February 12. The other three, Robert Shaw, Gabriel Spencer, and William Bird or Borne, Chambers inclines to believe,[60] came from the Chamberlain's company; it is possible that a "sewt agenst Thomas Poope" of that organization, for which Henslowe made a personal advance of ten shillings to Bird on August 30, 1598, may have been connected with the shiftings of the companies the previous year. Other members may have been Jonson, and Humphrey and Antony Jeffes, who appear in the Admiral's company in 1598.

Of their productions Chambers says:[61] "A study of the Admiral's repertory for 1597–98 suggests that some or all of the plays, *Black Joan*, *Hardicanute*, *Bourbon*, *Sturgflattery*, *Branholt*, *Friar Spendleton*, *Alice Pierce*, and *Dido and Aeneas* may have been brought in by Pembroke's men." We have already noticed several of these—*Hardicanute*, *Friar Spendleton*, *Alice Pierce*. Henslowe's inventory of properties in 1598 included "j frame for the heading in Black Jone"; so we know the play contained an execution and may surmise that it was a crime play of Halifax, the only locality where the process of "heading" at this time required anything easily described as a "frame." The Halifax guillotine was famous.[62] Fleay[63] suggests identifying *Bourbon* with the anonymous *Trial of Chivalry*, published in 1600; but since the title page assigns that

[60] Chambers, II, 131.

[61] *Ibid.*, II, 132.

[62] Cf. J. F. Fletcher, *Halifax*, 46 ff.; forty-nine were decapitated, 1542–1650, five of them women. For an amusing account of the "gibbet law" see Deloney's *Thomas of Reading*, published before 1600. The usual offense was stealing cloth. Dr. Ledsham, vicar of Halifax, was murdered in London in 1598; but his slayers suffered at Tyburn.

[63] *Chronicle History*, II, 318.

play to Derby's men, we naturally incline to consider it our only extant specimen of the Earl of Derby's writing for his own company. *The Trial of Chivalry* does indeed feature a Pembroke prominently and make Bourbon a villain, who poisons the heroine's face; and so *Bourbon* and *Branholt* may both have expressed more or less the Cecil attitude toward French politics, for Brunhalt is a prominent character in Fletcher and Massinger's *Thierry and Theodoret*, a very unpleasant depiction of that nation's character. *Sturgflattery* seems to be shrouded by Henslowe's spelling in an impenetrable mystery. "Stark Flattery" has been dubiously put forward. Or can it possibly be a corruption of some Irish name? For identifying *Dido and Aeneas* with Marlowe's *Dido* we have no reason other than the identity of subject. It may be that Pembroke's men ventured a popularizing of the classics resembling what Heywood had done for the Admiral's men in his *Ages;* or perhaps they revived the old play for the purpose.

But the career of Pembroke's men was short. Their rash venture with Nashe's lost *Isle of Dogs* brought disaster upon them, July 28, 1597. The Isle of Dogs was a marshy peninsula across the Thames from Greenwich. Like Cuckold's Haven, which faced it across Limehouse Reach, it seems to have been one of those frowsily dismal localities which naturally associate themselves with satire; and it is mentioned in *Satiromastix, Eastward Ho*, *The Return From Parnassus*, etc., often in connection with the cynical sort of criticism as in the last-named play:

> There where the blatant beast doth rule and reign,
> Renting the credit of whom it please.[64]

Nashe's satirical vein was, of course, notorious. Chambers (who is rather harsh to speculators about contemporary political references, yet quite bold in making such suggestions of his own) conjectures that the play contained some slur on the Polish Ambassador, who had complained to Elizabeth five days before the trouble, about a difference over contraband in neutral vessels, and had been answered by her extempore in vigorous Latin.[65] But is not the interval almost too short between the event and the satire if the satire was organic, as the play's title makes us feel? The Council can hardly have acted on the same day as a late-afternoon performance, and Nashe had time to get away. Can three or four days, at most, have been time enough to write, rehearse, and produce an extensive satire, constituting a considerable part of the play?

Possibly the basis of Nashe's allusions was heraldic. There were dogs on the arms of Talbot, Heneage, Devereux, and many others. In *Lenten Stuffe* he complains: "Talke I of a beare, O it is such a man that em-

[64] *2 Return from Parnassus*, V, iv.

[65] III, 455.

blazons him in his armes, or of a woolfe, a fox, or a camelion, any lording whom they do not affect is meant thereby." However, the fact that Topcliffe was the man who called to the Council's attention the sedition in the play strengthens the likelihood that there was more in it than mere lampoons on some of Cecil's enemies. As Chambers points out, Nashe, some years before, had been criticized for attacking (in *Pierce Penilesse*) another people with whom the Elizabethans were on uneasy terms, the Danes.

At any rate the satire, whatever its nature, made it necessary for Nashe to go into hiding, threw Jonson into prison as a collaborator, and brought on a general inhibition of stage plays, during which the Chamberlain's and at least part of the Admiral's men travelled,[66] while Henslowe busied himself in reorganizing his company by binding to him as his personal servants various actors, including several from Pembroke's men. In the autumn he records a few performances by the Admiral's and Pembroke's jointly. By the end of 1597 there was a separate Pembroke's company again, and in 1598–1600 it is heard of in the provinces. For a time Langley kept some sort of company together at the Swan, and there was litigation with the players who had joined or rejoined the Admiral's men over breach of covenant.

Two plays of Ben Jonson's may represent worked-over material from his 1597 writing for Pembroke's men, *The Case is Altered* and *A Tale of a Tub*. The former was published in 1609, the latter not until 1633. Both poke fun at cheap and popular Elizabethan writers, the former clearly at Munday as "Antonio Balladino, pageant-poet," the latter at "Diogenes Scriben," who is less easily identified. *The Case is Altered* treats the French well, shows an interest in warfare, and has an odd exclamation, "But a saint! Another Bridget!"[67] which may possibly refer to Bridget Vere. *A Tale of a Tub* shows even less connection with Pembroke. It deals with the same region in the northwestern suburbs of London into which Jonson is introduced as "Brabant Senior" in Marston's play for Paul's boys, *Jack Drum's Entertainment*, about 1600; and it shows various other connections with the drama of our period which need not necessarily be taken to prove an early dating.

On the whole, Pembroke's men cannot be seen to have exerted any distinct influence on the drama as practiced by the older, more stable companies. Whatever fashion of pert allusiveness they may possibly have encouraged must have been rather dampened by the serious trouble they drew down upon the whole London stage. It is true that the growing

[66] The Chamberlain's men were at Rye, Dover, Faversham in August; Marlborough, Bath, and Bristol in September. Cf. B. M. Ward, "The Chamberlain's Men in 1597," *R.E.S.*, IX, 55.

[67] IV, iii, 63; the context is ironical.

taste for satire was uncontrollable and showed itself very strikingly during the next few years both in non-dramatic publications and on the stage, in the latter case being especially affected by the boys, who seem to have enjoyed a sort of immunity not shared by the adult actors; but there is insufficient evidence that this ephemeral grouping of players under the name of Pembroke did anything important to start or to strengthen the satirical vogue.

The year 1597, then, was a disturbed one in the theaters. It seems probable that *The Isle of Dogs* was only the final aggravation which made the inevitable explosion of the Queen and her Privy Council a violent one, releasing a tension made up of many accumulated irritations over the personal and political satire in *Richard II*, *Henry IV*, *The Tinker of Totnes*, and numerous other plays by both the Admiral's and the Chamberlain's men. In the unstable conditions of 1597, then, the triumphant position the Shakespearean company had occupied at the end of the previous year was inevitably lost. The general reorganization of the companies during the period of "restraint" launched them upon a new period of intensified competition.

As I have said, Henslowe during the inhibition was binding some of the Admiral's actors to him under a new system as his own covenant servants, in one of his agreements saying "my company."[68] Some of the reorganized company were returning to the Admiral's men after their brief adventure with Pembroke's, others were new to the Henslowe troop. Martin Slater had left on July 18, perhaps to go to Scotland;[69] and about October the company suffered the great loss of Alleyn, who left the stage for three years. The leadership of the company, as indicated by payees for court performances, was thereafter taken by Shaw and Downton. The increased control of Henslowe over the company under the new arrangement, especially in the absence of Alleyn, appears to have favored a financial policy which was more profitable to Henslowe than to his players. The Diary shows a lavish policy in the purchasing of playbooks

[68] Chambers, II, 151. For the company's membership, autumn, 1597, see *Ibid.*, 156.

[69] After Slater's departure Downton sued him for thirty pounds damages for a playbook "found" and disposed of by him for his own profit, and was awarded the considerable sum of ten pounds ten. "Fletcher and Mertyn [Slater?] with their company" were building themselves a playhouse in Edinburgh, with the King's backing against the Kirk, in November, 1599. Perhaps this company's repertory was the intended destination of the playbook.

This suit is an important event for the student of the problems of Elizabethan dramatic publication. The sum claimed by the Admiral's representative, or even that awarded, is several times the usual value of old plays (about two pounds each) as we see them bought and sold by Henslowe and Alleyn. Perhaps it was an award of punitive damages. Or, if Slater was planning to take the book with him to Scotland, it is interesting to speculate on his willingness to risk staging it there, while fear of ridicule, reprisals, or legal measures might have restrained him from taking it to a London company.

and properties which saddled the Admiral's men with a debt they never fully discharged, although the return of Alleyn in 1600 appears to have made the administration comparatively economical once more.[70]

It seems probable that the Chamberlain's men, on their return to London, resumed playing at the Curtain rather than at the Theatre, where the Burbadges were disputing with the owner of the ground over a renewal of the lease. The Curtain stood not far away. Certainly the company had moved to it before the end of 1597, and Guilpin's *Skialetheia* in 1598 refers to "the unfrequented Theatre—darke silence and vast solitude."[71]

An approximate roll of Shakespeare's company at this time is given by the actor list of *Every Man in His Humour*, which was produced in 1598 (this, first published in the 1616 Jonson Folio, is the earliest extant list of the company).[72] Stage directions of *Much Ado about Nothing*, also performed in 1598, show that Richard Cowley played Verges to Kempe's Dogberry. No marked change in financial policy is evident in the Chamberlain's men at this time.

More plays got into print from 1597 on, especially from the Chamberlain's stock. This phenomenon is usually interpreted to mean theft in the case of garbled, corrupt quarto texts, and dire financial straits for the company in the case of good ones. But it has been observed that the boy companies a little later followed a policy of printing their plays almost at once, perhaps because their playwrights were literary men of marked vanity. It should be noticed, however, that the tone of their plays was prevailingly one of satire. A play satirizing a rival company is not one of which the rival company is likely to appropriate the theme the moment it appears in print; moreover, the amount of verbal political satire which the censorship[73] left in a play would only whet the reader's appetite and thus increase rather than diminish the audiences, which could be regaled with much in make-up, business, etc., of which censor,

[70] Chambers, II, 183.

[71] Leslie Hotson's recent discovery (cf. his *Shakespeare versus Shallow*) of Shakespeare's name in association with that of Langley goes far toward proving that the Chamberlain's men had moved by the autumn of 1596 to the Swan in Paris Garden, built in 1594–95. But they probably went to the Curtain a few months later, for Pembroke's came to the Swan in February, 1597.

[72] The principall Comoedians were.

WILL. SHAKESPEARE.	RIC. BVRBADGE.
AVG. PHILIPS.	IOH. HEMINGS.
HEN. CONDEL.	THO. POPE.
WILL. SLYE.	CHR. BEESTON.
WILL. KEMPE.	IOH. DVKE.

[73] Cf. *Sir Thomas More.*

reader, and posterity were deprived. The element of satire, especially of the political sort, in Shakespeare's plays, then, may be one explanation of the appearance in print of some of them and their rivals during this period, for instance *1 Henry IV* and *Oldcastle*, both in print within a year or two of their first production.

Wallace asserts that the Children of the Chapel, a company of boys, were revived in 1597; but I think it safest to follow Chambers (*The Elizabethan Stage*) and Hillebrand (*The Child Actors*), who hold that they did not reappear until 1600. The question has an important bearing on the dating of some of the work of Jonson and Marston, especially *The Case is Altered* and *Histriomastix*, and therefore on the history of the "Poetomachia" and of certain dramatic innovations of the last years of the century.

Politically the situation as the year 1597 drew to a close was unpleasant. The jealous dispute between Essex and Nottingham was at its height. Although England was once more released from fear of invasion and Count Maurice was successful against the Spaniards in the Low Countries, Parliament had been bitterly debating economic troubles, mainly agricultural,[74] and Tyrone's brewing rebellion was threatening Ireland's most prosperous district, the English plantation of Munster.

The Admiral's men, perhaps partly because of the waning of Essex's glory, partly because of the temporary reconciliation between him and the Cecilians at the end of the year, and partly because of a sprucing-up of their properties, costumes, casts, and plays, were once more called to court after nearly two years' absence, on December 26, January 1 and 6, February 26.

Among the Admiral's plays of this year which would seem most likely to please a court audience is *The Comedy of Humours*, which we know from Henslowe's inventories to be the same as Chapman's brilliant innovation, *A Humourous Day's Mirth*.[75] The remaining plays of the Admiral's repertory up to the end of July do not appear particularly promising. *Alexander and Lodowick* was popular, but may have been considered too old-fashioned, being based as we have seen on a popular romance. *Five Plays in One* is plausibly thought to have been made up from some of Heywood's *Pleasant Dialogues and Dramas*, drawn mostly from Lucian. Their mythological learning flavored with satirical tartness may well have been pleasing to the court taste at this time, for the vogue of this sort of thing was beginning; Hall's *Toothless Satyres* had been well received this year. Of later plays, after the reorganization, *Branholt* was probably tragical (see Fletcher's *Thierry and Theodoret*), *Alice*

[74] I.e., enclosures and statutes of tillage. But the even more ticklish issues of pluralities, patents, and monopolies were also touched upon.

[75] Greg. *Henslowe*, II, 184.

Pierce may just possibly have been unsuitable politically, as touching the reign of Richard II, and *Mother Redcap* looks too plebeian.[76] A play which the company had ready before the February court performance was Dekker's *Phaeton*, which may underlie the extant *Sun's Darling* by Dekker and Ford, quarto 1656, a masquelike piece well adapted to court showing.

Some of the characters in the latter piece are: Raybright (the Sun's Darling), Lady Spring and the other Seasons, Youth, Fortune, Detraction, a Spaniard, a French Tailor. Raybright, like Faustus, is led on unsatisfied from delight to delight. A few phrases may come from our period: "Poor Follie, honest Follie, Jocundary Follie forsake your Lordship?" sounds like Falstaff; "O sweat like pamper'd jade of Asia" quotes Tamburlaine; "This Apple John Kent" seems to mix *Henry IV* and *John a Kent*, possibly in a conscious identification of Falstaff and Cobham. Water's father is "one of the Dunce-table, and one that never drank strong beer in his life" (Dunstable's brewer figures prominently in *Oldcastle*, and small beer in *Henry IV*). Resemblances to Nashe's *Summer's Last Will*[77] are striking. But if there were any really stinging references to Essex in the original play, they seem to have been removed along with the identification of Raybright with Phaeton, always a stock example of the favorite who comes to disaster through his presumption.

Munday's *1 Robin Hood* is also a possibility. But I think *The Comedy of Humours* for December 27 and *Phaeton* for February 28 are the best selections for the Admiral's plays at court this season.

According to Baldwin, the activities of Shakespeare in 1597 consisted of the writing of *The Merchant of Venice*, summer, and the rewriting of *Love's Labour's Lost*, winter; the latter is thought to have been given at Christmas before the court, because of the claim to that effect made on the title page of the 1598 quarto. Its fairly probable presence on the stage this season affords an opportunity for saying something about the rivalry in plays which dealt more or less with French affairs.

The Rival Companies' Attitudes toward the French, 1594–1603

Love's Labour's Lost, of course, with its curiously fantastic distortion of French politics, is probably in its original form considerably before our period.[78] I am inclined to think that its unreal treatment of events and issues, however, is not due to ignorance on the part of the dramatist,

[76] *Mother Redcappe her last will and testament*, S.R. March 10, 1595, seems to have been a rowdy chapbook about some such character as Gillian of Brentford. Mother Redcap's "syne" is in Henslowe's inventory. Compare *The Wise Woman of Hogsdon*. [77] ?1593.

[78] But see Rupert Taylor's argument for a 1596 dating, *The Date of "Love's Labour's Lost,"* 1932.

but to a desire to remove the play from the realistic handling which would be bound to give offence, Elizabeth being especially sensitive about any literary interference with her foreign, above all her French, policy. The play, I think, must have been in the possession of the Chamberlain's men in 1594 and may have been revived then by them in opposition to the bloody and violently Protestant view of French affairs presented by Marlowe's *Massacre at Paris*, played by the Admiral's and Strange's in 1593 and probably held by the Admiral's men with the rest of Marlowe's plays. Revivals may have occurred in 1598, 1601, and 1602. The ownership of the play is made reasonably certain by Henslowe's purchase for the Admiral's men on July 18, 1602, of *The Massacre of France*, an old play, from Alleyn. Properties for a revival had been bought the preceding November.

Perhaps we should remind ourselves at this point that the partisans of Essex and of the Cecils were rather consistently opposed as to their French policies. The Admiral seems to have disliked the French; but the Cecils were following a traditional policy of alliance with Burgundy (which toward the end of our period meant alliance with the Archduke and his bride the Infanta) in order to keep France from becoming too powerful a rival across the Channel. Of course this issue was inextricably tangled with that of the war with Spain, against which nation England was allied with the Netherlands and France up to 1598, when King Henri made a separate peace; and it was in this, the last year of Burghley's life, that the wrangling between Cecil, for peace with Spain, and Essex, for war to victory, reached the point where the old man held before the eyes of his young opponent Psalms, 55:23.—"But thou, O God, shalt bring them down into the pit of destruction: bloody and deceitful men shall not live out half their days; but I will trust in thee." (Essex died at thirty-three, having lived not half his allotted three score years and ten.) Essex replied by writing to Anthony Bacon an *Apology*, intended for publication, which offended the Queen by its appeal to public opinion for sanction of his desire to continue the war. Essex was a personal friend, too, of King Henri and several of his great nobles, as we have already noticed; and his friend Southampton was doubtless very pleasantly received on his visit to France in 1598. His brother-in-law, Sir Robert Vernon, had been "bred up" with the Duc de Bouillon, who was interceding for him on that account after the Rebellion.[79]

Two or three lost plays of the Admiral's men; *The French Doctor*, 1595 (perhaps revived in 1602), *The French Comedy*, 1595 and again marked "ne" in 1597, probably continued in a comic and satiric vein the company's general attitude of hostility toward the French. The

[79] Cf. *Winwood's Memorials*, May 23, 1601; Winwood to Cecil.

French doctor was rather a stock type in the drama, and perhaps was in some way a descendant of the miraculous doctor of the mumming plays. Sometimes a character disguises as a French doctor, as does Angelo to help plot his own murder in Dekker's *Wonder of a Kingdom*, which may be the Admiral's *Wonder of a Woman*, 1595. Shakespeare has one, Dr. Caius in *The Merry Wives*, about 1598; and Philomusus in *2 Return from Parnassus*, 1601, disguises as one.

About 1595 we should contrast with this habitual representation of French physicians as ridiculous and villainous figures Shakespeare's markedly gentle treatment of the French in *King John*. Shakespeare does not seem inclined to tax the nation with anything worse than frivolity here, any more than in Portia's remarks on Monsieur Le Bon a year or two later,[80] in which Monsieur does not seem to me to fare worse than the Englishman or the Scot, and surely comes off far better than the Neapolitan, the puritanical County Palatine, or the German.[81] Frivolity, again, seems to be about the only vice of the French in *Henry V*, produced by the Chamberlain's men two years later still, from the sending of the tennis balls to Katherine's English lesson and the boasting.

In competition with the Chamberlain's revival of *Love's Labour's Lost* in 1597—and let us notice again that much of the satire is artfully turned against the Spanish, and that the weakness of the French is again the modish one of frivolity—the Admiral's men appear to have had from Pembroke's men the tragical *Branholt*[82] and possibly also Pembroke's *Bourbon*. The latter, as we have seen, may perhaps be identified with the *The Trial of Chivalry*, published in 1605 as Derby's, to which Heywood appears to have made the additions of "Cutting Dick" for Worcester's men in 1602. The Earl of Pembroke has a prominent part (in 1597 he appeared likely to become Derby's brother-in-law), and Bourbon a villainous one, including "poisoning" the heroine's face, a very popular trick of villains about 1600.[83] But the most lengthy contribution of the Admiral's men to the type, and important because of its nearness in date to *Henry V*, was the three-part play on *The Civil Wars of France*, written by Dekker and Drayton in the autumn of 1598.

[80] *The Merchant of Venice*, I, ii, 58 ff.

[81] The portrait of the last may be a lampoon due to the trade war with Germany which was going on at the time.

[82] Cf. the character of Brunhalt in *Thierry and Theodoret* by Fletcher and Massinger about 1617, a gloomy and violent play.

[83] See *The Gentleman Usher* and *Jack Drum's Entertainment*. It occurs also in two plays which may have been first played in 1594 and revised later, *Four Prentices* and *Match Me in London*. The device must have had a powerful effect on audiences all too familiar with what smallpox could do.

Unfortunately it is lost, but it must have been pro-Huguenot, and very likely stressed the wickedness of King Henri's turning Catholic for the sake of the crown, for that had been used by the Cecils as a convenient pretext for refusing him further English aid and dunning him persistently instead for the payment of his accumulated debts. The play was running in the following year, when Drayton provided it with an induction, thus directly competing with *Henry V*. At about the same time we get slight comic treatments of Frenchmen by both companies, in *The Merry Wives of Windsor* and *Englishmen for my Money*.

Various plays touched French affairs through glorification of English campaigns on French soil. *Henry I* may have done so, *Richard Cordelion's Funeral* doubtless did, *Edward III* and *The Famous Victories of Henry V* we know did; and note *2 Edward IV*, "containing his journey into France, for obtaining of his right there; the treacherous falsehood of the Duke of Burgundy and the Constable of France used against him, and his return home again."

An unknown company, perhaps the Admiral's men, produced the somewhat unpleasant depiction of the national life in *Charlemagne, or the Distracted Emperor*, about 1600. This may allude to the odd ceremonies for King Henri's mistress, Gabrielle d'Estrées: her body was placed under her bed, in which was a lifelike effigy to which meals were served for four days.[84]

In 1601 the Admiral's men are seen reviving the old *Massacre at Paris;* and about the same time the French were being more or less roughly handled by the boy companies, several of whose writers had worked for Henslowe and had been affected by the Admiral's politics, in such satirical plays as *Jack Drum's Entertainment*, *What You Will*, *Sir Giles Goosecap* (in which a French page is mistaken for a baboon), and *Monsieur d'Olive*. The French were uncomfortably aware of such slurs. Winwood wrote Cecil on July 7, 1602, that he had managed to block the Italian comedians' playing of "l'Histoire Angloise contre la Roine d'Anglcterre," although the playbills had been posted; but that "It was objected . . . that the Death of the Duke of Guise hath been plaied at London . . . and . . . that the Massacre of St. Bartholomew hath been publickly acted, and this King represented upon the Stage."

The fairly amiable picture of the French given by Shakespeare's *All's Well that Ends Well* about 1602 was rudely contradicted by Chapman's *Biron*, for which Henslowe records Worcester's men[85] as buying

[84] *S.P. Venetian*, April 25, 1599. At the same time it was being proposed to marry Henri to the eldest daughter of the late Ferdinando Stanley, Earl of Derby, to give his house a claim to the English crown.

[85] I shall try to explain this company's politics when I come to its organization.

properties in 1602—a black satin suit, a bar, and a scaffold. The parallel of Biron's fate to that of Essex had been widely observed,[86] and this play's presentation at this time seems markedly a taunt at the crushed Essex faction. Chapman's *Bussy d'Ambois*, probably about two years later, gives by no means a flattering impression of French civilization.

Shall we leave Shakespeare's rivals the last word? I think that perhaps we must. As far as I know, the Shakespearean company's kindly feeling toward the French lost its motivation when Essex died. Even in *The Fair Maid of Bristow* before 1604 the King's men had a clown called "Frog." The French were not particularly pleased by the peaceful accession of James, fearing disturbance of the balance of power, especially as he was known to favor peace with Spain.

In the 1597 repertory of the Chamberlain's men the two parts of *Henry IV* were still undoubtedly new enough to be popular. *Richard II*, *Richard III*, and *Romeo and Juliet* were published during the year,[87] the first two in good quartos (note that they contained political material)[88] and the last in a garbled, probably surreptitious version. The company may have had, too, the curious pastoral play *Mucedorus*, first published in 1598, and of doubtful ownership. The 1610 quarto assigns it to the King's men. The earlier quarto has an epilogue in which Envy yields to Queen Elizabeth—a fairly open reference, it seems to me, to the ending in Essex's favor of the controversy over Cadiz:

> *Co*[*medie*]. Then caitife cursed, stoope vpon thy knee,
> Yeelde to a woman, though not to mee,
> And pray we both togither with our hearts,
> That she thrice Nestors yeares may with vs rest,
> And from her foes high God defend her still,
> That they against her may neuer worke thir will.
> *En*[*uie*]. Enuie were he neuer so stoute
> Would becke and bowe vnto her maiestie,
> Indeed Comedie thou hast ouerrunne me now.
> And forst me stoope vnto a womans swaie.

The rewritten version of *Romeo and Juliet* which Baldwin assigns to 1598, and perhaps also *Much Ado about Nothing*, may have been ready before the end of the court season; but probably not the latter, unless it is *Love's Labour's Won*, for Meres does not mention it in his *Palladis*

[86] Chamberlain, writing to Carleton on November 4, 1602, discusses the matter interestingly. Biron's valor he calls "rather a French furie then true fortitude." Comparing the deaths of Essex, Biron, and Gowrie in three successive years, he points out the similarities of their careers and fates, and goes on, "A great part of the world rests unsatisfied in their deaths, and will not be persuaded . . . but *mundus vult decipi*."

[87] Chambers, IV, 385.

[88] In *Richard III* it bore chiefly on the claims of the candidates to succeed Elizabeth.

Tamia of that year. The most likely candidates for the Shakespearean company's four performances at court in the season of 1597–98 appear to be *Love's Labour's Lost, The Merchant of Venice, 1 Henry IV*, and *Mucedorus;* with *Romeo and Juliet* revised and *2 Henry IV* very possible. *The Merry Wives* more probably belongs to 1598.

The year 1598 was an important one in English politics. It opened, as we have seen, with a superficial harmony between Essex and his enemies; and in February Sir Robert Cecil took the Earl of Southampton with him on his important embassy to King Henri of France, first having secured Essex's promise not to alter state affairs in his absence. The Edict of Nantes in April was, of course, pleasing to English Protestantism; but the Treaty of Vervins in the following month brought about the peace between Spain and France which English policy, for safety's sake, naturally opposed; although the re-cession of Calais from Spain to France was a great relief, as was also the death of Philip II.

Through the spring Essex was in general on good terms with the Queen, but there appear to have been misunderstandings, one in May over Southampton's affair with Elizabeth Vernon; and new favorites, younger men than Essex, were coming into prominence, especially Lord Herbert, son of the Earl of Pembroke, and Sir Henry Carey, a younger brother of Lord Hunsdon. In August Southampton made a secret journey from France to marry his mistress. The Queen in November, when he returned again to England, had him committed to the Fleet, and very nearly sent the "new-coined Countess" there, too. This was the end of Southampton's favor with the Queen.

On August 4 died the old Lord Burghley. The Queen wept, and the passing of the elder Cecil was felt as a blow to the cause of peace throughout Europe. On August 10 Essex succeeded him as Chancellor of Cambridge, but most of his powers were gathered into the hands of his son.

In the summer Tyrone broke out in rebellion. He captured the fort at Blackwater, and by October Munster was aflame. The position of Lord Deputy had been vacant since Lord Burgh's death in 1597 and was the center of curious political intrigues. Long experience had taught politicians that the responsibility of quieting Ireland was almost certain to be disastrous to anyone who accepted it; and the object of maneuvers during the summer and autumn of 1598 seems to have been to discredit some leading figure of the opposite party by giving him the post, which, it appears, was settled on Essex finally in January, 1599, because his character, complex even for an Elizabethan, admitted as motives both an altruistic desire to pacify Ireland through his policy of tolerance, and jealousy lest anyone else should have the honor of leading England's great army thither. The jealous striving for glory is obvious; the altruism, I think, probable; we should add also a third motive, alleged by his enemies, an ambitious plan to lead back from Ireland an army perfected and inspired by his leadership into an instrument capable of making him either king or king-maker.

One of the most important stage events of the year 1598 was the production by Shakespeare's fellows, shortly before the twentieth of September, of Ben Jonson's *Every Man in his Humour*. The origin of the type may have been in the lost *Comedy of Humours* recorded by Henslowe for the Admiral's men in 1596, which is probably the same as Chapman's extant *An Humourous Day's Mirth*, written for the same company early in the following year. The same author's *Blind Beggar of Alexandria*, Admiral's 1596, also makes use of representative humours for comical and satirical purposes:

> *Irus* [*Cleanthes*]. Now to my wardroppe for my veluet gowne,
> Now doth the sport beginne,
> Come gird this pistole closely to my side,
> By which I make men feare my humor still,
> And haue slayne two or three as twere my mood
> When I haue done it most aduisedly.
> To rid them as they were my heauie foes,
> Now am I knowne to be the mad braine Count,
> VVhose humors twise, fiue summers I haue held,[89]
> And sayde at first I came from stately Rome,
> Calling my selfe Count Hermes and assuming
> The humour of a wild and franticke man,
> Carelesse of what I say or what I doe,
> And so such faultes as I of purpose doe,
> Is buried in my humor and this gowne I weare,
> In rayne or snowe or in the hottest sommer,
> And neuer goe nor ride without a gowne,
> which humor doth not fit my frencie wel,
> But hides my persons forme from beeing knowne . . . [90]

The rivalry between Jonson and Chapman, running as it does through rather complicated changes in company affiliations, is a matter of some interest though not quite important enough to the main rivalry of the leading companies to find place here.[91] The change in allegiance which chiefly concerns us at present is Jonson's from the Admiral's to the Chamberlain's men. This was accompanied by his killing of Spencer, Henslowe's leading actor, in a duel, and was followed by a spiteful allusion on the part of the Admiral's playwright, Porter, to his branding

[89] Essex first became a favorite in 1587; he had entered the court circle in 1584, in his seventeenth year, and had been in the Netherlands with Leicester during 1585–86. The "twice five summers" is a very good approximation of the truth, if Cleanthes is meant for Essex. [90] Sgn. C 3.

[91] I plan to publish an article on this subject in the near future.

for the deed.[92] After the failure of *Every Man out of his Humor* in 1599 Jonson left Shakespeare's fellows, traditionally with hard feelings which he expressed later in his work for the boy actors during the Poetomachia.

An even more successful 1598 production by the Chamberlain's men than *Every Man In* was probably Shakespeare's *Much Ado.* Dogberry and Verges, Benedick and Beatrice, as supreme examples of their types were often imitated. The resemblance of Friar Francis to Friar Lawrence has already been noted, and may have something to do with the surmised rewriting of *Romeo and Juliet* at about this time; but traces of condensed verse[93] and even of rhyme[94] in some of the prose passages of *Much Ado* hint that they may be underlaid by material dating back to the time of the first popularity of *Romeo and Juliet.* Signs of revision appear also in the plot and the characters, especially in the first act.

There is an interesting possibility that Shakespeare here took a dig at Sir Robert Cecil during his absence on an embassy to France.[95] When, in III, ii, the Watchman says, "I know that Deformed; a' has been a vile thief this seven years; a' goes up and down like a gentleman: I remember his name," the reference may be to Cecil, undersized and deformed, enemy to the Essex faction, whom his enemies were accustomed to call "Hunchback" in several languages. Francis Davison, poet, son of the unfortunate Secretary, wrote to his father from Lucca, November 6, 1596,[96] referring rather hopelessly to the troubles of his patron Essex with his enemies and calling Cecil "arch-enemy," "viper," "pigmy," "bumbasted-legs," and "St. Gobbo." If the nickname was current, the Gobbos in *The Merchant of Venice* must have been identified by audiences as the Cecils.[97] On November 20 Davison refers to Cecil's Secretaryship as "the late instalment and canonization of the venerable saint." The Essexian French ambassador, Boisisse, in an account of Essex's trial which got him into a great deal of trouble, called Cecil "ce petit Bossu." Cecil had in fact been serving informally as Secretary for just seven years, since the death of Walsingham in 1591, although not actually named Secretary until 1596. Moreover, the Cecils were of low origin

[92] See *Two Angry Women* (Q. 1599), Epilogue.

[93] III, iii, 161–173, for example.

[94] See v, ii, 101–106. I think that the latter part of Benedick's soliloquy, II, iii, about ll. 25 ff., is condensed from verse.

[95] But cf. *Hist. MSS. Com.* R. XIII-4, 109; the Mayor and Jurats of Rye to the Lord Warden [Cobham], May 4, 1594.—"On Wednesday last there came into our town one Paule Formosus, apparelled in such sort as we have sent him unto you, a very suspicious person and one who greatly abused the Lord Hounsden. We send you certain notes found about him." Possibly the "one Deformed" allusion was originated on a visit to Rye, and changed in 1598 to apply to Cecil. The Chamberlain's men were at Rye in August, 1597.

[96] Cf. Bullen's Intro. to his edition of Davison's *Poetical Rhapsody.*

[97] Cf. Chambers, *William Shakespeare,* I, 372.

and were troubled at times by taunts about the fact;[98] so the implication in "a' goes up and down like a gentleman" would be cutting. The later reference to his wearing "a lock" may refer to his doings in France, for the wearing of love-locks was considered a French fashion. Dogberry's remarks, allowances being made for his wonderful confusion of ideas, may contain some obscure satire on Cecil's governmental actions:

And also, the Watch heard them talk of one Deformed: they say he wears a key in his ear and a lock hanging by it, and borrows money in God's name, the which he hath used so long and never paid, that now men grow hard-hearted, and will lend nothing for God's sake.[99]

Cecil's father, Burghley, as Lord Treasurer had collected many of the "loans" which were one of Elizabeth's chief forms of taxation; and apparently the son had been prominent in this business during the past few years of Burghley's increasing incapacitation from gout and other infirmities. The Secretary also had charge of secret-service money. Moreover, Burghley had been Master of the Court of Wards and Liveries, a lucrative but annoying institution, for the suppression of which there was strong agitation. Essex was spoken of for the Mastership in 1598, but it went to Cecil in the following year.[100]

It may be more than a coincidence that the villain Conrade has a prototype in a real "Conrados" (a rare name in England), gentleman servant in the household of the Willoughbys of Wollaton, of whom I have spoken in connection with the Shelford affair and *1 Henry IV*. This Conrados played a dark rôle in the intrigues which alienated husband and wife during the 80's.[101] Lady Willoughby died about 1594.

A bit of Essex propaganda which Shakespeare may have inserted in

[98] Sir John Holles, for instance, in June, 1597, returned a spirited *tu quoque* to Burghley's slur on his ancestors—cf. *Portland MSS.*, IX, 91. Cf. also *S. P. Venetian*, July 21, 1599.—Cecil "has found a new pedigree, by his grandmother, from the Walpoles, and altered his crest from a sheaf of wheat between two lions to two sheaves of arrows crossed and covered with a helmet." But Holles's hint that the Cecils had tacked themselves onto another man's pedigree probably alluded to their claiming the Sytsyllts of Glamorgan for their ancestors.

[99] v, i. Queen Elizabeth's subjects found it useless to look for repayment of their unwilling lendings to her government. Cf. *S. P. Venetian*, 25 August, 1604.

[100] Chamberlain reports on October 20, 1598, that Essex is said to refuse the Court of Wards "gelded and maimed," or "finds scruple in the strictness of the othe, and wonders how the late Lord Treasurer could dispense so easilie and so largely with it and his conscience." For comparison we have Cecil's letter to Neville (*Winwood's Memorials*) on May 23, 1599: ". . . my self Master of the Wards, but so restrained by new Orders, as in the Office I am a Ward my selfe. But seeing yt was my Fathers Place, and that her Majestie hathe bestowed yt on me, I will undergoe yt with as muche Intergrity [sic] as I can, and yet I vow to you, I have resigned a better Place of the Dutchy [of Lancaster] for yt." See also *S. P. Venetian, 1603–7*, 507.

[101] *Middleton MSS.*, 561 and *passim*.

Much Ado between Essex's return from Ireland in September, 1599, and the publication of the play in 1600 is this reference:

> And bid her steal into the pleached bower,
> *Where honey-suckles, ripen'd by the sun,*
> *Forbid the sun to enter; like favourites,*
> *Made proud by princes, that advance their pride*
> *Against that power that bred it.* There will she hide her
> To listen our propose. This is thy office . . .[102]

The italicized lines are possibly a complaint against the hostile faction which Essex felt was barring his access to the Queen.[103] The passage, one observes, can be removed without injuring the context in metre or meaning. "There will she hide her" is obviously mere padding.

Southampton, too, was out of favor with Elizabeth after his marriage in 1598. Another connection between Shakespeare's friend and his dramatic work in this year rests on the possibility, as good as any of the several available, of identifying *Love's Labour's Won* with *All's Well that Ends Well.* Acheson points out certain resemblances between Southampton's domestic affairs and those of Bertram and asserts that *All's Well* reflects "Shakespeare's combined reproof and approval of Southampton's recent conduct toward Elizabeth Vernon, as well as a practical reflection of the actual facts in their case."[104]

Southampton was a better man than Bertram; it seems odd that Shakespeare should weaken his patron in dramatizing him. And other facts and well-founded speculations about the play appear to weaken Acheson's theory. The presence of older, rhymed material in *All's Well* has often been noted, and it is doubtless the reason for Baldwin's placing *Love's Labour's Won* in 1589, with its rewriting as *All's Well* in 1607; the more usual dating for our version of *All's Well* is about 1602, when it may be observed, Southampton was in the Tower to reflect upon his many indiscretions, including experiences with the cavalry in Ireland which may possibly be traced in the play.

[102] III, i, 7–12. Cf. Chambers, *William Shakespeare,* I, 387.

[103] Cf. Essex to Anthony Bacon, 1600, in *A Collection of Letters made by Sir Tobie Matthew,* 1660, 9: "And I believe . . . that, since the Sentence, she meant to restore me, to attend upon her Person. But they, who could use Occasions (which it was not in me to hinder) nay could amplifie Occasions, and practise upon Occasions, to represent to her Majesty a necessity to bring me to the one [public censure]; can and will do the like, to stop me from the other [access to her presence]. . . . But they, who know . . . that, if ever I recover the Queen, I will never lose her again, will never suffer me to re-obtain an interest in her Favour. . . . Sure I am, that the false Glasse of others must alter her, when I want accesse to plead mine owne Cause. . . . And they, who can hinder me from coming neer to her, cannot hinder me from drawing neer to [God]; as, I hope, I do daily."

[104] Arthur Acheson, *Shakespeare's Lost Years in London,* 194. He thinks also that Shakespeare imputed the young Earl's misfortunes to the bad influence of John Florio.

Pembroke, as we have remarked before, had an affair somewhat resembling Bertram's in 1601, when he refused to tie himself to Mary Fitton, who was with child by him, stood firm in spite of imprisonment in the Fleet, and after the Queen's wrath had been mollified went abroad. But the plot of *All's Well* is still more closely paralleled in the life of the Earl of Oxford, at least as common report had it. Married in 1571 to Burghley's eldest daughter Anne, he threatened to ruin her in revenge for his father-in-law's ruining Norfolk, wasted and sold his lands, and traveled to Italy. On his return Burghley was much disturbed over his refusal to live with his wife; but the matter was, in time, somehow patched up. Lady Anne died in 1588, having borne him three daughters: Elizabeth, 1575, married in 1594 to the Earl of Derby; Bridget, 1584, intended for William Lord Herbert in 1597 but married to Sir Francis Norris; and Susan, 1587, who married William Herbert's younger brother Philip. To Susan, Francis Osborne[105] refers as "that daughter of the last great Earl of Oxford whose lady was brought to his bed under the notion of his mistris, and from such a virtuous deceit she is said to proceed."[106]

As for Parolles, there is reason to suspect that his characterization is salted with the malice of the dramatist's jealousy. William Reynolds, informing Cecil after the Rebellion of fugitive Essexians, writes:

> I marvel also what became of Pearse Edmonds, the Earl of Essex's man, born in Strand near me, who had many preferments by the Earl. His villainy I have often complained of; he dwells in London, and was corporal general of the horse in Ireland under the Earl of Southampton. He ate and drank at his table and lay in his tent. The Earl Southampton would coll and hug him in his arms and play wantonly with him.[107]

Mrs. Stopes, in quoting this letter,[108] omits the last sentence, the very portion which throws light on the nature of Southampton's friendships and therefore upon the problem of Shakespeare's *Sonnets*. Edmonds may have been about Shakespeare's age, for he pleads[109] that he has spent twenty years in the Queen's service, which would probably bring him to his late thirties. He was a captain,[110] and Essex sent him as a confidential messenger "with messages into Wales, as before he had been with secret instructions into Ireland, to such as the Earl there best reckoned of. Him the Earl so favoured as he rode often in coach with

[105] *Traditional Memoirs*, I, 226. Compare Thos. Wright, *History & Topography of the County of Essex*, I, 516; Wright has Burghley contrive the stratagem, and a son as the result. Oxford's only surviving son was b. 1592 to his second wife, Elizabeth Trentham.

[106] The stratagem is in Shakespeare's source, but it is interesting to find it also as contemporary gossip about a Bertram-like figure.

[107] *Sal. MSS.*, XI, 93.

[108] *The Third Earl of Southampton*, 199.

[109] *Sal. MSS.*, XI, 99; to Mr. Wade, Clerk of the Council.

[110] *Ibid.*, 103.

him, and was wholly of his charges maintained, being a man of base birth in St. Clement's parish."[111]

I should be more inclined to see the lives of Shakespeare's friends mirrored in his plays if it were not for such an odd phenomenon as the Aumerle story in *Richard II*—an incident which looks as if it had been tacked on to point a political moral of 1599, but which, if the first quarto is correctly dated, actually was in print in 1597, two years before Essex came posting from Ireland to throw himself at the Queen's feet, and nearly four years before the implication of the house of Rutland[112] in the Essex Rebellion. Was Shakespeare prophetic, or did the romantic, self-dramatizing young nobles who drank in his plays sometimes use them as guides to conduct? Puritan reformers have always held that stage-plays influence their auditors' actions. If we could prove that the Bertram story dates before Southampton's marriage in August, 1598, we should have rather impressive evidence that the latter was the case. After all, where could one learn better than from Shakespeare's plays how, in an impossible situation brought about by one's own weakness, to act and speak like a gentleman and a poet?

The Domestic Crime Play, 1594–1603

The remaining production to be assigned to the Chamberlain's men in 1598 is their anonymous *A Warning for Fair Women*. Published in 1599, it was perhaps by Lodge, who had gone abroad to study medicine. This play seems to have launched an important revival of its type, the dramatization of actual domestic crimes, which had lapsed since *Arden of Feversham* (quartos 1592 and 1599), and which the Admiral's men now seized upon with apparent enthusiasm. The authorship of *A Warning for Fair Women* has been ascribed also to Kyd and to the mysterious "Robert Yarington," author of *Two Lamentable Tragedies*, and by J. Q. Adams to Heywood. In the Induction and elsewhere the play appears to refer to or to resemble the old tragedies *Arden of Feversham*, *The Spanish Tragedy*, *Hamlet*, *Edward II*, *Doctor Faustus*, *Locrine*, and *The Battle of Alcazar;* but this does not necessarily prove that the play was an old property of the Chamberlain's men, written before our period. Many of these plays were revived in the last years of Elizabeth's reign; and other resemblances to *Sir John Oldcastle*, Marston's Antonio plays, *Henry V*, *Macbeth* and *Julius Caesar* indicate at least a rewriting under the in-

[111] *Ibid.*, 107, John Bird to Cecil, March 4, 1601.

[112] The Duke of Aumerle or Albemarle, son of Edmund de Langley, first Duke of York, was Earl of Rutland during his father's life. Roger Manners, fifth Earl of Rutland, and two of his brothers, George and Francis, were imprisoned and fined for their part in the Rebellion.

fluence of some of these plays, and a revival in order to influence the others. To me the most interesting of these passages are the following: the contentious Induction, in which Tragedy whips Comedy and History off the stage, and serves in a bowl of blood, a type of induction seen in *Mucedorus*, c. 1597, and crudely varied in Yarington's *Two Lamentable Tragedies;* John Beane's premonitory dream about his murder in which he is "troubled with green meadows" like the dying Falstaff:

Nay, I cannot tell. But I like neither thy dream [of picking flowers] nor my own, for I was troubled with green meadows, and bulls fighting and goring one another, and one of them, methought, ran at me, and I ran away, that I sweat in my sleep for fear";[113]

the passage,

> . . . fifteen wounds
> Which now be fifteen mouths that do accuse me.
> In every wound there is a bloody tongue,
> Which will all speak;[114]

and the expression, "my eyes dazzle," so splendidly employed by Webster in his *Duchess of Malfi*. In general I believe that this play or its rewriting resulted from the company's sharing in that revival of interest in the Senecan type of tragedy which occurred at about this time.[115] After *A Warning for Fair Women* the playwrights of Shakespeare's company apparently were not interested to develop the domestic crime type itself further, at least until *The Yorkshire Tragedy*, after our period; yet the emotional values of the type appear, heightened and intensified, in *Hamlet*, *Othello*, and *Macbeth*.

But the Admiral's men saw a chance for easily secured popular appeal in this journalistic sort of device. Almost all their plays of the type have

[113] II, ii. Perhaps, since "a' babbled of green fields" is almost too good an emendation to be true, we may speculate of Falstaff that "a' trobl'd of Greine fields." Cobham had lands in the Isle of Greyne, Kent; cf. *P.R.O. Lists and Indexes*, XXXVII, 46. It is "Graen" on Norden's map. The Folio has "a Table of greene fields." The line is not in the quartos.

[114] IV, ii. Compare *Julius Caesar*, III, ii.

[115] *Arden of Feversham* may have been revived, too; at least both plays appeared in print in 1599. *Arden* was written before April 3, 1592; so its connecting of its villains with robberies on Gads Hill and with a Lord Cheyney on the Isle of Sheppey may allude to our old friend Sir Edward Hoby, whose castle of Queenborough was on Sheppey, and who was said by Sir Roger Manwood in 1590 to be harboring certain thieves who infested Gads Hill and Chatham Down. "This Curtall and Manwaring," he says, "kepte themselves aboute Sir Edward Hobbyes howse in the Isle of Sheppey, where no constable . . . from the partes about Canterburye durst there entermedle." (Cf. Henry Ellis, *Original Letters*, 2nd Series, III, 182 ff.; and the reference to "Sir John Oldcastle's bay hobbie," *The Famous Victories of Henry V*, 83.) It is noteworthy in view of our theory of a revival that the Chamberlain's men played at Faversham in September, 1597 (Cf. Lionel Cust in *Archaeologia Cantiana*, XXXIV, 101 ff.), the same year to which we assign *The Mayor of Quinborough;* indeed, the Admiral's men, also on tour, may have visited Hoby at about this time.

been lost; probably their literary value was extremely slight.[116] In 1598 Chettle, Dekker, Day, and Wilson collaborated for Henslowe on a *Black Bateman of the North*, in two parts. I have already shown this play's connection with the Admiral and the Trent navigation controversy. As we find it in Sampson's *Vow-breaker*, it has also interesting material on the siege of Leith, and some good comedy centering on Joshua, a Puritan painter-stainer pressed for the campaign, who goes solemnly to work to hang his cat Tybert on a Monday, for catching a mouse on Sunday (I think the scene may be older than *Barnaby's Journal*, in which the famous rhyme first appears). The "Black Bateman" part of the plot deals with Anne Boote, troth-plight to Bateman, who marries a widower for his money. Bateman hangs himself before her door, and his ghost haunts her until she drowns herself in the Trent. The play's many reminiscences of Shakespeare may be largely due to Sampson's seventeenth-century rewriting.

In the following year the Diary shows *The Stepmother's Tragedy*, Chettle and Dekker; *Page of Plymouth*,[117] Dekker and Jonson; *Cox of Collumpton*[118] Day and Haughton; *Thomas Merry* (entered in the Stationers' Register as *Beech's Tragedy* the following year), Day and Haughton; and *The Orphans' Tragedy*, Chettle.[119]

Two Lamentable Tragedies, published in 1601 as by "Rob. Yarington," a playwright otherwise totally unknown,[120] and without any ascription to a company, is oddly made up of two murder stories, dealing in alternate scenes with the realistic story of the London murder of Beech by Merry and the romantic Italianate story of the murder of one of two orphans—really an Italian setting of "The Babes in the Wood," on which a ballad with a Norfolk setting was licensed in 1595. The traditional home of the wicked uncle of the "Babes" was Griston House, Nor-

[116] Yarington's *Two Lamentable Tragedies* may have been in their 1594 repertory if, as R. A. Law thinks (*M.L.R.*, v, 167), it was written, at least in part, soon after the murder of Beech in August of that year.

[117] The title of one of the several ballads on the subject runs: "The Lamentation of Master Pages wife of Plimmouth, who being enforced by her Parents to wed him against her will, did most wickedly consent to his murder, for the love of George Strangwidge; for which fact she suffered death at Bar[n]staple in Devonshire." (Cited by Greg, *Henslowe*, II, 205.)

[118] Collier says this play related to a murder at Collumpton, Devon. I have found no definite record of such a crime.

[119] The *Orphans' Tragedy* for which Chettle received a payment in 1601 was probably the *Italian Tragedy* of the preceding year; the "orphan" part of *Two Lamentable Tragedies* is Italian in setting. Cf. Greg, *op. cit.*, 209 (but compare *M.L.R.*, XIII, 100).

[120] Save as a scrivener who finished his apprenticeship in 1603. Cf. B. M. Wagner, *M.L.N.*, XLV, 145.

folk,[121] and nearby Wayland ("wailing") Wood was the scene of the tragedy. There is Norfolk material in other work by Day and Haughton, as I shall point out in discussing *The Blind Beggar of Bednal Green.* Fleay conjectured that "Rob. Yarington" was a fictitious name, to cover the amalgamation of *The Tragedy of Thomas Merry* by Day and Haughton and *The Orphans' Tragedy*, by Chettle. This now seems improbable,[122] and the relationship of the plays stands in great doubt.

In 1602, after a gap of two years or more, Day wrote *The Bristow Tragedy* for the Admiral's men and Haughton *William Cartwright.*[123]

Thus a considerable series of journalistic domestic crime plays leads up to the first fictional domestic crime play, if we may call it so, *A Woman Killed with Kindness*, by Heywood for Worcester's men in 1603.

The fundamental difference in spirit between the rival companies (for Worcester's men were under Henslowe's control) is interestingly exhibited by their reception of the revived domestic-crime play: the Chamberlain's men produced one or two plays, perhaps both old, which seemed to them to represent the unsatisfactory best to which the type as dramatic literature could be carried, and then dropped the type to turn to the high tragedy "of Kesars and of Kings"; the Henslowe group for several years exploited the sensational appeal of the type to the utmost, and then their fellow Heywood, apparently only an observer through this period, produced his masterpiece, fictionalizing it and giving it a twist of honest sentiment which made it an entirely new thing in the drama, and yet in a way a development of the same desire to appeal to the lower middle class which had encouraged the ventures into sensational stage journalism.

During their direct competition in domestic crime plays in the season of 1598, the rivalry of the Admiral's and the Chamberlain's men was

[121] For various lords of the manor—Montchensy, de Griston, Clifton, Knevet, Grey, Dunthorn, Barney—see Blomefield's *Norfolk*, II, 294. It belonged to the Honor of Clare. The ballad is in Roxburghe, II, 216, "The Norfolk Gentleman's Last Will." According to the Rev. George Crabbe, "Robert de Grey, Recusant," *Norfolk Archaeology*, IX, 282–328, Wayland Wood passed in 1541 from Sir Edmond Knyvett to Edmund de Grey. The manor house nearby, built in 1597, contained carvings of the story. The next de Grey, Robert, was persecuted as a recusant and his lands injuriously farmed about 1598–1603 by Thomas Felton, backed by Sir John Stanhope and Chief Justice Popham. A "Babes in the Wood" drama may thus have done some service as a plea in justification of these oppressions.

[122] See R. A. Law, *M.L.R.*, V, 167; and Baugh's introduction to his edition of Haughton's *Englishmen for My Money*, 1917. The former's view, that *Two Lamentable Tragedies* must precede the works named by Henslowe, is accepted by Baugh, Greg (*M.L.R.*, XIII, 100), and S. R. Golding (*N.Q.*, CLI, 347). Cf. also Law, "Further Notes on Two Lamentable Tragedies," *N.Q.*, CLIII, 93.

[123] Nothing is definitely known of either of these plays; they may not even necessarily belong to this type. Cf. Greg, *op. cit.*, 221, 224.

narrowed and therefore intensified by the Privy Council's order restricting the London playhouses to just two. This order was imperfectly obeyed; ostensibly it left only Shakespeare's company at the Curtain and Henslowe's at the Rose. Hints as to repertories are given by Guilpin,

> Ile to the Rose
> Or Curtain, one of Plautus comedies,
> Or the pathetic Spaniards Tragedies,

and by Marston's juxtaposition[124] of "Juliet and Romeo" and "Curtain plaudities." The closer rivalry was accompanied by, perhaps resulted in, legal troubles. On August 30 Henslowe made his loan to William Bird to follow a "sewt against Thomas Poope," and on January 30 following, one to Thomas Downton "to discharge Thomas Dekker from the arrest of the Chamberlain's men."

Important plays published during the year were *1 Henry IV*, *The Blind Beggar of Alexandria*, Samuel Brandon's closet play *The Virtuous Octavia* (which may have had some slight influence on Shakespeare's Roman plays),[125] *Love's Labour's Lost*, *Mucedorus*, *The Famous Victories of Henry V*, and Bernard's translation of six comedies of Terence. *The Merchant of Venice* was entered, but was not published until 1600. The prominence of Shakespeare's work in this list is probably due largely to its popularity, but perhaps somewhat also to its political bearings. Apparently no play published this year was absolutely new; *Mucedorus* may have been the freshest.

At the end of the year the Burbadges were pulling down the old Theatre, now vacant a year or more, to incorporate its materials in the new Globe on the Bankside, across the Thames. An interesting literary event of the Christmas season was the production by the students of St. John's, Cambridge, of *The Pilgrimage to Parnassus*, containing allusions to Spenser, *George a Greene*, the Henry IV plays, the vogue of satire, and the clown Will Kemp and his methods. This alert interest of the St. John's students in literature and the stage was shown also in the two later Parnassus plays, 1599 and 1601 respectively.

At court that season the rival companies stood on even terms for the first time, each with three performances, the Admiral's men on December 27, January 6, and February 18, and the Chamberlain's on December 26, January 1, and February 20. (The fortunes of the Earls of Essex and Southampton stood in much the same state of uneasy balance against

[124] *The Scourge of Villanie*, XI, 37.

[125] For a Hannibal-Essex reference in this play, see Chambers, *Shakespeare*, I, 383. I might add that Essex's friend Peregrine Bertie wrote a curious letter praising the Countess of Cumberland for her "passionate Octavia." (*Hist. MSS. Com.*, R XI–7, p. 82). Did he think the Countess wrote the play?

those of their enemies.) *Much Ado About Nothing* and *Every Man in his Humour* seem very likely to have been given at court this season. The third performance can hardly have been *A Warning for Fair Women* which, after all, seems crude and unsuitable. Perhaps it was a revised version of *Romeo and Juliet*, a repetition of *Henry IV*, or even (by request of the Queen) "Falstaff in Love," for *The Merry Wives of Windsor* may easily have been ready early in 1599.

The Admiral's repertory shows Henslowe's lavish policy since the reorganization, with nearly two score new plays, of which very few are extant and most were probably worthless. The prominence of chronicle plays has already been noted. Probably the company's best productions of the year were Munday's *1 Robin Hood* and Munday's and Chettle's *2 Robin Hood*, now known by their publication titles, as *The Downfall* and *The Death, of Robert Earl of Huntingdon*. Chapman's lost *Fount of New Fashions* may have been enjoyed at court if not too satirical for the more conservative tastes. *Two Angry Women of Abingdon* was available, it seems, for Part Two was ready in February. The early weeks of 1599 do not show anything else very promising for the end of the 1598–99 court season excepting Heywood's *War without Blows and Love without Suit*. The Chamberlain's men must have made the better showing; and indeed a year later, in spite of the disgrace of Essex and his friends, they once more took the lead in court performances, with their three dates to the two of the Admiral's men and the one of Derby's.

CHAPTER IV (1599–1600)

CULMINATION OF THE RIVALRY IN HISTORY PLAYS

Paul's boys and their repertory. *Satire in the drama, 1594–1603.* The 1599 revival of Senecan tragedy. "Henry V." The disgrace of Essex. The Admiral's history plays. "Sir John Oldcastle." *Roman plays, 1594–1603.* Oxford's and Derby's companies. The Christmas season of 1599–1600.

THE most important event of dramatic history in 1599 was the revival of "Paul's Boys" as an organization of players, under their new master, Edward Pearce. They had been dissolved about 1590, probably largely because of the political allegory in Lyly's work for them.[1] Their revival of old romantic plays in a new dress of social and literary satire, and their production of important new work by the prominent young satirist, Marston, injected a serious new element of competition into the situation. Appealing as they did to a fashionable audience, the boy companies in general must have cut more deeply into the receipts of the Chamberlain's men than into those of the Admiral's; and in the culminating plays of the "Poetomachia" a little later the warfare of satire appears more bitter between the Chamberlain's men and the boys. Yet even in 1599 the performances of the boys appear to have reacted on the Admiral's men to stimulate the work of their playwrights, especially Chapman and Dekker; Chettle and Heywood appear more strongly influenced a little later. Paul's boys may also have threatened the pre-eminence of the adult companies at court, although they do not actually appear there until January 1, 1601.

The Wisdom of Doctor Dodipoll, published in 1600 as given by the Children of Paul's, is quite possibly an old romantic play by George Peele, with a new satirical title and a fairly thorough rewriting to bring it up to date. The folk-lore elements are interestingly characteristic of Peele; and Doctor Dodipoll himself, who boasts that he is able to slay and to revive, may be a modernization of the doctor of the mumming plays. The whole plot, as it consists of wandering lovers, madness, potions,

[1] H. N. Hillebrand, *The Child Actors*, 143, says that the offense was given by their mingling in the Marprelate controversy, rather than by their allegorizing the Queen's suitors or foreign politics. Any topical allegory would almost certainly touch on forbidden materials—"affairs of Church and State." But the ridiculing of the Martinists was a Cecil, or at least a Bancroft policy (cf. McKerrow, *Nashe*, v, 44), and Burghley himself advocated in the Star Chamber the exposure of cozening tricks on the stage (Cf. Hawarde, *Cam. Stel.*, 48; 1596, May 12). Probably if Marprelate meddling was the trouble, the child actors had merely gored the wrong ox.

sleep, enchantment, fairies, and a reassignment to proper partners at the end, closely resembles that of *A Midsummer Night's Dream* and that of *Two Angry Women*, but most of all that of *The Old Wives' Tale*. There are also important resemblances to *The Shoemakers' Holiday* by Dekker for the Admiral's men, 1599, in the noble lover's taking on a "mercenary" disguise for his wooing, and the comic use of Teutonic dialect; and resemblances to *Julius Caesar* by Shakespeare for the Chamberlain's men the same year, in the solemn fooling of Alphonsus in putting off by dreams and adverse portents a marriage to which he has no inclination, a burlesque of the first Caesar which closes with a mention of his name,[2] and a little later the well-known quotation, "Then reason's fled to animals I see."[3] In general *Doctor Dodipoll* shows a clever furbishing up of old romantic material to please the fashionable taste, and doubtless the same movement produced Shakespeare's great romantic comedies of about this time. The taste for romance was, of course, perennial; the period just before ours had liked it chivalric and pastoral, and treated rather simply, if often allegorically; the end of the sixteenth century preferred it spiced with social and literary satire; the later revival which produced *Philaster* and *The Winter's Tale* stressed the pastoral once more, but with a marked sensationalism not without traces (especially in Fletcher) of decadent eroticism.

Middleton's *The Old Law, or A New Way to Please You* as we have it has undergone a revision by Rowley and Massinger after our period; but the allusion in the text, "and now 'tis 99,"[4] and several references to plays of about the end of the century, especially, " 'I take thee, Beatrice,' says the bridegroom," indicate that its original version may have been presented in this year, possibly by Paul's boys or by the Chamberlain's men.

But the most important work for Paul's boys in this year of their revival was done by Marston. There is little doubt that it was he who rewrote for them *Histriomastix or The Player Whipt* from some earlier play which may have been written by Peele for performance by amateurs, for the piece is wholly a satire on the adult professional players. In its present form it is a poor hodge-podge interesting only for its satirical material, which seems to be aimed indiscriminately at the adult companies, with gibes at Munday, Jonson, and Shakespeare, and a detailed

[2] Act II, at end, Sgn. D2. [3] Sgn. E.

[4] In his *Tract on the Succession* (p. 104) Harington tells us that in 1598 both universities had public disputations on the proposition, "*Mundus senescit,*" and that their lack of tact was "ill taken." The "Old Law" decrees that all old people shall be put to death, men at 80, women at 60; Queen Elizabeth was well past the limit. Cf. also *Old Fortunatus*, 1599, for references to the world's growing old.

satire on some patched-up company in the provinces. Both this play and *The Old Law* appear to have references to Shakespeare's *Troilus and Cressida;* but as *The Old Law* was not printed until 1656, and *Histriomastix* not until 1610, the evidence for dating *Troilus* so early is not conclusive. The repertory of the players for whom Posthaste (Munday) writes appears to be a satire on the out-of-fashion plays of the Admiral's men, including as it does *The Lascivious Knight, Lady Nature, The Prodigal Child, Mother Gurton's Needle* (a tragedy), *The Devil and Dives* (a comedy), *A Russet Coat and a Knave's Cap* (an Infernal), *A Proud Heart and a Beggar's Purse* (a Pastoral) *The Widow's Apron-Strings* (a Nocturnal), and *Troilus and Cressida.*[5] The play is dated by its clear allusion to the London panic of August 7, 1599, caused by a rumor that the Spaniards had landed:

> *Perpetuana.* O sweet heart the Spaniards are come,
> We shall all be kild they say.

This play's attitude toward the scare is contemptuous and seems to reflect the general feeling that the rumors were worked up by the Cecil faction for their own purposes in Essex's absence. One of the current jests was to say that the "Invisible" Armada was surely coming.

Let us turn now to Marston's *Antonio and Mellida,* in which we see him launching out upon important original work. It is in two parts, of which the second is called *Antonio's Revenge.* Part One is a romantic tragi-comedy of a strongly satirical cast, ending with the sudden conversion of the villain and reconciliation all round; the second part, as if in protest against the sentimentality of that sort of ending, opens with the villain gloating over his feigned conversion and well in the midst of fresh plots which go on through ghastly horrors to a highly Senecan conclusion. The plays, as is usual with the productions of the boy companies, owe much to older plays which were the property of the adult companies; here the chief indebtedness appears to be to *Romeo and Juliet,* the old *Hamlet, The Spanish Tragedy, Titus Andronicus, Much Ado,* and *The Merchant of Venice.* There may be burlesque on *Love's Labour's Lost* in giving the name of Rossaline to a character who here is "everybody's mistress."

Yet in spite of its dependence upon other work, *Antonio and Mellida* has a manner all its own and an important position in the history of dramatic satire. To distinguish this original quality, we must go back and sketch, in the limited space we can give ourselves here, the development of satire in the plays of our period.

[5] Chettle and Dekker were writing a play with this title for Henslowe in April, 1599.

Satire in the Drama, 1594–1603

The earliest types of satire we have observed were two: the social-economic type in such plays as *The Cobbler's Prophecy*, *A Knack to Know a Knave*, and probably *Cloth Breeches and Velvet Hose;* and the religious-ethical in *The Seven Deadly Sins*, *A Looking Glass for London*, and probably *Seven Days of the Week*. Both these types were old-fashioned and bourgeois, better suited to the Admiral's repertories of our period than to the Chamberlain's.

Political satire came next into prominence; in our discussion of the chronicle plays we have seen how the Chamberlain's company affected incidentally an aristocratic and genealogical method of personal-political satire in their great series of histories culminating in 1599 in Shakespeare's *Henry V;* at the same time the Admiral's playwrights, while engaging the rival company to some extent on the same ground, appear to have ventured on several more obviously and offensively personal political satires which were suppressed after one performance—of these we have already noticed *The Mack*, *Paradox*, and *The Tinker of Totnes*. The affair of *The Isle of Dogs* which wrecked Pembroke's men was still more serious, and perhaps gave the Admiral's men a salutary fright.

The next type to come into vogue on the stage was social satire on manners, in the "humour" comedies of Chapman, followed by those of Jonson and later Marston. Although "humours" could be used for personal lampooning, they were allied to the earlier abstract figures in the history of satire, being naturally types rather than individuals; it is probably for this reason that the participation of the Chamberlain's men in this field of comedy is mainly represented by the plays of Jonson, only very slightly by those of Shakespeare; although of course he has in such comedies as *Love's Labour's Lost*, *As You Like It*, and *Twelfth Night* plenty of characters who are "humourous" by Elizabethan definitions. The general tone of this type of satire is that of the comedy of manners—light and frivolous rather than serious and bitter. Good examples of this sort of satire are: Chapman's *A Humourous Day's Mirth*, Admiral's, 1597; Jonson's *Every Man in his Humour*, Chamberlain's, 1598; and Marston's *Jack Drum's Entertainment*, Paul's, probably about May, 1600.

But a new satirical element, developed in non-dramatic writing, was injected at about this time into the drama, and was very important in the plays concerned in the so-called "War of the Theatres" or "Poetomachia," with their curious combination (seen in *Satiromastix* or *The Poetaster*, for example) of personal, literary, social, and ethical satire. The new element, it seems to me, was classical, cynical satire, and may, indeed, have appeared on the stage of our period as early as 1597, if the

Admiral's *Five Plays in One* consisted of some of Heywood's Lucianic adaptations.[6] But non-dramatic satire was developing in several types. That of the Nashe-Harvey controversy was medieval and closely related to the Scottish "flytings"; that of Sir John Harington was more specifically classifiable as Rabelaisian. Hall, in his *Vergidemiarum Libri*, 1597 and 1598, and Marston in his *Scourge of Villanie*, 1598, modelled their more bitter, less humorous satire on Juvenal and Martial; and the satire of the end of the century, on stage and off, was fond of Lucian and his misanthrope Timon, and of Diogenes the original cynic, snarling in his tub—now less amiably than in Lyly's *Campaspe*. The philosophy, indeed, of these satirists was cynicism, the language of their fools and madmen railing, the mood of their heroes melancholy. A morbid interest in vice and perversion permeates the writing of this type and time. We may typify the satire of the plays at about the period of the "Poetomachia," say 1599–1602, by saying that when personal it was literary (and based somewhat on Horace as well as the other writers named), when it was social it was "humourous" and dealt with manners, and when it was ethical it was cynical.[7]

The part played by Diogenes and Timon in the Elizabethan drama deserves a separate study. Marston's connection with the newly revived boy company would naturally have led him to make a careful study of the work of Lyly, and incidentally therefore of *Campaspe*. The anonymous, probably academic *Timon* which dates about 1600 has interesting parallels with *Cynthia's Revels* and *The Poetaster*, about 1601; but also with *The Wounds of Civil War*, published 1594, and of course with *Timon of Athens*, on which Shakespeare appears to have worked about 1607. There are important traces of early pre-Shakespearean work in *Timon of Athens;* but they belong to a different play from the academic *Timon*. It would not be at all surprising if the Chamberlain's men had had a version of the story (in which Apemantus is of course modelled on Diogenes), before 1597; and its misanthropy would well suit a revival at any time between the disgrace of Essex and Southampton in 1599 and the end of the reign.[8] The unfinished preparations for revival about 1607 would be due to the renewed vogue of cynical satire at that time which was suddenly brought to an end by the new pastoral romance.

Satire had a pronounced vogue at the end of Elizabeth's reign. In

[6] Among the pieces in his *Pleasant Dialogues* are some dozen from Lucian, including "Misanthropos," "Mausolus and Diogenes," "Diogenes and Crates."

[7] A non-dramatic publication of 1599 has a very characteristic title, *Micro-cynicon, Six Snarling Satyrs*, by T. M.

[8] For the play's Essexian interests see Dixon Wecter, "The Purpose of *Timon of Athens*," *PMLA*, XLIII, 706 ff.

1601 Marston was able to say in *What You Will*, "What's out of railing's out of fashion."[9] And satire remained in considerable favor until long after our period; perhaps the chief change to be perceived is a tendency about 1603, in Marston's *The Dutch Courtesan*, for cynicism to grow somewhat less aristocratic and classical, more democratic and realistic.

The attitude of Shakespeare's plays toward this type of satire was one of intense dislike, at least at first. Certainly Jaques in *As You Like It* is a cynic of the Marston type, and is rather harshly characterized:

> *Jaques.* Invest me in my motley; give me leave
> To speak my mind, and I will through and through
> Cleanse the foul body of th' infected world,
> If they will patiently receive my medicine.
> *Duke Senior.* Fie on thee! I can tell what thou wouldst do.
> *Jaq.* What, for a counter, would I do, but good?
> *Duke S.* Most mischievous foul sin, in chiding sin:
> For thou thyself hast been a libertine,
> As sensual as the brutish sting itself;
> And all the embossed sores and headed evils
> That thou with license of free foot has caught
> Wouldst thou disgorge into the general world.[10]

And Thersites in *Troilus and Cressida* may quite conceivably be a caricature of Marston himself. But the increasingly gloomy situation in politics and the drama, as well as the pressure caused by the type's popularity, soon had its influence on even Shakespeare.

The Admiral's men do not seem to have been able to keep up with this fashion of cynical satire; at least we have no extant play of theirs for this period which markedly belongs to the type. Perhaps the company had no good "railing fool" among its actors. Neither Jonson nor Chapman, moreover (both were especially able in this new type of composition), seems to have been available among their playwrights, although the former does appear briefly among Henslowe's records in 1601–02. It may be, as I have previously suggested, that the series of plays on Biblical subjects presented by the company in 1600–02: *Judas*, *Pontius Pilate*, *Jepthah*, *Tobyas*, *Samson*, *Joshua*, was their characteristic way of taking advantage of the current vogue of satire—by harking back to the religious-ethical type and justifying their scurrilities to their relatively unsophisticated audience by uttering them as jeremiads.

As *Antonio and Mellida* is important in the realm of satire, so does its sequel, *Antonio's Revenge*, take a prominent place in that of tragedy—not as a great play, to be sure, although it is a highly interesting one, but as a bold and successful experiment.

[9] II, i, 184. [10] II, vii, 58–69.

The year 1595, with the publication of *Locrine* and *The True Tragedy of Richard Duke of York* and probably the writing of Shakespeare's *King John* and the university play *Caesar's Revenge*, seemed to mark the dwindled and mollified end of the long vogue of the Senecan tragedy of horrors. The following year was altogether uneventful in that type of drama. But 1597, with its perturbed atmosphere and its upsetting of dramatic policies, produced a renewed activity in the type. *Richard III* and *Romeo and Juliet* (the latter is Senecan in the revenge spirit and the horrors of the tomb) were published; *The Spanish Tragedy*, *Faustus*, and probably *The Massacre at Paris* were revived; and the Admiral's *Hengist* and *Branholt* were probably new examples of somewhat Senecan tragedy. The year 1598 produced, apparently, renewed revivals of *The Spanish Tragedy* and *The Massacre at Paris*, and a revival of *The Battle of Alcazar;* while *James IV* and *Mucedorus*, both of which have certain Senecan elements, were published, and the new plays, *The Downfall of Robert Earl of Huntingdon*, with its scene of Lady Bruce starved to death after trying to feed her son on her own flesh, and *A Warning for Fair Women* were produced by the Admiral's and the Chamberlain's men respectively,[11] the latter bringing after it the whole train of domestic crime plays, which naturally would employ the Senecan method for sensational and tragic effect, as we actually see in the extant Merry-Beech portion of *Two Lamentable Tragedies*, where the murderer dismembers his victim on the stage. The last-named play was published in 1599, as were also *The Spanish Tragedy*, *Soliman and Perseda*, and *Alphonsus*, *King of Arragon*, all three probably old plays belonging to the Admiral's men. A new play with some small Senecan element at about this time was Lodge's (?) *Alarum for London*, given by the Chamberlain's men. But the important event of the year was Marston's *Antonio's Revenge*, produced by Paul's boys with the whole Senecan paraphernalia of ghosts, revenge, and bloody horror. Its production proves that there was still much life in the type of play defined by *The Spanish Tragedy* and carried in *Titus Andronicus* to an extreme almost equalled by Marston's effort, with its murdered man hanging outside a bride's chamber window, its poisonings, its betrayal of an accomplice as Pedringano is betrayed in *The Spanish Tragedy*, and its gory murder, in a church, amid the groans of ghosts above and beneath, of a little boy, whose flesh is then fed to his own father, the tyrant, who in turn is then trapped in a masque-device and assassinated. The whole is a bloody farrago not without tragic power, which apparently seemed as piquant to the Eliza-

[11] The lost *Madmen's Morris* written for Henslowe in July by Dekker, Drayton, and Wilson reminds us of an element of Senecan horror later adapted to fine tragedy in *The Changeling* and *The Duchess of Malfi*, to say nothing of the great storm scene in *King Lear*.

bethans as it would seem in ghastly bad taste to us when acted by the boys, some of them not over ten years old. Here also Marston introduced an air of sophistication from his satirical writings and combined, perhaps for the first time (for we do not know exactly what the mood was in Kyd's *Hamlet*) the part of the Senecan avenger with an ironical and cynical feigned madness, all this in an Italian setting which must have helped to keep the play from appearing as old-fashioned as it really was in fundamental type.

The success of Marston's play brought about, I believe, an immediate refurbishing and revival of *Titus Andronicus*, which was published in the following year with additions. It was also responsible, I have little doubt, for the interesting Senecan elements in *Julius Caesar* (written in 1599): the gaping wounds, the hands dipped in the victim's gore, the meteors, the opening graves, Caesar's revengeful ghost.

The following year, 1600, probably saw besides the quarto of *Titus Andronicus* the writing of *Charlemagne*, which may have been the Chamberlain's, of Fulke Greville's closet tragedy *Alaham*, and of the Admiral's *Spanish Moor's Tragedy*, which may be the very Marlovian *Lust's Dominion*. In 1601 the Admiral's men had revivals of *The Jew of Malta*, *The Spanish Tragedy* (with additions by Jonson), and probably of *The Massacre at Paris*. *Faustus* was entered but was withheld from publication, and *Two Lamentable Tragedies* published. The Chamberlain's *Thomas Lord Cromwell*, in all likelihood produced this year, has few or no Senecan elements; but this is one of the most favored dates for Shakespeare's rewriting of Kyd's *Hamlet*,[12] long the company's valued property, and doubtless especially prized for its direct rivalry to the same writer's *Spanish Tragedy*, so persistently revived through our period by the rival company.

In 1602 the Admiral's men, it is generally agreed, produced Chettle's *Hoffman* with its skeleton and red-hot iron crown, a good example of the Senecan type as revived by Marston; and we might go on to the tragedies of Chapman, Tourneur, and Webster to show how well Marston had recognized the affinity between the growing Elizabethan mood of cynical melancholy and the Senecan dramatic accessories. But we have seen clearly enough how *Antonio's Revenge* was of central importance

[12] On the relation of *Hamlet* to Marston's work see E. E. Stoll, "Marston and the 'Malcontent' Type," *Mod. Phil.*, III, 281 ff. The analysis of the type is most interesting, and hints, I think, at Shakespeare's politics, in which his interests were long with the opposition or malcontent party. Even as late as 1616, in *S. P. Venetian*, Southampton is mentioned as "head of the Malcontents." But it seems to me that Kyd's *Hamlet*, Chapman's *Humourous Day's Mirth* (the character Dowsecer), and Marston's *Antonio's Revenge* are sufficient to explain the traits of Shakespeare's Hamlet without dating Marston's *Malcontent* as early as Professor Stoll does.

in the revival which proved the perennial vitality of Senecan tragedy and probably was responsible for Shakespeare's rewriting of *Hamlet* and his following that success with the other great tragedies.

Now let us take up the theatrical events of 1599. Before September, perhaps as early as April, the Chamberlain's men opened their new theater, the Globe, on the Bankside, some think with a splendid production of *Henry V*. The new site was leased February 21. One moiety of interest in the new building was retained by Richard Burbadge and his brother Cuthbert, the other assigned to Shakespeare, Pope, Phillips, Heminges, and Kemp.[13] For the actors thus to share in the ownership of their playhouse was not according to the Henslowe policy. Soon after, Kemp made over his share to the other four players, and presumably now quitted the company, after playing Peter (as we know from a stage direction) in the revised *Romeo and Juliet* which was printed in 1599. His place seems to have been taken immediately by Robert Armin, formerly of Lord Chandos' men.[14] For playing the new type of fool Armin was much better suited than Kemp, as Baldwin makes admirably clear in his *Organization and Personnel of the Shakespearean Company*. Armin's place of playing before coming to the Globe and the dating of his *Two Maids of Moreclacke* are discussed by Baldwin in an article in *Modern Language Notes*.[15] Since in his *Fool upon Fool or Six Sorts of Sots*, 1600, Armin calls himself "Clonnico del Curtanio," he appears to have played with the Chamberlain's men before they moved to the Globe. Possibly a reason for Kemp's leaving[16] was jealousy caused by the popularity of the new type of clowning. Compare Peter and Touchstone, for instance, to appreciate the difference. Kemp's type is shown by Shakespeare's derogatory remarks in *Hamlet* to have been definitely out of the fashion by 1601.[17]

The foreign visitor Thomas Platter saw *Julius Caesar* at the Globe on September 21; and the Globe is named in the Epilogue of *Every Man Out*.

Fifteen ninety-nine was the culminating year of the chronicle-play rivalry. It saw the first production of Shakespeare's great patriotic historical drama *Henry V*, and almost certainly its fitting into a series of

[13] Chambers, II, 203.

[14] Grey Brydges, later fifth Lord Chandos, was imprisoned for being in the Essex rising. His father William visited Essex House on the fatal morning, but was not thought enough implicated to prevent his sitting on the trial commission. Elizabeth Brydges, Grey's cousin, who was a succession claimant, was beaten by the Queen for an affair with Essex. The seat of the Lords Chandos was at Sudeley Castle, Gloucestershire.

[15] XXXIX, 447.

[16] He appears to have gone to the Curtain for a while; see his biography in Chambers, II. His morris dance to Norwich was in the spring of 1600.

[17] III, ii, retaining the Quarto material omitted from the Folio.—"And let those that play your clowns speak no more than is set down for them; . . . Masters! tell him of it."

productions which involved the revision of the endings of *Richard II* and *2 Henry IV* to make the mighty cycle smoothly complete, from the banishment of Bolingbroke by the second Richard to the third Richard's downfall at Bosworth Field.

I have been tracing the rivalry in the writing and production of historical plays from *King John* through the Falstaff-Cobham incidents to its culmination in Shakespeare's *Henry V*. Nowhere, I believe, does Shakespeare show partisanship more clearly than in his version of the Battle of Agincourt, shown by the words of the Chorus preceding Act Five to have been on the boards during Essex's absence in Ireland. He had set out thither on March 27 with a fine force amid great acclamations. With him went Southampton, although Elizabeth, still piqued about his marriage, would not let Essex make him General of the Horse. John Harington was on the expedition and was knighted by Essex on July 30.[18] Rutland slipped away to join but was called back by the Queen. On April 19 Sir John Holles wrote to Lord Sheffield:

> I never saw the Court at so low an ebb as it is presently, for if the gentleman ushers should not let in a flood of serving men the channel would be empty notwithstanding the holidays which in times past have been accounted the high spring tides, and therefore, if ever you purpose your being there, a privater time you can never choose, none in effect but the withered leaves hanging upon the tree, the beautiful, attractive Spring being as it were 'racte' over into Ireland, greyheads and gravity only left, which countenance I am sure is more acceptable to your lordship, rather confirming a man in his solitariness than inciting to the vanity of action.[19]

The poetry of martial glory surely has few words as stirring as those of Shakespeare's hero-king before the fight:

> Then shall our names,
> Familiar in his mouth as household words,
> Harry the King, Bedford, and Exeter,
> Warwick and Talbot, Salisbury and Gloucester,
> Be in their flowing cups freshly remember'd.
> This story shall the good man teach his son;
> And Crispin Crispian shall ne'er go by,
> From this day to the ending of the world,
> But we in it shall be remembered;
> We few, we happy few, we band of brothers . . .[20]

It was a splendid thing to be able to boast an ancestor who had fought at Agincourt or to hold a title which had been carried to victory on that field. But it was fortunate for many such descendants that Shakespeare's play was not the only authority upon the Agincourt honor roll.

[18] Cf. N. E. McClure, *Letters and Epigrams of Sir John Harington*, 21.

[19] *Portland MSS.*, IX, 71.

[20] *Henry V*, IV, iii.

Of course the dramatist could not conveniently name all the men of note who were present; but a study of his selections and omissions discloses a partisanship more creditable to Shakespeare's loyalty to his friends than to his disinterested patriotism. Such a study involves comparing the lists of the heroes of Agincourt furnished by Holinshed, by the anonymous writer of *The Famous Victories of Henry V*, and by Shakespeare:

HISTORICAL CHARACTERS AT AGINCOURT

Holinshed	*Famous Victories*	*Henry V* (Folio)
King	King	King
York	York	York
Beaumont	. . .	. . .
Willoughby	Willoughby	. . .
Fanhope	. . .	. . .
Gloucester	Gloucester	Gloucester
Marshall	. . .	. . .
Oxford	Oxford	. . .
Suffolk	. . .	Suffolk
Exeter	. . .	Exeter
Erpingham	. . .	Erpingham
Kikelie	. . .	Ketley
Gam	. . .	Gam
. . .	Clarence	. . .
. . .	Bedford	Bedford
. . .	Northumberland	. . .
. . .	Derby	. . .
. . .	Kent	. . .
. . .	Nottingham	. . .
. . .	Huntingdon	. . .
. . .	. . .	Salisbury
. . .	. . .	Westmorland
. . .	. . .	Warwick
. . .	. . .	Talbot

As I have pointed out elsewhere,[21] we have the unknown author of *The Famous Victories* making numerous changes in Holinshed's account of Agincourt for no apparent literary or dramatic reason, but for numerous reasons connected with Cecil politics; and Shakespeare following in his turn with even more elaborate changes, also to be explained only by factional politics, this time on the Essex side. But if Shakespeare's handling of the battle of Agincourt shows partisanship, as I believe it does, it should be remembered in his favor that probably in his own eyes he was on the side of true patriotism with a liberal opposition party

[21] R. B. Sharpe, "We Band of Brothers"; *Studies in Philology*, April, 1929. The article needs, however, numerous corrections and amplifications which cannot receive space here.

that aimed at enlightenment and domestic peace through toleration,[22] at ridding the Queen of evil counselors, and at active, glorious war against England's still-dreaded enemy, Spain.

Yet Shakespeare's own personal politics may still be considered as mysterious as ever. He was too universal a man to be narrowly confined to the notions of one party, too conservative a man to go all the way with Southampton's radical young associates. One cannot help feeling that as an individual and as a poet he cared very little indeed what noble names he sounded in his roll call of Agincourt, so long as they sounded well. As a friend of Southampton, however, and a member of a company which was catering to the Essex faction, he had these matters forced upon his attention, and he handled them with characteristic efficiency; that was probably about all: and how far he really approved of King Henry the Fifth, and how far of Essex, are not problems to be settled by the discovery of political reasons underlying his choice of certain families for Agincourt honors.

Even while *Henry V* was being played at the Globe, Essex in Ireland was struggling on to foredoomed failure. His policies were fatally hampered by conflicting advice from London and from the Council in Ireland; Tyrone appeared sincerely anxious for peace if it could be had with toleration and partial independence, and these desires had the sympathy of the Essex party. Essex's enemies at court, on the other hand, managed to keep Elizabeth insistent upon the invasion of Ulster and the absolute crushing of Tyrone's rebellion. The Earl finally rode with inferior forces to the border of Ulster and conferred with Tyrone at a ford, arranging an armistice and agreeing to carry the Irish peace proposals to the Queen. Southampton was on guard to keep all others beyond hearing distance, but two treacherous Essexians managed to eavesdrop. Their reports to Cecil did Essex great damage.[23] Soon after, with Sir John Harington and two or three others, Essex returned hastily and secretly to court, and forced his way into the Queen's presence to put his affairs once more upon a personal basis with her, instead of having them seen by her as distorted by his jealous enemies. But things had gone too far. The Queen had been frightened by his enemies' whisperings about her favorite's ambition and their identification of her with Richard II, not only in Shakespeare's play, but also in Hayward's *History of the Reign of Henry IV*, dedicated to Essex in flattering terms, which had disturbed her at Easter time. Essex arrived at Greenwich in the morning, September 28. That evening he was ordered confined to his chamber; next day he was called before the Council, and on October 1 he was committed

[22] King Henry says, "Every subject's duty is the king's, but every subject's soul is his own."

[23] Cf. *Sal. MSS.*, IX, 375, 384.

to the custody of Lord Keeper Egerton at York House. His friends proposed to free him by force of arms, but he forbade them.[24] In order to prevent any public demonstration in his favor there emanated from the Star Chamber in November a defense of the Earl's imprisonment. Lord Treasurer Sackville, Chief Justice Popham, and Secretary Cecil vindicated the Queen in her attitude; and much was said against the currency of "libels" (lampoons) on Essex's enemies. Meanwhile Tyrone grew restive under the loss of Essex's aid[25] and broke the truce on Christmas day; his rebellion was not put down until the Queen's last days. There was much sympathy for Essex among the people and clergy of London, causing the Council a good deal of worry.[26]

Since in such circumstances they cannot well have helped touching at least somewhat on politics, the lost chronicle plays recorded by Henslowe in 1599 call for a few comments:[27]

1. *William Longbeard*, by Drayton, was evidently based on a historical pamphlet published by Lodge in 1593, *The Life and Death of william Long beard, the most famous and witty English Traitor, borne in the Citty of London.* Longbeard, who lived in the reign of Henry II, was an ingratiating villain, who led an array of "mechanicall rebels" against the forces of law and order, but was at length taken and executed. One would think that this material would make a play at least as obnoxious to the licensing authority as *Sir Thomas More;* yet possibly it was winked at because treated as sheer anti-Essex propaganda. But it is not certain that the play was ever allowed to be produced.

2. *The Spensers*, by Chettle and Porter, which certainly was staged, probably dealt with the days of Edward II and the great family of Despensers, ancestors of the Admiral on his mother's side. In this connection there is a family legend, worth repeating for the points on which it touches the materials of drama, that Owen Glendower took refuge, disguised, at Coity Castle, Glamorganshire, then held by his enemy Sir Laurence Berkrolles, who was so amazed when his guest revealed his identity that he was struck dumb for the remainder of his life—which was not long, for his wife, a Despenser, murdered him and for the crime suffered burial alive. There is small likelihood that this series of events was in the Admiral's play, since their patron's mother was a Gamage, of the family to which Coity had come by descent.

3. Wilson's *2 Henry Richmond*, which evidently dealt with matters in the reigns of Edward IV and Richard III not developed in any of the numerous other plays on that period, is of interest chiefly for the lack

[24] Cadwallader, 62 (Camden, *Elizabeth*, ed. 1629, 247).

[25] Cadwallader, 65. [26] *Ibid.*, 66.

[27] We have already considered *Brute Greenshield, Bear a Brain*, and *Robert II.*

of any trace of the play's first part. Of course the first Tudor's claim to the crown provided interesting as well as somewhat ticklish material.

This was the year of the appearance of *Sir John Oldcastle*, in two parts of which only the first is extant, cobbled together by Dekker, Hathaway, Munday, and Wilson to vindicate the memory of Cobham's sainted ancestor. The first performance of Part One was early in November (Part Two, lost, by the same authors, was ready in March, 1600).

> It is no pamper'd glutton we present,
> Nor aged Counsellor to youthful sinne,

says the Prologue. The title of the Quarto, promptly brought out the following year, is *The True and Honorable Historie of the Life of Sir John Oldcastle, the Good Lord Cobham*. In the play itself resemblances to Shakespeare's Falstaff plays have been noticed, but many of them can be explained as imitations of the Admiral's own *Longshanks*, or *Edward I*.

Cobham's habitual bounty to the beggars at his gates is carefully brought out. It was a virtue especially fostered by Elizabethan administrators because it helped to take care of the problem of destitution; and the nobility and gentry were therefore urged to live at home to support their tenants and the poor of the neighborhood by household employment and charity. Cobham, with his chief estates nearby in Kent, could conveniently make a virtue of retiring thither often when things went ill at court; and there may be here implied some condemnation of Essex, whose large holdings in Staffordshire, Herefordshire, and Pembrokeshire were so inaccessible that he could not afford to leave the center of affairs to live upon them. He sometimes threatened to do so, but the Queen usually gave in, or else a military expedition took him abroad. When *Oldcastle* was played he was under restraint and would not have been allowed to go to Chartley or Lanfey if he had wished, partly because the Cecils feared his influence over large and important groups in those parts. Barn Elms, on the Surrey side near Putney, was his mother-in-law Walsingham's; and he had sold Wansted, just over the Essex boundary, to Mountjoy in March,[28] doubtless to raise the money to fit out for Ireland.

The play opens with a scuffle in the streets of Hereford at assize time. Powys has quarreled with Herbert over religion, the former being a Wycliffite and a sympathizer with Sir John Oldcastle. In treating Oldcastle as a Protestant martyr, the Admiral's men had to go counter to current Elizabethan Catholic propaganda, which asserted that he had suffered as a rebel for treason against the crown. Their natural sources were the chief writings on Oldcastle's side of the controversy, those of Foxe (in his *Acts and Monuments*, commonly known as *The Book of Martyrs*), and those of John Bale, of which Foxe made use. Now in Bale[29]

[28] Cf. Chamberlain, March 15, 1599.

[29] John Bale, *Syr Johan Oldecastel*.

Oldcastle's great enemy is Thomas Arundell, Archbishop of Canterbury. Why did the Admiral's dramatists substitute the Bishop of Rochester? Probably John Whitgift, the contemporary Archbishop, a stern man to the Puritans and considered on the whole rather friendly toward Essex, was nevertheless too powerful and dangerous to attack. Queen Elizabeth called him her "little black husband" and treated him as her confessor. His power, through the Bishop of London, over the censorship of printed work, was almost complete. The Bishop of London, too, rather prominent in Bale among the persecutors, was now Richard Bancroft, who owed much to Cecil and was well disposed to repay. Moreover Munday, as an aid to Topcliffe in the persecuting of recusants, was dependent upon Bancroft. Hence the playwrights chose instead as their villain John Young, Bishop of Rochester, who in 1594 had refused the see of Norwich on the ground that Bishop Scambler had spoiled its possessions (he is said to have granted many of them to William Cecil, Lord Burghley).[30]

Some of the other characters may have had contemporary significance. Harpoole, Cobham's faithful steward, had a namesake, William Harpoole, Esquire, Constable of Carlo Castle in Ireland, who in 1601 was informing against the Essexian activities of the "Earl of Wormewood"[31]—he means Ormond. Clun, the sneaking Summoner whom Harpoole forces to eat his summons, bears the name of a lordship[32] in Shropshire, on the Welsh border, long associated with the earldom of Arundel, which in Shakespeare's time had been forfeited for treason by the Catholic branch of the Howards. Clun itself seems to have been at this time in the hands of either Lord Henry Howard, a secret Catholic and a probably treacherous Essexian, or still another relative of the Admiral, Lord Howard de Walden, also a Catholic. Can it be that the Admiral, like Cobham, was striving against the known facts of recusancy in his own house, to assert his Protestant sentiments? Such a move was especially desirable politically in the latter half of 1599, when Essex was under fire for favoring Tyrone's demand for toleration. Another protestation of loyalty may be read in the Duke of Suffolk's part here as an ally of Rochester. The Earl of Huntingdon is given a simply loyal rôle. As for the disreputable priest Sir John of Wrotham, the Byngs of that Kentish place had certain family connections (especially to Davison) which may have made them offensive to the Cecils.

The play is at least as interesting topographically as biographically. Like *Henry IV* it has its scenes on the road to Rochester, Canterbury,

[30] We know Young also a patron of Edmund Spenser, whose enmity to Burghley was far from a secret. See A. F. Pollard, "John Young," *D.N.B.* [31] Spedding, *Bacon*, II, 326.

[32] But cf. *Sal. MSS.*, VII, 174.—April 26, 1597, memorandum of the receipt by Edward Clunne of £40 from Henry Brooke, Lo. Cobham.

and Dover followed by scenes on the Northwest Road which Falstaff took to Daventry and Shrewsbury, and Essex to his house at Chartley in Staffordshire or to Ireland by way of Chester and Beaumaris. The Kentish "parsonages" of the robber priest are Barham Down, Chobham Down, Gads Hill, Wrotham Hill, Blackheath, Cocks Heath, and Birchen Wood. Numerous suburbs of London are mentioned, especially Greenwich, where the Queen had one of her favorite palaces. King Henry's easy democracy is stressed where he calls himself "Keeper of Eltham," an honor which went to Cobham in 1594. Being robbed by Wrotham on Blackheath, he asks, "Where the diuel are all my old theeues, that were wont to keepe this walke? Falstaffe the villaine is so fat, he cannot get on's horse, but me thinkes Poines and Peto should be stirring here abouts"; and Wrotham replies that Prince Hal "once robde me before I fell to the trade my selfe, when that foule villainous guts, that led him to all that rogery, was in's company there, that Falstaffe."[33]

At the Bell at St. Albans, on the Northwest Road, we have a calling for the hostler in the darkness before dawn, just as in *Henry IV*, with "A pox of this pigstie at the house end, it fills all the house full of fleas." The Lancashire dialect hereabouts may be done by Munday. The carrier Club complains that his horse, old Dicke Dun, "has bin moyred in a slough in Brick hil-lane." This must have happened within a stone's throw of Little Brickhill, a few miles beyond Dunstable, one of the chief manors of the Chamberlain, whose duties at court doubtless kept him from being a "housekeeper" up to the Cobham standard.

Murley the Dunstable brewer provides good sport, particularly for an audience which at *Belin Dun* had learned all about the founding of his town:

Mur. We come to fight for our conscience, and for honor, little know you what is in my bosome, looke here madde knaues, a pair of gilt spurres.

Tom. A pair of golden spurres? Why do you not put them on your heeles? Your bosome's no place for spurres.

Mur. Bee't more or lesse vpon occasion, Lord haue mercy on vs, Tom th'art a foole, and thou speakest treason to knighthood dare any weare golden or siluer spurs til he be a knight? no, I shall be knighted to morrow, and then they shall on: sirs, was it euer read in the church book of Dunstable, that euer mault man was made knight?

Here we see the Admiral's playwrights taking full advantage of Murley's story to poke fun at Essex's swarm of new-made knights, whose creation constituted one of the charges against his Irish administration, and whose knighthoods were in grave danger of shameful revocation by the Queen.

It seems to have been intended in the Second Part to transfer much of the action to those Welsh border regions with which Oldcastle legends

[33] Sgn. F 2.

were connected. The historical Oldcastle had been in charge there of the castles of Buelt, Kedwelly, Hay, and Dinas; and a portion of his family estate at Almeley, Herefordshire (very near Weobley, which belonged to Essex) was called "Oldcastle," perhaps because of some ruins there.[34] Saxton's map of Herefordshire shows no Oldcastle at Almeley, but an "old Towne" which his map of Monmouthshire calls "The old cast." a considerable distance to the south, and very near the Monmouthshire border and Allt-yr-yrnys, the place claimed by the Cecils as the home of their ancestors, where they were still actively interesting themselves in the affairs of certain Cecils who, because of their family's antiquity, found themselves unusually well situated for poor relations.[35] Paul de la Hay writes to Cecil on April 9, 1601, from "this your house" of "Alterenes," and on March 14 mentions a locality "betwixt Old Castle and Walterston," while informing against some local adherents of Essex.[36] It is amusing that the map shows a place called "The old court-Dowlas"[37] in the immediate neighborhood. We may have had, then, in the lost second part of *Oldcastle*, a connecting of Sir John Oldcastle, Lord Cobham, with the Cecils of Allt-yr-yrnys on the Monnow which would remind the Admiral's audience agreeably that Sir Robert Cecil, Principal Secretary, and Lord Cobham, Warden of the Cinque Ports (and prospective son-in-law of the Admiral) were brothers-in-law.

Turning from Essex's enemies, such as Cobham and the Admiral, to his sympathizers, we find the latter under great disadvantages. With Essex under arrest (and desperately ill in December), his enemies had practically a free field through the late autumn, deterred from going to whatever length they might please only by their fear of arousing too far the popular sentiment for him and against his opponents or of causing a revulsion of feeling in the Queen. If any sympathy for Essex was expressed in Shakespeare's *Julius Caesar*, which as we have seen was being played by the Chamberlain's men in September, it would have to be very closely veiled. We may guess that Cicero represented one of the elder members of the Cecil party from the fact that the Admiral's men the year before had staged *Catiline's Conspiracy*, by Chettle and Wilson, which must have given a favorable view of Cicero, since Cecil's partisans liked to call Essex "Catiline." The Elizabethan Sir Julius Caesar, a Master of the Court of Requests (for which he stood up against the Common Pleas, dedicating a little volume of his arguments to Burghley in 1596), although somewhat Cecilian was apparently not an important

[34] C. J. Robinson, *The Castles of Herefordshire*, 3.

[35] Cf. *Sal. MSS.*, VII, 250 and *passim*.

[36] *Sal. MSS.*, XI, 162, 123.

[37] Falstaff, "Dowles, filthy dowlas!" *1 Henry IV*, III, iii.

member of the faction.[38] Caesar's "Come on my right hand, for this ear is deaf"[39] reads amusingly enough with L'Estrange's anecdote of the Elizabethan judge:

> Sir Julius Caesar, Master of the Rolls, was reported none of the deepest men and had many slye jerks passed upon him; amongst others, he was once hearing of a cause somewhat too intricate for his capacitie, and his judgment beganne to incline the wrong way. The Court at that time being very lowde and clamorous, one of Councell to the adverse part steps up and calls out, 'Silence there my masters: yee keepe such a bawling the Master of the Rolls cannot understand a word that is spoken.[40]

Sir William Cornwallis, of whose connection with the drama I shall speak in my next chapter, seems, in spite of Cecil connections, to have preferred Shakespeare's version of the story; for in his essay "Of Traps for Fame" (1610) he is contemptuous of Cicero and his sort of "more witty cowards, of a higher reach and more profit"; while in "Of Life, and the Fashions of Life" (1601) he says: "The next division . . . is to advise and execute: my knowledge of these is by reading, not by experience, yet did I once touch [at Cadiz?] at the baye of Armes, but so short was my stay, that I trust more to my reading than to my experience." But he delights in reading of Caesar until shaken "out of my dreame with comming to, *Et tu Brute*." That he had seen Roman plays acted we may judge from "The Instruments of a Statesman" (1610), where he describes a Plautine comedy but considers even more instructive "the Tragicall matters of Princes, where the play is more deepe, and more earnest." The power of representation over the emotions, he says, is mighty; the action of Scaevola thrusting his hand into the brazier, "performed . . . lookes not madly, but beautifully."

Perhaps a careful study of *Julius Caesar* would show partisanship cogently; but one great difficulty in identifying the characters with contemporaries is that Shakespeare's sympathies here are unusually uncertain and seem to waver from Brutus back to Caesar after the latter's death. The clue to the general Elizabethan interpretation of the play may lie in Cornwallis's sympathy for Caesar as a man of action who nevertheless deserved death for his imperial ambition. If so, the play served as a warning to both factions not to carry matters to a pass which might well be utterly fatal to the players' fortunes.

[38] He had some association with the Admiral, being a judge of the Admiralty and M.P. for Reigate and Windsor, both places in which the Admiral was very influential. His father Cesare Adelmare, physician, was a graduate of Padua.

[39] *Julius Caesar* I, ii, 212.

[40] Sir Nicholas L'Estrange, *Anecdotes and Traditions;* Camden Society, 1839, 23.

Roman Plays, 1594–1603

A summary of the Roman plays of our period shows considerable activity, yet little of that activity in Shakespeare's company. Several of the Garnierites' closet plays found publication during these years: Kyd's *Cornelia*, in 1594 and 1595, Daniel's *Cleopatra* in 1594 and 1598 (Brandon's *Virtuous Octavia* was registered in 1598), the Countess of Pembroke's *Antonie* in 1595. At the universities *Caesar's Revenge* and *Nero* came somewhere within our period. The former is very Senecan and perhaps is burlesqued in *The Cobbler's Prophecy* for the strain its bloodshed puts on Charon's ferry and the capacity of Hades. Compare (*Caesar's Revenge*, the closing scene):

> *Caron* that vsed but an old rotten boate
> Must nowe a nauie rigg for to transport
> The howling soules vnto the *Stigian* stronde.
> Hell and *Elisium* must be digd in one,
> And both will be to litle to contayne
> Numberless numbers of afflicted ghostes,
> That I my selfe haue tumbling thither sent.—

with *The Cobbler's Prophecy*, lines 674–80:

> *Charon.* And there are shipwrights sent for too, to build me vp a bigger bote,
> A bote said I? nay a whole hulke:
> And that the same may safely flote,
> Cocytus, Lethe, Phlegeton
> Shal al be digged into Styx:
> For where one wont to come to hell,
> I tell thee now comes fiue or sixe.

Between *Titus Andronicus* and *Julius Caesar* we hear of no Roman play presented by the Chamberlain's men. The former is intensely Senecan, the latter somewhat so; naturally this element was long a traditional one in drama with a Roman setting.

Fifteen ninety-four had been a year of activity in Roman plays, with the publication of Daniel's *Cleopatra*, Lodge's *Wounds of Civil War*, Marlowe and Nashe's *Dido*, and Shakespeare's *Titus Andronicus*. There was also entered in the Stationers' Register a *Heliogabalus* which was probably an old play, of unknown provenance, and may have dealt somehow with the Earl of Leicester, whom the scurrilous *Leicester's Commonwealth* likened to Heliogabalus for his lust. In this year, too, the Admiral's men produced their lost *Dioclesian*, sometimes identified with Dekker's *Virgin Martyr*, which shows indications of being a revision of an earlier play. In its Elizabethan form the drama may have been localized in part at St. Albans—a favorite town with dramatists—for the

Emperor Diocletian's persecution caused the martyrdom of St. Alban, "Britain's Stephen and proto-martyr."

Fifteen ninety-four and the following year saw the production of the two parts of the Admiral's lost *Caesar and Pompey;* and 1596, their *Julian the Apostata*, on a subject which had been dramatized at Shrewsbury as early as 1556. The Apostate was a good subject for the same kind of crudely spectacular staging as was given *The Four Ages*, especially when he pushed the rebuilding of the Temple at Jerusalem as a blow against Christianity. The work, assigned to Alypius, who had been governor of Britain, was stopped by fearful globes of fire, that burst forth repeatedly from the earth close to the foundations and so scorched and terrified the workmen that they had to give up. Good comic relief would be afforded, too, by his feud with the snobs of Antioch over their satires on his lousy beard. And he died in Marlovian manner, exclaiming, "Thou hast conquered, Galilean; yet still do I renounce thee!"

Phocas, another lost Admiral's play of the same year, dealt with an Emperor of the East who began his career as groom for the general Priscus and won imperial rank by the brutal courage which made him popular with the soldiers. He was crowned in succession to Mauricius, against whose authority he had revolted and whom he caused to be put to death. His short reign saw bloody wars with the Persians under their king Chosroes, marked by reverses for the Roman arms; while Phocas himself remained in Constantinople, given up to sensual pleasures. Insurrections against him followed, put down with great severity, until Heraclius, son of the Exarch of Africa, stormed Constantinople and had Phocas beheaded. The seven performances of *Phocas* recorded by Henslowe, May 20–July 22, 1596, coincided with the absence at Cadiz from June 1 to August 10 of the Earl of Essex, Master of the Horse[41] to Queen Elizabeth, whose prowess and popularity in war and in love appeared very differently to his friends and to his enemies.

Fifteen ninety-seven was uneventful. Fifteen ninety-eight saw the reprinting of Shakespeare's poem *The Rape of Lucrece*, on a story later dramatized by Heywood, the playing of a *Dido*, perhaps Marlowe's, by the Admiral's men, and that company's production of *1* and *2 Hannibal and Hermes*,[42] and *Catiline's Conspiracy*. A translation of Tacitus also

[41] The post could be referred to insultingly. *Leicester's Commonwealth* has it that Essex's stepfather poisoned his former ally Throckmorton because he had written the Queen that it was common French gossip that she was going to marry her "horse-keeper," i.e., Leicester, Master of the Horse. Essex's mother's later marriage to Sir Christopher Blount, who had been Leicester's Master of Horse, was productive of similar sneers.

[42] Henslowe, "haneball & hermes other wisse called worse feared then hurte." Cf. my remarks on Count Hermes of *The Blind Beggar of Alexandria*. But of course Henslowe may mean "harms," to accord with the subtitle. The play, in two parts, is quite mysterious.

was published in this year. The following year produced Shakespeare's *Julius Caesar*. In 1600 one Will Boyle wrote a *Jugurtha* for Henslowe; and Holland's translation of Livy appeared, followed in 1601 by translations of Caesar's *Gallic Wars* and Pedro Mexia's *Roman Emperors*.[43] Early in January Hathaway and Rankins wrote *Hannibal and Scipio* for the Admiral's men, a play which must have borne upon partisan politics; for this work, ready for production on the eve of the Essex rebellion, dealt with a period in history with which Essex's career was constantly being compared. As Chamberlain wrote on February 22, 1600, "We lacke but a Plutarch to make him (the Adelantado) and my Lord of Essex parallels"; and it is but a step to his friend Perez's paralleling him with a Plutarchian worthy:

Lege Plutarchum in Marcello, & ibi quid tibi velim, quid tibi deberi intelligam, videbis. O invidia, virtutis aemula, Principum pernicies, Regnorum exitium, qua erumpes modo?[44]

Marcellus had fought well for Rome against Hannibal, and according to Heywood's *Apology for Actors* was a stock dramatic type of the noble general unappreciated at home; he may easily have been a character in *Hannibal and Scipio* (of Nabbes's extant play with this title I shall speak in my next chapter). The references to Essex in connection with the Punic Wars emphasize constantly the treachery of enemies. Harington[45] says that Doleman (who in 1595 dedicated to Essex his book on the succession) loved him as "did Hannibal love Fabius when he burned other men's corn and spared his to make him more suspected to the Romans." On September 12, 1596, Mr. Bruce wrote to Bacon from Edinburgh to congratulate him on the triumphant return of Essex from Cadiz, confessing that he had before thought his lordship's enterprise extremely difficult and dangerous, and had been of Fabius's opinion, that it was best and most expedient to fight within the country for the liberty thereof.

But as the Roman Scipio, by advice and action made it known to his commonwealth, that it was assuredly their best to fight Hannibal at Carthage; so has your English Scipio by this happy defeat of the Spaniard in Spain altered my judgment by his semblable experience. I wish his lordship Scipio's—,[46] and I trust he serves a queen and country will vouchsafe him a better fortune.[47]

And Essex identified himself with the leaders of the Punic Wars in 1599,[48] writing to Peregrine Bertie, Lord Willoughby,

[43] Statues of the Emperors were rather common Elizabethan garden decorations; for instance Cecil had at Theobalds a summer house embellished with "the twelve Caesars."

[44] Perez to Essex, probably 1599 or 1600, in Camden's *Historie of Elizabeth*, 112.

[45] *Tract on the Succession*, 1602, 74.

[46] A blank. Query, "virtue"?

[47] Birch, *Memoirs of Queen Elizabeth*, II, 138.

[48] Jan. 4; *Sal. MSS.*, IX, 9.

You did choose a solicitor that can procure nothing for himself nor any of his friends but once a year a breakneck employment . . . Into Ireland I go . . . And yet all these [drawbacks to the Irish campaign] were better endured than to have a Hanno at Carthage or a Cato at Rome, barking at him that is every day venturing his life for his country abroad . . . In the meantime enemies may be advanced; so I show who should be, let fortune show who be.

Willoughby replied on January 21:[49]

You have made already the conquest your own . . . Hanno is subdued alive, Hannibal from the senate throws his trifling enemy to the stairs' foot, Cato his poison ends himself, *you victorious shall see these new acted.*

The wavering nature of Elizabethan allegory, the great freedom it allowed itself to change from one identification to another, are well shown in these excerpts, where Essex is now Marcellus, now Scipio, now Fabius, now Hannibal; and Carthage stands sometimes for Spain, sometimes for London. But it becomes clear also, I think, that it was difficult for Shakespeare's contemporaries to see a play on the Punic Wars without thinking of Essex's affairs abroad and at home.

Roman material, the Augustan poets, was used for another sort of satirical allegory in the War of Theatres by Dekker in *Satiromastix*, produced by the Chamberlain's men and Paul's boys, 1601, and by Jonson in *The Poetaster*, played by the Chapel boys. In 1602 the Admiral's men had *Pontius Pilate* with additions by Dekker, and *Caesar's Fall or the Two Shapes* [or *Harpes*], by no fewer collaborators than Dekker, Drayton, Middleton, Munday, and Webster. Lodge's translation of Josephus appeared this year, dedicated to the Admiral. With Jonson's fine play *Sejanus*, produced by the King's men in 1603, we may close this brief survey of the Roman plays of our period. It is not easy to surmise why, unless for political content, this type of play should have appealed so mightily to the Admiral's men and their audience; perhaps the attraction was in part the Senecan ghosts and horrors, in part the sugar-coated instructiveness. Such a play as *Julian the Apostata* would have a strongly religious appeal, of course, as would *Pontius Pilate*. Like "Judas," "Pilate" was a natural political reference. For instance, the Reverend Stephen Egerton, Essexian, was in trouble soon after the Rebellion for a sermon on Mark 15:15, "So Pilate" . . . The reference somehow angered Bancroft and Cecil.[50] The Admiral's *Pontius Pilate* of 1602, like their *Hannibal and Scipio* a year earlier, may have been designed to turn the tables upon allegorizings by the opposite faction.

Catiline's Conspiracy may have fostered the Queen's suspicions of Essex, or it may merely have allegorized one of the numerous plots earlier in Elizabeth's reign. It seems to have been usually a retrospective refer-

[49] *Ibid.*, 34; from Berwick. Italics mine.

[50] Cf. *Sal. MSS.*, XI, 154, 157.

ence, for Camden in his *Britannia* speaks of "our Cataline, Simon Montford, Earl of Leicester," and Cecil refers in 1601[51] to Essex's "Catelyn army." Coke, fulminating before the Privy Council, June 5, 1600, accused Essex of treason in Cicero's terms, "Regina vidit, consul vidit," etc.[52]

Yet in general it seems evident that the Admiral's men catered somewhat to a thirst for easy education among their bourgeois audiences. Probably they presented the Greek mythology to them in the candied form of Heywood's *Four Ages* during our period,[53] and very likely they were doing somewhat the same thing with Roman history.

Some miscellaneous events of 1599 may be quickly mentioned. We have already noticed that the English comedians in Scotland were building themselves a playhouse, with King James's backing against the opposition of the Kirk. At their head was Laurence Fletcher, who stands first on the list of the newly patented King's men (formerly the Chamberlain's) in 1603. The Shakespearean company may have been in touch with Fletcher, as Essex certainly was with King James. Alleyn, as we shall notice, was using his influence with the Queen herself to cope with the opposition to his building near Golden Lane in the growing region beyond Cripplegate the new Fortune theater, on much the same plans as Burbadge's Globe, except that it was square rather than round.

At Christmas the second of the Parnassus plays (*1 Return from Parnassus*) was produced by the students of St. John's, Cambridge. The play is full of references to the new satirical mode which was displacing the old one of lyrical and amorous sweetness, satirized here in parodies on the "veins" of Spenser and "sweet Mr. Shakespeare." There is also a sample wooing, with bits from *Venus and Adonis* and *Romeo and Juliet;* apparently too sweet for Ingenioso, who resolves he'll "turn satirist."

In this year was published as "sundry times plaied" by the Earl of Oxford's men *The Weakest Goeth to the Wall*, an inn-yard play according to Lawrence, which in style somewhat resembles Dekker's work. As we have noted, it shows numerous resemblances to successful plays of the period belonging to various companies, and some slight Cecilian bias. Heywood's (?) *1* and *2 Edward IV* were published in 1599[54] and 1600, in quartos which ascribe them to Derby's men, and thus belong to their

[51] *Ibid.*, 138; Cecil to Nicholson (in Scotland), March 21, referring to Essex's design to bring over his Irish troops to enforce his will: "it now appeareth, if it had gone forward, what would have become of the state of England, which must have been made a prey for his Catelyn army, and have only sought the destruction not only of the possessor but of the successor to whomsoever God shall dispose it." [52] Whyte, June 11, 1600.

[53] I shall take this matter up in my discussion of "Greek Plays" in a later chapter.

[54] S.R. Aug. 28, 1599. We have noted their possible place in the Admiral's 1594 repertory.

1599 repertory, unless they are early enough to have belonged to the earlier Derby's men (Strange's) before 1594; still, we hear in 1600 that the Earl of Derby was "busy penning comedies for the common players," in all probability his own company. It is, moreover, altogether natural that Derby's men should have a play on Edward IV, from whom William Stanley, the present earl, was directly descended. His niece, Anne Stanley, was by the same descent an important figure in the succession situation, for if Edward Seymour, Lord Beauchamp, was illegitimate, as the Queen claimed (and as the Cecils were inclined to deny), the crown after Elizabeth's death vested in her issue, by the will of Henry VIII, which excluded the Scottish line. She was unmarried at this time; probably no one dared marry her; but after the accession of James she became the wife of Grey Brydges, Lord Chandos.

One of the attitudes to be expected in a Derby play of this period is, to judge from the rivalry which was mentioned in the Shelford Weir dispute, a dislike of the house of Hastings. Yet there seems to be no attempt to blacken Clarence, from whom the Hastings claim to the succession derived. Perhaps there is something of an indirect nature in the honoring of Sir Harry Morton (who executes Faulconbridge); since a Morton was an enemy of the Hastings clan in Leicestershire in 1599.[55]

Anti-Essex feeling is, as might be expected, quite clearly shown. Possibly the great play here made of King Edward's amours[56] is aimed at him, especially where the King is wasting his time thus in the midst of preparations for the French wars. When we remember that Derby himself had been cuckolded by Essex on the eve of the Islands Voyage, the great stress laid upon the tragic story of Shore and his wife here seems to exhibit a certain insensitiveness. But perhaps he thought the odium here was clearly transferred to Sir Robert Southwell, doubtless the "ancient noble husband" who died in 1598 after he had, like Shore, sold his property in despite at his wife's unfaithfulness with Essex. But we have been over these matters already, in connection with *The Blind Beggar of Alexandria*.[57]

Into the Second Part,[58] I suspect that Derby himself had Heywood insert this acid criticism of *1 Henry IV* and its appreciative audiences:

> Then comes a slave, one of those drunken sots,
> In with a tavern-reckoning for a supplication,
> Disguised with a cushion on his head,
> A drawer's apron for a herald's coat . . .
> With some such other tavern-foolery.
> With that, this filthy, rascal, greasy rout
> Burst out in laughter at this worthy jest,
> Neighing like horses.

[55] *Hist. MSS. Com.*, R VIII–1, 433. [56] *1 Edward IV*, V, ii. [57] Pp. 89, 90. [58] Sgn. M.

Numerous close imitations of Shakespeare's *Henry V* in this play point to a date early in the summer of 1599 for its writing or rewriting. Its French politics are not those of either party. King Lewis says:

> And it is better England join in league
> With us, his strong, old, open enemy,
> Than with those weak and new dissembling friends.[59]

Burgundy is made treacherous to the English, somewhat oddly in view of the Cecil policy and Derby's marriage to Burghley's granddaughter. But then, Derby was, like his father-in-law Oxford, alienated from his wife and inclined to be snappish and unruly with his Cecil connections.[60]

Huddled at the end of Part Two so undramatically as to make the reader suspect clumsy revision or ulterior motives are Buckingham's grievance about the earldom of Hereford (Essex was Viscount Hereford), and the founding of the Order of the Bath. I might add that the play contains a song on Agincourt which must be Drayton's and has informative blank verse choruses like those in *Henry V*.

Derby's men were at court on February 5, 1600; and this play or *The Trial of Chivalry* may have been their offering for the occasion.

Whyte writes to Sir Robert Sidney on October 26, 1599:

> Two daies agoe, the overthrow of Turnholt was acted upon a Stage, and all your names used that were at yt; especially Sir Fra. Veres, and he that plaid that Part gott a Beard resembling his, and a Watchett Sattin Doublett, with Hose trimed with Silver Lace. You was also introduced, killing, Slaying, and overthrowing the Spaniards, and honorable Mention made of your service, in seconding Sir Francis Vere, being engaged.

Turnholt had been taken from the Spanish by Count Maurice of Nassau, with the help of an English contingent, on January 24, 1598. The actors' unusual boldness in presenting living men under their real names was justified, it seems, by the complimentary nature of the performance. The play may have been given by some company which was occupying the Curtain since the Chamberlain's men had left it, or even by Shakespeare's company at the Globe. Sir Francis Vere had been a correspondent and staunch friend of Essex until after the Islands Voyage, on which some dissension appears to have developed which caused him to state definitely that he would no longer follow the Earl's fortunes. He was a nephew of the Earl of Oxford. Sidney was another friend and correspondent of Essex; when during the political disturbances of 1601 he was

[59] Sgn. M 2.

[60] Much might be said, for which I shall not take space here, about the minor characters in the play—Aston, Bowes, Darcy, etc.—and the connections of their families with county politics in Derby's part of England. The Tanner of Tamworth's part of the play, for instance, seems to glance at a certain Mr. Darcy's leather monopoly.

with the Admiral's forces attacking Essex House, he served, because of his connection with Essex, as an envoy to parley with the besieged rebels. Both these men, and particularly Vere, perhaps the ablest of Elizabethan generals, would have been valuable allies for the Essex faction to make firm at this time in any way possible.

The court season of 1599–1600 saw three performances by the Chamberlain's men; December 26, January 6, and February 3; two by the Admiral's; December 27 and January 1; and one by Derby's, February 5.

The repertory of the Chamberlain's company this season was unusually rich. It contained the great connected series of new and revised Shakespearean history plays, extending from the banishment of Bolingbroke to the death of Richard III and centering about the heroic figure of Henry V, victor of Agincourt, and that mighty comic creation, Falstaff. Other new plays of the year were *Julius Caesar*, *Every Man Out of his Humour*, *An Alarum for London* (?), and perhaps *The Merry Wives of Windsor*. *Turnholt*, as we have seen, is also possible. I am inclined to believe that *Two Gentlemen of Verona* was revived about this time. It appears to refer[61] to Chapman's play for the Admiral's men in 1599, *The World Runs on Wheels*. Note also the resemblance, in the situation of a girl disguised as a page wooing her rival in her own lover's behalf, to *Twelfth Night*, about 1600; and in the meeting in Friar Patrick's cell to the parts of the friar in *Much Ado*, 1598, and of Friar Laurence in *Romeo and Juliet*, thought to have been revived at about this time. If this sort of thing was popular this season, *Two Gentlemen* may have seemed very eligible for revival.

Thus there was a wealth of material to choose from for the company's performances at court. If the restriction of the Chamberlain's men to three showings was due to any difficulty in their repertory, it may have been the difficulty of choosing plays entirely free from offensive political implications. But it is quite possible that on at least one of these occasions two plays—both parts of *Henry IV*, say, or *The Merry Wives* and *Henry V*, were given. The practice of having several plays at a sitting, although much more common at King James's more lavish court, was not unknown to the subjects of Elizabeth, as we know from Whyte's letter of February 15, 1598:

> Sir *Gilly Meiricke* made at *Essex* House yesternight a very great Supper. There were at yt, my Ladys *Lester*, *Northumberland*, *Bedford*, *Essex*, *Rich;* and my Lords of *Essex*, *Rutland*, *Monjoy*, and others. They had 2 Plaies, which kept them up till 1 a Clocke after Midnight.

The Admiral's men had brought out about thirty new plays in 1599, among them a number which we have already mentioned in one con-

[61] III, i, 320.

nection or another, or which we shall have occasion to take up later in connection with special types of drama still to be discussed. Among the former are *Friar Fox*, *Thomas Merry*, and *Sir John Oldcastle;* among the latter, *Troilus and Cressida.* An interesting phenomenon of the year is Henslowe's payment on September 28 of earnest money to "Mr. Maxton, the new poet," for a book. It seems odd that Marston, who was so busy with Paul's boys, should have done anything at this time for the Admiral's men. Perhaps he was using his vogue to get rid of old work. Among the lost plays which may not have deserved to vanish are Chapman's *The World Runs on Wheels*, probably containing satire on current fashions including the new coaches, Porter's *Two Merry Women of Abingdon* (a reply to *The Merry Wives of Windsor?*), and Chettle's *Polyphemus.*[62]

But we need not waste time in speculation over what the Admiral's men may have given at court this season; for, oddly enough after so many years of pure guesswork, we are now practically certain in the case of each date. In December Henslowe records payments for a special ending for the court performance of Dekker's *Old Fortunatus*, probably a rewriting of an older play (see Henslowe's Diary for 1596); the piece was doubtless acted at court on December 27. The fact that it was played at Christmas before the Queen by the Admiral's men is mentioned on the title page of the 1600 quarto. The play has several interesting verbal echoes of *Romeo and Juliet:*

For sec, the Tapers of the night are already lighted, and stand brightly burning in their starrie Candlestickes.[63]

. . . at his skarres
They scoffe, that nere durst view the face of warres.[64]

. . . her Negro Paramour, grim night.[65]

. . . this skie
That's now so iocund, will mourne all in blacke.[66]

The other date was also taken by a play by Dekker, for whom this season seems to have been a great personal triumph—his excellent mingling of romance and realism, *The Shoemakers' Holiday*, based on Deloney's novel *The Gentle Craft.* The class appeal of the Admiral's men is strongly marked in this play; and it may well have been the administration's uneasiness over the political situation caused by Essex's imprisonment[67] which caused the London bourgeoisie and proletariat to be

[62] Possibly sometimes a political nickname; cf. Sir Edward Fortune in *Jack Drum*, 1600, decrying "popularity,"—"Nor do I envy Poliphemian puffes." [63] The Prologue at Court.
[64] Edition for John Pearson, London, 1873, p. 91. [65] *Ibid.*, 92.
[66] *Ibid.*, 128. [67] Cf. W. B. Devereux, II, 89–90.

flattered by the performance of this play "before the Queene's most excellent Majestie on New Yeares day at night last, by the right honourable the Earl of Notingham, Lord high Admirall of England, his servants," as the 1600 quarto declares. Prompt publication!

The fact that, in spite of the disgrace of the Essex faction, the Chamberlain's men still enjoyed this season a preëminence at court appears to need explanation. It may well be that Shakespeare's fellows now felt happier to have Lord Hunsdon as their patron than they had in 1597, when his signature to the petition had helped to block their occupancy of Blackfriars. For Hunsdon's high position of Lord Chamberlain, in which he appears to have stood aloof from any sympathies his younger brothers may have shown for the Essexians, was now a powerful help to his players at court. Yet the question of allegiance was a difficult one; Hunsdon's sister, Philadelphia Carey, Lady Scrope, was Essex's very faithful friend. Whyte tells us on October 11, 1599:

> At the Court, my Lady Scrope is only noted to stand firm to him; she endures much at Her Majesty's hands, because she doth daily do all the kind offices of love to the Queen in his behalf. She wears all black, she mourns and is pensive, and joys in nothing but in a solitary being alone. And 'tis thought, she says much that few would venture to say but herself.

Lord Hunsdon himself, although he acknowledged great obligations to Cecil, was not precisely hand in glove with him. We shall see in our remaining chapters how his company was yet to become seriously implicated in the Essex rebellion itself, and how it nevertheless survived this disaster to live through the last two years of Elizabeth's reign and triumph on the accession of King James.

CHAPTER V (1600–1602)

THE STAGE AT THE TIME OF THE ESSEX REBELLION

Repertories of 1600. "Jack Drum" and Cornwallis. *Pastoral elements in the drama, 1594–1603. The girl-page device, 1594–1603.* Contemporary references in "The Blind Beggar of Bednal Green." The Essex Rebellion. The court season of 1600–1: some reasons why the Chamberlain's men kept their position. Repertories of 1601. The "War of the Theatres." The Christmas season of 1601–2. *Greek plays, 1594–1603.* "Troilus and Cressida."

SOME time during 1601, in Jonson's play *The Poetaster*, which quite clearly lampoons the Chamberlain's men, the Chapel boys make the spokesman of the dramatic company they are satirizing say, "This winter has made us all poorer than so many starved snakes."[1] There is good evidence in *Hamlet*, too, that the first year or so of the new century had brought disastrous competition to Shakespeare's company in the form of child actors. We may well make our survey of the stage history of the year 1600 with this competition in mind, to detect if we can what qualities made it so dangerous.

All critics recognize Marston's style in *Jack Drum's Entertainment, or The Comedie of Pasquill and Katherine*, entered in 1601 and published in 1602 with an ascription to the Children of Paul's. The last line,

> Our Fortune laughs, and all content abounds,

points to performance at the Fortune, which was not completed until 1600 (the Admiral's men may have shared the play with Paul's boys as the Chamberlain's did *Satiromastix*); but the play may have been first produced in the preceding year, if we may judge by the allusion to the organ sent to the Sultan of Turkey in 1599, likening a character to "the instrument the merchants sent over to the Great Turk: you need not play upon him, heele make musick of himself, and he be once set going." However, I prefer to place it about May, 1600, partly because of its reference to Kemp's morris dance to Norwich, completed about Easter, as current news. The play had an important part in the Poetomachia, probably being the one in which, as Jonson complained to Drummond, Marston staged him, as either Brabant Senior or John Fo de King. The satire imitates Jonson's comedies of humours; has Fo de King apprehensive that he may "hang like de Burgullian," a fat rascal whose fate was sometimes used to taunt Jonson with his own narrow escape;

[1] III, iv, 345.

depicts certain intrigues which may refer to Jonson's own domestic affairs as he related them to Drummond; and uses some vocabulary which Jonson later makes Crispinus vomit in *The Poetaster*, doubtless by way of retaliation.

It has been suggested that Planet is Shakespeare. This does not seem really probable; yet it is true that some lines spoken by Brabant Junior (when he believes that he has procured the murder of his friend Planet) seem certainly to refer to the stage, especially when compared with Guilpin's mention of a malcontent, a "discarded intelligencer," who

> like the unfrequented Theater
> Walkes in darke silence and vast solitude,
> Suited to those blacke fancies which intrude,
> Vpon possession of his troubled breast.[2]

The lines in *Jack Drum* are as follows:

> *Brab. Jr.* Now haue I roome for murder, this vaste place,
> Hush'd silence, and dumb sollitude, are fit
> To be obseruers of my Tragedie.
> Planet accept the smoake of reeking bloud
> To expiate thy murder—Friend, I come,
> Weele troope together to Elizium.

With the exception, however, of various imitations of Shakespeare's plays, especially the burlesque of *Romeo and Juliet* in Puff's serenade of Katherine at three a.m., the satire in *Jack Drum* seems aimed mainly at Jonson personally.

It is notable how much stress *Jack Drum's Entertainment* lays upon the lavish out-of-door hospitality of Sir Edward Fortune at Highgate.[3] I believe that there is good reason to identify this jolly knight with Sir William Cornwallis, the essayist, a friend of Ben Jonson, who wrote for him (or his uncle of the same name) an entertainment for the occasion of his receiving the King and Queen at his house at Highgate on May 1, 1604. The guests are conducted through the house to a beautiful garden which seems to have been famous for its outlook toward the city.[4]

The difficulty of disentangling fully this Sir William Cornwallis, the essayist, from his uncle[5] is well illustrated by the cut in the *Essays* which

[2] E. Guilpin, *Skialetheia*, Satyre v.

[3] For a possible source of this character's name, cf. *Sal. MSS.*, v, 372; Sidney to Essex, Sept. 11, 1595.

[4] Nordon, *Speculum Britanniae,* says that on Highgate Hill is a pleasant and healthful dwelling, a fair house with a fine view over London, of — Cornwalleys, Esquire.

[5] Cf. the letters to *The Times Literary Supplement* on the Cornwallis problem by P. B. Whitt, C. E. Avery, and R. E. Bennett, Oct. 23, Nov. 6 and 20, Dec. 4, 1930, and Jan. 22, 1931. I do not feel that the confusion of identities has been entirely cleared up. Something definite might be established by comparison of hands.

shows uncle and nephew writing together in a classical summer-house (probably at Highgate) and looking as much alike as two peas in a pod. Apparently whichever Cornwallis dwelt at Highgate, the other, who had bought Fisher's Folly, Finsbury, from Oxford in 1588, spent much time in the garden on Highgate Hill. The best evidence that the essayist's uncle was the one at Fisher's Folly is old Sir Thomas's letter to Burghley, December 20, 1588,[6] disclaiming any part in his *son's*[7] purchase of the house from Burghley's son-in-law, Oxford. It seems unlikely that the elder Cornwallis owned both places.

As for the Cornwallis politics, let it suffice here to say that Sir William the younger, in the first series of his Essays, published in 1601, writes "Of Friendship and Faction" in such a way as to reveal himself quite clearly as a reluctant adherent of Cecil, regretting being forced by the other party's distrust into the faction to which he is allied by kinship.[8] But *Jack Drum* seems to show his house as the resort of men of many minds; and we learn from the essay "Of Censuring" that he knew Southampton's protégé Florio.[9] He (or his uncle) writes often from Highgate to his friend Sir Robert Cecil, once inviting him thither a-maying;[10] so it is possible to see in the foolish John Ellis of the play the real John Ellis, son of the landlord of the Three Kings, Canterbury, a candidate for employment as a spy, of whom Cecil writes to George Kendall in 1600,[11] "he seemeth too weak to commit any matters of her Majesty's service." The Queen herself came to Highgate on May Day, 1601.[12]

Although Marston's depiction of Sir Edward Fortune is jolly enough it is perhaps a little too highly colored to be fully satisfactory to its model. His dialogue with Mammon the miserly old usurer can be paralleled, almost thought for thought, from the Essays;[13] but it is going somewhat beyond the complimentary to have Sir Edward cry, when his daughter Katherine has just made an alarming disappearance:

> Broach me a fresh Butt of Canary Sacke,

[6] *Sal. MSS.*, III, 377. [7] The essayist was his grandson. [8] Cf. Whyte, Sept. 23, 1595.

[9] Cf. A. H. Upham, *French Influence on English Literature*, 266 ff. Mr. Upham rather exaggerates a possible doubt.

[10] *Sal. MSS.*, XI, 543; cf. also in the *Sal. MSS.* letters of July 9, 1598, Sept. 24, 1599, May 11 and 16, 1601.

[11] *Sal. MSS.*, X, 410 (& 428); also *S. P. Dom.*, 1598–1601, 491, 495, 502, 524.

[12] Chambers, IV, 113, n. 17.

[13] Cf., on news and gossip, "Of the Observation & Use of Things," on lavish housekeeping, "*Of Traps for Fame*," "Of Entertainment," "*Of Knowledge*"; on amassing wealth for heirs, "*Of Traps for Fame*," "*Of Keeping State*"; on court life, "Of Ambition"; on the acclaim of the populace, "*Of Popularity*." The italicized essays are from the second series, issued in 1610. But for the dates of these essays, cf. R. E. Bennett, "Sir William Cornwallis," *Times Literary Supplement*, XXIX, 1042.

> Lets sing, drink, sleep, for thats the best reliefe:
> To droune all care, and overwhelme all griefe.[14]

Perhaps Cornwallis's own reply to this play's exaggeration of his hospitality and enjoyment of life is in his essays; "Of Praise and Glory," which extols temperance, abstinence, and fortitude, and "Of Entertainment," which, although it does not use the words, draws a sharp contrast between liberality and prodigality in the entertaining of guests. So it is, after all, not surprising to find that the play, *Liberality and Prodigality*, which Greg claims was given before the Queen by the Chapel Children on February 22, 1601,[15] has the following passage:

> Thou art indited here by the name of Prodigality, for that thou, on the fourth day of February, in the three and fortie yeere of the prosperous raigne of Elizabeth our dread Soueraigne,[16] by the Grace of God . . . together with two other malefactors yet unknowne, at High-gate in the County of Middlesex aforesaid, didst felloniously take from one Tenacity of the parish of Pancridge yeoman, in the said County, one thousand pounds.[17]

Liberality in this play is chief steward to Virtue. The love affairs of Money, Fortune's son here, resemble those of Lady Argurion (Money) in Jonson's *Cynthia's Revels*, 1600.

In "Of Knowledge," one of his essays of the second series, Cornwallis sums up his views on the use of money in a manner which shows him fond of playing with these abstractions:

> Morall reasons will shew how excellently Liberality becomes plenty, and plenty without knowledge is not liberality, but a cheat that unnecessarily maketh much of his store without use; or else prodigality, which in consuming is no less vitious then covetousnesse is in sparing: what have we that use makes not pretious?

The good man, the wise man, he says with a reminder of *Jack Drum*, "playes not fortune, dispersing blindfold." Finally, as if commending the plot of *Liberality and Prodigality*, he marvels "how covetousnesse preyes upon unthriftinesse, which shewes the wisdome of the eternall goodnesse; who hath given one sinne leave to lash another to death." Can Cornwallis have written this belated morality play himself?

Cornwallis's *Essays* contain many interesting verbal resemblances to Shakespeare, especially to *Hamlet;* but I think I have brought forward here enough evidence to indicate that his relationship to the drama is worthy of careful and detailed study.

Before leaving *Jack Drum's Entertainment* we should notice one thing more: Pasquil's madness expresses itself in political terms:

[14] Compare Merrythought in *The Knight of the Burning Pestle* and the singing senator in Heywood's *Lucrece*.

[15] Cf. his edition of the piece for the Malone Society.

[16] Feb. 4, 1601.

[17] Sgn. F 3.

When shall old Saturne mount his Throane againe?
See, see, alas how bleake Religion stands.

"Saturn" was a common nickname for Burghley,[18] who had died in 1598, a champion of the established religion.

Come yons the Capitoll of Iupiter,
Letts whip the Senate, els they will not leaue
To haue their Iustice blasted with abuse
Of flattering Sycophants.

In Elizabethan parlance the "Senate," I think, was usually the Privy Council. The Essexians often made such charges. It is natural enough that a character whose name signified a political squib[19] should rave on such matters. The play's soberer—and safer—attitude has been stated earlier by Sir Edward Fortune:

The summe is this, beare only this good thought,
The Council-chamber is the Phoenix nest,
Who wastes it selfe, to giue us peace and rest.

Paul's boys, now in their second year, may have had, too, Chapman's *Bussy d'Ambois* in some form, at least Chambers thinks so;[20] the play as we have it, of course, is considerably after our period, but there are traces—for instance the praise of the orderliness of the English court—which seem to be Elizabethan. If they did have it, this play with its splendid fiery part of Bussy, like a Stukeley in the midst of an *Antonio's Revenge*, was a fine asset to the boys' repertory. Their *Doctor Dodipoll* was published in this year, as was also the anonymous *Maid's Metamorphosis*, an interesting romantic pastoral fashioned out of the Greek mythology,[21] somewhat in the manner of Lyly, although it is in heroic couplets. It may have been the play given by Paul's at court this Christmas season. Whether it is an old play rewritten or a new play in an imitative manner, it is interesting for its resemblances to *As You Like It*, probably of this same year, and Lyly's *Love's Metamorphosis*, written for Paul's boys about 1588 and now revived by their rivals, the Children of Her Majesty's Chapel. Notice the characters' names, Silvio, for instance, and a mention of Ganymede—*Love's Metamorphosis* has Montanus a character in Lodge's *Rosalynde*, Celia, Silvestris—; the pastoral setting; the vying of ranger and shepherd to lodge Eurymine; Joculo's aping of courtly humours, and his realistic bondage to this flesh,

Here's old transforming, would with all his art
He could transform this tree into a tart;

[18] Cf. *Sydney Papers*, I.—Sir Thos. Lake to Sidney, Oct., 1591.

[19] Chamberlain, Jan. 31, 1599.—Encloses "certain odde epitaphes and epigrammes that go under the name of pasquills."

[20] II, 20; but compare III, 258, where he prefers to date the play, with Parrott, 1604.

[21] Ovid's story of Iphis and Ianthe, *Metamorphoses*, IX.

a reference to women's wearing the breeches in leap year which may indicate a certain timeliness in the vogue of girl-page plays in 1600; the repentant Duke's sending for his son.

Love's Metamorphosis is doubtless aimed at by Jonson when in the Induction to *Cynthia's Revels* he refers to the ghosts of old plays seen on the Chapel stage:

They say, the *vmbrae*, or ghosts of some three or foure playes, departed a dozen yeeres since, haue bin seene walking on your stage heere: take heed, boy, if your house bee haunted with such *hobgoblins*, t'will fright away all your spectators quickly.

Burbadge leased Blackfriars, which it will be remembered he had been unable to use since his reconstruction of the place for a theater, to the Chapel boys' manager Henry Evans on September 2, 1600. The company's only other play which may be assigned to this year is the one I have just quoted, Jonson's bizarre combination of masque, morality, and humour elements, *The Fountain of Self-love, or Cynthia's Revels*. It is noteworthy especially for the eight character-sketches in the second act, which has been called "the first English character-book." Cynthia's speech, v, vi, 19–36, is supposed to reprove the discontented "outs" of the Essex party:

When hath Diana . . .
Denying to the world, the precious vse
Of hoorded wealth, with-held her friendly aide?
Monthly, we spend our still-repaired shine . . .
To giue the mutinous kind of wanting men,
Their look't-for light. Yet, what is their desert?
Bountie is wrong'd, interpreted as due;
Mortalls can challenge not a ray, by right,
Yet doe expect the whole of Cynthia's light.
But if that Deities with-drew their gifts,
For humane follies, what could men deserue
But death, and darknesse?

These boys appeared at court twice during the ensuing winter season, but rather late, when they may have had available one or more of their productions of the following year; *The Poetaster*, *Sir Giles Goosecap*, and perhaps *May Day*. Possibly, as we have seen, their court play of February 22, 1601, three days before the death of Essex, was the old-fashioned morality *Liberality and Prodigality*, published in 1602 as "played before Her Majesty."

These companies of boys are usually thought of together in considering the appeal which seems to have drawn the courtly patronage away from the Chamberlain's men to them, but perhaps we should try to differentiate them a little. Both no doubt charmed by their youth and pretty precocities, the piquancy of their adult clothes and ways; they must have stolen much of the allegiance of the ladies at once. We have already seen Paul's boys exploiting the novelty of their playing Senecan tragedy of the most horrifying sort, carrying off audacities of satire which the adult actors would hardly dare, and making a great point of burlesquing the most popular plays of the adult repertories. The Chapel boys, on the other hand, although historically no more a singing organization than their rivals,[22] may possibly have made slightly more of a special appeal with music, to which they found a pastoral mood particularly suitable.[23] Of course each company used the other's successful methods as much as possible, and the rivalry between them would make an interesting study—but outside our present realm of interest, which is concerned with these boy companies only as their competition weakened the Shakespearean company in its warfare against the Admiral's men.

As a result of too much impoverishing competition, or the example of the boys' playwrights in hurrying their productions into print, or the great political tension during this year of Essex's disgrace and confinement, or an intense energy of the booksellers caused by the boys' playwrights' demonstration of profits to be had from playbooks, the year 1600 saw a great publishing of plays. Of the Chamberlain's stock the following plays appeared in print, of which we have seen all but the first and last to contain anti-Cecilian matter: *Every Man Out*, *Henry V*, *Much Ado*, *2 Henry IV*, *The Merchant of Venice*, *A Midsummer Night's Dream.* The last named of these may have been too old to be of much acting value; although the present vogue of the pastoral play would excuse, one would think, its revival as well as its publication. *Every Man Out* was probably a play which the company had no expectation of reviving; *Every Man In* was "stayed" on the Stationers' Register on August 4 and did not get into print until 1601. Perhaps Jonson wished it printed and after Essex's disaster was able to override any influence the company could muster against him. *Henry V* and *Much Ado* were both stayed, but appeared, the former in a bad quarto, very likely surreptitious.

The company also registered its lost "moral" of *Cloth Breeches and Velvet Hose*,[24] mentioned in my first chapter, *A Larum for London*,

[22] Cf. Harold Hillebrand, *The Child Actors*, 106.

[23] Compare their *Cynthia's Revels*, *Poetaster*, *Goosecap*, *Liberality*, with Paul's boys' *Dodipoll*, *Antonio & Mellida*, *Histriomastix*, *Jack Drum*. But Paul's boys seem to have had a couple of the revived pastorals by Lyly or his imitators.

[24] S.R. May 27; John Roberts was prohibited from printing it until he could bring proper authority. Essex was seen walking in his garden, dressed all in cloth (i.e., not silk) this spring (Whyte, Feb. 9); a twelvemonth later, fustian (*Gawdy Letters*, 92, misdated) was all the fashion; cf. also Cornwallis's essay "Of Opinion," published in 1601, on the fad of wearing fustian, which was a cloth.

published in 1602, and *As You Like It*, seemingly a genuine case of staying to prevent publication, for it did not appear until in the Folio.

Plays of the Admiral's men appearing on the Register this year are *Old Fortunatus*, *1* and *2 Sir John Oldcastle* (Part Two is lost), *Look About You*, and *The Shoemakers' Holiday*, all published in 1600, though all valuable as acting properties; *Patient Grissell*, published 1603, *1* and *2 Robert Earl of Huntingdon*, published 1601, and *Captain Thomas Stukeley*, published 1605. None of these is recorded as stayed.

Plays belonging to Paul's boys which are registered are *The Maid's Metamorphosis* and *The Wisdom of Doctor Dodipoll*, published 1600, and *Jack Drum's Entertainment*, published 1601, but without great delay, for it was not registered until September 8, 1600. The Chapel boys' *Love's Metamorphosis* was registered November 25 and published in 1601. Oxford's *The Weakest Goeth to the Wall* came out in 1600. Two lost plays of unknown provenance appear on the Register this year; *Give a Man Luck and Throw Him into the Sea* (the proverb meant, "You can't down a lucky man"), and *The Tartarian Cripple, Emperor of Constantinople*.[25]

For all the winter season's being unprosperous, 1600 appears to have been an active year for the Chamberlain's men, and by no means one without social recognition, at least of an honorary sort, in spite of the disgrace of Essex and Southampton. On March 6 the company rendered direct service to Lord Hunsdon by playing *Henry IV*, still significantly called *Sir John Oldcastle*, after a dinner to the Flemish ambassador, presumably at the Chamberlain's house in Blackfriars. Chambers[26] thinks it also likely that they prepared *The Merry Wives* for a special performance with the aid of the boys of Windsor Chapel (in the dance of the elves and fairies) at the Garter Feast on April 23. It is interesting to notice that in the spring of 1599 Southampton had barely failed of election to the honor of the Garter, Northumberland, Worcester, Mountjoy, and Henry or Thomas Lord Howard voting for him in spite of the Queen's "special bar with special injury."[27] We should remind ourselves also of the great authority of the Admiral in Windsor Castle and Forest, that we may be conscious of the chief ironies in the assumed situation.

Shakespeare probably wrote *As You Like It* and *Twelfth Night* for his company in 1600, the former in the spring or summer, the latter in the autumn or winter. It may easily have been felt that the basic situation in *As You Like It* alluded to the position of Essex in 1600, banished from the court. In this play Shakespeare appears to have found his op-

[25] Some version of the story of Timur the Lame?

[26] II, 204. But compare *Shakespeare*, I, 434, where he is less definite.

[27] Stopes, 143; Lord Henry Howard to Southampton, April 27.

portunity to turn the tables on the boys who had been burlesquing his work so scurvily, by inserting some burlesque upon the pastoral convention of hanging verses and scutcheons on trees, represented by the Chapel boys in their revival of Lyly's *Love's Metamorphosis.*[28] With the exception of some extreme romanticism in the handling of the characters of its villains,[29] *As You Like It* displays in its whole tone a sturdy realism quite uncommon in the pastoral drama. Shakespeare's forest is far more real than Lodge's; in fact, for all its lions, serpents, and palm trees, and its lack of local gags, it is more real than Munday's Sherwood.

Pastoral Elements in the Drama, 1594–1603

A consideration of the pastoral during the companies' rivalry seems in order here. Under the influence of Ariosto and Tasso the English stage had long been accustomed to the occasional lightening of the conventional pastoral with humor. Lyly had adapted the form to courtly allegory of a political sort, and Greene had given it some praiseworthy realism in the depiction of character; while Peele's *Old Wives' Tale* succeeded in catching the magical atmosphere Shakespeare lets his puppets breathe in *A Midsummer Night's Dream.*

The Admiral's men were particularly fond of using the pastoral atmosphere in their folk-lore chronicle plays, such as those on Robin Hood. About 1596, probably to some extent under the influence of Lyly, they produced several plays giving events from the Greek mythology in pastoral settings, probably the material later published as the first three of Heywood's *Four Ages.* In this type of play we see the pastoral element closely associated with its original source. The Henslowe company, moreover, as we have seen, frequently produced a type of drama despised by Shakespeare's company—the old-fashioned romance of chivalry, which, partly because of its connection with the Greek romances through Sidney's *Arcadia,* was almost inevitably pastoral in setting.

Shakespeare's principal uses of pastoral materials before 1598 were in *Two Gentlemen of Verona,* for the rather perfunctory and unreal setting of the later scenes; in *A Midsummer Night's Dream,* where a surprising amount of realistic detail is employed with consummate skill to make the atmosphere all the more magical; and in *Love's Labour's Lost,*

[28] *Love's Metamorphosis,* I, i; *Ramis.* I will hang my Skutchin on this tree in honour of Ceres, and write this verse on the tree in hope of my successe.

[29] The wicked Duke's sudden conversion, however, represented to Shakespeare's audience an up-to-date humour rather than an old-fashioned romance, to judge from what Chamberlain writes on March 15, 1599: "The Duke of Joyeuse is once more become humerous, and, surrendring all his state into Montpensier (his sonne and lawes) handes, is returned again to be a Capuchin." One of Essex's own threats was to turn monk at a moment's notice, while turning "hermit" was a commonplace of Elizabethan public life.

which ridicules various pastoral cults and notions,[30] and has a strong infusion of realism.

I am inclined to believe that the pastoral convention, with its artificial treatment of human problems and human character, was essentially distasteful to Shakespeare—that when he did employ it as a concession to the exigencies of his source material and the demands of the dramatic competition to meet the tastes of the times, it was always with a partially unsuccessful effort to adapt it to his own realistic view of life and character. This conflict is, it seems to me, particularly observable in *As You Like It,* with its clash between reality and convention in Old Adam and Oliver, in "Blow, blow, thou winter wind!" and lions and palm trees.

The fact was that, for all the unreality of the pastoral convention and the vulgar popularity of the old romances among the lower classes, the pastoral had a persistent hold upon the taste of the court through its social usefulness as a love-making convention and its connection with the masque and the masque-like shows of the "barriers" or traditional and ceremonial tiltings. About 1597 the pastoral play *Mucedorus,* very likely produced by Shakespeare's own company, seems to have been distinctly successful. The Admiral's men did well in 1598 with their *Five Plays in One* (which probably contained Heywood's *Amphrisa, the Forsaken Shepherdess*[31]), and with their Robin Hood plays and their realistic adaptation of some of the materials of *A Midsummer Night's Dream* in *Two Angry Women of Abingdon.* Yonge's translation of Montemayor's *Diana* came from the press this year, as did Sidney's entertainments, *The Lady of May* and *A Pastoral Dialogue* (in the third edition of his *Arcadia*). 1599 saw Chapman writing a *Pastoral Tragedy* for Henslowe, and Chettle and Haughton an *Arcadian Virgin,* possibly on the story of Atalanta. Even the "Orphans' Tragedy" portion of *Two Lamentable Tragedies* is curiously pastoral in atmosphere; and Oberon and the fairies are most incongruously brought into the Marlovian *Lust's Dominion,* which is perhaps the Admiral's *Spanish Moor's Tragedy,* 1600. *The Merry Wives of Windsor* contrasts here in the way its hearty realism of treatment is extended even to the realistic explanation of the summer-night apparitions at Herne's Oak. The Admiral's *Look About You* returns to the manner of *John a Kent.* In 1600 was published a drama belonging to Oxford's men which shows a somewhat pastoral setting for a theme of rural exile, *The Weakest Goeth to the Wall.* Haughton seems to have returned to a successful vein of his company's in writing for Henslowe the lost *Robin Hood's Pen'orths* in the same year. Greg says,

[30] The chastity rules, for instance, are to be found in the Robin Hood plays of 1598 and in Fletcher's *Faithful Shepherdess* after our period.

[31] Published in his *Pleasant Dialogues and Dramas.*

"Nothing is known of this piece";[32] but I think we may fairly surmise that it was based on the ballads which have Robin play at potter or butcher and win all the Nottingham ladies' hearts by his gallant way of selling large quantities for small prices.[33] Derby's men may have had *The Trial of Chivalry.* But it seems most probable that it was the boy companies' *Love's Metamorphosis* and *The Maid's Metamorphosis* which most strongly influenced Shakespeare to make his first play of the year a pastoral comedy. The boys' choice of dramatic materials and types and their success with them would be watched with especial attention by the Chamberlain's men, whose dependence, far more than the Admiral's, was upon the favor of the upper classes; for the boy companies aimed their productions entirely at those classes and not at all at the "groundlings," for whom there was no place at their performances, as they take pains to tell us themselves:

> *Sir Ed. Fortune.* I saw the children of *Powles* last night,
> And troth they pleas'd me prettie, prettie well:
> The Apes in time will doe it handsomely.
> *Planet.* I faith, I like the audience that frequenteth there
> With much applause: A man shall not be chokte
> With the stench of Garlick; nor be pasted
> To the barmie Iacket of a Beer-brewer.
> *Brabant Jr.* 'Tis a good, gentle audience, and I hope the boys
> Will come one day into the Court of requests.[34]

The protection from the weather which they were able to offer, the greater accessibility of their theaters, and the better social character of their surroundings seem to have enabled them to charge a higher admission fee than that at such "public" theaters as the Globe and the Fortune.

It is interesting to notice that later in the same year as his successful (because largely unconventional) handling of the pastoral convention in *As You Like It,* Shakespeare reworked material which he had formerly used in the Julia-Silvia episodes of *Two Gentlemen of Verona* into the Viola-Olivia scenes of *Twelfth Night,* with almost obvious relief at ridding it as far as possible of pastoral elements.

Many plays both before and after 1600 exhibit odd incongruities between their pastoral conventions and the basically realistic and satirical spirit of the time. William Percy's plays, submitted to Paul's boys about 1600–1603, though probably never produced by them, appear to be full of satire of various sorts, although their very interesting stage directions are for pastoral settings, calling for such properties as a fawn trap, a hollow oak, etc. Pastoral elements are present in, but do not go harmoniously with the Senecan horrors of, *Alphonsus, Emperor of Germany* and

[32] *Henslowe,* II, 215.
[33] I.e., remarkable "pennyworths."
[34] *Jack Drum,* V, i, 102 ff.

Chettle's *Hoffman*. The universities express the dominance of the satirical over the pastoral mood in *2 Return from Parnassus*, 1601, and in the very amusing burlesque *Narcissus* (which owes much to *A Midsummer Night's Dream* and *Venus and Adonis*), produced at St. John's, Oxford, on Twelfth Night, 1603. Daniel's pastoral *Philotas*, partially written during the last years of our period and produced by the Revels boys shortly after it, caused him trouble by reason of its political implications in regard to Essex.[35] In his "Apology" for the "wrong application and misconceiuing of this Tragedy," Daniel says at the close:

> And for any resemblance, that through the ignorance of the History may be applied to the late Earle of Essex, it can hold in no proportion but only in his weaknesses, which I would wish all that loue his memory not to reuiue. And for mine owne part, hauing beene perticularly beholding to his bounty, I would to God his errore and disobedience to his Souereigne, might be so deepe buried vnderneath the earth, and in so low a tombe from his other parts, that hee might neuer be remembered among the examples of disloyalty in this Kingdome, or paraleld with Forreine Conspirators.[36]

The serious pastoral in a rather morbidly erotic form came back into vogue several years later, with *Philaster* and *The Faithful Shepherdess*. But this has been as long a discussion as we can afford the pastorals. With the next play taken up we must trace the girl-page device.

The Girl-Page Device, 1594–1603

Shakespeare's second play of 1600, *Twelfth Night*, was probably written in the autumn, and was produced before the lawyers at the Middle Temple feast on February 2, 1601. Its touching, wistful romance, mainly freed of the artificialities of the pastoral convention; its near-reincarnation of Falstaff in Sir Toby Belch; its charming part of the singing clown, Feste, for Armin; its great, gently satirical creation of Malvolio, so popular that he gave his name to the play in some early references—all were important elements in its success. The chief point in which it resembles his other play of the year should be noted; it is the use of the girl-page motive, long popular on the Elizabethan stage.

An early use in English drama of the piquant device of having a boy actor playing a girl part "disguised" as a page is by Lyly in his *Gallathea*, written for Paul's boys, and entered in the Stationers' Register in 1585. The trick was taken up, probably by the Admiral's men, in Kyd's *Soliman and Perseda*, registered 1592, and by Shakespeare in *Two Gentlemen of Verona*, probably written for Strange's men in the early nineties, although not printed until in the Folio. It may be noted that

[35] Cf. for example, lines 1135–63.

[36] Are not the last five words a *tu quoque* allusion to anti-Essex material in the plays on Biron, Gowrie, and Catiline?

this device must have been particularly exasperating to the Puritans who objected on Biblical grounds to players' masquerading as members of the opposite sex, for in spite of all the suggestiveness with which this sort of rôle was sometimes played, these "girl-pages" were technically guiltless of any such masquerade.

The period before 1594 was probably one of experimentation rather than keen rivalry in the type. In the anonymous *Wars of Cyrus*,[37] the motive of escape, very common for this sort of disguising, is well developed; the heroine escapes in her page's clothes; and he fleeing in hers slays a villain who thinks him a defenseless girl. (Compare Sir Toby's misadventure in *Twelfth Night.*) In his *Four Prentices of London*, probably an Admiral's play of about 1594, the ingenious Thomas Heywood rather burlesques the girl-page situation, although probably not intentionally, by having the girl serve her lover intimately as his page for long period without his detection:

> *Lady.* Thus haue I maskt my bashful modesty
> Vnder the habite of a trusty Page . . .
> My loue and Lord, that honoured me as woman,
> Loues me a youth; employes me euery where . . .
> And now I haue learnt to be a perfect Page,
> He will haue none to trusse his poynts but me,
> At boord to waite vpon his cup but me:
> To beare his Target in the field, but me:
> Nay, many a thing, which makes me blush to speake,
> He will haue none to lie with him but me,
> I dreame and dreame, and things come in my mind:
> Onely I hide my eyes; but my poore heart
> Is bard and kept from loues satiety . . .[38]

Finally Heywood introduces the new twist of having the "page" re-disguise as a girl, thus bringing about a double dénouement.

In the spring of 1595, Boas thinks, a group of Queen's College, Cambridge, students, playing before the Earl of Essex, revived the Latin *Laelia*, new in 1590, based on *Gl'Ingannati*, and containing the plot of *Twelfth Night*, but with a little more emphasis than Shakespeare's on the girl-page's brother and his amorous success. Shakespeare may have been present at this performance; at least it is very probable that some account of it reached him through friends, revealing to him through this example of the universities' traditional cultural linking to Italy some possibilities in the girl-page motive as yet undeveloped on the public stage. But he did not avail himself of these possibilities at once. In *The Merchant of Venice* a year or so later he merely uses Jessica's dis-

[37] Q. 1594; perhaps first given by a company of boys.

[38] Edition for John Pearson, London, 1874; II, 205.

guise to make her elopement a little more charming, and extracts some comic irony from the other girls' disguise as men. In 1598 he must have been reminded of the device by the Admiral's men's use of it in Haughton's *Englishmen for My Money*, where the girl escapes to her lover in boy's clothes. In this year, too, Greene's *James IV*, probably a property of the Admiral's men, was published. In it a girl disguised as a squire is wooed by a woman. Yonge's translation of Montemayor's *Diana*, on which a lost girl-page play, *Felix and Felismena*, had probably been based about 1585, was also published this year. And this, rather than 1595, may possibly have been the year of the revival of *Laelia*.

Sir Clyomon and Sir Clamydes appeared in print in 1599, an old play of the Queen's men in which a girl follows her lover in male attire and thinks him dead as in *Cymbeline*. There is also a business of rings, as in *The Merchant of Venice*, *Two Gentlemen of Verona*, *All's Well*, and *Twelfth Night*. The material here released for publication may have been staged by the Admiral's men this year in their *Four Kings*, which has been very doubtfully identified with the published play. In the same year Paul's boys, in Marston's *Antonio and Mellida*, use the escape form of the device; and the Latin *Labyrinthus* at Cambridge[39] represents the type in its lowest aspect, closest to the Italian manner, with a young man who passes as a woman, and a girl who is supposed to be a man; there is extreme confusion of sexes with such consequences to the play's moral tone as might be expected.

I believe that at about this time *Two Gentlemen of Verona* was revived by the Chamberlain's men, with a certain amount of revision. This revision, I suspect from the present state of Act Four, Scene Four, was to strengthen—perhaps even to introduce—the element of pathos, lacking among recent uses of the device. The disguised Julia, who has just been employed by her love Proteus as his page Sebastian,[40] soliloquizes:

> Yet will I woo for him, but yet so coldly
> As heaven it knows, I would not have him speed.[41]

Now this sort of promise, here apparently of a rather comic scene to ensue, is usually kept by Shakespeare. But when Silvia enters we have the famous pathetic scene which so closely resembles certain scenes and situations in *Twelfth Night*. It is introduced in this curious fashion, which I think reveals the place where the scene has been patched and the substitution made:

> *Jul.* If you be she, I do entreat your patience
> To hear me speak the message I am sent on.

[39] The 1599 dating is not certain. See Boas, 317.
[40] The name of Viola's brother in *Twelfth Night*, 1600.
[41] 113, 114.

> *Sil.* From whom?
> *Jul.* From my master Sir Proteus, madam.
> *Sil.* O! he sends you for a picture?
> *Jul.* Ay, madam.
> *Sil.* Ursula,[42] bring my picture there.

Does not the break come with Silvia's exclamation and question about the picture, which prevents our hearing Julia's "cold wooing" in the message she has asked to be allowed to speak? The sportsmanlike warmth of Viola's wooing of her rival is in interesting contrast. And observe that the girl-page is allowed to be humorously pert in *Twelfth Night*, the play which contains enough pathos elsewhere. The latter drama seems the best possible handling of the girl-page motive. And yet it can hardly be called unconventional; note, for instance, that it uses the ring and wooing devices, which were common, and the twin brother as in *Laelia*.

Earlier in the same year, in *As You Like It*, Shakespeare had disguised Rosalind as a youth, and had burlesqued the hanging of verses on trees,—a feature of Lyly's *Love's Metamorphosis*, just revived by the Chapel boys. An interesting parallel between this play of Lyly's and *Twelfth Night* shows, I think, a complimentary verbal borrowing from a dramatist Shakespeare admired for his literary qualities. Lyly has, "Thy face as fair as the damask rose shall perish like the damask rose; the canker shall eat thee in the bud." Is not Shakespeare's,

> She never told her love,
> But let concealment, like a worm i' the bud,
> Feed on her damask cheek,

close enough to Lyly to be a compliment rather than a plagiarism?[43]

Yet another girl-page on the boards in 1600, this one in *The Maid's Metamorphosis*, given by Paul's boys, presents herself as her own brother and in answer to her prayer is actually altered in sex by the gods.[44] This play may, like Lyly's, be an old one revived; but in any case, as if despairing of improving on Shakespeare's handling of the traditional materials of the type, playwrights soon appeared to be striving for novelties. Perhaps it was in 1601 that the Chapel boys presented Chapman's *May Day*, in which for the first time the disguise is unknown to the audience, although hinted at, and the dénouement therefore some-

[42] The name of Hero's waiting-woman in *Much Ado*, 1598. Moreover, a Friar Laurence is mentioned in *Two Gentlemen of Verona*, and Baldwin believes *Romeo and Juliet* to have been rewritten in 1598.

[43] Lyly had been seeking for years the office of Master of the Revels, and it seems just possible that the Chamberlain's men thought it best to be on his good side.

[44] The story, of course, is that of Iphis and Ianthe, *Metamorphoses*, IX, 668 ff. And compare the jolly Scotch dramatic poem, *Philotus*.

thing of a surprise. Of course much of the audience's interest in the characters' efforts to maintain the disguise unpenetrated is thus given up for the sake of the dénouement; possibly, however, in such cases part of the actor's technique was to allow the disguise to be suspected by the audience. As usually in Chapman's comedy, there appears to be a strong element of burlesque too, and of needless masquerading of the girl-page type. Heywood in his *Wise Woman of Hogsdon*, probably given by Worcester's men before the end of our period, again employs his device of re-disguise as in *The Four Prentices*, with a girl disguised as a boy re-disguising as a girl for a "mock" wedding which thus proves to be a real one. In the anonymous *Fair Maid of Bristow*, perhaps owned by Shakespeare's company before they became the King's men, a girl disguises to save her lover by taking his place on the gallows, a strangely sensational variant of the Sidney Carton motive. Jonson in *The Silent Woman*, played by the Revels Children, uses Chapman's device of surprise by keeping secret from the audience the disguising as a girl of a boy who unmasks at the end. And four or five years after the accession of James, Shakespeare's company produced Beaumont and Fletcher's *Philaster*, a pastoral play which, in the girl page who in serving her lover is wounded by him, uses rather morbidly the motives handled with such healthy, common-sense humor and pathos in *Twelfth Night*. Yet even Shakespeare makes concessions to sensationalism, for instance where in *Cymbeline* Posthumus hurls the disguised Imogen from him.

But let us return once more from pastorals and girl pages to the dramatic events of 1600 and the fortunes of the Admiral's men. At the beginning of February they bought a drum and trumpets "to go into the contrey." But they do not appear to have gone until July; probably the musical instruments were a bargain; perhaps they came through Henslowe's pawnshop. On April 27 they visited Windsor for the Garter installation (by proxy) of King Henri IV of France. Probably it was some time in the early autumn, after a tour, that they crossed the river and occupied Alleyn's recently built Fortune, on the northwestern boundary of the City. At the express desire of the Queen, Alleyn now returned to the stage after three years' absence. His presence appears to have brought about considerable economies in the management of the company.[45] Fewer new plays were brought out; thus the expense for playbooks and properties was less. And, as Chambers remarks, it may well have been the case that Alleyn, who had created parts in the eighties and early nineties, had a tendency toward revivals.[46]

The play for the opening of the new theater probably was *Fortune's*

[45] Chambers, II, 183.

[46] *Ibid.*, II, 177.

Tennis, for which Dekker was paid on September 6. On June 22, when the Privy Council gave authority for opening the Fortune, they understood that it would replace the old Curtain, which would be "ruinated" or turned to "some other good use." This arrangement seems to suggest that the Curtain was now somehow under the control of Alleyn or Henslowe. But it was not insisted on. Henslowe now had to find a tenant for the vacant Rose. He records Pembroke's men as there October 28, but only for two unprofitable performances.[47] Possibly the Privy Council, who had decreed on June 22 a limitation of houses to one on each bank, interfered; although this limitation shows no permanent effects.

Henslowe records that Chettle and Day were paid in full for *The Blind Beggar of Bednal Green* on May 26, 1600. Between January 29 and July 30, 1601, Day and Haughton were paid for two more parts of the play. Not until 1659 did a quarto appear in print, a long and somewhat hacked-about single play ascribed simply to John Day and the Prince's Servants. This, our only extant version, probably contains material, if not from all three of the original Bednal Green plays, at least from the first two. The play as we have it is of a sort we have learned to recognize as typical of the Admiral's men, with its royal and noble historical characters who take part in the intrigue, its semi-historical romance of contemporary Elizabethan interest, its manifold disguisings, its picaresque roguery, its broad and sharply-localized comedy. Here we have the Admiral's men handling romantically a portion of the life of Eleanor Cobham preceding that which Shakespeare treats of in *Henry VI*, just as in *Look About You* they give the romance of Lady Faulconbridge which antedates her appearance in *King John*. In both cases it happens that a pleasanter impression of the lady is given. We learn near the end of the play of Eleanor's marriage to Gloucester; but some important scenes in her romance have been omitted, probably in the process of condensing two or more plays into one.

The play, as I have indicated, is carefully and precisely localized at Bednal Green, in the parish of Stepney, at the eastern gates of London, where the road led out to Essex, Suffolk, and Norfolk. The Admiral's dramatists seem to have brought the story nearer their own times by changing a ballad about Simon de Montfort's hiding after the battle of Evesham in the reign of Henry III into this tale of the days of Henry VI; so it is not impossible that we are to look for some of the play's significances in events nearer still. Bishop Bonner, notorious in the Marian persecutions, lived at Bishop's Hall near the Green; and Stow relates how lies told at Bednal Green in the days of Edward VI procured the hanging of good men for treason.

[47] They gave *Roderick* and *Like Unto Like*, the latter probably Ulpian Fulwell's old play.

At least two mentions of localities in the play must have been taken to refer to contemporary Elizabethans. The slander about Calais best known to the Admiral's audience must have been the old rhyme:

> Who built Brome Hall? Sir Thomas Cornwallis.
> How did he build it? By selling of Calais.

Sir Thomas, 1519–1604, one-time Comptroller of the Household to Queen Mary, was the grandfather of the essayist. The family names of his two wives are both mentioned in drama: Jerningham (a connection of the Cecils and the Brookes) in *The Merry Devil of Edmonton*, Mewtas (a Howard connection) in *Sir Thomas More*. We have already seen that the Cornwallis family had Cecil connections which would make such an effort as this to kill the Calais slander a reasonable one for the Admiral's men. It is a question whether the dramatists would wish the audience to go a step further and parallel the domestic troubles of Momford, whose daughter is cast off by her troth-plight husband in the play, with those of Sir Thomas Cornwallis, whose daughter Mary was the repudiated wife of the Earl of Bath. In 1600 Francis Davison, a follower of Essex, wrote out of gratitude to the Russells for many favors, *An Answer to Mrs. Mary Cornwallis pretended Countess of Bath her Libel against the Countess of Cumberland; being a Defence of the Marriage of William Bourchier, Third Earl of Bath, with Elizabeth Russell, daughter of Francis Earl of Bedford.* Essex, himself connected with the Bourchiers, had been interested in the dispute, and in 1594 had written to the Earl of Bath congratulating him on escaping "bonds that were not worthy to hold" him, but reproving him for ill-treating his present lady "of a noble house."[48]

The prominence of Harling in the play would remind the Elizabethan audience of two families, the Gawdys of West Harling and the Lovells of East Harling, interrelated but not guiltless of mutual ill-feeling. Sir Bassingbourne Gawdy, head of his house, was a prominent man in the administration of Norfolk and highly serviceable to the alleged ring of recusant-squeezers headed by Chief Justice Popham and Cecil's very good friend Sir John Stanhope, which I have mentioned in connection with Wayland Wood. His younger brother Philip, whose gossipy letters I have quoted more than once, went adventuring as was the way of younger brothers, was captured in the Revenge, languished in a Spanish prison, was finally ransomed, became a retainer of Essex, and was especially assigned because of his linguistic attainments to wait upon Perez. He did all he could to be a friend at court to his elder brother. Apparently by the time of Essex's fall he was so good a friend of the

[48] *Hist. MSS. Com.*, XIII, R-2, 19.

Chamberlain and his family that he did not go down in that disaster. He married a dowerless East-Anglian girl; and his life and connections make it seem not impossible that he is made fun of here as the brave but bumpkinish Tom Strowd, who may not aspire to wed a Momford.[49] But we know that the Gawdys sided with the Cornwallis family in at least one important matter; for Philip refers to Mary Cornwallis as "her honor of Bathe."

Of the play's authors, John Day at least was well qualified to write of Norfolk places and people and of the road through Suffolk and Essex to London, for he was the son of a husbandman of Cawston, Norfolk, some score of miles beyond Norwich.[50] Between his father's home and London were Wayland Wood, the Harlings, Bury St. Edmunds (where Humphrey Duke of Gloucester died, perhaps in one of the last scenes of the Blind Beggar trilogy), and Bednal Green. His associate William Haughton, too, was very likely of a Norfolk family,[51] a relative of Robert Haughton of Norfolk, to whose chambers in Lincoln's Inn Philip Gawdy succeeded. Several of the plays in which he had a hand show Norfolk and Suffolk material more or less plainly: *Englishmen for My Money*, entered in 1601, his only independent play, has characters with the family names Harvey, Heigham, Walgrave, all mentioned in the Gawdy letters; *Beech's Tragedy*, on which he worked with Day late in 1599, is, as we have seen, mysteriously related to the *Two Lamentable Tragedies* ascribed to the scrivener Yarington, together with the Babes in the Wood story located by tradition not far from Day's birthplace; *The English Fugitives*, April, 1600, if it was the same as the extant *Duchess of Suffolk*, dealt with the adventures of Peregrine Bertie's mother, whose home was at Parham, Suffolk, and who owned Norfolk lands.

And these Norfolk associations of Haughton's give us, I think, a little more information about the mysterious "Mr. Pett" who shared with him Henslowe's payment on May 17, 1600, for *Strange News out of Poland*. In 1599 the Polish ruler had been opposing the peace between Russia and Turkey which English diplomacy was promoting (one probable result of the negotiations being a play called *Vaivode* by Chettle for Henslowe, 1598), and had seized English merchant ships for use in his war against Charles of Sweden, with whom England was on friendly terms.[52] Details for dramatic use may well have come through a member

[49] Cf. *The Letters of Philip Gawdy*, ed. by I. H. Jeayes; and *Hist. MSS. Com.*, VII, R., App., 518 ff.—The MSS. of Geo. E. Frere, Roydon Hall, Norfolk.

[50] Upon the passages against rapier-duelling in this play, as expressing John Day's regret for having slain his fellow-dramatist Porter, see Leslie Hotson, *Atlantic*, CXLVIII, 26.

[51] Cf. A. C. Baugh's biographical introduction to his edition of Haughton's *Englishmen for My Money*, Philadelphia, 1917.

[52] Cf. *S. P. Dom.*, 1598–1601, 134; *Sal. MSS.*, IX, 227; X, 169.

of the great Pett shipbuilding family. There were Petts at Deptford, Wapping, Limehouse, Chatham; but probably our playwright was Peter, younger brother of the Admiral's protégé Phineas, whose extremely interesting autobiography has been edited by W. G. Perrin for the Navy Records Society (1917). On their mother's re-marriage to the Reverend Thomas Nunn, minister of Weston, Suffolk, Peter had been "put out to a gentleman's house in Suffolk to teach his children"; but the course of his life was changed by a tragedy. Nunn was brutal to the younger stepchildren living in his house and beat Peter's sister Abigail so severely that she died. The stepfather was tried at the assizes at Bury in Lent, 1599, convicted and condemned, but secured a reprieve and was later pardoned; Phineas tells us that "great means was made for him," and indeed he had influential connections if he was one of the Nunns of Bury who were kin to the Gawdys.[53] And this, by the way, was not the only link between the Gawdys and the Petts, for there were Petts at Harling, and our Peter's elder half-brother Peter, shipwright of Wapping, wrote in 1598 a letter to Sir Bassingbourne Gawdy[54] which makes it clear that he was well known in Gawdy's neighborhood and presumably related to the Thomas Pett living there. In 1599 this elder Peter (?) published a poem entitled *Time's Journey to seeke his Daughter Truth; and Truth's Letter to Fame of England's Excellencie*, dedicated to the Admiral.

For some reason Phineas, who now took charge of his younger brothers and sisters, brought Peter to London in November and placed him with a lawyer, Dr. John (?) Hone, in the Court of Arches. But the younger man, it seems, did not care for the law; he became dissolute (doubtless associating with such persons as Day, classed by Jonson among "rogues and base fellows," and Haughton), and died in June, 1600, at the Dolphin in Water Lane. His first appearance in Henslowe's Diary was his last.

Before we leave *The Blind Beggar of Bednal Green* a few miscellaneous remarks may be of interest. That the play was ultimately printed from one or more prompters' books is indicated by the marginal direction, "Ready for a Hangman's Will."[55] Imitation of the successful Falstaff scenes appears, as so often in the Admiral's plays, when the clown Swash is terrified by the thieves about whom he has just been bragging that he "killed seven of the six and the rest carried away the money."[56]

The Admiral's repertory this year contained several more plays surely or possibly of the chronicle type, at least in part: *Fortune's Tennis* may have had something to do with the famous gift of tennis balls to Henry V; the extant "plot" of the second part, perhaps of about 1602, appears

[53] Cf. *Hist. MSS. Com.*, x, R-2, 7, 10, 84, and *passim*.

[54] *Ibid.*, from Limehouse, Oct. 22.

[55] Sgn. E3.

[56] Sgn. E3.

to be somewhat concerned with French history.[57] It would indeed be a parallel significant of the companies' rivalry if the new Globe really was opened with a Henry V play in 1599 and the new Fortune with another (of opposite political implications) in 1600. Possibly there was here some satire on Essex, an ardent tennis player, or on Southampton, who lost money at the game on his visit to Paris in 1598;[58] but interest in the sport was general. *Owen Tudor* must have dealt with Queen Elizabeth's ancestor, the victim of Richard III, executed after the battle of Mortimer's Cross in Herefordshire. *Truth's Supplication to Candlelight*, by Dekker, if we are to identify it with his later *Whore of Babylon*, was an elaborate exposure of the Catholic plots against Elizabeth's life, and therefore of somewhat the same political tone as the same company's *Massacre at Paris*. The extant play owes much to *The Faerie Queene*, especially in the characters' names: Titania, Florimel, Paridel, Elfiron, etc. In the allegorical treatment of the defense against the Armada both the elder Hunsdon, in command at Tilbury Fort, and the Admiral are honored; of course the latter actually got the glory (and, more important, the earldom). In the Prologue, the reference to the theater as a square may be an allusion to the new Fortune, built in 1600, for its shape was its chief point of difference from the Globe.

Then the company had, too, the lost *2 Oldcastle*, doubtless a tragedy showing Powys's treachery and Oldcastle's trial and martyrdom; *Ferrex and Porrex* by Haughton which, as a revival of *Gorboduc* would compliment that play's author, now Lord Buckhurst and Lord Treasurer, a staunch Cecilian, and also, if that dangerous portion was not excised in revision, would urge upon the Queen the necessity of settling the succession;[59] and the same dramatist's *English Fugitives*, which has been plausibly identified with *The Duchess of Suffolk*, 1624, a strongly Protestant account of Bishop Bonner's persecutions in the days of Queen Mary. But of course these "English Fugitives" may be the contemporary Roman Catholic exiles in Flanders, whose gatherings were a continual source of Jesuit propaganda, schemes for a Catholic succession, and plots against the Queen's life. A play on their affairs may have provided a supplement, then, to *Truth's Supplication*. *Strange News out of Poland*, by Haughton and Mr. Pett, the latter of whom perhaps furnished the information, looks like an interesting experiment in journalism. Haughton's *Robin Hood's Pen'orths* probably had some historical setting; the

[57] Greg, *Henslowe*, III, 143; among the characters are Orleaunce, Mauritius, Boniface, Bertram, Lewes; as well as Somerton and Edwine. The plot is, however, extremely fragmentary.

[58] Cf. Chamberlain, Nov. 8, 1598, reporting that he has lost 1800 crowns.

[59] The material in *Gorboduc* which is specifically against the Scottish succession needs not have been left in the play for a revival at this time.

natural one would be Nottingham in the reign of King John. But the collaborated *1* and *2 Fair Constance of Rome*, although they may have contained passages of legendary British history (we remember Constance's adventures with Alla, King of Northumberland in "The Man of Lawes Tale"), may perhaps be better classified as romances. Nearly all the other plays of the year's repertory have been mentioned.

Since the machinations of Grey had lost Southampton his command and brought him home from Ireland in disgrace, the Earl had been malcontent. In the autumn of 1599 he was idling in London with his young friend Rutland and "passed away the time merely in going to plays every day." In 1600, Essex, still imprisoned, escaped a Star Chamber trial, and was granted lighter confinement in his own house. On June 5 he was reprimanded before a commission; and he was given his liberty on August 27, but forbidden to approach the court. Pleading letters failed to make the Queen relent toward him. At Michaelmas his chief source of revenue, the monopoly of the importation of sweet wines, lapsed; and his supplications, now despairing, could not move the Queen to renew it. Meanwhile Lord Mountjoy was pressing his campaign in Ireland, and Sir John Hayward was belatedly imprisoned for his authorship of *The History of Henry IV* (1599) with its dedication to Essex couched in ambiguous but fulsome Latin. The Earl's own *Apology* for his stand against peace with Spain, which again seemed near that summer, was printed and suppressed.

Essex's last fruitless plea to the Queen was on November 17, Queen's Day. He then became suddenly and violently malcontent, declaring that the Queen's "conditions" were "as crooked as her carcass."[60] Malcontents of all sorts began to gather at Essex House. There were sermons by extreme Puritan divines who were in the habit of justifying resistance to authority. Agents were dispatched to Scotland urging James to take steps against the influence which Ralegh, Sackville, the Admiral, and Cecil were using against his claim to the succession, all favoring the Infanta of Spain.[61] Southampton went to Ireland to induce Lord Mountjoy to come with troops to the aid of Essex, but failed in his mission and went on to the Low Countries, where Lord Grey had challenged him to meet him. He soon returned again to London and there engaged in a street fray with his enemy in January, 1601. In the same month consultations of the Essex faction were being held at Drury House, the Earl of Southampton's lodging. On February 7 the Queen (at least the move was ostensibly hers), anxious to stop these suspicious and dangerous

[60] *Reliquiae Wottonianae*, 192; *cit.* Cadwallader, 73 n. 1.

[61] Cadwallader, 74. This view conflicted with that of the English Catholic fugitives, who feared the Protestant claimants, especially Beauchamp and Arabella.

gatherings, precipitated the rebellion by an order to Essex to come before the Council.

The story of the brief outbreak, the trial which followed, and its tragic aftermath, is well known. It is dramatically told by Strachey; clearly, although very briefly, with good biographical notes, by Cadwallader; more fully by Stopes. It has never been told with an adequate use of the material now calendared and easily accessible.

For us a little of the chronology of these events is necessary because they parallel the latter part of the court dramatic season of 1600–1601: At the request of some of the conspirators *Richard II* was played at the Globe on February 7. The rebellion occurred on Sunday, February 8. The trial of Essex and Southampton was held on February 19. Essex was beheaded in the Tower on February 25. Captain Thomas Lea's subsidiary plot to seize the Queen and force her to release Essex failed on February 13; he was hanged the eighteenth; and the executions of Blount, Danvers, Cuffe, and Meyrick took place on March 13 and 18.

With these dates in mind, let us consider the unusually large number of court performances this season. They were apportioned as follows:

December 26, Chamberlain's. (*As You Like It?*)
December 28, Admiral's. (*The Blind Beggar of Bednal Green?*)
January 1, Paul's. (*Jack Drum's Entertainment?*)
Derby's. (*The Trial of Chivalry?*)
January 6, Admiral's. (*Phaeton?* Properties for court Jan. 2.)
Derby's. (Aid with *Phaeton?* or an unknown play?)
Chapel. (Songs and dances for *Phaeton?*)
Chamberlain's. (*Twelfth Night?*)
February 2, Admiral's (*Hannibal and Scipio?*)
February 22, Chapel. (*Liberality and Prodigality?*)
February 24, Chamberlain's (*Richard II?*)

As You Like It, the past summer's play, would have given a more amiable picture of Essex in "exile" than was now justified by the actual situation. I have merely guessed at the Admiral's play of December 28 as probably their best and most suitable production of the year. It was sufficiently popular to call for two sequels, and its politics and personalities were harmless enough and yet designed to please the dominant party. For January 1 *Jack Drum's Entertainment* was probably fairly new; at least it had not been published; and as a lighter, more satirical thing it would go well on the same day as Derby's *Trial of Chivalry*, the only play we can assign to that company's 1600 repertory.

On January 6 no less than four companies were present at court. Now until the reign of James two plays in one day appear to have been the limit in lavishness;[62] for the court was small and orderly; the Queen was inclined to be penurious; and probably much the same auditors, including Elizabeth herself, saw all the plays given at court. For these reasons I argue that instead of four plays' being given on January 6, 1601, entirely too many for the endurance of Elizabeth's court, there was a joint performance, probably in the afternoon, by the Admiral's and Derby's men with the aid of the singing Chapel boys, of Dekker's *Phaeton*, which I believe to have been in its original form a spectacular mythological play reflecting on the rashness and downfall of Essex, although we now possess to represent it only the gentle, masque-like *Sun's Darling*. Of course Derby's men may have given a separate play of their own, of which we have no clue to the title or nature, in the evening, preceded or followed by the Chamberlain's men. They appear to have been paid the usual sum for a court performance at this time, ten pounds, as were the Admiral's and the Chamberlain's men. The other payment for the day[63] was five pounds to "Nathanyell Gyles, M^r^ of the children of the Chapple, for a showe wth musycke and speciall songes p'pared for the purpose." *The Sun's Darling*, a "moral Masque" by Dekker and Ford, was published in 1656 as played "by their Majesties' Servants at the Cockpit in Drury Lane." It is full of songs and "shows," and in revision may have been deprived of the topical political material which had justified Henslowe's calling it *Phaeton*. A side-light on the original date of writing is given by the fact that in its allegorical organization by means of the successive seasons it bears a marked resemblance to Nashe's *Summer's Last Will*, published in 1600. The name of Shakespeare's *Twelfth Night* seems best accounted for by assuming its performance on the evening to which it is here assigned, Twelfth Night.

I have surmised that the Admiral's play of February 2 was the lost *Hannibal and Scipio* for which Hathaway and Rankins were paid in full on January 12. The story of the defeat of the elder Scipio by Hannibal, the cautious campaign of Fabius, and the crushing of Hannibal by the younger Scipio might be so handled, conceivably, as to shadow, as clearly as could be dared against the looming crisis, less than a week before the Essex Rebellion, the political events of the preceding years, with the elder Cecil kneeling to Essex after Cadiz, the Admiral moving cautiously from defeat to stalemate in his rivalry of the leader of the opposite faction, and the younger Cecil (here in true prophecy) finally

[62] For the records see Chambers, IV, App. A & B. Arabella (cf. E. T. Bradley, *Arabella Stuart*, II, 190) wrote of the Christmas season of 1603, "It is said there shall be thirty plays." At Christmas, 1605, there were ten plays by the King's men, apparently in a rather brief period, and two by Paul's boys (Chambers, *op. cit.*, 173).

[63] Chambers, IV, 166.

victorious over the great enemy. But it is desirable that someone should make a study of the interrelations among the Admiral's *Hannibal and Scipio* (1601), Marston's *Sophonisba* (for the Blackfriars boys, quarto 1606), and Thomas Nabbes's *Hannibal and Scipio* (Queen's, 1635). The Prologue of the last-named work apologizes to some who

> . . . would taske
> His [i.e., Nabbe's] borrowing from a former play.

Marston's play, containing many of the same events and characters and similarly stressing romantic elements, may be referred to: but *Sophonisba* exalts Sophonisba and Massinissa, while Nabbes favors their opponents, Scipio and Syphax. The differences, indeed (although both plays contemn Carthaginian treachery), are sufficient to hint at opposed politics, whether those of Marston and the Admiral's men or Marston and the later Queen's men is not clear. It is perhaps noteworthy that Nabbes's actor-list names several who played in Shirley's *Wedding*, 1629; Heywood's *Fair Maid of the West*, 1631; and Davenport's *King John and Matilda*, printed in 1655, at least two of which plays had Elizabethan ones underlying them.

It is supposed that the Chapel boys' performance of February 22, just after the trial of Essex, was their old-fashioned morality play *Liberality and Prodigality*, published in 1602 "As it was playd before her Majesty." I am inclined to think that the play contains an expression of the widespread desire and general hope of Elizabeth's commuting the sentence of Essex to imprisonment, as she did Southampton's,[64] in the part of the Lame Soldier who has served "In France, In Flaunders: but in Ireland most."[65] There was plenty of time between the eighth and the twenty-second to write in and rehearse so brief a part. Prodigality is tried for the murder of Tenacity on "February 4 in the Year of Elizabeth 43"—oddly near the date of the rebellion.

It seems exceedingly strange that there should be a play at court at all on February 24, the eve of Essex's death under the axe. That the Chamberlain's men should be the ones to give it seems still more remarkable. But Elizabeth was perfectly capable of both bravado to conceal her real feelings and a very grim sort of humor. It may be that as a gesture of contempt, triumph, and warning, she called Shakespeare and his fellows before her that evening in the presence of her uneasy court and commanded them to perform the play in which she believed they had pointed out her weakness and foretold her deposition by Essex, the play of which they had given a special performance by request of the Essex conspirators on the eve of the Rebellion—*Richard the Second.*

[64] By refraining from signing his death-warrant.

[65] v, iv.

Such a gesture could certainly have been accompanied by an inhibition of public performances. But another explanation is possible; that Essex's enemies procured the acting of this very play at this time to keep firm the Queen's wavering purpose. Even if there is nothing in the ring story, Essex seems to have held, not without reason, some hope of reprieve to the very last. On the morning of the execution,

> The Queene, by reason of her good will alwaies to him, somewhat now moued in mind, commanded that he should not die, by Sir Edward Cary.[66] But then on the other side, weighing his contumacy and stubbornesse, that scorned to ask her pardon; and that he had said, that as long as he liued, the Queene could not liue in safety;[67] she altered her resolution, and by Darcy commanded the execution to proceed.[68]

Recalling for a moment the *Poetaster* allusion to the financial disastrousness of this winter season to the Chamberlain's men, should we not decide that it would be unwise to accept as the only explanation Shakespeare's own reference to the damaging competition of the boy companies? The novelty of the boys, of course, and their specialty of singing were dangerously attractive to that aristocratic audience on which the Chamberlain's men chiefly depended. We have seen nothing in their repertories, however, which ought not to have been matched, novelty, singing, and all, by Shakespeare's delightful plays of the season —evidently designed to use the charm of the company's own boy actors and the singing of Jack Wilson and Robert Armin to meet the boy companies on their own ground. But in addition to the boys' competition, which by itself Shakespeare's company probably could have coped with, there was the political situation. By the end of the season some of the chief patronizers of their plays were dead, many were imprisoned or impoverished by fines; some had fled since the Rebellion, to say nothing of those who had deserted the sinking ship before and after the eighth of February. Indeed, from the middle of November on, the character of the malcontent faction regularly attending the Globe may well have had such a reputation as to frighten away the more conservative or timorous of that theater's clientele. It seems that tact would have forbidden Shakespeare to mention this political difficulty in *Hamlet*, but his having the players travel because of an "inhibition" which "comes by means of the innovation"[69] comes at least perilously close to being such a reference. Editors[70] make great efforts to reject such an inter-

[66] Probably Sir Edmund, son of the Chamberlain.

[67] The reverend Abdias Ashton, for working the Earl into this fatal state of repentant frenzy, was paid forty pounds on the day before the execution, out of the special emergency fund. Cf. *Acts of the Privy Council*, 1600–01, 180.

[68] Camden, *Elizabeth*, 324.

[69] II, ii, 355.

[70] E.g., J. R. Crawford, in the *Yale Shakespeare*.

pretation of the passage, which did not appear in print until the 1604 quarto; yet "inhibition" surely is a term used in connection with such a forced closing of the theaters as resulted from the *Isle of Dogs* trouble, while "innovation," although Chambers[71] says it "does not seem a very obvious term for a seditious rising," was not uncommonly used by the Elizabethans to mean "change of government," as when Camden says:

But most of all being discontented at the preferment of his enemie Cecil, to his place of the Master of the Wards, hee [Essex] began to cast himselfe into darke and cloudie stormes of melancholy; he secretly thought some vndirect course to take in hand, as, to returne againe into *England* with his choisest Bands, and so to bring vnder his power by force those his great enemies; being perswaded that great store of concourse out of loue of him, and desire of innouations, would easily and quickely flocke vnto him.[72]

These political difficulties must have contributed greatly to the poorness of the season and made up exactly the factor over which Jonson, with his glances at the Essex affair in *The Poetaster*, appears to gloat, making the player lament, "No bodie comes at us; not a gentleman . . ."

But why were not the Chamberlain's men more actively concerned in the rebellion? And even implicated only as deeply as they were with their special revival of the politically dangerous *Richard II*, why were they not imprisoned and shattered as Pembroke's men had been for their far less dangerous *Isle of Dogs?* One or two of their members were examined in regard to the matter, but apparently with all gentleness, and with a certain disinclination to dig deep for unpleasant facts.[73] That was all. The company did not even suffer obviously in its standing at court. How is this to be explained?

The party which followed Essex into London in his attempt to rouse the City consisted of about two hundred "lusty young men of stout Courage, but no ways provided of arms like Souldiers, most of them having their Cloaks wrapped about their Arms, and only Swords by their Sides."[74] Judging by such evidence as we can gather, these were almost all nobles and gentlemen with a few of their personal retainers. There do not appear to have been any of the Chamberlain's men with them or at Essex House;[75] as a class distrusted by the citizens, the players would have been kept out of sight, anyway, until the revolt was well started. Moreover, Shakespeare and his fellows were officially the servants of Lord Hunsdon, who was not an adherent of Essex. In fact, a

[71] II, 206.

[72] *Elizabeth*, 244.

[73] Chambers, II, 205, n. 1, gives references to the documents in this affair.

[74] Caldwallader, 78 and notes.

[75] There are extant several gaol-lists, which with their discrepancies give us a total of considerably over a hundred names, to which we should add those who escaped and were rounded up later. Cf. *S. P. Dom.*, 1598–1601; *Sal. MSS.*, XI; *Acts of the Privy Council*, 1601.

lampoon on the Cecil faction which was circulated soon after the Rebellion, makes fun of the Chamberlain with the rest.

Chamberlin, Chamberlin
hees of hir graces kinne
foole hath he euer bin
with his Joane siluerpin

She makes his cockescombe thin
and quake in euerie limme
quicksiluer is in his head
but his wit's dull as lead—
Lord for thy pittie.[76]

As a business organization, too, for all their dramatist's personal feeling for the Earl of Southampton, the Chamberlain's men would naturally be hesitant about committing themselves to so desperate an enterprise, although if the City had actually risen—Essex fully expected that it would, and only Cecil's careful preparation and resolute action kept it from doing so—, I believe they would have cast in their lot with the Essex party. Shakespeare himself seems to have been the reverse of turbulent, but rather a gentle, philosophical person of naturally conservative feelings, who could sympathize with his friends' stand for tolerance and for war with Spain, but not with their rebellion. That he was not altogether unambitious, we have a right to judge from the discontent with his profession which he expresses in the *Sonnets*, from his buying of land at Stratford, and from his efforts to secure for his family heraldic recognition as an offshoot of the ancient and noble Ardens; but these are, after all, conservative ways of asserting ambition, and there may easily be something in Acheson's suggestion that he looked on Southampton as a rash young man, misled by his own passions and prejudices and by unsafe advisers (Essex was generally so considered, and Southampton followed Essex almost blindly). This seems to me especially probable after the faction's sudden turn toward dangerous insurgency in November, 1600. Shakespeare's own political principles, if they are anywhere expressed at all, seem to be stated by King Henry the Fifth on the eve of Agincourt, "Every subject's duty is the king's; but every subject's soul is his own."[77] This statement draws the line very neatly between tolerance and rebellion.

The conflict between Shakespeare's judgment and his gallant impulses, between his duty to his monarch, his lord, and his fellows, and his loyalty to his patron-friend,[78] must have been a bitter one. I believe

[76] Cf. Stopes, 235.

[77] IV, i, 189.

[78] I hold that Southampton was this friend, in spite of what Chambers says (Shakespeare, I, 565): "The case for Southampton as the friend of the sonnets is now very generally accepted, and has been well put recently by Fort. I do not think it a convincing one. If it were sound, one would expect to find some hints in the sonnets of the major interests of Southampton's early life, his military ambitions, his comradeship with Essex, the romance of his marriage. There are none."

My comment on these remarks would be that the first two major interests Sir Edmund

that it is this conflict which, forcing Shakespeare, among loyalties, to choose the material one, lent to *Troilus and Cressida* its acrid pessimism, and that it is this tragedy of politics and friendship—not the six-years-old affair of the "Dark Lady"—which gave his "dark comedies" their sympathy with the generally satirical, disillusioned spirit of their times.

But we have not yet found a sufficient explanation of the company's escape from the natural consequences of its abetting the Rebellion by performing *Richard II*. There must have been some potent reason why Essex's fall did not end the dramatic rivalry by leaving the Admiral's men unchallenged masters of the London stage. We should look, I think, to the Queen's own attitude. For one thing, she would not wish to impugn the faith of her Lord Chamberlain, whose sister, the wife of the Lord Admiral, was her oldest and best friend among her ladies. The Hunsdons' loyalty to her had been unswerving. She liked plays, too; and the evidence is very good that she especially liked Shakespeare's plays as acted by Burbadge and his fellows. Moreover, there was her politic dislike of letting one faction get supreme and unchallenged control of her administration, which may help to explain the Cecil faction's failure to go all the way in extirpating the Essex faction, as well as Cecil's willingness to have the credit for securing the tacit commutation of Southampton's sentence of death to one of imprisonment. Then, after the execution of Essex, the Queen's reaction was one of remorse; toward the end of 1602 she was grieving over him and could not be comforted. Harington wrote to his wife:

> It was not manie daies since I was bidden to her presence . . . and founde her in moste pitiable state. She bade the archbishope aske me if I had seene Tyrone? I replied with reverence, that "I had seene him withe the Lord Deputie." She lookede up, with much choler and greife in her countenence and saide, "Oh, nowe it mindeth me that you was one who sawe this manne *elsewhere*":—and hereat, she droppede a teare, and smote her bosome. She helde in her hande a goldene cuppe, whiche she often put to her lippes; but, in soothe, her hearte seemethe too fulle to lacke more fillinge.[79]

Not long after, we are told,

---

names conflicted with both of the major interests Shakespeare displays in the earlier sonnets—his great fondness for his friend, and his desire that he should marry some suitable person and perpetuate his line. Indeed, Shakespeare may have been actually jealous of Essex. As for "the romance of his marriage," his affair with Essex's cousin did not develop until 1598 into anything that looked like matrimony; and since it was not considered an alliance worthy of Southampton's rank, the same influences, whatever they were, which made Shakespeare urge marriage on his friend can hardly have impelled him to press for this particular union.

[79] December 27, 1602. Printed by N. E. McClure, *The Letters and Epigrams of Sir John Harington*, 96.

. . . the *Queenes weaknesse* did appeare mortall, hastened by the wishes of many, that could not in reason expect pardon for a fault they found she had so severely punished in her selfe, as to *take comfort in nothing after*. But upon all occasions of signing Pardons would upbraid the movers for them with the hasty anticipation of that brave mans end, not to be expiated in relation to the Nations losse by any future indeavour.[80]

We should mention, too, the conservatism of Shakespeare's plays themselves. Once the Cecil faction had ceased to point out their veiled or wholly imaginary political insinuations, Elizabeth, especially as her perceptions dulled with age, would no longer be likely to imagine any disloyalty in their tone.

The policy of the head of the Cecil party, also, altered decidedly although not publicly, soon after the execution, when the Earl of Mar, arriving from Scotland to aid the cause of the Essex, was secretly met with assurances of Cecil's aid to the cause of his King's succession, and returned to the North with this good news for James. Hereafter magnanimity was the most politic attitude the Cecil forces could show toward the remnants of the Essex faction, whom King James counted as his original friends at the English court.

Thus although the Admiral's men may have been surprised in the spring of 1601 at not having their rivals taken permanently out of their way, the fact that the Chamberlain's men were spared was not, after all, really very surprising. My explanation of the court performance on February 24, the eve of the final act of Essex's tragedy, is, of course, not incompatible with the theory that Shakespeare and his fellows may have been forced to take the road by a brief punitive closing of the Globe that spring. Or, indeed, such an inhibition could have been a prudential measure. For weeks, probably months, after the eighth of February, Her Majesty's Government was taking steps to avert a threatened sympathetic rebellion. Until Essex's head fell, on the twenty-fifth, the danger was of a rising to release him from the Tower;—such an exploit was planned, for instance, by a group of London apprentices, but discovered by Cecil's excellent spy system and nipped in the bud.[81] Numerous "libels" frightened the authorities.[82] The troops called up from the shires to the defense of the Queen's person were mostly dismissed by the end of February, but it was not until after the seventh of March that the Mayor was permitted to release the special day watch over the London gates.[83] On April 8 there were rumors that Cecil would be killed if the Queen left London.[84] Informations purporting to reveal the extensive

[80] Francis Osborne, *Historical Memoirs*, ed. of 1658, 95.

[81] *Sal. MSS.*, XI, 77. The ringleaders were still in prison on July 7 (*Ibid.*, 270).

[82] *Ibid.*, 75, 88, 99, 132, 148, 284 (Jul. 12), 321 (Aug. 4).

[83] *Ibid.*, 111.

[84] *Ibid.*, 170.

ramifications of the Essex plots kept coming in until midsummer; and seeking, arresting, examining, and fleecing of his followers went on.[85]

So it is quite believable that the Chamberlain's men were quietly advised by their patron to go on tour, and that on this circuit they gave those performances of *Hamlet* at both universities which are claimed by the 1603 quarto. And they may even have gone as far as Scotland.[86]

The Admiral's men this year, apparently because of the return of Alleyn, showed comparatively little enterprise in the production of new plays, bringing out only some eighteen, of which four or more were sequels. They staged numerous revivals, of which we can more or less doubtfully identify the following: *The Blind Beggar of Alexandria*, *The Jew of Malta*, *The Massacre at Paris*, either *The Battle of Alcazar* or *Hiren*, *The Mayor of Quinborough* (*Valteger*), *Hercules*, *Crack Me This Nut*, and *The Wise Man of West Chester*. Several of these plays were bought of Alleyn at the current price for old plays of two pounds each. Their new productions of the year have all vanished—an indication of their old-fashioned materials and poor quality which is supported by an examination of their titles, such as *Scogan and Skelton*, *Friar Rush*, *Judas*. Yet it should be admitted, in justification of the Admiral's policy as not altogether oblivious of court requirements, that the Queen herself was always fond of "merry tales" and sprightly scandal, patronizing Harington's Rabelaisian jests and insisting that her envoys at the court of Henri IV keep her supplied with news of "accidents,"— by which she meant the comical scandals which Henri provided so plentifully.

As for *Judas*, by Birde and Rowley, begun perhaps in May and completed in December, the subject can easily have had a topical treatment, for speculation was busy as to the betrayer of Essex.

> It is said by Thuanus, that a young man of good family, a domestic of the Earl, who had been educated with him, and was so much trusted by him, that in his hearing he discussed his most secret designs, at this time turned informer, and revealed to the Secretary everything that passed at Essex House.[87]

Various men were subsequently mentioned as the traitor, Sir Ferdinando Gorges so prominently that he issued a special apology in defense of his name.[88] But Manningham's friend "Martin" in his anagram, DAVIS = IVDAS,[89] gave, I believe, the true solution. I shall not take space here

[85] *Ibid., passim.*

[86] Chambers (II, 205) thinks such a visit unlikely if not impossible; yet it would have been quite in accordance with Cecil policy at this season to wink at their being smuggled quietly across the Border by Essex's friend Lord Willoughby at Berwick, thus pleasing James and getting rid at a ticklish time of a disturbing element in the situation in England.

[87] W. B. Devereux, II, 137.

[88] *A Breefe Answer;* cf. *Archaeologia*, XXXIII, 241–261.

[89] Manningham's Diary, 18.

to blacken the forgotten name of this Captain John Davis, but merely refer anyone interested in the historical problem to his offer to confess;[90] Carleton's remark, "Sir J. D. is thought to have saved his life by telling first;"[91] Davis's letter to Cecil, from prison, suing to escape trial, urging that he has been promised his life by Ralegh, and promising great services;[92] his thanks and renewed promises of faithful services when these boons have been granted;[93] and the fact that, pardoned but his Somersetshire house confiscated, he was somehow able in 1602 to retire to Pangbourne, Berkshire, where he bought an estate.[94]

A ballad representing Ralegh's supposed agonies of conscience over his part in Essex's downfall shows a belief that the Earl's betrayer had served his enemies also as *agent provocateur:*

> And now I find it doth my conscience gall,
> That wee suborned a Judas to betray thee
> Who tould thee, when the Council did thee call,
> That I and Cobham by the way would slay thee . . .
> And thus by fraud we forced thee to offend . . .[95]

Quite possibly we should make an exception to our statement that the Admiral's new plays of the year have all vanished, in favor of Chettle and Dekker's *King Sebastian of Portingale*, April-May. If, as seems very likely, it was based on Munday's tract, *The strangest adventure that ever happened . . . containing a discourse concerning the successe of the King of Portugall Dom Sebastian from the time of his voyage into Affricke . . . in the year 1578 unto the sixt of January this present 1601*,[96] the play probably underlies Massinger's *Believe As You List*, where on the demand of Master of the Revels Herbert the author has thinly disguised his characters as Romans and Carthaginians.

We have a political issue here, and in translating and publishing Teixeira's tract Munday was doing the government a service; for it was the Cecil policy to uphold the genuineness of the pretender Sebastian, who claimed that he had survived the battle of Alcazar and years of Moorish slavery and desert wanderings, against both the King of Spain's claim to Portugal and the claim of the Essex-backed pretender, Don Antonio.[97]

[90] *Acts of the Privy Council*, 1600–01, 165.

[91] *S. P. Dom.*, March 25, 1601.

[92] *Sal. MSS.*, XI, 101.

[93] *Ibid.*, 161; and see also 413 and 421.

[94] Birch, *Memoirs of Queen Elizabeth*, II, 494. For Davis's efforts to make his peace with Southampton at the beginning of the new reign, cf. Stopes, 261–263.

[95] Ballad Society, *Ballads from MSS.*, II, 256.

[96] S.R. March 30, 1601, and printed the same year.

[97] Cf. *Venetian S. P.*, 1603–7; 17, 18; *Sal. MSS.*, X, 406; Chamberlain, Oct. 20, 1598; Jan. 17, 1599; Oct. 10, 1600 ("as freshly talked and believed in the Exchange as ever it was"); Dec. 22, 1600 (rumor that Sebastian is secretly at the English court); *Winwood's Memorials*, 289, 430 (Aug. 28, 1602—Sebastian, in the galleys in Spain, recognizes a sword once given him by Medina Sidonia, an incident which is in Massinger's play).

Therefore we have in this play a fairly clear case of the Admiral's men's lending themselves to propaganda in furtherance of the administration's foreign policy. Their great interest in the subject appears also in their playing of *Alcazar* and *Stukeley*.

Dekker's name does not appear in Henslowe's Diary this year after May 22; therefore such an apparent imitation of his *Shoemakers' Holiday* as *Six Clothiers* (doubtless based on Deloney's *Thomas of Reading*) had to be done by Hathaway, Haughton, and Smith, whose skill was necessarily inferior to Dekker's in the vein of bourgeois romance. For some unknown reason—was Shakespeare under some temporary restraint, or grieving in retirement?—Dekker had gone over to the Chamberlain's men, for whom he hastily prepared *Satiromastix* this year in competition with *The Poetaster*, which Jonson was writing for the Chapel boys as a lampoon on the Shakespearean company. Dekker's play was staged, probably in the autumn,[98] by the Chamberlain's men "publickly" and the Children of Paul's "privately." It is mainly aimed at Jonson.

The whole affair of the Poetomachia or "War of the Theatres," which centers upon this play and Jonson's *Poetaster*, though highly interesting, is altogether too intricate to be justly treated within the proportions of this present study. The best work upon it has been done by R. A. Small.[99] It was mainly a "flyting," literary and personal, among the playwrights of the day. Its inception seems to have been in some of Marston's satirical scurrilities which offended the vanity of the dictatorial Jonson. But Marston also, as spokesman of the boy company of Paul's, had taken advantage of his comparative independence as a dramatist to cast slurs on the old-fashioned balladizing of Munday for the Admiral's men[100] and on the adult companies in general. Jonson's attacks on the Chamberlain's men in *The Poetaster*, which he wrote for the Chapel boys after leaving that organization, possibly with some ill feeling toward them over the failure of *Every Man Out*, were not without a trace or two of malicious political allusion, and brought Shakespeare's fellows into action against him with *Satiromastix*. Shakespeare himself, if we may take as well informed the famous statement in *2 Return From Parnassus* that he gave Jonson a pill which made him bewray his credit, may have taken a hand, in *Hamlet*, *Troilus and Cressida*, or elsewhere. But the whole affair, as far as it had anything to do with the serious competition between the rival companies, was merely a rather frivolous result of the frictions incident to that competition,

[98] The Epilogue refers to "this cold weather," and the play was entered on the Stationers' Register on November 11.

[99] *The Stage Quarrel, Between Ben Jonson and the So-called Poetasters*, Breslau, 1899.

[100] The dramatizations of Deloney, also, would be considered on a par with ballad-stuff.

and can have had little practical effect on the fortunes of the companies. The "throwing about of brains," indeed, seems to have been amusing to the play-going public, and may have drawn a small amount of patronage away from the Admiral's men, who were, through their playwrights and repertories, the indirect objects of many gibes, and yet did not take part in the affair, at least with any play that is extant, perhaps because their clientele was not of a sort to be interested in a literary squabble. One would expect some retort from Munday, the chief butt of Jonson and Marston in several of the early plays of the Poetomachia; but nothing is evident in the extant plays in which he had a hand—*John a Kent*[101] *Robin Hood*, *Oldcastle;* or in the titles representing his lost work, unless, with the cheerful irrelevance displayed by Dekker in preparing *Satiromastix*, he worked something into *Mother Redcap*, *Chance Medley*, *2 Oldcastle*, *Owen Tudor*, *Fair Constance of Rome*, or *Cardinal Wolsey*. But the absence of any real heat from the affair makes it quite possible that, having no talent for personal scurrility, he refrained from any attempt to retaliate. The "stage quarrel" did not even result in any lasting personal enmity between the two bitterest participants, Jonson and Marston, who collaborated with Chapman in *Eastward Ho* a little later.

A brief summary will show the direction in which the often good-natured and usually harmless satire of each of the principal plays of the Poetomachia was aimed:

The Case is Altered, Jonson, for Pembroke's? 1597? Antonio Balladino = Munday.[102] Satirizes the Admiral's men indirectly.

Every Man In, Jonson, for the Chamberlain's, 1598. Poet Nuntius = Munday. Satirizes the Admiral's men indirectly.

Histriomastix, Marston (rewriting) for Paul's boys, 1599. Posthaste = Munday. Chrysoganus = Jonson. Satirizes the Admiral's and the Chamberlain's men.

Jack Drum, Marston, for Paul's boys, 1600. Brabant Senior = Jonson. Decius = Drayton. Satirizes the Admiral's and perhaps the Chamberlain's men.

Cynthia's Revels, Jonson, for the Chapel boys, 1600. Anaides = Dekker. Hedon = Marston.[103] Satirizes indirectly Paul's boys and the Admiral's men.

What You Will, Marston, for Paul's boys? 1601. Lampatho = Jonson. Satirizes the Chapel boys indirectly.

The Poetaster, Jonson, for the Chapel boys, 1601. Demetrius = Dekker. Crispinus = Marston. Histrio = one of the Chamberlain's men. Satirizes Paul's boys indirectly and the Chamberlain's men directly.

Satiromastix, Dekker, for the Chamberlain's men and Paul's boys, 1601. Horace = Jonson. Crispinus = Marston. Satirizes the Chapel boys both directly and indirectly. Paul's boys may have appropriated this play without leave.

[101] Possibly there was something here in the rustic playmaking.

[102] I am using only the identifications of which Small feels certain.

[103] It is probably just a coincidence that Sir Christopher Heydon, a fiery Norfolk Essexian who fought several savage duels with Vice Admiral Sir Robert Mansell, the latter a relative of the Gawdys and Gamages, sometimes had his name spelled "Hedon." Cf. *Sal. MSS.*, VII, 27.

Hamlet, Shakespeare, for the Chamberlain's men, 1601? Satirizes the boy companies, possibly rather the satirical and burlesquing boys of Paul's than the singing boys of the Chapel.

2 Return from Parnassus, anonymous, at Cambridge, 1601? Satirizes the London dramatic companies rather indiscriminately and appears to be amusedly neutral in the stage quarrel. Its statement that Shakespeare took part in the "War" and routed Jonson may be due to something which was once in one of the acting versions of *Hamlet*;[104] or the university playwright, unaware of Dekker's temporary and possibly secret connection with the Chamberlain's men, may have assumed that *Satiromastix* was by their chief dramatist, Shakespeare.

It seems highly probable that *Hamlet* was part of the repertory of the Chamberlain's men in 1601, for numerous reasons which we need not go into here. *Twelfth Night*, belonging to either this year or the preceding, was new or still on the boards. It was performed before the lawyers of the Middle Temple at their feast on February 2, 1602, as we know from Manningham's Diary. The company's only other play of the year, as far as we know, appears to have been *Thomas Lord Cromwell*, published in 1602 with an ascription to them.[105] The connections of this play and the later *Henry VIII* of the King's men with the political affiliations of the company might repay a careful study. For our present purpose we should at least observe that the policies of the Howards had been hostile to Cromwell, who is here depicted as highly virtuous and generous, and that in particular the Lord Admiral's uncle, the third Duke of Norfolk, had been the implacable enemy of Wolsey, Cromwell's master, and had headed the opposition to Cromwell himself.[106]

The play, like *Two Maids of Moreclacke* and *Westward Ho*, is interestingly localized a little way up the Thames from London, in the neighborhood of Putney. There seems to be a reference to Shakespeare's version of *Troilus and Cressida* in Bedford's saying that Hector was killed by the Myrmidons and his speaking of "sweete tong'd Ulisses that made Ajaxe mad"; and Cromwell, like Caesar, fails to receive Bedford's warning messages. As Essex feared to be, he is hurried to the Tower by his enemies and condemned without trial; when he asks to see the King, his enemy Gardiner tells him:

> The King is so advertised of your guilt
> He will by no meanes admit you to his presence.

Gardiner will not carry a letter to him; Cromwell tricks him with an

[104] Cf. Tucker Brooke, *Tudor Drama*, 383 ff.

[105] Its ascription also to "W.S." has placed this play among the Shakespeare apocrypha.

[106] Thomas Wriothesley, Southampton's grandfather, was Cromwell's kinsman and servant, did the work he left, and stepped into his shoes (Stopes, 486). Edward, Lord Cromwell, the great-grandson of Henry VIII's minister, deserted the Essex rebels with Bedford, but was heavily fined all the same.

oral message, but his reprieve from the King comes just too late.[107]

The Admiral's men produced one or perhaps two plays dealing with the same period and the same politico-religious issues—*The Life of Cardinal Wolsey*, for which Chettle was paid, perhaps in full, on August 8, 1601; and *The Rising of Cardinal Wolsey*, for which Chettle, Drayton, Munday, and Smith were paid in full on November 12. We hear also of this play or these plays in 1602. In this group of plays on the reign of Henry VIII it seems possible that the rival companies, now both for the Scottish succession, were competing to show their parties' ancestors in the most favorable light, the Admiral's men by blackening Wolsey and exalting Norfolk, the Chamberlain's by showing the Howards' enemies in a more agreeable way. The Admiral's playwrights, it may be observed, were now laboring under very special difficulties; for while their rivals of the Chamberlain's men had merely to be as pro-James as they dared, the Cecil partisans did not know just where they did stand. Down to the very end of the reign Cecil kept secret from almost everyone, possibly even from the Admiral himself, the fact that he had abandoned the Suffolk claim and gone Scottish; therefore the Admiral's playwrights were in grave danger of blundering into anti-Cecil policies with the best will in the world, and must have suffered many a puzzling check from the licensing authorities.

Sir Thomas Wyatt, on the other hand, which is reasonably thought to be the *1* and *2 Lady Jane* recorded by Henslowe as written by Chettle, Dekker, Heywood, Smith, and Webster for Worcesters's men in October, 1602, shows about the succession politics one would expect under the circumstances: a distinct Protestantism; an advocacy, as first choice, of the nearest claimant by blood—probably meant to be applied to King James in case of dangerous question—; and a sympathetic adherence to the descendants of Lady Jane Grey, i.e., the Suffolk claim. It was bold indeed to deal at all with this period while Queen Elizabeth was yet alive. I imagine that the playwrights had assurances of protection before they went into the undertaking.

Of the plays given by Paul's boys this year we have already discussed one, *Satiromastix*. They probably produced also Marston's *What You Will*, which appears to have appropriated the subtitle of *Twelfth Night*. It is a comedy of disguises and humours, with numerous bits of burlesque, such as this one on *Hamlet*,

> To kill one's self, some ay, some hold it no.

[107] The style of the play, it must be admitted, seems rather old-fashioned for a new production of 1601 by the Chamberlain's men; but perhaps there was a revival with revision this year, and the old version got into print.

Their *Blurt Master Constable*, published in 1602, is probably this year's. It was written for them by Thomas Middleton and is in the usual burlesque vein of the company. Very lively, bawdy, amusing, with a Venetian setting which does not disguise the English humours of the constable and the lazy watch, it has an unusually large number of allusions to other plays—contemptuous ones to such old-fashioned assets of the Admiral's men as "most terrible Tamburlain," the "puppet show" of Nineveh (*A Looking Glass for London?*), Mephistophilus (*Faustus*) "Go by, old Jeronimo (*The Spanish Tragedy*)," "The Seven Wise Masters of the world" (*The Seven Wise Masters*, a lost play on the Seven Sages). Such witty echoes of the Chamberlain's repertory occur as: "I have heard that some men have died for love—So have I, but I never could see't" (*As You Like It*); "Sir Pandarus, the broking Knight of Troy" (*Troilus and Cressida*);

> Bid him whose heart no sorrow feels
> Tickle the rushes with his wanton heels (*Romeo and Juliet*);

"Say he scorn to marry me, yet he shall stand me in some stead by being my Ganymede" (*As You Like It*); "I'll hang a jewel at thine ear, sweet night" (*Romeo and Juliet*); "I smell a rat, I strike it dead" (*Hamlet*); and so on. And the play imitates a number of the situations of Shakespeare's romantic comedies.

The Chapel boys had Jonson's *Poetaster*, already mentioned. *Sir Giles Goosecap*, an anonymous comedy of humours, probably by Chapman, is ascribed to this company by the quarto of 1606 and was therefore played before the death of the Queen (the company's name in the new reign being "The Queen's Revels"). The melancholy of Clarence seems to burlesque that of Hamlet; but perhaps Chapman was merely imitating. The Pandarus motive from the Troilus and Cressida story is used here, not merely as a reference or for a bit of action as frequently in plays of about this period, but organically; indeed, in such details as the lady's being brought to her uncle's house where her lover is "sick" it appears to follow Chaucer more closely than Shakespeare did. It is possible that Chapman's *May Day* was a Chapel play of this year. The 1611 quarto says that it was "divers times acted at the Blacke Fryers." Fleay's dating for it, 1601, has, I believe, been generally rejected; but the general tone of burlesque and the dates of the plays burlesqued or referred to[108] seem to me to make it very possible. Chapman's jest at

[108] *Twelfth Night, Romeo and Juliet* (revival?), *Hamlet, Much Ado,* the rival boys' *Antonio's Revenge* (a burlesqued quotation); and especially the burlesque of the rival boys' *Maid's Metamorphosis:* Lucretia, really a man disguised, exclaims:

> O my Theagine, not Theagines,
> Thy love hath turned me woman like thyself. (II, i, 38, 39.)

his own *Blind Beggar of Alexandria*, already quoted in another connection, would be particularly apt in view of the fact that the Admiral's men, now his rivals, were reviving that play this year.

On May 10 of this year the Council instructed the Middlesex justices to suppress a libelous play at the Curtain, which presented

> the persons of some gentlemen of good desert and quality that are yet alive, under obscure manner, but yet in such sort as all the hearers may take notice both of the matter and of the persons that are meant thereby.[109]

The year saw few plays published. We have *Cynthia's Revels* and *Two Lamentable Tragedies* in 1601 quartos. *1* and *2 Antonio and Mellida*, *Satiromastix*, and *The Poetaster* were entered, and appeared in print in 1602. The Admiral's men entered *Doctor Faustus* and *Englishmen for My Money*, the former of which was not printed until 1604, the latter not until 1616. It seems odd, if the Chamberlain's winter season had been as impoverishing as Jonson asserted, that they did not have to sell any plays; but it is likely that the political situation deterred the booksellers from issuing any.

The Chamberlain's men appear to be securely back in favor at court this season, with four performances in addition to their engagement by the Templars. These were on December 26 and 27, 1601, January 1 and February 14, 1602. Their nearest competitors were the Chapel boys with three performances, on January 6 and 10 and February 14.[110] The Admiral's men were given only one date, December 27; and the newly formed Worcester's men, with Kemp and Heywood as their payees, appeared at court on January 3. Worcester's men began playing for Henslowe at the Rose the following August; I shall discuss them as a factor in the stage rivalry in Chapter Six. In addition to these performances before the Queen and her court, Elizabeth and her maids of honor were present at a play at Blackfriars after dining with Lord Hunsdon on December 31; this play would naturally be furnished by Hunsdon's own players, perhaps with the aid of the Chapel boys, who were occupying Burbadge's theater there.

It is of little use to speculate as to what plays the Chamberlain's men gave before Elizabeth this season. *Cromwell*, *Hamlet*, and *Twelfth Night* may have been new; but the ageing Queen may have been in a mood for revivals. Perhaps it is too fantastic to suggest that Ophelia's

[109] Chambers, I, 324. I suspect that this play slandered some members of the Essex faction in a way which was thought unseemly, Southampton, for instance, who was "yet alive" in the Tower under sentence of death.

[110] Greg, *Henslowe*, II, 337, appears to disagree with Chambers by holding that the second company on Feb. 14 was Worcester's. But Chambers (IV, 167) seems to be right, as he summarizes the warrants, and the recorded payments bear him out.

snatch of a Valentine's Day ballad may have something to do with the date of her first appearance at the English court. Neither do I find any clue to what the Admiral's men played; it was somewhat more probably a revival than one of their meager and inferior stock of new pieces. As for Worcester's men, probably we should look for a Heywood play with a good part for Kemp, the new company's chief histrionic asset. The Chapel boys seem likely to have given *May Day* and *Sir Giles Goosecap*.

It is in this winter season that I shall try to place the performance of Shakespeare's *Troilus and Cressida*, as a joint performance by the Chamberlain's men and the Chapel boys on either December 31 or February 14. But the play was the culmination of a long rivalry in "Greek plays" which I shall first pause to sketch.

Greek Plays, 1594–1603

Before our period these plays fell into two main types, the academic and the allegorical, according to their audiences; the former, such as *Hippolytus* and *Ulysses Redux*, being given at the universities, chiefly for didactic and literary reasons; the latter, represented by the plays of Lyly, being prepared for a sophisticated courtly audience who enjoyed seeing the myths with which they were familiar manipulated so as to reveal a gossiping sort of topical significance, especially in regard to the Queen's love affairs. But Lyly seems to have gone too far with this, so that the activities of his company, Paul's boys, were suppressed.

It seems not improbable that Shakespeare in some way handled the love scenes between Troilus and Cressida early, before those of *Romeo and Juliet*, which resemble the scenes in the extant *Troilus* that reveal the older style. That this romantic rather than sardonic version of the story was acted may perhaps be inferred from the fact that Heywood in his *1 Iron Age*, which may plausibly be identified with the *Troy* given by the Admiral's men in 1596, seems to show his usual deference in regard to matters already treated by Shakespeare by giving only the slightest attention to Troilus and Cressida. But I believe that this early *Troilus and Cressida* was given before the organization of the Chamberlain's men, for whose audience the story of Pyramus and Thisbe was a banal thing most enjoyable in burlesque, and the reference to Troilus in *The Merchant of Venice* was to be appreciated simply as an allusion.

The Admiral's men, for an audience whose nature has been sufficiently defined, affected early in our period two types of Greek play: the romantic, which belonged to a dramatic type which was not really concerned with ancient Greece and its mythology, and which we have already discussed; and the didactic, represented by *Selio and Olimpo* and *1* and *2 Hercules* in 1595, *Pythagoras* and *Troy* in 1596, and *Five Plays in One* in 1597. At least we judge from Heywood's *Four Ages* published in 1611, 1613, and 1632, that he was responsible for *Olimpo*, *Hercules*, and *Troy*, and from his *Pleasant Dialogues and Dramas* that he wrote *Five Plays in One*. The didactic purpose we can read in the manner of the Heywood plays themselves, as well as in the explicit statement of Homer at the end of *The Brazen Age:*

> All we have done we aim at your content,
> Striving to illustrate things not known to all,
> In which the learn'd can only censure right:
> The rest we crave, whom we unlettered call,
> Rather to attend than judge; for more than sight
> We seek to please.

This would have been insulting to Elizabeth's court or the Chamberlain's audience; whereas the relatively uncultivated court of James, on January 12, 1612, could be regaled with *The Silver Age*, performed jointly by the King's and Queen's companies.[111] The episodic nature of these plays made it possible to perform them with a cast of ordinary size by "doubling"; but they were most effective when put on with a large cast to take full advantage of the spectacular nature of many of the scenes. In his Address to the Reader of *1* and *2 Iron Age* in the quarto of 1632, Heywood gives us the explicit information that

> These were the plays often (and not with the least applause) publicly acted by two companies, upon one stage at once, and have at sundry times thronged three several theatres with numerous and mighty auditories.[112]

In his foreword to the second part he says, "These ages have been long since writ, and suited to the time then."

A brief characterization of these important plays seems in place here. *The Golden Age* contains "the lives of Jupiter and Saturn, with the deifying of the heathen gods." Calisto, Danae, and Ganimed are important figures. *The Silver Age*, which is identified with Henslowe's *Selio and Olimpo*, has the loves of Jupiter and Semele, of Jupiter and Alcmena, the birth of Hercules, the rape of Proserpina, and the arraignment of the Moon. Both these plays present mythology in a didactic way, but with a naïve exploitation of the spectacular and the risque which appears at its height in the latter piece. *The Brazen Age*, to be identified with Henslowe's *Hercules*, has Nessus, Meleager, Jason and Medea, Vulcan's net, and the labors and death of Hercules. I believe that these three plays were first presented before 1596, and that the cynical spirit which

[111] Cf. Chambers, IV, 126, 178.

[112] The three theaters were probably the Rose, Blackfriars, and the Red Bull. There appears, however, to have been a revival of *Hercules* in 1601 at the Fortune. On these plays see J. Q. Adams, "Shakespeare, Heywood, and the Classics," *M.L.N.* XXXIV (1919), 336.

appears in *The Iron Age* is better suited to a slightly later period, say about 1602. Some of it is probably due to the conventional view of the age so named, some to the influence of Henryson's continuation of Chaucer's *Troilus and Criseyde,* some to the vogue of satire in the last years of the century and the predominance of the "railing fool," some to the influence of Shakespeare's version. The first part contains the rape of Helen, the siege of Troy, and events, including the death of Troilus, down to the death of Ajax. Thersites "rails" the Epilogue.[113] The second part of the play has the fall of Troy, treated in much the same Marlovian manner as the passage in *Hamlet,*[114] and much Senecanized material from the Agamemnon tragedy, including scenes between Orestes and Clytemnestra which closely resemble those between Hamlet and Gertrude. Cressida is shown degenerating and finally leprous; she is called "a traitor to all womankind." Cethus is a character of the malcontent type. There is an unconsciously farcical piling up, at the end of the play, of dead bodies, which Cethus uses as a promenade. Finally Ulysses says:

> Of all these Princes,
> And infinite numbers that opposed Troy,
> And came in *Hellen's* quarrel (saue my selfe)
> Not one suruiues (thankes to the immortal powers) . . .
> And since I am the man soly reseru'd,
> Accept me for the Authors Epilogue.

I suspect that Heywood's unintentionally ludicrous venture into Senecan tragedy here was the result of an order from his fellows, the Admiral's men, in 1599, that he help them meet the demand for that dramatic type revealed by the public reception of Marston's *Antonio's Revenge;* and that he was hurt by his failure, especially as it was advertised by the assignment in the same year of several portions of the material he considered his own to others of the company's playwrights —*Orestes' Furies* to Dekker, *Agamemnon* and *Troilus and Cressida* to Chettle and Dekker. Fleay suggests that this was the reason for Heywood's leaving the Admiral's men. We have noted his appearance with Worcester's at the beginning of 1602; he had not been paid by Henslowe for a play since February 12, 1599; did he too, like Dekker, do some work for the Chamberlain's men about 1601?

The Admiral's *Troilus and Cressida* may have been considered an infringement of the Chamberlain's right to the material. The extant

[113] In the earlier part of *The Iron Age* Heywood makes Thersites a wise, if cynical, courtier, of much higher rank and character than in Homer or Shakespeare; in the second part, perhaps under the influence of the rapidly increasing scurrility of the popular railing fools of the stage, he degrades him.

[114] Compare Henslowe's entry of *Dido and Aeneas,* Jan. 8, 1598.

"plot," fragmentary and lacking a title,[115] has some names of actors which bear out its identification with the 1599 play. Greg remarks[116] that the female characters are somewhat prominent for so warlike a theme, and that the plot does not agree with either Shakespeare's *Troilus and Cressida* or Heywood's *Iron Age*. In one scene we have Troilus and Pandarus and "to them Cressida and a waiting maid with a light." This may be the source of the reference in *Histriomastix*, 1599:

> Come Cressida, my Cresset light,
> Thy face doth shine both day and night,
> Behold, behold, thy garter blue
> Thy knight his valiant elboe weares,
> That when he shakes his furious speare
> The foe in shivering fearful sort
> May lay him down in death to snort . . .

In view of the current sophistication and cynicism of the stage, especially as it appealed to the fashionable class, it would not be to the credit of the Chamberlain's men or to their advantage in their competition with the boys for court favor to assert their claim to the Troilus and Cressida story by a revival of their early, romantic, and perhaps somewhat didactic play. Someone must rewrite it in the cynical manner, and this Shakespeare found himself in the mood to do in 1601.

Baldwin declines to cast Shakespeare's *Troilus and Cressida* on the ground that the important rôles are too numerous. I believe that this difficulty is to be explained by assuming that Shakespeare wrote the play for a joint performance by his company and the Chapel boys, the adults to play the Greeks, the boys the Trojans. An examination of the evidence may make this theory seem not altogether fantastic.

The Trojans, of course, because of the legendary founding of Britain by Brutus, had the British sympathies. London was often spoken of as "Troynovant." Sir John Harington writes in 1602, "Now for an *Ultimum Refugium*, all is suddenly turned French." and that there is a plan afoot among the Cecilians to marry Arabella to the illegitimate son of King Henri, aged fourteen, and thus to make her "a new Helena to burn our Troy novant and run away by the light."[117] The natural aim of the dramatist was to show the Greeks as bullying brutes, winning by main force and Machiavellian politics. It appears to me that the play might have been exceedingly pleasing to a courtly Elizabethan audience if the leading boy actors (several of whom were well grown, to judge by scandal)[118]

[115] Cf. the type facsimile in Greg, *Henslowe*, III, 142.

[116] *Ibid.*, 144.

[117] *Tract on the Succession*, 42.

[118] " 'Tis said my La. of *Lester* [Essex's mother, widowed for the third time by the execution of Sir Christopher Blount] hathe marryed one of the playing boyes of the chappell." (Philip Gawdy's gossip, c. 1602.)

were cast as the Trojan heroes, Æneas, Hector, and Troilus, so that their youthful gallantry could appear shining but hopeless against the huge bulk of Pope as Ajax or the mature force of Burbadge as Achilles. Indeed, there appears so much parallelism in the characterizations of the figures in the Greek and Trojan camps that a tabulation shows clearly how the play could be cast using two whole companies, each having its actors trained to about the same traditional "lines." In this table I have tried to follow as far as I could Baldwin's ascriptions of "lines" to the Chamberlain's men:

Venerable old men	Nestor (Shakespeare?)	Priam
Martial heroes	Achilles (Burbadge?)	Æneas
Champions	Ajax (Pope?)	Hector
Effeminates	Patroclus (Phillips?)	Paris
Railing fools	Thersites (Armin?)	Alexander
Plotters	Ulysses (Sly?)	Pandarus
Cuckold and bastard	Menelaus (Cowley?)	Margarelon
Lovers	Diomedes (Cundall?)	Troilus
Secondary old men	Agamemnon (Heminges?)	Calchas

The women present more difficulty; but if we may classify Cressida as a Greek because of her defection, as the pro-Trojan Elizabethans would have been glad to do, we have an interesting little study in contrasts:

Unmarried women	Cressida (Gilburne?)	Cassandra
Married women	Helen (Ned?)	Andromache

A few very small Trojan parts are left over. But the Chapel organization may have been somewhat larger than the adult company, or the latter may have used its hired men to make the nameless numbers of the Myrmidons seem more overwhelming.

Much of the fun in such a performance would be in the direct comparison between the adult actors in their accustomed "lines," i.e., the types of characters which they habitually acted, and the boys playing opposite them in the same "lines" which, we assume, they had been trained to imitate and burlesque. The Chapel boys had gone in for burlesquing Shakespearean rôles a good deal in the past year or so, as we have remarked in regard to *The Poetaster* and *Sir Giles Goosecap*, the former of which actually lampooned individuals of the Chamberlain's men, and the latter of which had a very interesting, somewhat idealized adaptation of the Troilus and Cressida story.[119]

I believe that the boys aiding the Shakespearean company in presenting this play would be those of the Chapel, not those of Paul's, for several reasons. For one, the Chapel boys occupied Blackfriars,

[119] For Chapman's handling of Chaucer here cf. G. L. Kittredge, "Notes on Elizabethan Plays," *Journal of English and Germanic Philology*, II, 10–13.

which they leased from Burbadge, and thus were convenient to Lord Hunsdon's lodgings and accessible to financial dealings with the Burbadge interests. Other reasons are the popularity of the Chapel boys at court this season, and the convenient place and date afforded by Lord Hunsdon's entertainment to Queen Elizabeth. There is, of course, the objection that *Satiromastix*[120] appears to have been shared by the Chamberlain's men with Paul's boys; but this alliance was specifically against the Chapel's *Poetaster*, and must at any rate have been brief.

I think it likely that Shakespeare's fellows were far from wishing to crush the Chapel boys at this time, although no doubt they would have liked to see the competition kept within bounds. The Burbadges were receiving the good rental of forty pounds a year from them for a theater which their own company could not use. In a law suit[121] one of the brothers, explaining why he had exacted a bond of four hundred pounds surety of Evans for the lease of Blackfriars, said,

> . . . except the said Evans could erect and keepe a companye of Playinge boyes or others to play playes & interludes in the said Playhouse in such sort as before tyme had bene thus used, that he was lykelye to be behind with the said rent of fortie pounds.

Would the Burbadges wish to see anything done to imperil this rent money? Dekker, in his "Address to the World," says explicitly that his lines "are free from conspiring the least disgrace to any man, but onely to our new Horace." And Tucca, speaking the Epilogue, asks the audience not to hiss the play, for that would be sufficient vengeance for Jonson and the Chapel boys, but "if you set your hands and seals to this, Horace will write against it, and you may have more sport"—an interesting indication that the Poetomachia was a box-office attraction of (financially) a singularly non-competitive sort.[122] Obviously here

[120] When it first occurred to me that *Troilus and Cressida* might have been given jointly by the Chamberlain's men and a boy company, it was my natural impulse to suppose the boy company Paul's, because of the seeming "alliance" for the lampooning of Jonson with *Satiromastix*, and to consider *Satiromastix* also as a joint performance. But the title page of Dekker's play does not bear this out; it indicates definitely separate performances: "Satiro-mastix. Or The vntrussing of the Humorous Poet. As it hath bin presented publikely, by the Right Honorable, the Lord Chamberlaine his Seruants; and priuately, by the Children of Paules." And the characters are not so numerous as in *Troilus and Cressida*, nor can they be so symmetrically parcelled out among the actors of the two companies.

[121] Cf. H. Hillebrand, *The Child Actors*, 153.

[122] Cf. also Jonson's *Poetaster* (early in 1601), III, iv, 334 ff.:

Tvcca. Stay . . . what's he . . . ?

Histrio. O, sir . . . hee is . . . one Demetrius, a dresser of plaies about the towne, here; we haue hir'd him to abuse Horace, and bring him in, in a play, with all his gallants. . . .

Tvcc. And: why so, stinkard?

Shakespeare's fellows are not trying to decrease the Chapel boys' revenue, but to foster a device which was bound to add to the revenues of all the companies that used it.

Evans had a twenty-one year lease. With the accession of King James and the change of the temper of the court, the Burbadges' hopes of getting the use of the Blackfriars theater for their own company revived; and although they did not succeed until 1609, they no longer feared the breaking of the lease—very likely they rather hoped for it. Thus the King's men's appropriation of *The Malcontent*, a really dangerous financial blow to the Blackfriars boys, would appear quite consistent with their policy in 1604 and after.

Two dates are available for the joint performance of *Troilus and Cressida* when it would not be "clapper-clawed with the palms of the vulgar;"[123] December 29, 1601, at Blackfriars as the Lord Chamberlain's entertainment to the Queen, and February 14, 1602, when both companies were at court and each was paid the full sum of ten pounds for itr performance. I think the earlier date more probable because of the promise of Pandarus, spoken to the audience at the end of the play:

> Brethren and sisters of the hold-door trade,
> Some two months hence my will shall here be made:—
> It should be now, but that my fear in this,
> Some galled goose of Winchester[124] would hiss.
> Till then I'll sweat, and seek about for eases;
> And at that time bequeath you my diseases.

This promise for "two months hence" here indicates that the performance was in December and therefore possibly at Blackfriars, for February was the last month of the court season; and that the play promised was to be either a joint or a Chapel production, probably the latter.[125]

Hist. O, it will get vs a huge deale of money (Captaine) and wee haue need on't; for this winter ha's made vs all poorer, then so many starued snakes: no bodie comes at vs; not a gentleman, nor a—.

Tvcc. But, you know nothing by him, doe you, to make a play of?

Hist. Faith, not much, Captaine: but our Author will deuise, that, that shall serue in some sort.

[123] Cf. the Address to the Reader in one of the 1609 quartos.

[124] The reference is to the bawdy-houses on the Bankside in the Bishop of Winchester's liberty, and possibly to some such real estate interests of Henslowe's. The efforts of some writers to whiten the character of this region in Shakespeare's time show a rather naïve faith in the permanent efficacy of various rulers' acts of suppression.

[125] My supposition is that the play promised is Chapman's *Gentleman Usher*. The titular character plays the pandar in a particularly ludicrous fashion, and his occupation was one with a scandalous taint of "pandarism" about it. Pandarus's will itself is lost, if it ever existed; but we have the unfulfilled promise of the Epilogue of *2 Henry IV* and Jonson's excision of matter not written by him from his published works to help us understand the

I believe that the play was written and presented with a general feeling that the Trojans typified the gallant Essex faction,[126] defeated by superior force and guile; thus it would be more tactful that the boys should take the Trojan parts. Yet through the atmosphere of defeat and gloom which pervades the play we may see the adaptable and reasonable spirit of Shakespeare working to rationalize the actual state of affairs—to justify the peace party in Troy, the practical wisdom of Ulysses. But he is far from making any effort to justify the murderous practicality of Achilles.[127] One can imagine Queen Elizabeth's enjoying this thoroughly as a transference of all blame for the death of Essex to the shoulders of his vindictive enemies in the Cecil faction. Manningham tells us that she forbade Dr. Barlow access to her because in April, 1602, he preached against Essex at Paul's: " 'O, Sir,' said she, ' we heare you are an honest man! You are an honest man,' etc."[128]

One other Greek play should be mentioned before we leave the type and bring this long chapter to an end—Daniel's *Philotas*, upon one of the generals of Alexander the Great, produced by the Queen's Revels in the autumn of 1604, but worked on by him from as early as 1596. Mrs. Stopes[129] calls him Pembroke's "family poet," but points out that he wrote the noblest praise of Southampton on his release from the Tower. It was suspected in very high quarters that the early part of *Philotas*, in which a trial for treason is dramatized, alluded to the Essex trouble; and although we have seen that Daniel denied the charge, his denial has not been altogether believed.

---

loss of one more Elizabethan example, such as we have in *Gillian of Brentford's Testament* and *Two Wise Men and All the Rest Fools*, of this medieval device employed by Chaucer and Villon.

[126] Cf. Tucker Brooke on *T. & C.*, *Yale Review*, April, 1928.

[127] Arabella to the Queen, Ash Wednesday, 1603 (the anniversary of Essex's execution).—"And how over-violently hasty he was this fatal day, Ash Wednesday, and the new dropping tears of some, might make you remember, if it were possible you could forget. *Quis talia fando temperet a lacrimis? Myrmidomina Dolopumae aut duri miles Ulisses?*" (E.T. Bradley, *Arabella Stuart*, II, 158; the editor hazards no explanation of Arabella's treatment of Virgil, *Æneid*, II, 7.)

[128] Diary, 51. Her irony seems reminiscent of *Julius Caesar*.

[129] *The Third Earl of Southampton*, 277.

CHAPTER VI (1602–1604)

THE STAGE DURING THE TRANSITION FROM ELIZABETH TO JAMES

Worcester's men. 1602 repertories. Christmas at court, 1602–3. Some reasons for the King's special favor to the Chamberlain's men. Sir Robert Carey's ride. 1603 repertories. *"Family Drama" during the plague interim.* King James's initial court season, 1603–4.

ON March 31, 1602, Worcester's men received permission to set up at the Boar's Head[1] in a merger with Oxford's men. The latter company was under a patronage which we have seen to be pro-Cecil, or at least anti-Essex; but Worcester himself requires special comment.

Edward Somerset, Earl of Worcester, born about 1550, was connected through his ancestors with many great houses, including those of Percy, Beauchamp, Herbert, Browne (and thus Wriothesley), Courtenay, Delawarr, Dudley, Hastings. His father had died in 1589 at his house "by St. Johns near London,"[2] and lay buried at Raglan; his mother was a daughter of Lord North. The new Earl had married before 1575 Elizabeth, daughter of Francis Hastings, the puritan Earl of Huntingdon. Edward, Earl of Worcester, was, according to Naunton, "in his youth a very fine gentleman and the best horseman and tilter of the times . . . and when years had abated these exercises of honour he grew to be a faithful and profound counsellor." He had also a reputation as a favorer of learning and good literature; and the Queen, who liked him, said that he "reconciled what she believed impossible, a stiff papist to a good subject."[3]

Up to about 1600 Worcester's chief connections seem to have made him an ally of Essex. It was the marriage of two of his daughters at Essex House in 1596 which called forth Spenser's *Prothalamion.* In 1597 he became the Queen's Deputy Master of the Horse, serving immediately under Essex, who, on leaving either for the Islands Voyage in that year or for Ireland two years later, recommended him strongly to the Queen.[4] In 1599 he supported his kinsman Southampton for the Garter against

[1] Not the famous inn but a theater according to Chambers, II, 444; still there remains at least a doubt.

[2] *The Blind Beggar of Bednal Green* makes prominent mention of this locality as the stronghold of the good Duke of Gloucester.

[3] Lloyd, *State Worthies.*

[4] *Sal. MSS.*, XIV, 106.

the Queen's opposition.[5] But an effort by Essex's mother, Lady Leicester, to retain him in the faction by marrying his second son, Henry, now his heir, to a daughter of Lady Knollys[6] failed; and on June 16, 1600, Henry Somerset, Lord Herbert, was married in the presence of the Queen at St. Martin's, Ludgate, to Anne, daughter and heiress of John Russell, styled Lord Russell (the heir of Francis Earl of Bedford) by Elizabeth, daughter of Sir Anthony Cook. The wedding was followed by a feast at Cobham's house in Blackfriars to which the Queen was borne on a litter by her nobles; and among those present, as Lady Russell put it, "of the bride's and bridegroom's blood and alliance" were Lady Warwick, Sir Robert Cecil, Lord Thomas Howard, and Lord Cobham.[7]

At Essex's hearing before the Council on June 11 Worcester had been the only one who delivered no opinion "touching the sequestration of the offices."[8] He could not decently say anything, for he was, of course, next in line for the Mastership of the Horse. On the following February 8 he was among the councilors imprisoned at Essex House; on April 21 he became Master of the Horse, in 1602 lord-lieutenant of two Welsh counties. He retained the royal favor under King James, whom he had invested with the Garter at his marriage in 1590.

From August 17, 1602 on, Worcester's men were playing for Henslowe at the Rose, and are shown by his records to have shared playwrights and at least some plays with the Admiral's men. As we have already seen, they had Kemp and Heywood with them from the beginning of the year; and this presence of Kemp in a rival organization may have had something to do with Shakespeare's lampooning him in *Hamlet.*

Whether from their patronage or from their connection with Henslowe and the Admiral's men, the repertory of Worcester's showed a rather strongly and vindictively political tendency. They raked up old scores by performing *Sir John Oldcastle* in August, with additions by Dekker, and *Biron* in October.[9] Later in the autumn they had *1* and *2 Lady Jane*, which are probably closely related to the extant *Sir Thomas Wyatt*, a play which favors the Suffolk claim, now secretly abandoned by Cecil in favor of that of James, but perhaps still espoused by Worcester—who, we recall, though a Catholic was a firm and perhaps insular patriot and had married a daughter of the puritan Huntingdon. I am rather loth to believe that Worcester, who seems on the whole a very fine sort of man, actively promoted this sort of thing in his company; yet human

[5] *Ibid.*, IX, 438. [6] *Ibid.*, XIV, 165.

[7] *Ibid.*, X, 175; Lady Russell to her nephew Cecil, c. June 9, asking him to act as man of the house at a marriage supper she intended to give.

[8] *Ibid.*, 178; Meyrick to Southampton.

[9] Marshal Biron had been condemned on July 28. His fate was generally seen (and indeed had been foreseen by Elizabeth herself) as parallel to that of Essex.

nature has been known to display cases of resentment and self-justification against the man by whose downfall one has profited.

A play which may have belonged to Worcester's men is the anonymous *Fair Maid of the Exchange*, a bourgeois comedy which many think Heywood's. It was not published until 1607, but the imitations of Shakespeare and Jonson in it point to a date about 1602. We have noted that Heywood had left writing for the Admiral's men some time before and was with Worcester's at the beginning of the year. In the prologue a tragedy is promised from the author's muse in case this comedy pleases. It may be that this was the play performed at court by Worcester's men on January 3, 1602, and that Heywood here promises his bourgeois tragedy *A Woman Killed with Kindness*, produced by the same company a little over a year later—a work which might be considered inspired by the same muse as *The Fair Maid of the Exchange.*

Also during 1602, *How a Man May Choose a Good Wife from a Bad* was published with an ascription to Worcester's men. It is a combination of Griselda and Prodigal Son motives, rather creditably done. It has been ascribed to Joshua Cooke, whose name is printed in by hand on the title page, and to Heywood, and was very popular, six quartos appearing down to 1634. I shall have a little more to say about this production presently.

Heywood's *Wise Woman of Hogsdon* is usually dated about 1604, and may have belonged to the Queen's men, formerly Worcester's. The Wise Woman, an old fortune-telling bawd, dwells in the London suburb of Hogsdon, (or Hoxton) near Edmonton and Bednal Green, where the young Essexian Tresham held lands.[10] Here Lord Mounteagle, former Essexian, received the message which revealed the Gunpowder Plot. The play's hero is Young Chartley, "a wild-headed gent," whom an audience might very naturally connect with Essex, one of whose chief seats had been Chartley in Staffordshire, especially since his name is "Robin."[11] Other characters are Boyster, "a blunt fellow," and Sir Boniface Absee, a schoolmaster (descriptive names), Sir Harry, an ignorant justice, Sencer, "a conceited gent."[12] and Haringfield "a civil gent," and two Luces, both of whom Chartley woos. The historical background is ostensibly about the time of Richard II, for one Luce's father, a pathetically gallant old man, says he was in Spain with John of Gaunt. The play probably added a spice of allegory to its lively plot of mistakes and disguises.

The *Marshal Osric* written by Heywood and Smith for Worcester's

[10] Cf. *Hist. MSS. Com., Var. Coll.*, III, 112 ff. [11] I, ii.

[12] Possibly a Spencer, for he is "a Northamptonshire gentleman, borne to a thousand pound land by the yeare." So Haringfield may be a Harington.

in September, 1602, has been very plausibly identified with the former playwright's extant *The Royal King and the Loyal Subject*, published in in 1637 as a Queen's play, with an Epilogue describing it as "old." The Marshal, who is the "Loyal Subject," is a sort of Patient Griselda under the successive trials laid upon him by some unidentified King. Chester and Clinton are sycophants and plot against him, using methods much like those employed by Cecil, Cobham and Ralegh against Essex, the famous Marshal of Elizabeth's last decade; using his popularity, for instance, to frighten the king and make him envious. Bonvile, his cousin (or uncle), and Audley, his friend, reject him in his supposed poverty; but Lady Mary Audley is loyal. Cast down, deprived of his staff, and banished from the court, he is called "Phaeton," and later is tried before "a bar and jury of his peers" including, as did Essex's jury, his enemies and the holders of his honors. The localities are in London and Wales.

The politics seem inconsistent here, whether or not the Marshal is intended for Essex. Chester was a favored character with the Admiral's men, and therefore, one would judge from their general policy, with Worcester's. Clinton was the family name of the earls of Lincoln, as had formerly been Lacy, another favorite name with the Admiral's playwrights. The contemporary Clinton earl, however, in 1602, was a treacherous and morose madman who seems to have had, like Oxford, few friends in either party. The Audleys were connected with Lord Thomas Howard, acting Chamberlain from late in 1602 until Elizabeth's death and Lord Chamberlain thereafter under King James, whose mother was the heiress of Lord Audley de Walden. Second son of the Duke of Norfolk, he was knighted at sea by the Admiral in '88, was drawn by his wife into a quarrel with Essex over Cadiz spoils, was a vice-admiral on the Islands Voyage the next year and sat in Parliament as Lord Howard de Walden. He tried to help reconcile Essex and Ralegh in 1598, and was made lieutenant of Cambridgeshire. He was marshal of the forces which besieged Essex House, and sat at Essex's trial. On July 21, 1603, he was made Earl of Suffolk, and a little later served as joint commissioner to execute Essex's office of Earl Marshal. His first wife was one of the Dacres of the North, long persecuted by the Queen for their Catholic connections and valuable lands on the Border; his second, whom he married about 1585, was a Knyvet, noted for her beauty and her ways of making her husband's offices bring money into her coffers—she even took a pension from Spain for influencing foreign policy.

The puzzle offered us by this obscure and inconsistent connection of two real Marshals with this Marshal on the stage may be due to a revision which partially adjusted the play's allusions to changed political conditions—before *The Royal King* was published Suffolk had become

Lord Treasurer and then had been disgraced by the efforts of his enemies at court—and carelessly left older allusions to complicate matters. Of course, reared upon Plutarch, the Elizabethans and Jacobeans were fond of historical parallels, especially of unfortunate great men; as, for example, Wotton's parallel of Essex and Buckingham bears witness.

Worcester's company did not appear at court this last season of Elizabeth's reign.

The Admiral's men this year produced some twenty new plays and staged ten or a dozen revivals. As we have already observed, they had several biblical plays this year and may have used them for satirical purposes. A play like *Jepthah* may have had some allegory about the Queen, who was often flattered by comparisons with Biblical heroines, as in Clerke's *Polimanteia*, where she is called "more courteous then the churle-saving *Abigal:* more courtly then the friendes-honoring *Hester:* more valiant then prince-killing *Judith.*"[13] Two lost plays of fascinating political possibilities in their repertory of 1602 are *Malcolm King of Scots*,[14] for the book of which Henslowe paid Massey five pounds on April 18, and *The Earl of Hertford*, for which "new play" Henslowe records the purchase of properties in September. Since the Earl of Hertford, whose company appeared at court this season, was father of Edward Seymour, Lord Beauchamp, inheritor of the Suffolk claim to the succession, and since Hertford's second wife (who had died in 1598) was Frances Howard, sister of the Lord Admiral, one wonders whether at this time the Admiral's players sided with Cecil in his new adherence to the cause of James, or indeed whether they knew anything about that wily statesman's change of policy. We have already noticed that outsiders thought the faction to be supporting Beauchamp and Arabella. Indeed, the presence of Hertford's men at court on January 6, as well as much in the Admiral's and Worcester's repertory, may have been managed by Cecil to cover his secret pact with James, which it would

[13] Wm. Clerke, *Polimanteia*, in Grosart's *Occasional Issues*, XIV, 57.

[14] Lord Henry Howard to Bruce, c. July, 1602 (*Secret Corr. of Cecil with James*, ed. *Dalyrymple*, 1766, 139), says a delay in receiving letters from Scotland "did move some scruples in the mind of Cecil and me, that somewhat had miscarried, considering our earnest instance for present satisfaction to the admiral, who thought every day a year till he heard from thence. . . ." Probably the same writer speaks of the Admiral, also, to King James on August 24: "The letters written by your Majesty to 40 and 50, have wrought their effects, according to their wishes and desires that humbly advised you. 50 was no less delighted with that cordial, than if he had been possessed of America; and no man can blame the man, for he hath most to hazard; and having carried himself very strangely toward you and yours in former times, is glad of a *quietus est*, which may secure him and the state which he may leave after him. He promiseth to bind that favour more assuredly by future desert; and so I think he will, so long as he is guided by that spirit that in his present fear and future ticklishness is predominant. . . ." (*Ibid.*, 183).

not do to have the Queen, still unwilling to discuss the succession, know anything about.[15]

The company's other chronicle plays this year were: *The Massacre of France* (Paris), revived: *The Rising of Cardinal Wolsey*, altered by Chettle; *Richard Crookback*, Jonson, perhaps never finished; *Philip of Spain*, and *Longshanks*, older plays bought from Alleyn; *Mortimer*, properties bought September 10; and *Randal Earl of Chester*, by Middleton. Any of these plays might easily have passages bearing on the succession.

The production of *Tasso's Melancholy*, with alterations by Dekker January 16 and November 3, may have been a revival of the old play (1594), written in competition with the Chamberlain's Kydian *Hamlet*, with cynical and realistic "mending" to meet the new Shakespeare version of the play. The payment of earnest money to Chettle, July 7, for his *Danish Tragedy* appears to show the influence of *Hamlet* on the original title of his *Hoffman*, which appears in the Diary on December 29. But Greg[16] thinks *Hoffman* a sequel to *The Danish Tragedy*.

Some clues to the nature of the Admiral's court performances this season are offered by Henslowe's entries, which show that *Merry as May Be*, finished in November by Day, Hathaway, and Smith, was designed for the court (it seems an ominous title); that Middleton was paid five shillings on December 14 for a prologue and epilogue for the court presentation of *Friar Bacon;* and that Chettle received the same sum on December 24 for the same service, performed for an unnamed play which was probably his and Heywood's *1 London Florentine*. But the company actually appeared at court only twice.[17] Very likely the failing powers of the Queen caused the cancellation of an engagement.

The general policy of the Admiral's men appears unchanged.

The Chamberlain's repertory in 1602 may have included the following:

1 Jeronimo, if written to ridicule this year's revival of *The Spanish Tragedy* by the Admiral's men.

The play on the capture of Stuhl Weissenberg seen by the Duke of Stettin on September 13.[18] The play was recorded by the Duke's secretary as a "comedy" depicting the capture of the place by the Turks and its recapture by the Christians. We do not know at what theater this was performed, but it may have been at the Globe.

[15] Cf. the well-known story told by Wotton, of the packet of secret Scotch correspondence which Cecil escaped opening in the Queen's presence by pretending that it stank.

[16] *Henslowe*, II, 226.

[17] December 27 and March 6; the latter date is doubtful.

[18] Captain John Smith of Virginia fame (see his biography by E. K. Chatterton) gives a vivid account of a night attack on this town with "fiery dragons," a sort of incendiary bomb of his devising. He was wounded in the Turkish counter-attack. His father was a tenant in Lincolnshire of Lord Willoughby d'Eresby.

Hamlet, doubtless popular.

Troilus and Cressida, if we may assume a series of semipublic joint performances at Blackfriars with the Chapel children, a sort of run which would not conflict with the statement of the quarto that it was "never clapper-clawed with the palms of the vulgar."[19]

All's Well that Ends Well, if our version of the play does not belong, as *Love's Labour's Won*, before *Palladis Tamia*, or as Baldwin would have it, after our period. Baldwin's datings, by the way, which he promises to defend in a later publication,[20] show a gap of about eighteen months in which Shakespeare wrote no plays, between *Troilus* in the summer of 1601 and the rewriting of *Hamlet* in the summer of 1603. Dekker and possibly Heywood may have been called on by the Chamberlain's company to fill the earlier part of such a gap. This cessation of playwriting, if it took place, would appear to indicate an even deeper wounding by the tragic events of the Essex rebellion than the nature of Shakespeare's plays of this period reveals in their usual datings. These show nothing from his hand in 1603, a shorter interim which might have been caused simply by the public mourning for Elizabeth and by the prevalence of the plague.

Richard III, a revival. Manningham's Diary this year relates the famous anecdote concerning Burbadge's winning the heart of a citizen's wife by his performance in the part of Richard III.

The Freeman's Honour. (Wentworth?) Smith, in the Epistle to the Reader of his *Hector of Germany*, about 1613, says, "I have begun in a former play, called 'The Freeman's Honour,' acted by the now-servants of the King's Majesty, to dignify the worthy company of the merchant-taylors." Although the merchant-tailors may possibly have been of better class than others of the London companies, it was not according to the policy of the Chamberlain's men as we have observed it to glorify the bourgeoisie. They left that to the Admiral's men, who did it supremely well in Dekker's *The Shoemakers' Holiday*. It is possible, however, that in 1601 or 1602, deprived of much of their cavalier clientele by the Essex disaster, Shakespeare's fellows were forced temporarily to seek a patronage which they had formerly despised.[21]

[19] The statement that it was "never stal'd with the stage" remains a stumbling block. It may be denied, or interpreted to mean that the play was given only at Blackfriars—or perhaps only after Hunsdon's dinner, with no admission charge. How many stagings would be required to "stale" a play is a question, too.

[20] Cf. *Organization and Personnel*, viii and 229.

[21] In this connection I should like to say just a word about realism as concerned in the rivalry of the Admiral's and the Chamberlain's men. The subject calls for more elaborate definition and discussion than I am now prepared to give it; but we should observe that in general what we call realism when we speak of "realistic comedy of contemporary Lon-

The Chamberlain's men appeared at court but twice this season, on December 26 and February 2. Perhaps in deference to the Queen's mood they revived a couple of their older comedies.

We come now to the repertory of Paul's boys. They may have had *Wily Beguiled*,[22] probably an old romantic play fitted up with new comic material. It was not published until 1606. Like most of this company's plays it has very numerous similarities and allusions to productions of other companies, but here they extend over so long a period of dramatic history as to make the play's dating very doubtful. Fleay[23] makes it an elaborate literary satire. A sneering reference to the "gentleman usher to the Great Turk"[24] may be significant. Paul's boys may also have had Marston's very effective play *The Malcontent*, apparently written strongly under the influence of *Hamlet;* but the fact that an allusion shows this to be a Blackfriars play causes Chambers to conclude that it was the first one written by Marston for the Queen's Revels in 1604.[25] Paul's boys appeared at court once this season, on the first of January.

The Chapel boys, as we have remarked, may have had Chapman's combination of romance and humours, *The Gentleman Usher*. The self-healing by faith and resignation in the play is a curious element. The company did not appear at court this season.[26]

On November 6 of this year occurred Richard Vennar's interesting hoax of *England's Joy* at the Swan.[27] Vennar's prospectus worked upon what seems to have been a growing popular desire to see the masques and shows which the court enjoyed, and promised a summary of English history from Edward III down to date, with chief emphasis on Elizabeth's reign, in a series of spectacles to be performed by gentlemen and gentlewomen. The play as promised was to avoid the Essex trouble, although it was to honor Lord Mountjoy's success in Ireland, and was

---

don life" belonged in the province of the Admiral's men. As far as realism was a matter of social materials, a question of the social standing of one's heroes and heroines, the Admiral's men often adopted it, the Chamberlain's almost invariably eschewed it, whether in comedy or in tragedy. But we should note that the best play of bourgeois appeal, *The Shoemakers' Holiday*, was romantic in plot; and that the finest realism of our period, whether in the form of contrasting details, as in *A Midsummer Night's Dream*, or of genre pictures, as those centering about Falstaff or Sir Toby, or in truth of character in action, is to be found in the work of that incorrigible aristocrat and romanticist, William Shakespeare.

[22] Baldwin Maxwell (*S.P.*, XIX, 220) thinks Ward right in calling it a University play originally. [23] *Shakespeare Manual*, 272. [24] Sgn. F3.

[25] See Chambers, III, 432. Sly says in the Induction, "This play hath beaten all your gallants out of the feathers; Blackfriars hath almost spoiled Blackfriars for feathers." So the allusion to "Jeronimo in *decimo-sexto*" points to the Chapel children, too.

[26] See Chambers, II, 45, for the change in the Chapel management this year.

[27] Cf. *New Shakespeare Society Transactions*, 1887–92, I.

to show Elizabeth's ascent into Heaven at the end. The open staging of such recent and even prophetic subject-matter would have been unprecedented. Vennar fled, and the common people wrecked the theater. In his *Apology*, 1614, the shifty promoter asserted that the project was all in good faith, but spoiled by beadles arresting him for debt. Yet it seems impossible that such a performance was ever seriously planned or that it would, if so planned, have been permitted by the authorities.

Publications of the year were the Chamberlain's *Merry Wives*[28] and *Cromwell*, Paul's boys' *Blurt Master Constable*, Worcester's *How a Man May Choose a Good Wife from a Bad*, and the Chapel boys' *Liberality and Prodigality*. *Hamlet* was entered, and published in 1603 as of the King's men. If the selling of plays for publication is really evidence of a company's financial straits, 1602 must have been an even harder year for the Chamberlain's men than the preceding.

We have noted that the remnant of the Essex faction was still busily plotting for the succession of James, and that Cecil, with the knowledge of but few of his friends, had secretly gone over to James, too. Therefore when Northumberland, by spying on his wife, found that "all Essexians were Scottish, and that the widow daily prayed for King James," and that all the party resorted constantly to Southampton in the Tower, by the Lieutenant's sufferance, and that Northumberland's own brother, Sir Josceline Percy, ordinarily lay with him there, Cecil refused to make use of the information, ostensibly because to do so would be "raking in the bowels of a man half dead"—but really, as Howard goes on frankly to say, because "the practice meant against Southampton formally, did pierce himself through the other side."[29]

The "Triplicity of Hell" were finally forced to make advances to James also, Northumberland coming over on a promise of toleration for his faith.[30] The appearance of Hertford's men[31] at court on January 6 may, as we have remarked, indicate that the Suffolk claim was being given some encouragement, at least for show. Tyrone surrendered to Mountjoy about Christmas; and Elizabeth, much to her distaste, was forced to pardon him early in 1603.

The Queen was merry on November 17 over the antics of the clown

[28] Possibly let out to hurt Cobham, whom Cecil and Howard were at this time trying to injure underhand with King James.

[29] Dalyrymple's ed. of *Cecil's Secret Corr. with King James;* Lo. Hen. Howard to Bruce Dec. 4, 1601.

[30] Cf. Sidney Lee, "Henry Percy, 9th Earl of Northumberland," *D.N.B.*

[31] Their payee was Martin Slater, whose presence has been suspected with the English comedians of King James in Scotland. Possibly James had arranged for the secret support of the Seymours; or he may have been using Slater to keep in touch with these curious events of this crucial court season.

Gerard. But she was growing very infirm and melancholy and could be cheered only by "old Canterbury Tales." At the end of the year she had the coronation ring she had worn so long filed from her finger.

Chamberlain says on December 23 that there is "no shew of any great doings at Court this Christmas," many courtiers spending the holidays in the country; but on January 17 he reports that Court is better than ordinary after all. Sir Edward Wotton, the new Comptroller, "Hath put new life into it by his example (being allwayes freshly attired, and for the most part all in white *cap a pied*)." He reports dancing, bear-baiting, many plays, much gambling, with Cecil a heavy loser. On January 27 he relates that the acting Chamberlain, Lord Thomas Howard, has feasted the Queen at Charterhouse.

The records show, however, that fewer plays than of late were given at court this season, only six in all, of which the Chamberlain's and the Admiral's men each gave two. Thus the two leading companies appear to be neck and neck at the end of their decade of rivalry. But one of the two remaining dates (the other went to Paul's boys) was given to the company patronized by the Earl of Hertford, whose connections we have noticed; so the preponderance was politically at least with the Admiral. And of course this season was, after all, not particularly significant; England and Scotland were only waiting for the Queen to die, and plotting for the patronage of the new reign which was bound to begin soon.

It is possible to ascribe King James's favor to the Chamberlain's men, shown so promptly and decisively upon his accession to the English throne, to three motives: first, his own and the general estimation of the company's supreme merit; second, his recognition of the company's notorious Essexian sympathies; third, his old friendship for the Careys. The first motive seems to me indisputable. The second is weakened somewhat by what we know of James' rather skeptical attitude toward the Essexians and their advocacy of his claims, especially after the failure of the rebellion and the commencement of his secret correspondence with Cecil. Gratitude for past and futile good intentions can hardly be thought to have moved James much. But in historians' accounts of the succession intrigues of 1600–1603, James is given, I think, too complete a trust in Cecil, so that a possible dependence upon the Careys at the critical moment of Elizabeth's death is likely to be overlooked. Thus a strong and immediate motive of gratitude to the Careys is obscured; and one thing that obscures it is the common romantic treatment of Sir Robert's ride northward with the great news—according to which Lady Scrope drops him the ring from a window at the moment of the Queen's last gasp, between two and three in the morning; Carey picks it up and sets out immediately. It is hard to see why Sir Robert's own circumstantial account in his well-known *Memoirs* is not used. It has the sound of truth and is well corroborated by existing documents and known family and political connections.

Sir Robert tells us that, during the Queen's last illness, he wrote to warn King James not to stir from Edinburgh until he heard from him. ". . . if of that sickness she should die, I would be the first man that should bring him news of it." His sister, Lady Scrope, who was with the Queen when she died, sent word to him in the Jewel office, which was kept by a brother, at about two in the morning. The Council, met in the Privy Chamber, forbade him to go to Scotland until they had conferred further at Whitehall, and tried to leave him locked in at Richmond; but his eldest brother, the Chamberlain, "said angrily to the porter, 'Let him out, I wil answer for him.' " At Whitehall the Council again tried to trap him, this time employing Sir Arthur Savage;[32] but Sir William Knollys[33] and the Knight Marshal[34] checkmated them, and got him away about ten o'clock, at least eight hours after the Queen's death. That night he reached Doncaster, the next Witherington; next morning he gave commands that James be proclaimed King of England on the Border; and delayed by a fall, he reached James the third evening.

. . . he asked what letters I had from the Council? I told him, none: and acquainted him how narrowly I had escaped from them. And yet I had brought him a blue ring from a fair lady, that I hoped would give him assurance of the truth that I had reported. He took it and looked upon it, and said, "It is enough: I know by this you are a true messenger . . ."

Meanwhile, proclamation of King James was made in London and Westminster within an hour after Carey rode out of the city; and late that night the Council's missive Letter of Allegiance, signed also by the Lord Mayor and some nobles and dignitaries of the Church, was sent by Sir Charles Percy, brother of the Earl of Northumberland, and Mr. Thomas Somerset, son of the Earl of Worcester, who reached Holyrood on Monday the twenty-eighth. With their formal missive the Council sent a complaint which reads amusingly in the Scots transcript:

Forther, we have thocht meit and necessar to adverteis your Hienes that Sir Robert Carie is this morning depairtit frome hence towardis your Majestie, not onlie without the consent of any of us quha wer present at Richmouth at the tyme of our lait Soveranes deceis, bot also contrarie to such commandement as we had power to lay upone him, and to all decencie, guid maneris and respectis quhilk he aucht to sa mony persones of our degrie. . . .[35]

[32] A friend of Ralegh, and Southampton's rival for the Governorship of Connaught in 1600.

[33] One of the Council, and Essex's uncle.

[34] Sir Thomas Gerrard, kinsman and partisan of Essex: cf. Whyte, Michaelmas Day, 1599; and *Sal. MSS.*, XI, 109.

[35] *Register of the Privy Council of Scotland*, 1603, 551.

But why did the Careys, including the Chamberlain, patron of Shakespeare and his fellows, act thus counter to Cecil at this most critical time? The first, most direct explanation would be that they distrusted Cecil, whose policy as it appeared to a highly intelligent outsider and partisan of James we have already summarized from Sir John Harington's *Tract on the Succession*, 1602.[36] If Hunsdon, not admitted to the secret of Cecil's correspondence with James, believed that the delay in letting him have the news of the Queen's death was in order to put Beauchamp on the throne (and perhaps to marry him to Arabella at once), he was acting logically and according to his own long family record of loyalty, in moving for James. Note that Sir Robert did not merely carry good news, in such hope of reward as a lady-in-waiting might cherish in bringing word to a new-made royal father[37]—he proclaimed him King of England on the Border, an act in which he exceeded all authority in order to give James a time advantage if he should have to assert his right by force.

There is another possibility—a little more intricate, but for that very reason more probable, I think, as an interpretation of this, Cecil's masterpiece of the Machiavellian statecraft: that Hunsdon was made to appear (consciously or, more subtly still, unaware that he was a tool) to act against Cecil's wishes. The Secretary, it must be remembered, had been running with the hare and hunting with the hounds. A sudden revelation of perfidy to the Seymours and Talbots and their many friends might easily have caused a flareup into the anarchical disorders he was striving to avert. Those who hail his work for James and treat the business as triumphantly completed the moment the King was proclaimed, allow their readers to forget that the "secret correspondence" really was kept secret for many years.

The situation appears, then, thus: Cecil took measures (surprisingly inefficient ones for him) to keep back the news until steps could be taken to insure a native ruler. A day or two might have married Arabella, conveniently near at Wrest House, to Lord Beauchamp, who was rumored to be in the field at the head of his retainers,[38] and have brought the pair to London, surrounded with ample forces from the southern shires and the navy, to be proclaimed king and queen: before James could move, Arabella's friends might have made the North strong against him. But at ten o'clock word came that Carey had slipped away and

[36] In connection with the Cecilians' flirtations with the Suffolk Claim.

[37] Cf. *Henry VIII*, v, i.

[38] Cf. Manningham's Diary (Camden Soc.), 154; also *Hist. MSS. Com.*, XIII, R-4, 126; Corporation of Rye, March 30, 1603; the deposition of several "common players of interludes" that at Hastings one Holland on March 25 said that Lord Beauchamp had been proclaimed King by the Earl of Southampton.

was riding north. We imagine that the Admiral, in the secret, and Cecil appeared frightened and beaten; that they urged the other councilors and nobles that it was too late now, because King James had long been ready on his side of the Border, and the northern Marches would join him now at once; that the proclamation of James must be drawn up and dispatched instantly.[39]

By some such tactics the English claimants, none of them personally noted for bravery and decision, were thoroughly frightened. Their protestations of loyalty, especially the Earl of Hertford's,[40] were almost frantic. Harington's prognostications concerning Arabella's relatives, that they would not take any risks, were fully justified, and the general attitude toward James became completely submissive so suddenly that Northumberland and Ralegh, who had wished to hold out for concessions were left unsupported, their futures in the new reign adroitly ruined.

Those who have followed the career of the efficient, remorseless, but generally non-vindictive Secretary through the later years of the Queen, will be a little amused at the naïve triumph Sir Robert Carey expresses over his succession of victories over Cecil. I, for one, cannot believe that it was against the little statesman's secret will that Carey made his famous gallop, and later triumphed over opposition to become honored and ennobled under the Stuarts.

There remains the problem; did James understand Cecil's tactics? The latter's interests, it would seem, required that he should, although not necessarily in advance. Could the ring which Sir Robert Carey tells us he presented, to be received by James as a complete assurance, have been a Cecil token? Carey didn't know it, if so; and indeed the tradition seems most believable, that it was an Essexian token from Lady Scrope, Carey's sister, the lady for whom the other Essex ring of romantic story was intended. That James had allowed arrangements to be made for information of Elizabeth's death from anti-Cecilian sources also is not at all unlikely, the persons and circumstances considered; it would have been most imprudent for James to entrust himself wholly to Cecil's

[39] Compare the instant proclamation of treason against Essex, to see how Cecil could have acted had he wished.

[40] Cf. *Venetian State Papers*, 1603–7, 2: King James is reported as angry because the Council, to strengthen its own position, had suppressed in their Proclamation the Queen's deathbed acknowledgement of him as her heir. "The action of the Earl of Hertford is attributed by rumor to the French [who did not wish to see James on the throne of England]. . . But the younger is beginning to yield to the elder, and the rumor is dying away, for the elder Earl of Hertford, crippled as he is, swears that he will have himself carried to London, and there sign the proclamation himself and pledge his son's hand to the same. Arabella, too, no longer mad, writes in all humility from her prison that she desires no other husband . . . than . . . King James may assign her."

hands. As I have pointed out, there was suspicion, probably signified to him by Harington among others, that Beauchamp and Arabella might be popped in between the election and his hopes. And he could not well have escaped feeling some gratitude thereafter to the Careys for providing him, at their own peril, this anchor to windward. The result was naturally a kindly feeling toward Lord Hunsdon's servants, the fellows of Shakespeare, based on something more closely connected with the situation of May, 1603, when he took them into his own service, than were the events of the Essex rebellion in February, 1601.

Only ten days after Carey stumbled into Holyrood, King James wrote the letter which released Southampton from the Tower. Since the siding of Cecil with James which thus resulted in a bloodless accession had evidently been an unexpected coup to all but the very few who were in the secret,[41] Shakespeare could write in Sonnet CVII:

> Not mine own fears, nor the prophetic soul
> Of the wide world dreaming on things to come,
> Can yet the lease of my true love control
> Suppos'd as forfeit to a confin'd doom.
> The mortal moon hath her eclipse endur'd
> And the sad augurs mock their own presage;
> Incertainties now crown themselves assur'd,
> And peace proclaims olives of endless age.

In the face of the current interpretation which refers this sonnet to Elizabeth's "climacteric year," I agree with those who see here Shakespeare's joyful surprise at the peaceful and happy accession of King James and his congratulation of Southampton on his release.[42]

The King's triumphant progress toward his new capital immediately began. But the worst visitation of the plague since 1594 soon broke out, delaying the coronation and closing the theaters.

[41] Cf. Harington's *Tract on the Succession;* also *Venetian State Papers*, 1603–7, 15; "For years all Christendom held for certain that it [the change of rulers] must be attended with trouble and confusion."

[42] Cf. Garrett Mattingly, "The Date of Shakespeare's Sonnet CVII," *PMLA* XLVIII (1933), 705–721. I agree in general with Mr. Mattingly, who stands for the 1603 dating. But I disagree when he says (p. 709): "Only a perverse ingenuity can make ll. 1–4 refer to a release from imprisonment. What Shakespeare says is: Neither my own fears nor the widespread prophecies (of coming disaster) have power to control (i.e, to set a term to) the lease of my love (for you) which has been supposed to be doomed (like all leases) to expire." Shakespeare obviously intended this cryptic sonnet to be interpreted with ingenuity; and it does not seem to me perverse to suggest that in ordinary course leases *terminate*, but they may be broken off prematurely by *forfeiture;* and that Southampton while the Queen lived had been under a "confined doom" of death in the Tower, either from natural causes in that unhealthful place or on the block in the Tower yard where his friend Essex had perished.

We still have to consider the fraction of the 1603 dramatic season which was broken off by the death of the Queen on March 24.

The repertory of the Admiral's men was slight. Chambers[43] thinks they were probably not playing in January and February. They produced Heywood's *The Blind Eats Many a Fly*—the title is proverbial—finished by January 7. *Singer's Vallentary*, for which Singer was paid five pounds on January 13, has been supposed to have been prepared as his valedictory performance on retiring from the stage. He was an ordinary Groom of the Chamber at Elizabeth's funeral. A little later Henslowe paid Shaw the usual sum of two pounds for an old romance, *The Four Sons of Aymon*. On March 12, Day, Hathaway, and others were paid in full for *The Boss of Billingsgate*, evidently a city comedy; the Boss was a fountain, and there was an early ballad of its marriage to London Stone.[44] The Elizabethans derived "Billings" from Belinus, the mythical British king; Henslowe's spelling is "bellensgate."

Two plays for which earnest money was paid, but which were halted by the Queen's death, were Massey's *Siege of Dunkirk*[45] and Chettle's *2 London Florentine*.

The company went on the road after the death of the Queen. The tour ended October 21, but the plague kept the actors out of London. About Christmas the company, under the King's new policy of keeping the patronage of the players in his own family—he had doubtless been informed of the political dangers of the old one of allowing it to the nobles—was taken into the service of Prince Henry.

Chambers remarks[46] that the years 1600–1603, on the evidence of private debts paid off by Jones, Downton, Bird, and Shaw, had probably been prosperous ones for the Admiral's men, but that it is doubtful that the playwrights reaped any benefits from this prosperity. T. W. Baldwin[47] points out a decline in the Admiral's gallery receipts about 1597–98, indicating that the company was perhaps "gradually losing its courtly clientele." By 1600 it had seemingly adjusted itself to any loss of that nature which it may have suffered.

Worcester's repertory closely corresponds to that of the allied company. Early in January, Day, Hathaway, and Smith were paid in full for *The Unfortunate General*, the properties for which included a "citizen's coat."

[43] Chambers, II, 174.

[44] Cf. Greg, *Henslowe*, II, 227.

[45] Dunkirk, in Spanish hands, was a thorn in England's side throughout our period, swift galleys based there raiding shipping and even the coast villages; toward the end of the reign they seem to have been especially obnoxious. It was on the way to besiege Dunkirk that the Dutch and English troops won the battle of Newport, July 2, 1600; but the siege was given up. Nearby Ostend, besieged for three years by the Archduke, fell at last in September, 1604.

[46] Chambers, II, 174.

[47] "Posting Henslowe's Accounts," *J.E.G.P.*, XXVI, 42 ff.

It had something to do with French history. The same writers provided *2 Black Dog of Newgate*, a city play. It was doubtless based on a chapbook ascribed to Luke Hutton, executed in 1598 for robbery, who was a scapegrace relative—Harington says the son—of Matthew Hutton Archbishop of York, Essexian.[48] Luke dedicated his *Repentance* to Huntingdon, and his *Black Dog* to Popham. Matthew, the Archbishop, was a more tolerant man than Whitgift, befriending both Catholics and Puritans. He acted as President of the Council of the North between the terms of Huntingdon and Burghley. Harington tells a good story of his bold sermon before the Queen at Whitehall, probably about 1595, in which he "thundered" a text on Nebuchadnezzar, and spoke openly for the succession of James.[49]

Smith was paid in full for an *Italian Tragedy*,[50] apparently new, on March 12, about a week after the completion of Heywood's bourgeois tragedy, *A Woman Killed with Kindness*, of which the deserved run was cut short by the end of the reign. On May 9, Henslowe, recording the payment of earnest money to Chettle and Day for *Shore's Wife*, also records Worcester's men as "beginning to play again by the King's license." But the theaters were almost immediately closed again by the plague, and the general license to reopen them did not come until April 9, 1604. The company, which had been taken under the patronage of Queen Anne, went on the road during the inhibition.

The Lord Chamberlain was relieved of his duties on April 6, on account of illness, and died on September 9. Strictly speaking, his players became Lord Hunsdon's men once more for a short time on the lapse of the Household appointments with the Queen's death; but on May 19 the company received its patent, the first to any company from King James as the King's men.

Jonson's *Sejanus* may possibly have been acted publicly by the company before they became the King's men; and it may have been given at court in the first autumn or winter of the new reign. Jonson said in the 1604 quarto that he had excised the work of a collaborator, whom he praises so highly that he may have been Shakespeare himself. The fact that Jonson was now back with the company is notable.

It was from Mortlake that the King's men were called in December, 1603, to perform a play before their patron at Wilton.[51] What were they doing at Mortlake? Doubtless keeping out of the way of the plague as

48 Cf. *Sal. MSS.*, XI, 208.

49 *Nugae Antiquae*, II, 248.

50 Cf. Greg, *Henslowe*, II, 234.—"This can have nothing to do with Day's 'Italian Tragedy of—'." He thinks that Day's play may be the *Orphans' Tragedy;* see *Ibid.*, 208.

51 Chambers, IV, 168. They may have given *As You Like It:* cf. II, 209, n. 3; a lost letter is involved in the problem.

best they could, and probably striving to keep their company together by playing here and there in the general neighborhood of London, wherever they could find an inn-yard or a mansion hall with an audience. On February 8 a warrant for thirty pounds was handed to

> Richard Burbadg one of his ma*tes* comedians . . . for the mayntenaunce and releife of himselfe and the rest of his company being prohibeted to p'sente any playes publiquelie in or neere London by reason of greate perill that might growe through the extraordinary concourse and assemble of people to a newe increase of the plague till it shall please God to settle the cittie in a more p'fecte health by way of his mat*ies* free gifte.[52]

There seems to be no way of telling whether the restriction on playing near London extended to such places as Mortlake; if so, the players may have had to eke out their resources with the king's bounty until the spring sun had dried the roads enough to allow them to stroll the provinces. But however this may have been, it is to be noticed that the long plague interim at this time must have placed a special premium upon drama sharply localized at places relatively near London.

Perhaps we can even pick out from among the plays of about this time certain ones which belong to a type a little different from any with which we are familiar, something not exactly chronicle play, romance, satirical allegory, or domestic comedy—a type which has not as yet received a name. Indeed, it blends so easily along its borders with other accepted types, and it has so few really good examples, that it may hardly deserve a name of its own, or at any rate may not deserve a better than the unsatisfactory one I shall tentatively use, "Family Drama."

"Family Drama" during the Plague Interim

One of the best examples of the type is *The Merry Devil of Edmonton*, written by an unknown dramatist (traditionally Drayton) about 1603, mentioned in T. M.'s *Black Book*, 1604, and published in 1608 as acted by the King's men at the Globe. Among the characters, Fabell, the Merry Devil, whose grave is in Edmonton church, gives about the only indication of the play's historical date and therefore about its only link with the chronicle-type. He was a scholar-magician of the time of Henry VII, and connected with Cambridge as Friar Bacon was with Oxford. Smug the smith and some of his group's pranks come from a prose piece by Anthony Brewer.[53] But the gentlemanly Clares, Jerninghams, and Mounchenseys, involved in a plot resembling the marriage part of *Bednal Green*, appear to represent real county families.

[52] *Ibid.*, 168, 169.

[53] *The Life and Death of the Merry Deuill of Edmonton. With the Pleasant pranks of Smug the Smith*, etc. Fabell has a small part.

As nearly as I can tell, the Elizabethan representatives of these names who would interest the dramatist or his audience were, on the whole, Cecil connections. The chief contemporary descendants of the great earls of Clare were the daughters of the late Lord Burgh[54] (direct descendant of Hubert de Burgh of *King John* and the Robin Hood plays): Elizabeth, wife of George Brooke, Cobham's younger brother, and therefore a connection of the Jerningham family; Ann, wife of Sir Drue Drury, probably a connection of the Gawdys, long persecuted by Leicester,[55] replacer of the Essexian Sir Michael Blount as Lieutenant of the Tower in 1595, Gentleman Usher of the Privy Chamber in 1599, one of Essex's keepers in 1600; Frances, wife of Francis Copinger, another relative of Cobham; and Katherine, wife of Thomas Knyvet, and thus married into an important Norfolk family which was connected with the Howards and favored by King James.

The Mountchenseys were ancient barons of Swanscombe, near Gravesend, Kent;[56] and a branch at Edwardeston, Suffolk, married into the families of Pembroke and Waldgrave:[57]

> Sir *Guarin Mont-chensy*, as he was a right honourable person, so he was a man exceedingly wealthy, in so much as in those dayes they accounted him the most potent Baron, and the rich *Crassus* of England.[58]

The Jerninghams were related to both Cobham and Cornwallis; indeed, they also had some family connection (through Scrope) with the Careys, as well as a religious one with Southampton; on August 27, 1601, John Byrde, informing Cecil of Catholic doings in London, says that Father Gerrard, "who brake the Tower," stays at Southampton House with "old Lady Cornwallis," at Mr. Roper's, and at St. John's (a place prominent in *Bednal Green*) with "Mr. Jaringham."[59]

Yet in general these families seem to be Cecilian; and so, on the whole, are the localities here made much of: Enfield Chase was in charge of Sir Robert Cecil himself, who held the offices of ranger, forester, keeper of the lodges, master of the game, and chief steward of the manor, and had a good deal of trouble with deer-stealers; for instance, in 1601 the following were complained of: Tyndall Perte of Fryan Barnet; William Terry, servant to Mr. John Ashe; Mr. Robert Hayes of Enfield; Launcelot Fox and Mr. Myners, of Waltham Abbey.[60]

It is possible that Banks, the miller of Waltham, who has difficulty

[54] Died as Lord Deputy in Ireland, Oct. 14, 1597, leaving also a son, Robert, three years old, who died before 1601.

[55] Cf. *Leicester's Commonwealth.*

[56] Camden, *Britannia*, 329.

[57] There is a Walgrave or Waldegrave in *Englishmen for My Money.*

[58] Camden, *op. cit.*, 463.

[59] *Sal. MSS.*, XI, 362.

[60] *Ibid.*, 542.

when drunk in negotiating the bridges over the Lea, is a lampoon upon Sir Edward Denny, who had married about 1599 Mary, daughter of Thomas Cecil, Lord Burghley. Sir Edward carried matters in his neighborhood with a rather high hand. The weirs connected with his mills on the Lea at Waltham Abbey had caused controversies and even riots in 1593 and for twenty years preceding.[61] In 1601 a William Purveye complained to Cecil that he had been cowardly assaulted while hunting by a bravo, well appointed and vizarded; the procurers of this, he says, are easily discerned, as Sir Edward Denny has confessed to an intention of meeting him at Waltham Cross and stabbing him, and also has confessed that before the above assault his (Denny's) brother, called Captain Cecil, lay two mornings in the Strand with ten soldiers to have taken him in his passage to Westminster Hall, and by presumption to have murdered him; for Captain Cecil then had a ship ready for the passage of himself and company to Flanders.[62] In 1602 there were complaints that Denny's potent connections had made him Sheriff of Hertfordshire; his residence was not in that county, but across the river Lea in Essex.[63] In 1604 King James made him Lord Denny de Waltham.

Blague was a very common Elizabethan name; this Blague says constantly that he serves "the good Duke of Norfolk," i.e., a Howard; and from 1600 on, the manor house at Enfield was held by Lord William Howard.[64] Smug and Bilbo appear to be comic names of the ordinary descriptive type which sometimes runs into satirical allegory. Coreb, the stupid devil so easily tricked by Fabell, has a name which makes an easy anagram of "BROKE."

We have here the not-uncommon Elizabethan obscurity of purpose—is this play meant to be complimentary or the reverse to the familes to which it alludes? I think we may judge in this particular case, from the traditional anti-Cecil policy of the company that gave the play—although times had greatly changed, men like Southampton and Sir Robert Carey still held a grudge—and from the somewhat undignified motives and situations allotted to the characters, that a good-humored neighborly satire was intended, to be presented perhaps at Lord Mountjoy's house at Wansted, or the Careys' at Hunsdon, or some other mansion near enough to the Lea and the North Road so that the local references would contribute to the mirth of the occasion.

The peculiarities of the Family Drama begin to appear: The leading rôles are given to real families, some of them openly named, of solid rather than lofty Elizabethan importance, and of secondary importance in earlier history. Domestic scenes of a nature somewhat romantic,

[61] Cf. Hawarde, *Camera Stellata*, Appendix I.
[62] *Sal. MSS.*, XI, XI, 562.
[63] Chamberlain, Dec. 4; cf. *Sal. MSS.*, XII, 534.
[64] Lysons, *Environs of London*, II, 288.

somewhat realistic, are placed in a very slight frame of history, and made interesting to a local audience by detailed local references and an underplot of lower and coarser comedy. Such plays may very possibly have grown out of a practice of adapting, by the use of family and local traditions and color, the strolling company's repertory of romances, comedies, and chronicles to such situations as would be constantly met on tour—a chance to perform in the guildhall of a town bursting with local pride, or in the great hall of a proud county family. In the latter case the players may have found it more tactful, when there was the slightest tartness in the satire or moral dubiety in the plot, to assign names from the neighboring families, not from those present. Such a policy would not be likely to lose a company much good will, either; since the great families in their factional alliances had all England sharply marked out into spheres of influence and pocket-boroughs, and since a family which was traditionally or factionally hostile to a company's patron would not be very likely to entertain his players.

Unfortunately for the establishment of "Family Drama" as a recognized Elizabethan type, none of our other examples, I think, exactly follows our tentative definition, although some diverge little from it.

Two Maids of Moreclacke (i.e., Mortlake), for instance, attracts our attention because it is by Armin, who had taken Kemp's place as the chief clown of Shakespeare's company, and because its title indicates that it is localized at the place whence that company was called to court at Wilton.[65] But the characters' names are not, like those in *The Merry Devil*, obviously those of well-known families. Sir Robert Toures may represent the Tower family of Lancashire or the Towers family of the Isle of Ely; but Humil and Vergir are names not easily found in the records, and indeed seem descriptive, like Filbon, and Tutch, the clown. John of the Hospital and his Nurse are real Elizabethan characters, described by Armin in his *Nest of Ninnies;* and Ferris the Waterman and Henry, priest of Putney, may be real persons. "The Earl of Tumult" looks like a descriptive name also; I suspect, however, that he is Donagh O'Brien, "The Great Earl" of Thomond, County Clare, Ireland, who was often in London as a privy-councillor to Elizabeth and James, commanded at Kinsale in 1601, was President of Munster in 1605, and Governor of Clare and Thomond. He was related to Ormonde and Clanricarde, and he himself had married about 1585 as his second wife Elizabeth, daughter of Gerald Fitz Gerald, Earl of Kildare (and therefore a connection of Cobham and the Admiral) by Mabel, daughter of Sir Anthony Browne, Southampton's great-grandfather. In 1600 Southamp-

[65] The Elizabethan dating of this play is established by T. W. Baldwin, *M.L.N.*, XXXIX, 454, and Harold Hillebrand, *J.E.G.P.*, XXI, 328 ff.

ton applied for the Governorship of Connaught, but was denied the post by the Queen. Cecil writes Carew on August 2:

I pray you comend me afectionately to the Erl of Thomond, of whom the Queen is infinitely satisfied. For the feare he had to be comanded by any other named to Conagh, let him be assured he shold neuer haue come under him; but that is dissolved, for the Erl of S. is come away, and goes into the Low Contrey.[66]

Thomond can have become "Tumult" by the same sort of punning corruption which made Angus "Anguish" to the Elizabethans, Ormonde "Wormwood," Munster "Monster." Cecil himself calls Ireland "The Land of Ire."[67] A descriptive justification for calling Thomond by such a name is to be found in Spenser's *State of Ireland*.

But a brief allusion needlessly dragged into the romantic portion of the plot gives us our clue to the Vergirs. Toures, eloping with Mary, daughter of Sir William Vergir, "the Knight of Moreclacke," takes her, supposed dead of the hardships of the voyage, ashore at Scilly to bury her in a chest on the sea strand. He is hurried away by a renewed onset of the storm; and George, Sir William's "brother" (brother-in-law may be meant), who happens to be Governor of Scilly, chancing along, has the chest opened and his niece restored to life.

Now throughout our period the defense of the Scilly Islands was in the hands of Sir Francis Godolphin, wealthy Cornish landowner and tin miner.[68] In 1598 he was thanking Essex for favors to himself and his son William, whom he sometimes used as his deputy on Scilly;[69] but four years later he thanked Cecil for taking his son into his service.[70] Godolphin tells Cecil on October 8, 1601, speaking of the Spaniards at Kinsale, "I needs must write of the present dangerous estate of the isles of Scilly under my charge, being the fairest inn in the direct way between Spain and Ireland."[71] Compare the play:

Gentle. I haue not seene a better glasse to looke in,
What country call you yon, whose cliffes are as
The cloudes, smoake, and all shadowing mists?
Gouer. Sir that is *France*, a faire beseeming friend,
On yonder continent stands *Ireland*,
On this side *Brittaine*, and on that side *Garsie*,
Islands besides of much hostillitie . . .

[66] Camden Society, *Letters of Sir Robert Cecil*, 14; a confidential holograph postscript.

[67] Cf. *Cal. S. P. Carew*, Index.—Thomond spelled Thomant, Tomon, Twomont, Towmone. For "Anguish" see *Sal. MSS.* x, 386; "Wormwood," Spedding, *Bacon*, II, 328, 336; "Monster," *Carew Papers* (Camden Soc.), 88; "Land of Ire," *Sal. MSS.* x, 344.

[68] Cf. S. Baring Gould, *Cornish Characters and Strange Events*, 705; and W. H. Tregella, *Cornish Worthies*, 340 ff.

[69] *Sal. MSS.*, VIII, 478; cf. also XIV, 168—W. Godolphin apparently serving Essex.

[70] *Ibid.*, XII, Oct. 6, 1602. [71] *Ibid.*, XI, 412.

> We that all neighbour, must so strength our being,
> As fearlesse we may frolicke, yet not seeing.[72]

In 1602 he was offering Cecil his expert services in the recovery of treasure from Spanish ships wrecked near Dunkirk.[73] The play makes treasure-hunting the motive of his finding the buried heroine:

> Ha, what scrambled ends heape vp confusedly?
> New digd and ript vp is this plot of ground,
> Some Shipwrack on my life, hid to deceiue
> The Queene and me of our aduantages.

Sir Francis Godolphin's second wife was Margaret Killigrew, apparently a Killigrew of Hanworth, a few miles west of Mortlake, across the Thames, whence Godolphin dates a letter to Cecil on March 18, 1597,[75] and whence Sir William Killigrew, Gentleman of the Privy Chamber, befriender of Sir Robert Carey when neither Cecil nor his own brother would help him, dates letters in 1598 and 1601.[76] The Queen visited William Killigrew at Hanworth on September 4, 1600, and about August 7, 1601; and during her last three years she was often at nearby places, some of them mentioned in *Two Maides of Moreclacke.*

Our play, then, seems to have been somehow contrived to interest relatives of the Godolphins, probably at Hanworth, while the Shakespearean company was in quarters at Mortlake—or rather, if we follow the theory we applied to *The Merry Devil,* it was to amuse neighbors of the Godolphins and Killigrews by showing them in undignified—though sometimes pathetic—situations. James Humil, after falsifying his own funeral, returns in disguise to find his wife about to marry the Knight of Moreclacke. She, on learning that he is alive, agrees to cozen the Knight. Humil's son, thinking he has discovered her adultery with a servant (really his father), raves against her in Hamlet-like terms; Shakespearean echoes are numerous in the serious portions of the play:

> Who knowes the hearts affection by the face?
> . . . .
> Scarlet is scarlet, and her sin blood red
> Will not be washt hence with a sea of water.
> . . . .
> More ugly then is vulcans tithye.
> . . . .
> The diuell has scripture for his damned ill.

As might be expected in a play written by a great clown, there is much disguising; old Humil as a servant, Toures as "The Tinker of Twitnam," Tutch as a Welsh knight, and Filbon as his servant, young

[72] Sgn. G. [73] *Sal. MSS.*, XII; October 6, 1602. [74] Sgn. G2.
[75] *Sal. MSS.*, VII, 118. [76] *Ibid.*, VIII; July 8, 1598; XI; July 7, 1601.

Humil as a 'pothecary. The comedy is lively, the romance often prettily pathetic, the ravings of young Humil not without power. Altogether *Moreclacke* deserves more attention than it has ever received.

Another play which gives its characters descriptive names but unmasks them as real people by a local allusion is *The London Prodigal*.[77] Here much of the plot revolves about the three daughters of Sir Launcelot Spurcock, of Lewsome (Lewisham), in Kent—whither, Chamberlain writes on May 8, 1602, "On May-day the Queen went a-maying, to Sir Richard Buckleys at Lewisham, some three or four miles off Greenwich." (She was on the way to Croydon, where the play has a scene at the Fair.) The characters' names, many of them, would serve well for a maying entertainment: Flowerdale, Daffidill, Hartichoak, Greenshood (or Greenshield), Weathercock, Civet. Oliver, a Devonshire clothier, speaks the dialect better known as "Zummerzet." Sir Launcelot himself says "shuters" for suitors, "shue" for sue, and "A vild upon thee," thus perhaps being made to show traces of Welsh dialect; for his prototype, Sir Richard Bulkeley, was of Beaumaris, Anglesey, at the end of the Northwest Road. He had three sons and (as in the play) three daughters, some of whom appear in the Lewisham parish register.[78] His father Sir Richard, who died in 1573, left among other children, *Launcelot*,[79] Tristram, and Grisel, our Sir Richard's half-brothers and sisters; Richard's own mother was of the good family of Savage, of Rocksavage, Cheshire. Sir Richard had been violently hated by Leicester, and once rowed down to Greenwich in the Lord Mayor's barge to avoid being drowned by Leicester's retainers. He quarreled with his eldest son for marrying a poor cottager's daughter. He was tall and fair, very hospitable to travelers who stopped at Beaumaris on their way to Ireland, but "temperate in his diet, not drinking of healths"—see the play:

> *Lance.* A pinte of sacke, no more.
> *Drawer.* A quart of sack in the three Tunnes.
> *Lance.* A pinte, draw but a pinte.[80]

"In his habit he never changed his fashion, but always wore round breeches and thick bombast doublets, though very gallant and rich." This idiosyncrasy would certainly make him easy to caricature on the stage. Possibly some Kentish neighbor—Lewisham manor, for instance, seems to have been held by Henry Knollys, a relative of Essex—jealous because the Queen did not come to his house a-maying, encouraged this cheerful travesty on Bulkeley and his daughters' suitors.

[77] Quarto, ascribing it to the King's men, 1605. Like *The Merry Devil*, it is one of the Shakespeare apocrypha.

[78] Cf. J. P. Earwaker, *East Cheshire*, I, 182; and Lysons, *Environs of London*, IV, 516.

[79] Launcelot Bulkeley went to Brasenose, in 1593 became deacon at Bangor, and some years later archdeacon (archbishop in 1619) at Dublin.

[80] I, ii, 104–106.

Before King James, probably at Hampton Court at Christmas, 1603, his players gave *The Fair Maid of Bristow.* I think that it may have been written for a Bristol visit during the plague interim. This play differs from *The Merry Devil* by introducing King Richard I and the great nobles Leicester and Richmond, all for small parts; but it follows the Family Drama type by weaving its romantic plot from the adventures of more obscure gentlefolk whose names represent real families, some of them easily identifiable among Shakespeare's contemporaries: Challener, Vallenger, Sir Godfrey Umphrevil and Lady Ellen his wife, Sentloe and his friend Herbert who serves him disguised as "Blunt," and Mr. Chambers of Bristol.[81] The clown Frog has a wench named Douce, but these are comic-descriptive names. Unlike other plays of the type, this has little or no local color.

A. H. Quinn,[82] editing the play, points out the resemblances among the characters of *The Fair Maid of Bristow*, *The London Prodigal*, *How a Man May Choose a Good Wife from a Bad*, and *The Miseries of Enforced Marriage*, remarking on the "probable interdependence of the dramas of the time, rather closer than is now generally supposed." His interesting table is partly based on character types; but we notice, too, certain resemblances in names and places which hint at their interchangeability: Lusam, a character in *Choose a Wife*, and Lewsome, a place in *The Prodigal;* Challoner, of near Scarborough, in *Bristow*, and characters named Scarborow in *Miseries of Enforced Marriage;* Chartley, one of Essex's principal seats, as the name of the chief character in *The Wise Woman of Hogsden.* The closest resemblance shown by Professor Quinn is between *Bristow* and *Choose a Wife*, a play given by Worcester's men in 1602, and may perhaps be due to disputed ownership of an underlying older play. We shall have no more to say about *The Miseries of Enforced Marriage;* since it is based on an actual crime and belongs after our period. In *Choose a Wife* only Christian names are used for most of the characters—Mr. Arthur and his wife and son, Mr. Anselm and his son, Mrs. Mary, Sir Aminadab. It may be remarked that "Lusam" was, like "Lewsome," a not-uncommon spelling of the name of the Admiral's son-in-law, Vice Admiral Sir Richard Leveson of Trentham, Staffordshire. Sir Richard's father Sir Walter was somehow out of his son's favor. He was in the Fleet for debt in 1598 and died there in 1602.[83]

[81] The Sussex Challoners were intimates of Henslowe and Alleyn; Sir Thomas, of Guisborough, was a friend of Cecil and a favorite of King James; a William Challoner was Sheriff of Bristol in 1609. There were Umfrevilles in Bucks., and St. Loes in Somerset a few miles from Bristol.

[82] *Pub. of the U. of Penn.*, VIII, 1 (1902), p. 29.

[83] Chamberlain, Dec. 8, 1598, and Nov. 4, 1602.

Perhaps the family was divided by faction, since John and Walter Leveson are mentioned as Essexians in 1601.[84]

If we dismiss the greater historical characters, we have in *Bednal Green*, already discussed at length, a good example, presented by the Momfords, Westfords, and Strowds, of the Family Drama with hidden real names which are given away by connecting them with localities—here especially Harling and Stepney.

I have already said something, too, about Haughton's *Englishmen for My Money*. Its central figure, Pisaro, a rich Portuguese Jew settled in London, has three daughters whom he wishes to marry to three foreigners whose names seem of the descriptive type—Delion, a Frenchman; Alvaro, an Italian; Vandalle, a Dutchman. But they are won by three English suitors; Harvie, Ferdinand Heigham, and Ned Walgrave, with the aid of Anthony, a schoolmaster, who is "of the same country," an ambiguous expression which here probably means both England and Norfolk-Suffolk; for Philip Gawdy in 1591 sends regards to Mr. Harvey and his wife, apparently of Norfolk or Suffolk, and Mr. Harvey, minister at West Harling, had been recommended thither by the Gawdys' relative Elizabeth Nonne or Nunn of Tostock. The Heighams of Suffolk and Essex were related to the Gawdys;[85] so were also the Waldegraves of Smallbridge,[86] (who were descended from the Montchenseys, prominent in *The Merry Devil*). Here we have, then, another case of close relationship between Haughton's writings and the Gawdys; and so just possibly Anthony, the young adventurer-schoolmaster and tutor of rich men's children is Haughton's unfortunate young collaborator, Peter Pett.

Masters Moore, merchant, and Browne, clothier, as well as Goodman Buttericke the Belman may be identifiable; and Master Towerson appears to stand for a real London merchant who was in trouble over his refusal or inability to pay his share, in 1598,[87] of one of those forced "loans" to the Queen of which we hear mutters of complaint in *Much Ado*.

As we go on looking for Family Drama, we find cases still more closely allied to already recognized types, such as the old romantic chronicle *Fair Em*, with its adventures of William the Conqueror and his group of nobles, but also with appeals to the local patriotism of the burghers of Manchester and references to the important local families of Goddard and Trofferd, the latter mentioned by Camden as still in his day a good Lancashire family.[88] Interestingly linked to it by one of Greene's personal jealousies[89] is another old play, *Friar Bacon and Friar Bungay*,

[84] *Sal. MSS.*, XI, 387.
[85] Philip Gawdy, *Letters*, 168, n. 1.
[86] *Ibid.*, 97, n. 1.
[87] *Acts of the Privy Council*, 1598–99; 433, 444, 463, 467.
[88] Cf. Alwin Thaler, "Fair Em (and Shakespeare's Company?) in Lancashire," *PMLA*, XLVI, 647 ff.
[89] Cf. Chambers, III, 329; IV, 11, 12.

which displays a great interest in the Suffolk squirearchy in its mentions of Fressingfield, Laxfield, Crackfield (now Cratfield,) Bungay, Fram[l]ingham, Harleston, and Beccles. These places can all be connected[90] with Elizabethan families of more or less importance which were probably known to Greene, who came from Norwich, and who made at least two dedications to Robert Carey, whose elder brother Sir George, later Lord Hunsdon and Lord Chamberlain, was granted by the Queen a twenty-one-year lease of Framlingham manor in 1591.

George a Greene, too, appears to have mixed in with its chronicle and ballad materials a good many allusions to county families of the North. But I shall not take the space here to discuss these references.

Henry Porter's *Two Angry Women of Abingdon* is so very well localized that one naturally suspects it of family allusions; and very likely someone on the ground can fill out such slight identifications as I am able to make from the localities mentioned. Young Barnes goes "over the meads" to Milton, Goursey's house; but the Milton a few miles south of Abingdon is so nearly surrounded by meads that we cannot easily identify Barnes's house with any one of the possible manors nearby: Sutton Courtenay, Drayton, Steventon, Hendred, Ham, Harwell, Didcot, etc. Perhaps young Barnes came from Steventon, where the Wisemans were lords of the manor, to see one of the Caltons.

Heywood's *A Woman Killed with Kindness* is well localized in Yorkshire and probably contains in its Actons, its Mountfords, Frankfords, Wendolls, Malbys, Cranwells, and Shaftons a good number of more-or-less well concealed personal identifications. Another play he may have had a hand in, *The Fair Maid of the Exchange with the Pleasant Humours of the Cripple of Fanchurch*, very likely in the 1602 repertory of Worcester's men, has London characters whose names seem real rather than descriptive: Berry, Bobbington, Gardiner, Flower, Bennet, Barnard, Bowdler, and three Goldings. There were Goldings, of course (the family of the translator of Ovid), related to the Earl of Oxford. Bennet's mention of "that worthy arts-master, Lionel Barnes" may be significant; Gardiner is a Cambridge man, and a real Richard Gardiner, M. A. Peterhouse 1568, was probably rector of St. Mary's, Whitechapel, 1570–1617; while another who matriculated at Trinity in 1587 was also admitted to the Inner Temple that same year. There were numerous Cantab Barneses, but I find no Lionel.

But it is unnecessary to discuss here all the plays which show traits which we have found in Family Drama. *Eastward Ho*, *Westward Ho*, and *Northward Ho* all celebrate numerous localities near London as well as some probably identifiable names, open or concealed. And we have

[90] Cf. W. A. Copinger, *The Manors of Suffolk.*

mentioned the crime plays, such as *Arden of Feversham, A Warning for Fair Women, The Yorkshire Tragedy*—the truest journalism of all, but appealing even in their local details to much more than a local interest, and of course not at all of a complimentary nature. Another related type of which we have said nothing is the masque, with its fashion of local compliment to persons and places, which is well illustrated in several Elizabethan and early Jacobean productions of that sort, as well as in the late but supreme example, *Comus.*

Now to leave Family Drama and mention two miscellaneous plays. *The Wit of a Woman,* of unknown authorship and ownership, appeared in print in 1604. It is a rather amateurish bourgeois play and may possibly have belonged to Worcester's men. An excellent little amateur burlesque was *Narcissus,* given by the students of St. John's, Oxford, on January 6, 1603. It parodies *Venus and Adonis* and in its burlesque of Ovid owes much to *A Midsummer Night's Dream.*

In spite of the plague, the initial court season of James I was more lavish in plays than any of Elizabeth's. Twenty plays were given, nine of them by the King's men (counting the performance before the King on December 2 and the two plays given on January 1, the one "of Robin Goodfellow" being probably *A Midsummer Night's Dream*),[91] five by Prince Henry's men (formerly the Admiral's),[92] two by Queen Anne's men (formerly Worcester's), and one each by the Queen's Revels (the Blackfriars or Chapel boys) and Paul's boys. The Prince's men and Paul's boys both appeared on February 20, giving two different plays, the latter organization perhaps Middleton's *The Phoenix.*

The idea that King James may have been encouraged to favor the Shakespearean company by their reputation of having a fine stock of old plays which would bear revival, is borne out by the fact that the company is known to have performed a number of such plays before him in the course of the first two seasons of his reign: *As You Like It* and *A Midsummer Night's Dream* of the 1603–04 season are uncertain; but in 1604–05 performances are recorded of *The Merry Wives, The Comedy of Errors, Henry V, Every Man Out, Love's Labour's Lost, Every Man In,* and *The Merchant of Venice* (twice), in addition to the new *Othello* and *Measure for Measure* and the lost *Spanish Maze.*

[91] That there may have been even more plays given this season is indicated by Chambers, IV, 117 n. 17; at Christmas, 1603, "It is said there shall be thirty playes . . . Manie plaies and dances with swords." One of the King's men's plays was *The Fair Maid of Bristow.*

[92] Prince Henry had been the center of an eddy of English politics since long before his father came to the English throne, and there may be hidden reasons for his being assigned the patronage of the Admiral's players.

Of the total number of court performances during Elizabeth's last decade the Chamberlain's men had given thirty-two, the Admiral's twenty. Probably the lead of the Shakespearean organization would have been still more clearly marked, and much more consistent as well, if political considerations had not sometimes complicated matters. And we can only guess how far the plays of Marlowe had been a factor in keeping the Admiral's men within sight of their rivals.

From 1603 to 1616 the supremacy of the King's men was undisputed. Of 299 plays at court[93] the King's men gave 177, their old rivals the Prince's 47, the Queen's men 28, the Duke of York's 20, Lady Elizabeth's 9, the Queen's Revels boys 15, and Paul's boys 3. The King's men, Chambers remarks, were usually selected for playing before James himself; but it is possible that the Red Bull and the Fortune were better able to hold their own against the Globe with a popular audience.

And after the King's men got possession of Blackfriars in 1609, they themselves catered less and less to the taste of the Globe patrons, who were now deprived of their leaven of gentility. Their complete contempt for this audience ultimately is well indicated by the "Prologue Spoken at the Globe" which Shirley prefixed to his *Doubtful Heir*.[94]

[93] I am using the summary in Chambers, II, 8.

[94] S.R. 1640.

CHAPTER VII

CONCLUSION

A defense of moderate topical identifications. General effects of the decade's stage rivalry upon the work of the dramatists concerned.

IN the course of this study we have had an opportunity to observe closely the decade of rivalry between the two leading companies which ended thus in triumph for Shakespeare and his fellows. We have watched the influence upon the fortunes of the dramatic organizations exerted by various forces, such as their patronage, their politics, the social classes to which their clientele belonged, the skill of their actors, and the genius of their playwrights. We have seen the standing of the Chamberlain's men at court rise and fall with that of the Essex faction, recover itself from utter disaster with the aid of their lord's loyalty to Queen Elizabeth, and attain to something resembling supremacy with the coming to the English throne of King James.

In his recent book *William Shakespeare*[1] Sir Edmund Chambers makes a general denial of the influence of politics on Shakespeare's plays and those of his fellow dramatists with which I feel obliged to take issue, in spite of my own great obligations to his solid and invaluable work *The Elizabethan Stage*. Sir Edmund has been, I think, goaded, by those who try to make of Shakespeare a violent partisan personally and an inveterate political allegorist artistically, into saying things which conflict not only with the facts of history, political and dramatic, but also with his own willingness to ascribe, in particular instances, political implications to a number of plays. No doubt, also, he is too modest to realize what great weight many of his readers, justly convinced of his authoritative knowledge of dramatic history, will ascribe to his remarks upon Elizabethan politics, a field over which he extends no claim. Therefore, in taking up these anti-political remarks of Sir Edmund's, I shall not imagine that I must join issue with him in a carefully documented case, but shall merely, with a few allusions as I press on toward the end of this study, endeavor to correct a wrong impression which might be formed by a hasty reader of only a portion of his work, and to summarize what I have shown about a decade of political allusions on the stage by placing the political relations of Elizabethan drama to the censorship in a somewhat clearer light than recent controversies have left upon them.

Sir Edmund holds that, aside from "some passages of obvious satire

[1] I, 66 ff.

in the comic scenes," there is not "much of the topical in Shakespeare, whose mind normally moved upon quite another plane of relation to life." Notice the important exception made here. We really know very little indeed about the planes favored by Shakespeare's mind, excepting that they are to be found at great heights and depths. On the whole I think it is reasonable to assume that he had only a very human interest in personalities and politics; yet I think that I have shown in the foregoing pages that the minds of Shakespeare's patrons and audience, at least, moved upon levels which were not always above partisanship.

Shakespeare's characters, of course, says Sir Edmund, were built up partly from persons he knew or had heard about, "but this is a very different process from the making of portraits." Perhaps it is different chiefly in degree; moreover, the Elizabethan allegorical "portrait" was meant to be an elusive and shifting thing, of which we have many good examples in *The Faerie Queene*, where the same literary figure stands now for one political figure, now another; and the same political figure acts now one character, now another, in the allegory. Under such rules the allegorical "portrait" itself can be little else than a character built up partly from the writer's knowledge of reality.

But we come now to more debatable statements. "For topics of political controversy . . . there was no room in the Elizabethan theatre." Our study has shown them as seldom openly and seriously discussed, but continually allegorized, paralleled from history, hinted at, and, especially, jested about. "You could beat the patriotic drum against the Spaniards, of course." Well, not if the dominant party chanced to be for peace with Spain. I have not much doubt that the influences which suppressed Essex's *Apology* were able to keep down the martial ardor of the stage, or at least to turn it, in such plays as *Henry V*, ostensibly against the French. It has often been remarked upon as strange that we have no good contemporary dramatic treatment of the Armada or Cadiz victory. Perhaps we possess here the reason for the lack. "You could flout the Scots." Again only if your party wished you to, and the other party was unable to prevent it. Sir Edmund admits that "even here there might be a risk as the wind of diplomacy veered."

"But," says Sir Edmund, "you could not ventilate the grievances of the subject, of which indeed there were few except the monopolies." Perhaps I should leave this minimizing of the grievances of the Elizabethan subject to the historians;[2] it is my impression that there were many, including taxation and forced loans, compulsory foreign military service, unfit justices, corruption, favoritism, bribery in every depart-

[2] On grievances in mass, said to number sixty, see *S. P. Venetian*, March 18, 1610; on Elizabeth's packed parliaments, *Ibid.*, May 12, 1604, and August 25, 1605.

ment of church and state, restrictions on commerce, harassing of recusants and Puritans, purveyance, the Court of Wards, the packing and muzzling of Parliament, and in general the absolute rule of a peevish and failing old woman, hemmed in by a close little knot of sycophants and flatterers from almost all contact with the people whom she ruled. And it is my impression, too, that almost every one of these grievances, as well as many another I have not named, was touched upon somewhere in the drama of the decade. See *Edward IV* and *1 Richard II*, for instance, for propaganda to break down the public hostility to the war "loans" to the Queen, and *Much Ado* for a comment on the way in which those loans were repaid; *A Knack to Know a Knave* for satire on the noxious privileges secured by greedy courtiers, and so forth.

Nor could you, says Sir Edmund, if you were an Elizabethan dramatist, "touch upon ecclesiastical affairs," (and yet prelates take part in practically all the historical plays and have their full share in the politics; see *Henry V*, *Oldcastle*, *Ironside*, *Wyatt;* did these affairs never have the slightest contemporary bearings?)—"or champion the conflicting views of Essex and Burghley as to bringing the war to an end" (I have already spoken of this matter),[3] "or above all meddle with the dangerous arcana of the succession problem." But, as we have seen in every preceding chapter, it was simply impossible for the Elizabethan writer to keep off the succession problem, whether dealing with history as in *Edward II*, *Richard II*, *Henry VI*, *Richard III*, or with romance as in *The Weakest Goeth to the Wall* or *The Old Law;* for where the lives of rulers are dramatized, there must inevitably be succession problems. And I have already expressed my opinion that as long as the suspected discussion of such matters drew audiences, the players themselves made little effort to avoid the suspicion; and indeed that the factional struggle made the pressure upon them to deal with the most ticklish portions of English dynastic history so great that they underwent great risks of suppression and even imprisonment for the sake of bulging money bags and the approval of their patron. *Sir Thomas Wyatt* is an especially interesting case, in its connection with a faction so powerful that its attitude appears semi-official.

Sir Edmund goes on, "Least of all could you do this, if you were in a company which, since the Queen's men were never in London, had practically become an official part of the royal household with a privileged and remunerative position, the preservation of which depended entirely on the avoidance of offence." There does seem to be a mystery here. But there were deep political rifts in the Household itself. We have noticed the politics of the Lords Chamberlain—Cobham's hatred of Essex,

[3] And see *Jack Drum's Entertainment*, Sgn. A3.

Hunsdon's rivalry of Cobham and his opposition to Cecil at the end of the reign, the change to a Howard again in 1602. The Admiral, one of the chief partisans against Essex, was a Household officer (Lord Steward) from 1597 on. So was the Secretaryship a Household office. In *Reliquiae Wottonianae*[4] there is an illuminating passage, written, we remember, by a man who had been one of Essex's secretaries and later one of Cecil's, upon the extent to which Queen Elizabeth allowed factionalism to flourish, even among the officers closest to her:

> 'Tis true, he [Essex] was rivall'd by a strong and subtile faction, which cared and consulted for his ruine, as a foundation they must build upon; and were intent to betray him abroad, and misinterpret him at home: yet the danger was thus allay'd, that they were all his publique and professed enemies, and so known unto the Queen, that they durst never impertinently urge ought against him, since they were sure their malice was concluded, when the reason of their objection happily might not be considered.
>
> And indeed, that trick of countenancing and protecting factions (as that Queen almost her whole Reign did with singular and equal demonstration of grace look upon several persons of most distinct wishes one towards another) was not the least ground of much of her quiet and success. And she never doubted but that men that were never so opposite in their good will each to others; nor never so dishonest in their projectments for each others confusion, might yet be reconciled into their Allegiance towards her. Insomuch, that during her whole Reign, she never endeavoured to reconcile any personal differences in the Court, though *the unlawful emulations of persons of nearest trust about her*,[5] were even like to overthrow some of her chiefest designs. A Policy seldome entertained by Princes, especially if they have issues to survive them.

"I do not know," says Sir Edmund, "what the topical theorists suppose that the censorship was about. They have a dilemma to face." So has Sir Edmund, for such flagrant violations as *Richard II* apparently went unpunished. He gives an impression of Elizabethan censorship much better based upon the facts in *The Elizabethan Stage*.[6] He goes on, "Either the portraits must have been so veiled as to be unrecognizable to the naked Elizabethan eye . . ." The Elizabethan eye saw when it chose; indeed it was greatly sensitized by the official suppressing of news and discussion; on other occasions it could wink—see the Induction to *The Malcontent*. . . . "or alternatively the playwright would have tasted the Marshalsea and the players would have gone to pad the hoof in the provinces." Well, sometimes these very disasters did happen. The best-known example is the *Isle of Dogs* trouble in 1597.

The censorship, we must not forget, was an instrument held in the hands of partisan politicians, and therefore could be used as a partisan weapon whenever the opposing party was too weak to shield itself against it. Thus in 1600, soon after Hayward had been examined and

[4] Ed. 1672, 188. [5] Italics mine. [6] I, 322–325.

jailed for suspected Essex partisanship in his year-old history of the usurpation of Henry IV, and Essex himself had tried to turn aside trouble about the surreptitious issue of his *Apology* by accusing his enemies of bringing it out to do him harm, the fallen favorite implored the Queen not to allow the censorship to be relaxed still further:

> As if I were thrown into a corner like a dead carcass, I am gnawed on and torn by the vilest and basest creatures on earth. The tavern-haunter speaks of me what he lists. Already they print me, and make me speak to the world; and shortly they will play me in what forms they list upon the stage. The least of these is a thousand times worse than death.[7]

There was a sort of poetic justice in treating Essex thus; for it seems to have been his influence which had kept the censors from punishing Shakespeare's lampoons on Cobham as Oldcastle-Falstaff and Cecil as Gobbo and "One Deformed."

We have noticed the partisan use of the censorship in the Marprelate affair, for example, and Burghley's notion that the drama might be used as propaganda against such social abuses as usury and cozenage. During our period it was used, one is forced to believe, chiefly to suppress what the dominant faction in the Privy Council wished suppressed. During Essex's ascendancy, with him and several friends in the Council, it was difficult for the Cecils to punish the indiscretions of his sympathizers; the chief suppression of these years was Pembroke's men's *Isle of Dogs*, and Pembroke was Essex's enemy. The Admiral's *Tinker of Totnes* and *Merchant of Emden* appear, also, to have felt a heavy hand.

Essex partisans had a very fair chance in any case involving the censorship during most of our period; for Bancroft did not appear very staunchly Cecilian until he had been Bishop of London for a year or two, and his predecessor Fletcher was an Essex protégé. The Bishop's superior, Whitgift, Archbishop of Canterbury, was considered a mild Essex sympathizer and seems to have been rather friendly to the Earl until his death.[8] But he was above all loyal to the Queen, as was the other great official chiefly concerned with the censorship of plays, the Chamberlain; for Hunsdon, not especially fond of either Essex or Cecil, seemingly refused, like the modern opponents of the "topical theorists," to see any politics in his players' productions. The Master of the Revels himself, the immediate licenser of plays, was as we have seen forced by his position into a certain neutrality, being a relative of the Admiral and a subordinate of the Chamberlain.

One other remark in defence of the more reasonable of those whom Sir

[7] Birch, *Memoirs of Queen Elizabeth*, II, 445.

[8] On the part played by these church dignitaries in the censorship, cf. E. P. Kuhl in *The Library*, IX, 388 ff.

Edmund calls "the topical theorists." There were living in Queen Elizabeth's last decade certain persons who might, since they suspected the players of seditious personal lampooning and public propaganda, be called topical theorists. Among them were Queen Elizabeth herself, King Henri of France, King James of Scotland, King Philip of Spain, the Pope, Sir Walter Ralegh, Lord Burghley, Sir Robert Cecil, the Earls of Essex and Lincoln, Whyte, Sidney, Sir Frances Vere, Coke, Bacon, Lambarde, and the members of the Privy Council, besides the regular officials of the censorship. To give just one example; on April 15, 1598, George Nicolson wrote from Edinburgh to Burghley,

> It is regretted that the comedians of London should scorn the king and the people of this land in their play; and it is wished that the matter should be speedily amended lest the king and the country should be stirred to anger.[9]

Was the play *James IV*, published in 1598, *George a Greene*, *Edward III*, or something which has been lost? *Black Bateman* showed the Siege of Leith, but it does not appear to have been on the boards quite so early. Perhaps there was something obnoxious in the Admiral's *Henry V*.

We cannot spare more space for this discussion. The Elizabethan playwright, as an individual, might be interested in politics or not; as a dramatist he was in politics willy-nilly, for the actors served partisan patrons and catered to partisan audiences. As for Shakespeare, everything we know about his life, his associations, his ways of working, shows him as a practical and adaptable, not an egoistic, Art-for-Art's-sake person—rather as the solid type of man who might be relied upon to be loyal to his fellows' interests, whether these interests restrained in him a flaming desire to allegorize Elizabethan politics (which I do not believe he had), or urged him (as I believe they did) to give them in each new play one or two characters whose resemblance to contemporary figures might be safely on the hither side of libel, and yet sufficient to start that profitable sort of gossip which would swell the audience; and perhaps also a few of those political generalizations the Elizabethans so loved, which might have the same effect. A dramatist who displays Shakspeare's easy attitude toward his sources and his art cannot have cared much whether he named a character Oldcastle or Falstaff, Gobbo or something else. The political generalizations are a greater matter; but Shakespeare's ideas of this sort would naturally be strongly influenced by those of his friends. It is my belief that the politics and personalities in Shakespeare's dramas derive naturally from his loyalties. Therefore

[9] *Cal. of Scottish Papers*, II, 749, cited by Chambers, I, 323 n. 2; and also in *William Shakespeare*, I, 65. See Ruth Hudson, "Greene's *James IV* and Contemporary Allusions to Scotland," *PMLA*, XLVII (1932), 652 ff.; and Edith Rickert, "Political Propaganda and Satire in *A Midsummer Night's Dream*," *M.P.*, XXI, 53–87, 133–154.

when these loyalties conflicted, as when the collapse of the Essex party sent his company and their patron scuttling, temporarily, to the side of safety, while his personal patron went to the Tower, Shakespeare's soul was troubled and his art was darkened.

But although I assert the reality and importance of the influence of Elizabethan politics upon Elizabethan drama, I am very willing to admit the danger of overestimating the relative importance of political considerations in any given case. After all, the ultimate excuse for the writing of this book must be found in the fact—now evident I hope—that this whole complex rivalry, the real War of the Theaters, has left its mark on the Elizabethan drama as literature. The literary effect was, in the case of the playwrights for Henslowe and the Admiral's men, in general a bad one; in the case of their great rival Shakespeare, in general, I think, very good.

The Admiral's men, their leadership, patronage, and clientele being what they were, reached the summit of their literary achievement in this decade with the bourgeois tragedy, written by Heywood for Worcester's but under the Henslowe aegis, *A Woman Killed with Kindness. The Shoemakers' Holiday*, too, is fine work; and the company also produced such enjoyable plays, excellent in their kind, as *John a Kent*, *Look About You*, and *Two Angry Women of Abingdon*. But dramatists such as Chapman, Jonson, and Webster did their best work after they had broken away from what was to their genius the stultifying influence of Henslowe and his policies. John Marston, one of the most important playwrights of the decade, did his work independently of Henslowe and appears in his records only in one doubtful entry.

And as for Shakespeare—it is impossible to estimate the value to his work of the privilege of aiming at an audience possessing cultivation and literary taste. We can see him through our period stimulated to some of his best efforts by the competition of the companies, rejecting some types and themes of drama which seemed unsuitable or unworthy, and developing others to a perfection the rival playwrights could not hope to touch; urged toward the creation of a Falstaff by a political rivalry, and to the perfection of a Hamlet by a literary one; glowing more brightly in his active, striving genius as time drew gradually its veil of gray ashes over the great plays of Kyd and Greene and Marlowe, who even from the grave had been his mightiest rivals through the decade; and emerging into the new reign the favorite playwright of the King, and the unchallenged master of the living drama.

THE END

ABBREVIATED REFERENCES

Arch. Cant. = *Archaeologia Cantiana: Being Transactions of the Kent Archaeological Society*. London, 1858—.

Atlantic = *The Atlantic Monthly Magazine*. Boston, 1858—.

Baldwin = Baldwin, T. W., *The Organization and Personnel of the Shakespearean Company*. Princeton University Press, 1927.

Birch = Birch, Thomas, *Memoirs of the Reign of Queen Elizabeth from the Year 1581 till her Death*. London, 1754. 2 vols.

C. H., *C. H. E. L.* = *The Cambridge History of English Literature*, ed. by A. W. Ward and A. R. Waller. Cambridge University Press, 1907–16. 14 vols.

Cadwallader = Cadwallader, L. H., *The Career of the Earl of Essex from the Islands Voyage in 1597 to his Execution in 1601*. Philadelphia: The Univ. of Pennsylvania, 1923.

Cal. Scot. Papers = *Calendar of the State Papers Relating to Scotland and Mary, Queen of Scots, 1547–1603*, ed. by J. Bain and W. K. Boyd. Edinburgh and Glasgow, 1898—.

Camden, *Britannia* = Camden, William, *Britannia*, translated by Philemon Holland. 2d edition. London, 1637.

Camera Stellata = Hawarde, John, *Les Reports del Cases in Camera Stellata, 1593–1609*, ed. by W. P. Baildon. London, 1894.

Carew-Cecil Cor. = *Letters from Sir Robert Cecil to Sir George Carew*, ed. by John Maclean for the Camden Society, 1864 (no. 88).

Cecil Cor.—See *Carew*.

Chamberlain = *Letters Written by John Chamberlain during the Reign of Queen Elizabeth*, ed. by S. Williams for the Camden Society, 1861 (no. 79).

Chambers = Chambers, E. K., *The Elizabethan Stage*. Oxford, 1923. 4 vols.

Chambers, *Shakespeare* = Chambers, E. K., *William Shakespeare; A Study of Facts and Problems*. Oxford, 1930. 2 vols.

Cokayne = Cokayne, G. E., *Complete Peerage of England, Scotland, Ireland, Great Britain, and the United Kingdom*. London, 1887–98. 8 vols.

D. N. B. = *The Dictionary of National Biography*, ed. by Leslie Stephen and Sidney Lee. London, 1908–09. 22 vols.

Devereux = Devereux, W. B., *Lives and Letters of the Devereux, Earls of Essex, 1540–1646*. London, 1853. 2 vols.

D'Ewes = D'Ewes, Sir Simonds, *A Compleat Journal of the Votes, Speeches, and Debates, both of the House of Lords and House of Commons throughout the Whole Reign of Queen Elizabeth, of Glorious Memory*, 2d. edition. London, 1693.

Encyclo. Brit. = *The Encyclopedia Britannica*. 14th edition. London, c. 1932. 24 vols.

Fleay, *Biographical Chronicle* = Fleay, F. G., *A Biographical Chronicle of the English Drama, 1559–1642*. London, 1891. 2 vols.

Fleay, *Chronicle History* = Fleay, F. G., *A Chronicle History of the Life and Work of William Shakespeare*. London, 1886.

Fleay, *London Stage* = Fleay, F. G., *A Chronicle History of the London Stage, 1559–1642*. London, 1890.

Gawdy = *The Letters of Philip Gawdy, 1579–1616*, ed. by I. H. Jeayes for the Roxburghe Club. London, 1906.

Greg, *Henslowe* = *Henslowe's Diary*, ed. by W. W. Greg. London, 1904–08. 2 vols.

Hist. MSS. Com. = *Reports of the Historical Manuscripts Commission*. London: H. M. Stationery Office, 1870—.

J. E. G. P. = *The Journal of English and Germanic Philology*. Urbana: The University of Illinois, 1897—.

Lloyd, *State Worthies* = Lloyd, David, *State Worthies: or, the Statesmen and Favourites of England from the Reformation to the Revolution*. 2d edition. London, 1766.

Lodge's *Illustrations* = Lodge, Edmund, *Illustrations of British History, Biography, and Manners in the Reigns of Henry VIII, Edward VI, Mary, Elizabeth, and James I*. 2d edition. London, 1838. 3 vols.

Lysons = Lysons, Daniel, *The Environs of London*. 2d. edition. London, 1811. 2 vols.

M. L. N. = *Modern Language Notes*. Baltimore, 1886—.

M. L. R. = *The Modern Language Review*. Cambridge University Press, 1906—.

M. P. = *Modern Philology*. Chicago University Press, 1903—.

Manningham's Diary = *The Diary of John Manningham, 1602–3*, ed. by J. Bruce for the Camden Society, 1868 (no. 99).

N. Q. = *Notes and Queries*. London, 12 Series, 1850—.

PMLA = *Publications of the Modern Language Association of America*. New York, 1886—.

P.R.O. = The Public Record Office, London (publications as specified).

Parrott = Parrott, T. M. (ed.), *The Plays and Poems of George Chapman*. London, 1910–14. 2 vols.

Privy Council = *Acts of the Privy Council of England*. New Series, ed. by J. R. Dasent. London, 1890–97. 32 vols.

R.E.S. = *The Review of English Studies*. London, 1925—.

S.P. = *Studies in Philology*. Chapel Hill, North Carolina, 1904—.

S. P. Dom. = *Calendar of State Papers: Domestic Series, of the Reigns of Edward VI, Mary, Elizabeth, and James I*, ed. by R. Lemon and M. A. E. Green. London, 1856–72. 12 vols.

S. P. Venetian = *Calendar of State Papers and Manuscripts relating to English Affairs, existing in the Archives and Collections of Venice and in other Libraries of North Italy*, ed. by R. Brown and others. London, 1864—.

S.R. = *Transcript of the Registers of the Company of Stationers, 1554–1640*, ed. by E. Arber. London, 1875–94. 5 vols.

Sal., Sal. MSS. = *Calendar of the Manuscripts of the Marquis of Salisbury at Hatfield House, Hertfordshire*. London: H. M. Stationery Office, 1883—.

Speed = Speed, John, *The Theatre of the Empire of Great Britain*. London, 1676.

Stopes = Stopes, C. C., *The Life of Henry, Third Earl of Southampton, Shakespeare's Patron*. Cambridge: The University Press, 1922.

Stow = Stow, John, *A Survey of London*, ed. by C. L. Kingsford. Oxford, 1908. 2 vols.

Sydney Papers = Collins, A., *Letters and Memorials of State. Written and Collected by Sir Henry Sydney, Sir Philip Sydney, Sir Robert Sydney, etc.* London, 1746. 2 vols.

T.L.S. = *The Times Literary Supplement*. London, 1902—.

W. B. Devereux—See Devereux.

Whyte—See *Sydney Papers*, which contain the letters of Rowland Whyte to Sir Robert Sidney.

Wilson = Wilson, V. A., *Queen Elizabeth's Maids of Honour and Ladies of the Privy Chamber*. London, 1922.

Winwood's Memorials = Sawyer, E., *Memorials of Affairs of State in the Reigns of Queen Elizabeth and King James I. Collected from the Original Papers of the Right Honourable Sir Ralph Winwood*. London, 1725. 3 vols. (Contains correspondence of Sir Robert Cecil with Sir Henry Neville.)

INDEX

NOTE: Since the Admiral's and the Chamberlain's men are mentioned on almost every page, I have not indexed them; and since there are so many anonymous and collaborated plays, I have listed all by title. Characters from plays are indexed in only a few special instances. The nobility appear usually under both title and family name.